In Times of Crisis

In Times of Crisis

ESSAYS ON EUROPEAN CULTURE,

GERMANS, AND JEWS

Steven E. Aschheim

THE UNIVERSITY OF WISCONSIN PRESS

The University of Wisconsin Press
2537 Daniels Street
Madison, Wisconsin 53718

3 Henrietta Street
London WC2E 8LU, England

Printed in the United States of America

Some of the chapters in this book originally appeared in the following publications: *Journal of Contemporary History* 28 (4): "Friedrich Nietzsche, Max Nordau, and *Degeneration*," reprinted by permission of Sage Publications Ltd.; "Excursus" was originally published under the title "The German-Jewish Legacy beyond America," in *American Jewish Archives* (November 1988); *LBI Year Book XLIII* (1998): "German History and German Jewry: Boundaries, Junctions, and Interdependence," reprinted by permission of Leo Baeck Institute; *German History* 15 (2): "Archetypes and the German Jewish Dialogue: Reflections Occasioned by the Goldhagen Affair," reprinted by permission of the German History Society; *New German Critique* 70 (Winter 1997), 117–41: "Nazism, Culture, and *The Origins of Totalitarianism*: Hannah Arendt and the Discourse of Evil"; *Tel Aviver Jahrbuch für deutsche Geschichte* 26 (1997): "Post-Holocaust Mirrorings of Germany: Hannah Arendt and Daniel Goldhagen"; *Tikkun* 11, no. 4 (July/August 1996): "Reconceiving the Holocaust?"; an earlier version of "George Mosse at 80: A Critical Laudatio" appeared in *Journal of Contemporary History* 34 (2), reprinted by permission of Sage Publications Ltd.; *History & Memory* 4, nos. 1/2 (Fall 1997): "On Saul Friedlander." Unless otherwise noted all articles are reprinted here by the permission of their respective journals. "Assimilation and Its Impossible Discontents: The Case of Moritz Goldstein" was originally published under the title "1912 The Publication of Moritz Goldstein's 'The German-Jewish Parnassus' Sparks a Debate Over Assimilation, German Culture and the 'Jewish Spirit,'" © 1997 Yale University Press, in *Yale Companion to Jewish Writing and Thought in German Culture,* edited by Sander L. Gilman and Jack Zipes (New Haven, Conn.: Yale University Press, 1997), reprinted here by permission of Yale University Press. "Hannah Arendt in Jerusalem," © 2001 Regents of the University of California, will be published in *Hannah Arendt in Jerusalem,* edited by Steven E. Aschheim (Berkeley & Los Angeles: University of California Press, 2001), reprinted here by permission of the University of California Press. "Nazism, Normalcy, and the German *Sonderweg*," © 1988 Oxford University Press, Inc., was published in *Studies in Contemporary Jewry, Volume IV, The Jews and the European Crisis,* edited by Jonathan Frankel (New York: Oxford University Press, 1988), reprinted here by permission of Oxford University Press, Inc.

Library of Congress Cataloging-in-Publication Data

Aschheim, Steven E., 1942–
In times of crisis: essays on European culture, Germans, and Jews / Steven E. Aschheim.
    pp.   cm.
    Includes bibliographical references and index.
    ISBN 0-299-16860-3 (cloth: alk. paper)   ISBN 0-299-16864-6 (pbk.: alk. paper)
    1. Jews—Germany—Intellectual life. 2. Jews—Europe—Intellectual life. 3. Jews—Cultural assimilation—Germany. 4. Jews—Cultural assimilation—Europe. 5. Germany—Ethnic relations. 6. Europe—Ethnic relations. 7. Antisemitism—Germany. 8. Antisemitism—Europe. 9. Germany—Civilization—Jewish influences. 10. Europe—Civilization—Jewish influences. I. Title.
DS135.G33 I4655   2001
305.892′4043′09—dc21   00-010301

For Hannah, again . . .
and Ariella, Yoni, and Daniel . . .
and now Yonatan
and to the memory of my Mother ז״ל

Contents

vii

Contents

Part IV: Historians, History, and the Holocaust

    Willing Executioners* 147
14. George Mosse at 80: A Critical Laudatio 155
15. On Saul Friedlander 171

    Notes 197
    Index 265

Preface

This work explores flashpoints of the nineteenth- and twentieth-century relationship between European culture, German history, and the Jewish experience. Here was a complex triangular encounter that proved to be of immense historical import. Out of this confrontation emerged some of the West's most powerful and paradigmatic intellectual creations and, perhaps in subtly paradoxical and interrelated ways, the century's darkest genocidal moments.[1] Ultimately wrapped up with the rise of Nazism and the Holocaust—an overwhelming datum that often tends to distort our portrait of the preceding years—it raises political, ethical, and interpretive issues that still reverberate powerfully in post-Auschwitz culture. This collection touches upon past dimensions of the meeting and present dilemmas of grasping and representing it. It concentrates upon the junctions—those multiple sites of sensitive contact—where its most creative and lethal dimensions, its achievements and tensions, ambiguities, nobility and meanness, ironies, and hidden subtexts are best uncovered. In the essays contained here, I seek to portray the contexts and dynamics of these interconnections and the ideas and biases of some of the personalities caught up in this taut nexus. I seek also to illuminate the ubiquitous, charged inscriptions of Nazi genocide within our own culture and the projects of some later thinkers and historians who—in various and highly contested ways—have wrestled with its problematics and sought to capture its animating essence.

These then are the themes that give this collection its rationale and unity. The essays included here were written for a variety of academic venues and public occasions. Chapters 3, 4, and 7 have not been previously published, and Chapter 2 has heretofore appeared only in Hebrew, in *Historia* 5 (2000). Although the others have been published before—the sources and permissions are given at the beginning of each chapter's notes—I have been persuaded to put them together not only because many of them appeared in journals not always easily accessible but because they are bound by a continuity of method, issues, and con-

cerns. At the same time, they also reflect a certain change and development and, one hopes, a responsiveness to emerging problems and controversies. Placing these essays together may, therefore, be useful in providing
a perspective over time on such continuity and change. I would hope that
any repetition that may occur—and an attempt has been made to cut this
to a minimum—will be compensated for by the variety of issues raised
and perspectives offered in the course of this work.

Over the years I have benefited immensely from the wisdom and advice
of countless friends and colleagues. I have gratefully acknowledged such
help in the notes and hope that I have not inadvertently omitted anyone.
I must, however, also acknowledge the support of Raphy Kadushin, ac-
quisitions editor of the University of Wisconsin Press, who showed immediate interest in the book, and thank Hannah Nyala for her skillful
and sympathetic editing of the work. Juliet Skuldt has guided *In Times of
Crisis* to publication with remarkable warmth, good spirit, and compe-
tence. John Landau, acute as always, suggested the title of the book. It is
quite obvious to me that if these essays have any merit at all it is due to
the warmth and boisterous support of my ever-growing family, to whom
this volume is dedicated. It is also dedicated to the loving memory of my
mother who passed away in June 2000. Last, but certainly not least,
I want to thank Saul Friedlander and Anson Rabinbach, both of whom
read *In Times of Crisis* in manuscript form. They were embarrassingly
generous in their encouragement.

Part I

The Crisis of Culture—Then and Now

One

Friedrich Nietzsche, Max Nordau, and Degeneration

Max Nordau (1849–1923) was a household name to educated late-nineteenth-century Europeans. It is a telling fact that most late-twentieth-century readers will have little or no idea who he was or what he repre-sented. A famous journalist, physician, dramatist, novelist, polemicist and, later, Zionist activist, his thought and work appears today to have achieved widespread popularity among the middle classes precisely be-cause it was so time-bound and tied to the conventions and postures of a positivist outlook that ceased to be relevant after World War I. The hun-dredth anniversary of the publication of his famous, or rather infamous, work *Degeneration* (1892)—a veritable diatribe of cultural criticism that characterized virtually every modernist fin-de-siècle trend as a symptom of exhaustion and inability to adjust to the realities of the modern indus-trial age—provides an opportunity for reassessment.[1] This can perhaps be most helpfully done through a comparison of Nordau to a thinker whom he despised, yet one whose relevance to and imprint upon twentieth-century intellectual sensibility could not have been greater: Friedrich Nietzsche.

Judging by contemporary intellectual fashions and the highly anti-positivist cultural tenor of the times, it appears, of course, that Nietzsche has defeated, indeed routed, Nordau. With the possible exception of his later Zionist career, Nordau's work has been accorded a fate worse than neglect: he is typically treated as little more than a "symptom," a textbook example of hopelessly outmoded and misguided cultural and intellectual postures built upon thoroughly discredited psycho-physiological prem-ises.[2] A recent historian of degeneration, for instance, has summarily dis-missed Nordau's work as "the best-known instance of bizarre 'social di-agnosis.'"[3] The story appears dotted with ironies and tables turned: as, for example, when Nordau predicted that his fin-de-siècle degenerates would "rave for a season, and then perish,"[4] a prediction that apparently

3

applied more to himself than it did, for instance, to the objects of his scorn—Ibsen, Wilde, Baudelaire, Nietzsche, and so on.

These perceptions notwithstanding, this essay will seek to analyze and reassess the Nietzsche–Nordau relationship in terms of a contemporary perspective. On one level, clearly, it is tempting to regard both thinkers as almost archetypal figures, extreme personifications of an epochal parting of the ways, the point at which an indignant, rather bewildered and un-comprehending, yet aggressively self-assertive European positivism con-fronted the incipient modernist revolution intent on radically questioning, indeed destroying, all its revered postulates. The clash of the Nordauian and Nietzschean sensibilities can then be taken as historical evidence of a particular cultural turning point. Nevertheless, appearances apart, there were not only differences: there were also certain interesting, if limited, affinities that need to be identified and analyzed. I shall document both the clash and the commonalities and then attempt to evaluate the compet-ing legacies of these two thinkers from our own present historical per-spective. We may yet uncover some unsuspected relevancies contained in Nordau's heritage.

At the very center of what Max Nordau described as a "severe mental epidemic . . . a sort of black death of degeneration and hysteria,"[5] stands the figure of Friedrich Nietzsche. In *Degeneration* it is Nietzsche who, more than anyone else, provided the philosophy behind what Nordau de-scribed as the prevalent "ego-mania" and who furnished the grounds for an ongoing "deification of filth, . . . licentiousness, disease and corrup-tion."[6] Nietzsche represented nothing less than the quintessence of intel-lectual and moral degeneration. Indeed, Nordau's definition of the ethical climate of the fin-de-siècle is marked by what appears to be its essentially Nietzschean characteristics:

> a contempt for traditional views of custom and morality . . . a practical emancipation from traditional discipline. . . . unbridled lewdness, the unchaining of the beast in man . . . disdain of all consideration for his fellow-men, the trampling under foot of all barriers which enclose brutal greed of lucre and lust of pleasure . . . to all, it means the end of an estab-lished order, which for thousands of years has satisfied logic, fettered de-pravity, and in every art matured something of beauty.[7]

Nordau's cultural analysis explicitly extended the Morelian and Lom-brosian analyses of psycho-physiological degeneration to an area where, as he stated, it had not yet been applied, "the domain of art and litera-ture."[8] "It is not necessary," he wrote, "to measure the cranium of an author, or to see the lobe of a painter's ear, in order to recognize the fact that he belongs to the class of degenerates."[9] Authors and artists, Nordau

proclaimed, as much as criminals, prostitutes, and lunatics (those classical outsiders labeled with the condition), demonstrated all the familiar
mental characteristics and very often the somatic features that symp-
tomized the degenerate condition.[10]

Critics were, from the beginning, skeptical of and sometimes appalled
by Nordau's application of quasi-medical categories to artistic and philosophical matters.[11] Yet in the case of Nietzsche and his well-known illness
(his insanity dated from January 1889), it was particularly easy and plausible to frame not only the man but also his thought within a medico-
pathological frame, a connection that for many of the others that Nordau
pilloried—such as Wagner or Zola—seemed forced or at best metaphorical. Linking the craziness of Nietzsche's ideas to his (later) insanity was a
general technique of those who, in the history of Nietzsche-reception,
sought to defame the philosopher and outlaw his arguments. The fact of
Nietzsche's derangement was regularly incorporated into the philosophical critique, explanatory of its "perverted" contents.[12] Nordau phrased
it thus:

> From the first to the last page of Nietzsche's writings the careful reader
> seems to hear a madman, with flashing eyes, wild gestures, and foaming
> mouth, spouting forth deafening bombast . . . So far as any meaning at all
> can be extracted from the endless stream of phrases, it shows, as its funda-
> mental elements, a series of constantly reiterated delirious ideas, having
> their source in illusions of sense and diseased organic processes. . . . Here
> and there emerges a distinct idea, which, as is always the case with the
> insane, assumes the form of an imperious assertion, a sort of despotic
> command.[13]

More than his fellow "degenerates," Nietzsche was not only considered
as insanely perverted but, as Sander Gilman has persuasively shown, a
thinker uniquely and consistently endowed with almost supernatural po-
tency, a "'dangerous thinker'—not merely that he espoused dangerous
thoughts, but that he caused dangerous acts. . . ."[14] In this respect, Nordau's comments fitted into an ongoing tradition, a strategy not only for
dealing with Nietzsche himself but for coping with what many contemporaries regarded as even more disturbing phenomena: the remarkable
influence that Nietzsche had begun to exert and the perplexing prolifera-
tion of Nietzsche cults (often quite contradictory in nature and outlook)
that increasingly dotted the cultural landscape of the 1890s.[15] Nietzsche,
wrote Nordau, was

> obviously insane from birth, and his books bear on every page the imprint
> of insanity. It may be cruel to insist on this fact. It is, however, a painful,
> yet unavoidable, duty to refer to it anew, because Nietzsche has become

the means of raising a mental pestilence, and the only hope of checking its propagation lies in placing Nietzsche's insanity in the clearest light, and in branding his disciples with the marks most suited to them, viz., as hysterical and imbecile.[16]

Nordau, like other nineteenth-century liberals, had no doubts about what constituted sanity and the nature of moral standards: these were largely defined through the norms of bourgeois respectability. Moreover, he did not fret about the imperceptible nature of "reality." Survival meant quite simply the adjustment to a clearly accessible reality. That adjustment was attainable through clear observation, rational self-discipline, a lucid sense of right and wrong, and a balanced integration of the faculties of will and judgment.[17] Those who lacked these qualities were degenerates: Nietzsche was perhaps the ultimate incarnation of its egomaniacal form. "The ego-maniac," Nordau confidently proclaimed, "is an invalid who does not see things as they are, does not understand the world, and cannot take up a right attitude towards it."[18] Inexorably it was this incapacity to come to terms with reality that destroyed these degenerates.[19]

There would not be much point to rehearsing Nordau's refutation of Nietzsche nor his almost point-by-point analysis of the way madness entered Nietzsche's writings or his logic, thought, and style. What distinguished Nordau's analysis from other anti-Nietzsche tracts of the day, however, was the way he integrated it into a systematic, overarching positivist framework. It is, indeed, as exemplifier of the clash between nineteenth-century positivism and an emerging twentieth-century modernist sensibility that the Nordau–Nietzsche comparison and confrontation retains its historical interest.

Nordau was acutely and anxiously aware of the apparently "modern" appeal of the artists and writers he attacked. Though they presented themselves as avant-garde, they were not, he sought to persuade his readers, "heralds of a new era. They do not direct us to the future, but point backwards to times past." Their spurious, irrational modernity had to be distinguished from his own authentic kind:

> The "freedom" and "modernity," the "progress" and "truth," of these fellows are not ours. We have nothing in common with them. They wish for self-indulgence; we wish for work. They wish to drown consciousness in the unconscious; we wish to strengthen and enrich consciousness. They wish for evasive ideation and babble; we wish for attention, observation and knowledge. The criterion by which true moderns may be recognised and distinguished from impostors calling themselves moderns may be this: Whoever preaches absence of discipline is an enemy of progress; and whoever worships his "I" is an enemy to society.[20]

From his perspective Nordau was quite correct to single out Nietzsche as a key articulator of this new modernist current with its assault on the objective foundations of reality, its radical problematization of truth, and its highly developed expressivist sense of subjective consciousness. Nietzsche is today, as we know, almost consensually viewed as foundational to both the modernist and postmodernist projects.[21] Who symbolizes better than Nietzsche—who once scoffed, "All ordered society puts the passions to sleep"[22]—the frontal attack on those values that Nordau held to be most sacred: rationality, discipline, science, and order?

Nietzsche, of course, was instrumental in questioning the basic premises of a widespread nineteenth-century liberal faith that Nordau had articulated: the belief in advancement based upon potentialities of the natural sciences. He fundamentally disputed the very idea of "progress." Even more radically, he railed against the presupposition that there was a prior, objective reality "out there." For Nordau and the many others whose views Nordau mirrored, there could be no doubt about reality's existence: the laws of an objective natural and social world could confidently be revealed through clear thinking and patient observation. "Culture and command over the powers of nature are solely the result of attention; all errors, all superstition, the consequence of defective attention. False ideas of the connection between phenomena arise through defective observation of them, and will be rectified by a more exact observation." Only through their "want of attention" did degenerates produce "false judgements respecting the objective universe."[23]

While Nordau sought to grasp and then adjust to objective reality, Nietzsche spoke about reality as a construct of the self. It was the will to power that created reality (a reality which, in some of his moods, Nietzsche regarded as wholly fictitious). What could have been further removed from the Nordauian conception of knowledge than Nietzsche's definition of his Dionysus ideal: "the force in all life that *wills* error; error as the precondition even of thought. Before there is 'thought' there must have been 'invention'; the *construction* of identical cases, of the appearance of sameness, is more primitive than the *knowledge* of sameness."[24]

Nothing could have been more alien to Nordau's way of thinking than the radical perspectivism of Nietzsche, who denied the validity of any stable, fixed viewpoint and who had written: "The world with which we are concerned is false, i.e. is not a fact but a fable and approximation on the basis of a meager sum of observations; it is in 'flux', as something in a state of becoming, as a falsehood always changing but never getting near the truth: for—there is no 'truth.'"[25] "Truth," he wrote elsewhere, was a "mobile army of metaphors . . . illusions about which one has forgotten that this is what they are."[26]

In the confrontation between Nordau and Nietzsche, middle-class sobriety, discipline, and realism encountered its Dionysian opposite. For
Nietzsche the withdrawal from positivist reality became a goal, an ideal:
"To spend one's life amid delicate and absurd things; a stranger to reality;
half an artist, half a bird and metaphysician; with no care for reality, except now and then to acknowledge it in the manner of a good dancer with
the tip of one's toes."[27] For Nordau such withdrawal was unequivocal evidence of a clinical condition, what he described as "coenaestheses, or sys-
temic sensations."[28]

In Nietzsche's Dionysian world, ecstasy was transformed into a fundamental fructifying force. Under its charm, he wrote, man

> has forgotten how to walk and speak and is on the way toward flying into
> the air, dancing. His very gestures express enchantment. Just as the ani-
> mals now talk, and the earth yields milk and honey, supernatural sounds
> emanate from him, too: he feels himself a god, he himself now walks
> about enchanted, in ecstasy, like the gods he saw walking in his dreams.
> He is no longer an artist, he has become a work of art.[29]

But for Nordau ecstasy was regarded quite simply as "a consequence of
the morbid irritability of special brain-centres,"[30] and dance and art
(those most liberative and expressive of Nietzschean activities) were dismissed as "pure atavisms" to be practiced in the future only "by the most
emotional portion of humanity—by women, by the young, perhaps even
by children."[31] Where Nietzschean man sought to transform himself into
a work of art, then, Nordau more or less banished art from his future
order.[32] "Observation . . . triumphs ever more and more over imagination
and artistic symbolism—i.e., the introduction of erroneous personal interpretations of the universe is more and more driven back by an understanding of the laws of Nature."[33]

The alternative to Nietzsche and his ilk was quite evident to Nordau.
"The normal man," he wrote, "with his clear mind, logical thought,
sound judgement, and strong will, sees, where the degenerate only gropes
. . . Let us imagine the driveling Zoroaster of Nietzsche, with his card-
board lions, eagles, and serpents, from a toyshop in competition with
men who rise early and are not weary before sunset, who have clear
heads, solid stomachs and hard muscles: the comparison will provoke
our laughter."[34]

Yet we need to pause here for, all the obvious differences between
Nietzsche and Nordau notwithstanding, it is precisely in their common
emphases on "normalcy" and "abnormalcy," "sickness" and "decadence," their common advocacy of the manly ideal, and their desire for
healthy, regenerated "men with hard muscles" that certain important

underlying affinities may be discovered. What united these apparently diametrically opposed figures was the fact that they were key participants, both as makers and beneficiaries, in a wider nineteenth-century discourse of "degeneration." Here was a highly flexible, politically adjustable tool able simultaneously to locate, diagnose, and resolve a prevalent (if inchoate) sense of social and cultural crisis through an exercise of eugenic labeling and a language of bio-social pathology and potential renewal.[35] The rhetoric of degeneration cut across the ideological spectrum. Linked to the optimistic language of evolutionary naturalism but marked by a belief in imminent breakdown and a search for ever more drastic corrective measures, it was employed by conservatives, liberals (like Nordau), the incipient radical right, and materialist socialists of all kinds.

Although Nordau and others had marked him as a major symptom and exhibit of the condition, degeneration was also perhaps the key constitutive ingredient in Nietzsche's *Lebensphilosophie*. "Tell me, my brothers," Zarathustra asked, "what do we consider bad and worst of all? Is it not *degeneration?*"[36] In Nietzsche's world, the reassertion of all that is natural and healthy is dependent upon the rootless extirpation of those anti-natural *ressentiment* sources of degeneration which have thoroughly weakened and falsified the natural and aristocratic base of life. "The species requires," he declared in various ways, over and over again, "that the ill-constituted, weak, degenerate, perish."[37] Both Nordau and Nietzsche, each in his own way, regarded culture and civilization as under threat; both were fundamentally concerned with the sources of decadence, a debilitating loss of energy and vitality, and the possibilities of recovery. Both constructed a world of ideal- and anti-types and looked forward to a cleansed world purged of the lower, degenerated elements they posited. Both envisaged new, non-decadent forms of humanity. Both employed naturalistic, quasi-biological language. There was even something quite Nietzschean in Nordau's eugenic suggestions: "Those degenerates," he wrote, "whose mental derangement is too deep-seated must be abandoned to their inexorable fate. They are past cure or amelioration. They will rave for a season, and then perish."[38] Nor did what Nordau proposed for his degenerate Nietzschean enemies differ significantly from the measures Nietzsche advocated for his, as can be seen when Nordau writes, ". . . whoever looks upon civilization as a good, having value and deserving to be defended, must mercilessly crush under his thumb the anti-social vermin. . . . To him who, with Nietzsche, is enthusiastic over the 'freely-roving, lusting beast of prey,' we cry, 'Get you gone from civilization!' . . . There is no place among us for the lusting beast of prey; and if you dare return to us, we will pitilessly beat you to death with clubs."[39]

There were other, at times rather striking, rhetorical resemblances.

Thus Nordau's evocation of *his* ideal type, of "exceptional" man—written eight years before *Degeneration*—bears a striking resemblance to the heroic *uebermenschlich* Nietzschean counterpart.

> The human race rarely produces an individual who, realizing his power, and upheld by an exalted self-appreciation, is prepared to enter alone upon life's battle-field, on which he must wield his sword and shield with might and skill to come out as victor or even alive. These exceptional men . . . offer the finest and most perfect types of our race . . . They look with contempt upon the beaten paths, and open new highways for themselves.[40]

These similarities notwithstanding, it should be clear that over the years it was with Nietzsche, far more than with Nordau, that the notion of degeneration was most intimately associated and assimilated into European political culture. This applied to left as well as radical right and racist circles. Thus, when the sexologist Magnus Hirschfeld employed the term, he did not invoke Nordau but rather, in an almost taken-for-granted way after writing "*entartete*," he added: "to use a Nietzsche-word."[41] The crucial point is that in the mediated (and at some points horribly fateful) political history of "degeneration," it is the impact of Nietzsche and not Nordau that has been decisive. To be sure, Nietzsche's influence, like his writing, was always multivalent and never reducible to any single political or cultural current or direction of thought.[42] This diversity of reception should not, however, obscure the fact that in the first half of this century various European political circles came to regard Nietzsche as perhaps *the* philosopher of degeneration.

As was his wont, he employed the concept in multiple, shifting ways: as metaphor and irony,[43] but most often and most crucially as a substantial literal danger whose overcoming through drastic measures was the precondition for the urgent re-creation of a naturalized, non-decadent humankind. "Let us look ahead a century," Nietzsche wrote, "and assume that my attempt to assassinate two millenia of anti-nature and human disfiguration has succeeded. That new party of life which would take the greatest of all tasks into its hands, the higher breeding of humanity, including the merciless extermination of everything degenerating and parasitic, would make possible again that excess of life on earth from which the Dionysian state will grow again."[44]

This kind of language—suitably integrated, of course, into National Socialist ideology—was constantly repeated and hammered home into every nook and cranny of the Nazi world. There are innumerable sources demonstrating that in formative ways the Nazi bio-political understanding of and obsession with degeneration was explicitly inspired by Nietzsche.[45] Of course, given Nordau's background, regardless of what he had written about degeneration, the Nazis could never have acknowledged that their diagnoses and widely advertised exhibitions of degenerate art and music owed anything to this Jewish author.[46] But the matter went beyond this merely formal consideration. There *were* obvious building blocks in Nietzsche's radically transvalued world that, if suitably interpreted and annexed, could be taken as inspirational to the Nazi *Weltanschauung* in a way that Nordau's most definitively could not.[47]

Nordau's views were, in many ways, an articulation of the conventional opinions of his class and time; indeed, their typicality and respectability constituted the source of their attraction.[48] Nowhere had Nordau preached a healthy barbarism "beyond good and evil," nor was his New Man to be unfettered by the chains of traditional morality and an anti-life rationalist intellect. If both men thought in generalized terms of socio-political hygiene and heavily employed the language of degeneration, they nevertheless placed such concerns into radically opposed epistemological and ethical frames.

Nordau, it is true, like Nietzsche, thought in naturalistic terms, and, like the author of *The Antichrist*, was an outspoken critic of all established religion; he was, in fact, considered so subversive that his *Conventional Lies of Mankind* (1883) was banned by the Imperial Council of Vienna.[49] Like Nietzsche too, not only did he propose taking exceedingly tough steps against those he regarded to be the agents of degeneration, but also he advocated a hierarchical "aristocratic" society consisting "of the best and most highly qualified human material."[50] But all these harsh emphases fitted into a wider philosophy of a positivist evolutionary humanism characteristic of a nineteenth-century European liberalism that valued order, traditional discipline, progress, respectability, and rationality—all of which Nietzsche openly despised and attacked.[51]

Above all, Nordau's toughness was softened by his ultimate aims. As were so many other liberals of the time, he was indubitably an elitist yet, quite unlike Nietzsche, the avowed purpose of his elitism was humanitarian. Elites and leaders had to act for the betterment of all of mankind. This formed part of Nordau's concept of human solidarity, a notion which, needless to say, was entirely absent from Nietzsche.[52] Similarly, for all of Nordau's disdain for organized religion, and quite unlike the author of *The Antichrist*, his critique was enunciated as part of an affirmation of the progressive nature of European civilization, not its overall denial. His positivist vision represented itself as part of a direct continuity, an advanced stage even, furthering the classical humanizing axioms of Western morality, rationalist Enlightenment, and liberal notions of progress. These were, one by one, Nietzsche's announced enemies and what he considered to be the sources of European life-denying slave-morality and its nihilism, decadence, and degeneration. While Nordau ultimately sought to defend the Western rational and moral tradition, then, Nietzsche's post-nihilist goal was to demolish or at least radically problematize and trans-value it.

Ultimately the prophet of *The Birth of Tragedy* longed for the Diony-sian condition, "a passionate-painful overflowing into darker, more fuller, more floating states,"[53] while Nordau sought to "abolish all laws which can not stand the criticism of natural science, and to have reason and logic govern all the relations between man and man."[54] If Nordau's mor-ality, like Nietzsche's, was immanent and not transcendental with its content constantly in flux, then, unlike Zarathustra's asocial, even anti-social, bias, its essence lay in its communal species-nature whose aim was the overcoming of selfishness and "consideration for one's neighbour."[55] While Nietzsche insisted that "not the corruption of man but the extent to which he has become moralized is his curse," Nordau proclaimed the aim of morality to be "the humanization of the animal, the spiritualiza-tion of the man, the exaltation and enrichment of the individual by means of sympathy, neighborly kindness, a sense of joint responsibility, and the subjection of Instinct to Reason, which . . . is the noblest product of Nature."[56]

Perhaps, in the end, Nordau does not come out quite as grotesquely anachronistic as he at first sight may appear. To be sure, his monochro-matic positivism and aesthetic traditionalism narrowed his vision and openness to the point that he had no capacity to absorb vital new devel-opments of a nascent modernist culture. Nietzsche's playful perspectivism and indeterminate epistemology was indeed to become the wave of the intellectual future, though even here Nordau more faithfully reflected the ongoing tenor and more conservative tastes of popular culture. For all that, even if Nordau wrote, together with Nietzsche, from within what today we consider the highly dubious presuppositions of the discourse of degeneration, he was determinedly skeptical of moral relativism and integrated his naturalism into an evolving progressive social morality. Nietzsche's immoralist, vitalist ethics "beyond good and evil" may have been more exciting and experimental, but they played a part in unthink-able political developments, the nature of which should reawaken us, in our *own* species-threatened, fin-de-siècle situation, to the importance of Nordau's message of universal human solidarity.

Two

Thinking the Nietzsche Legacy Today
A Historian's Perspective

To speak of "Nietzsche today" perforce alerts us to the historicity of the topic.[1] For, presumably, the Nietzsche of today differs from the Nietzsche or indeed, the Nietzsches, of the past and—if you believe, as I do, that his protean relevance remains strikingly alive—of the future as well. Today's Nietzsche—at least in this respect so different from the one that reigned in Europe during the 1930s and 1940s—is among other things the "playful" one. So in that spirit let me playfully suggest that every culture, every generation, and every political movement constructs the Nietzsche it deserves. Or, to put it in less facetious fashion: Nietzscheanism—the nature and extent of Friedrich Nietzsche's impact upon politics, culture, and our collective and individual sense of self—has always functioned as a historically dynamic phenomenon simultaneously influencing, reflecting, and being reshaped by the fluid political and cultural circumstances of which it was a part.[2]

The history of the still vibrant Nietzsche legacy must be regarded as the dynamic history of its manifold appropriations and as the product of an ongoing dialogue between the peculiarly accessible, relevant, and multifaceted qualities of Nietzsche's *oeuvre* and its various interested mediators (sympathetic or otherwise) acting within diverse institutional frameworks and changing cultural and political contexts. This has always been a relatively open-ended, reciprocal, creative process that entailed selective filtering and constant interpretive reshaping of Nietzschean thematics according to divergent perceived needs. In the spirit of the Stefan George circle, Nietzsche's most important *Völkisch* interpreter Ernst Bertram succinctly summed up the process. "Great men," he wrote in 1918, "are inevitably our creation, just as we are theirs."[3] Yet who, in the climate of today's Nietzsche, remembers or even wants to remember the *Völkisch* Nietzsche shaped during World War I—and how militantly triumphant it became in the Weimar Republic?

13

If we are to gain any perspective on today's Nietzsche we should keep in mind that the challenge and significance of his legacy has throughout resided precisely in its pervasiveness, in its manifold and often contradictory penetration of crucial cultural and political arenas. There have been not one, but many "Nietzschean impulses" influencing and reflecting their changing times. Only a *Rezeptionsgeschichte* (reception history) sensitive to the fluid and transformational nature of this legacy will be able to appreciate its rich complexity. "Today's Nietzsche" must be located as part of this ongoing history and made amenable to the kind of historical analysis applicable to all other Nietzsche annexations. Nietzsche today must be considered precisely that—contemporary yet historically situated—without foreclosing on who or what he will be tomorrow.

Nietzsche-reception has always possessed scavenger-like, casuistic properties. Only thus has it been possible to construct the remarkable variety of Nietzscheanisms (some more outrageous than others) revealed by the historical record: vegetarian, expressionist, socialist, feminist, Zionist, anarchist, sexual libertarian, nationalist, and so on. If we are to get a proper historical handle on today's Nietzsche and understand the elasticity and manifold implications of the legacy, we have to remind ourselves of something which twenty years ago was blatantly obvious but which today has been (or stands in danger of being) almost forgotten. If today's Nietzsche is, above all, the post-structuralist Nietzsche, during the 1930s and 1940s the not entirely implausible Fascist and Nazi Nietzsche virtually (though never completely) eclipsed every other version.

If each generation constructs its own most appropriate Nietzsche, during the years of the Third Reich and immediately after, Nietzsche appeared to be paradigmatically Nazi, while National Socialism itself seemed best understood as a kind of Nietzschean project.[4] Both National Socialists and many of their opponents tended to agree that Nietzsche was the movement's most formative and influential thinker, the key visionary of a hierarchical, biologized *Lebensphilosophie* society fueled by regenerationist, post-democratic, post-Christian impulses in which the weak, decrepit, and useless were to be legislated out of existence. For those interested in making the case, any number of prophetic themes and uncannily appropriate (and always selectively enabling) quotes were available. "From now on," Nietzsche wrote in *The Will to Power*, "there will be more favorable preconditions for more comprehensive forms of dominion, whose like has never yet existed. And even this is not the most important thing; the possibility has been established for the production of international racial unions whose task it will be to rear a master-race, the future 'masters of the earth.' The time is coming when politics will have a different meaning."[5]

The paradigmatic Nietzsche of the 1930s, 1940s, and early 1950s, then, was the Nietzsche regarded as the thinker most crucially and intimately definitive of the Nazi order. To be sure, there were always dissenting voices both within and without the Nazi camp. Indeed, as many contemporaries were aware, Georges Bataille—who later admitted that he and his friends shared a certain "paradoxical Fascist tendency"— articulated the major themes of the "French" Nietzsche that was to erupt in the 1960s.[6] Nevertheless the prevailing wisdom held that Nietzsche was proto-Nazi, that he prefigured and even in some way "caused" National Socialism, and that in fundamental ways the movement itself had to be regarded as "Nietzschean."[7]

This perception began to shift in about the mid-1950s and, although there have always been counter-challenges, it has proceeded so apace that, for many younger people educated from about the 1970s on, the identification seems virtually incomprehensible. Not only Nietzsche's de-Nazification—and a corresponding de-Nietzscheanization of Nazism— but also his disassociation from the political right has become close to a fait accompli within English-speaking countries and France.[8] This, in the main, has been the product of two quite different intellectual forces that in consonance with wider political changes have rendered the only other early major competitor and counter-interpretation, Georg Lukács and his *Destruction of Reason*, less compelling. With good reason: Lukács's guiding thesis that "Hitler . . . was the executor of Nietzsche's spiritual testament and of the philosophical development coming after Nietzsche and from him"[9] easily sounds if not downright quaint then certainly a little anachronistic.

I am not sure if it is an exaggeration to claim that the basic aim of Nietzsche's most insistent and influential post-war expositor, translator, and popularizer, Walter Kaufmann, was to exegetically rid Nietzsche of these sullied associations and to provide him with the kind of liberal-humanist face consonant with American academic values of the time. Kaufmann's 1950 masterwork portrayed the Nazified Nietzsche as a pure, virtually inexplicable distortion. Essentially a good European, Nietzsche was a thinker who had to be grasped in terms of his emphases on creativity, culture, and critical individualism, and one whose contempt for nationalism, racism, and anti-Semitism could not have been more apparent.[10]

Kaufmann was, of course, a more or less systematic philosopher who insisted upon pressing Nietzsche's thought into a comprehensible and comprehensive system. Such systematization is, however, an anathema to many scholars in a different, less liberally certain and determinate age—exponents of postmodernism or post-structuralism and deconstructionism, for example, who have functioned as notable colonizers of Nietzsche while at the same time being crucially shaped by him. Unlike Kaufmann, for these circles (with some conspicuous exceptions such as Jacques Derrida)[11] the issue of the connection to National Socialism by and large goes quite unmentioned, unnoticed, and the very need to even engage the putative Nietzsche-Nazi link has been virtually obliterated. This Nietzsche is quite dissimilar to Kaufmann's. Here he is the radically skeptical perspectivist, the anti-totalizing prophet of heterogeneity, fragmentation, and discontinuity.[12]

But the post-structuralists, like Kaufmann,[13] have also fashioned an ultimately epistemological[14] and rather sterilized Nietzsche, shorn of all vestiges of his vitalist *Lebensphilosophie* and his Great Politics of degeneration and regeneration.[15] If anything he appears not as the embodiment of National Socialism, but as the therapeutic answer and the antithetical response to it. This postmodernist Nietzsche is one with postmodernism's larger agenda, so often presented as an explicit antidote to the Nazi experience. For Lyotard, Auschwitz reveals the bankruptcy of the grand metanarratives of the Enlightenment and their accompanying belief in progress and reason. In a post-Auschwitz world, such totalizing, homogenizing, and manipulating modes must give way to non-privileging heterogeneous, pluralistic, and ironic narratives.[16] This, of course, is very much open to question. Lyotard's is a reductive treatment of the Enlightenment project in which, as one analyst provocatively notes,

> all narratives suffer a certain spurious homogenizing: "modernity" for Lyotard would seem *nothing* but a tale of terroristic Reason and Nazism little more than the lethal terminus of totalizing thought. This reckless travesty ignores the fact that the death camps were among other things the upshot of a barbarous irrationalism which, like some aspects of post-modernism itself, junked history, refused argumentation, aestheticized politics and staked all on the charisma of those who told the stories.[17]

The harnessing of Nietzsche to these new sensibilities and cultural and political agendas, his post-war de-Nazification, occurred above all in France from where it was imported to the United States. It was not so simple to loosen him from these moorings in Germany where, after all, he had been so intimately tied to the Nazi regime. Among upholders of the new German liberal-democratic regime, committed to models of renewed Christian values or humanist Enlightenment, the resistance to Nietzsche was perhaps the greatest.[18] We should remember that the most vociferous contemporary critic of Nietzsche, indeed of postmodernism itself, and what he considers to be its parallel irrationalist, anti-Enlightenment thrust, is Jürgen Habermas.[19] It is tellingly symptomatic that when, in March 1983, Habermas gave a series of lectures at the College de France, they were a disaster partly because they were delivered in garbled English (!) but also because in the presence of France's most famous living Nietzscheans, Paul Veyne and Michel Foucault, he devoted time to uncover what he claimed to be the fascist implications of Nietzsche's way of thinking. By then the distance between the "old" and the "new" Nietzsche seemed so great that, as one reporter put it, Habermas' line seemed a strange proposition: especially "in a place where two prominent Nietzscheans teach, neither of whom can be mistaken for anti-democrats."[20]

The post-war resuscitation of Nietzsche and his appropriate reconstruction into a prophet eminently suited to our own times (as he is thus refitted for all other times) required therefore that he emigrate into more hospitable waters. France and the nascent, politically ambiguous, post-structuralist revolution of the 1970s seemed to have been tailor-made for this. It is still not clear *why* the deconstructionist impulse was born in France and at that particular moment. Numerous explanations, some more persuasive than others, have been offered.[21] Whatever the explanation, there can be little doubt about the obviously dominant role of Nietzsche within this new dispensation. In paradoxical fashion, Nietzsche came to possess canonic status within a body of thought that sought to problematize the very notion of canon. As a recent volume "Nietzsche as Postmodernist" puts it: "Nietzsche paved the way for the philosophical concept of postmodernism" itself. In this view Lyotard's increasingly authoritative definition of postmodernism as a "distrust of metanarrative" can be seen simply to be drawn from a particular strain within Nietzsche's thought.[22]

To be sure, it would be an error to lump all the so-called post-structuralist trends and thinkers together. Not all its exponents are equally enthusiastic Nietzscheans and not all use him in the same way. Moreover, at times they critique each other on the basis of a kind of implicit Nietzschean purity. Derrida once accused Foucault of "confirming metaphysics in its fundamental operation," perhaps the most dire anti-Nietzschean deed in the entire deconstructionist lexicon.[23] Whatever the differences, however, there can be little doubt that—together perhaps with another old Nietzschean, Martin Heidegger—Nietzsche and what has been called his "unremitting interrogation of Western civilization"[24] is most central to this project and its sensibility.

Nietzsche's genealogical conception of history, and what is not always convincingly taken to be its radical problematizing of origins;[25] the emphasis on the discourse of power; the radically skeptical perspectivism; the experimental quest for self-creation; the fascination with the outer reaches of human experience (the realms of madness, cruelty, violence, and pain repressed by metaphysics and reason); the transgressive "Dionysian" impulses; the dissolution or the problematization of the very category of the self; the notion that truth is alternatively illusory, metaphorical, and institutional; the sense of stylistic play, heterogeneity, indeterminacy, and rupture: these Nietzschean echoes are all crucial constituent parts of the postmodernist project.[26] This Nietzsche, we should note, is not all that new. Already in 1950—in his post-Nazi phase—the German expressionist poet Gottfried Benn wrote that Nietzsche had destroyed philosophy, theology, causality, eros, truth, being, and identity. There was no transcendental, binding Archimedean point. Nietzsche had demonstrated the error of assuming that humans had an intrinsic or metaphysical content. There was, in fact, no such thing as the "person": there were only symptoms.[27]

Unlike in the 1930s and 1940s, Nietzscheanism today is not most clearly and officially represented in the life and ideologies of radical political movements but more as an infiltrative, atmospheric presence informing the culture and defining the lives of particular individuals. The case of the most famous Nietzschean of our time, Michel Foucault, is too familiar to bear repeating in detail here but it does exemplify the themes we have just outlined and perhaps reveals some of the hidden connections with Nietzscheans of an allegedly quite different political order.[28] The centrality of Nietzsche to Foucault's project has been attested to by all who have examined it. His analyses of the historicity (rather than fictitiousness) of the constructed self as it emerges within shifting discourses and institutional settings and his perception that power creates its subjects (rather than being exercised by them) were explicitly inspired by Nietzsche as was his own individual quest to understand "how one becomes what one is." What could be more Nietzschean than his description of his later aestheticized personal vision that there could be only one practical consequence flowing from the idea of self not being given to us: humans must create themselves as works of art.

Increasingly it has been established to what degree, however, his work and life—as an ultimate Nietzschean, Foucault considered the two utterly intertwined—consisted not, as so many of his admirers believed, of a critique or an attempt to escape the grasp of power, but as a celebration of it. His sadomasochism was a kind of exercise of the will-to-power, a fascination with the domination of self and other. What could be more resonantly Nietzschean than his disdainful definition of the humanist, Enlightenment tradition as "everything in Western civilization that restricts the desire for power." His *Discipline and Power*, as various commentators have recently pointed out, is replete with vitalistic reveling in blood and cruelty that stands in clear contrast to the demonization of the coolly efficient institutions of modern life.[29] The internalization of surveillance is condemned, as Mark Lilla has put it, not because it subtly perpetuates power but because it seeks to displace it from body to soul.[30] In Foucault's work, then, the question of nihilism is left wide open. In the absence of any unchangeable rule or norm, the positive and destructive capacities of which Nietzsche spoke coalesce as permanent possibilities.

There is a veritable rush in various feminist quarters to render this postmodernist Nietzsche as inspirational source. Jacques Derrida has spectacularly demonstrated the radical heterogeneities, the reversals, the encoded complexities of Nietzsche's treatment of women ("Nietzsche might well be lost in the web of his text, lost much as a spider who finds he is unequal to the web he has spun"), and their centrality to his project.[31] But its politicization too often elides such complexities. Here Nietzsche is simply invoked "to find ways of understanding and affirming sexual differences that do not imply social relations of domination and subordination; . . . conceptions of power and practices of criticism which are not confined to the reactive perspective of slave morality; . . . the desire . . . to find . . . forms of relations to others, to knowledge and to self which might provide bases for less oppressive social relations."[32] The mighty exegetical efforts involved in suitably transforming the Zarathustrian whip and the explicitly and radically anti-democratic, anti-egalitarian Nietzsche into this soft humanizing role have not been lost on even the most enthusiastic members of these circles.[33]

Contemporary feminist Nietzscheanism may have its own particular emphases, but we should remind ourselves it is no new creation. The same interpretive imperatives and tensions between Nietzsche's apparent dismissal of women and its exegetical interpretive overcoming, his radically emancipatory and transvaluative side,[34] and his emphasis on a biologistic, essentialist conception of the "identity" of women beset its advocates, many of whom flirted openly with various forms of bio-eugenic politics, as early as the 1890s.[35] It may be salutary to remember that historically there have been feminist Nietzscheans of all stripes. For example, the futurist vitalist Valentine de Saint-Point, who sought "to make lust into a work of art" and who argued that after battle *"it is normal for the victors, to turn to rape in the conquered land, so that life may be re-created,"* translated the notion of the *Übermensch* into a new myth of the masculinized superwoman. Give woman, she proclaimed, "a war cry and with joy she will ride again on her instinct and lead you towards undreamed of conquests . . . *Let woman rediscover her own cruelty and violence that make her turn on the beaten . . . and mutilate them."*[36] While for some de Saint-Point's construction may have been less attractive, can we say that it was less plausible than the rival feminist appropriations of her own or the present day?

In many obvious ways the Nietzschean corpus has formed and influenced contemporary sensibilities, but it is equally true that the Nietzsche(s) of our own times could only arise, like those of other times, because changed circumstances induced and encouraged him to be read and emphasized in this particular way. Nietzsche has simultaneously influenced but also been appropriately reconstructed to fit what his champions take to be our own age of radical ideological and epistemological indeterminacy. Like other constructions—including my own—all interpretations of Nietzsche are particular and historically conditioned. Indeterminacy is in many ways a Nietzschean legacy, and the deconstructionists are surely correct to highlight historical and textual contingency. Yet they do not differ in kind from the multiple Nietzscheanisms that form the history of the ongoing Nietzsche legacy. The making of this particular Nietzsche, like all other Nietzscheanisms, involves a series of selective interpretive operations. They too have constructed their own privileged, "meta"-Nietzsche: the self-subverting, paradoxical one of indeterminacy.

If many contemporary critics are to be believed, this Nietzsche simply consists of another, not always persuasive, reading: one, they argue, that entails not the jettisoning of metaphysics but rather the elaboration of yet another one. Of course, the post-structuralists continue to teach us much that is valuable about the textual and perspectivist nature of language and truth, and several have done so by apparently drawing sustenance from Nietzsche's formulations. As Avital Ronell has put it: "The question of the text erupted with Nietzsche, everything appears to be organized around the absence of an oeuvre."[37] But equally plausible counter-interpretations have been made that Nietzsche was the first to see through such claims and that his intra-linguistic play "does not amount to an absence of origins and absence of foundation," a mere play of signifiers, but an overabundance of plastic forces, a surplus of force, part of the *physics* of the will to power.[38] Furthermore, some have argued that for all Nietzsche's iconoclasm, and indeed, perhaps because of it, he remains, after all, within the classical philosophical mode a "seeker after truth."[39] One critic has recently gone so far as to suggest a "Nietzsche who is merely rehashing familiar Kantian themes, minus the rigor of Kant's exposition."[40] Be that as it may, others claim that Nietzsche's insistently judgmental stance posits the principle of rank-order as overriding. This presupposes the "supra-perspectival" truth that postmodernists deny.[41]

They point to the fact that the canonic postmodernist Nietzschean text—"On Truth and Lie in an Extra-Moral Sense"—was only published posthumously and that many other similar musings appeared in the unpublished notes to *The Will to Power*.[42] They argue that Nietzsche attacked specific modes of logic and rationality rather than Western thought as such, that he disavowed particular conceptions of truth, not the possibility of truth as such, and that he very much insisted both upon the notion and the possibility of "incorrect reading."[43]

The deconstructionist Nietzsche, on the other hand, is intentionally self-subverting. As one author puts it, rather than denying or ignoring the contingency of his own textual authority, especially in *Zarathustra*, Nietzsche "forges a deconstructive relation between himself and his readers . . . [and] forces his readers similarly to acknowledge their contingent construction of their own claims to authority."[44] But if the postmodernist Nietzschean paradigm emphasizes self-subversion, one wonders whether it leaves room for its own self-subversion (especially by Nietzsche, its purported champion and incarnation).

This is not the place to examine some of the more obvious transparencies involved in some of the postmodernist popularizations and political annexations of Nietzsche. Still, it is worth quoting the conclusions of one recent commentator, Mark Warren. Nietzsche's philosophy, he writes, when appropriately purged of subjective political views (!), implies "a pluralistic society in which egalitarianism underwrites individuality."[45] The Nietzschean collapse of any metaphysical source of authority is held to bring liberation from repressive closures in discourse and practice, undreamed-of transvaluations, and a newfound freedom going beyond all previously sanctioned limits.

But only a very slightly developed historical sense will remind us of the irony that the advocate of the "merciless extermination" of the weak, the degenerate, and the parasitic—a man whose thought, whether parodistically or not, could be regarded as foundational to and definitive of the Nazi order—should now be commonly heralded as a powerful advocate of tolerance and *difference*, as spokesman for the emergence and protection of the powerless Other, and as prophet of relationships shorn of domination.[46] In good deconstructionist manner we cannot know what Nietzsche *really* meant when he wrote that the Jews were "the most catastrophic people of world history," guilty of nothing less than the radical falsification of "all nature, all naturalness, all reality, of the whole inner world as well as the outer."[47] Good scholarship and Nietzsche apologists no doubt can casuistically explain and contextualize such remarks. But that is just the point. The history of Nietzsche appropriation is replete with just such casuistry by all interested sides and when anti-Semites of the most radical kind invoked and were influenced by such passages they did not concern themselves with the finer points of textual emendation.[48] The current liberationist Nietzsche thus fits into a long tradition of Nietzsche appropriation by socialists and other egalitarians. It demonstrates the ongoing remarkable capacity to filter out an enormous amount of many very unambiguous and extreme anti-democratic, anti-socialist, anti-egalitarian, elitist, and even eugenic and racist convictions.

Most Nietzscheans, and especially historians of the Nietzsche legacy, have sought to press the rich complexity of his appropriations into a narrow essentialist framework, classifying the various deployments either as deviations from or faithful representations of the "real" Nietzsche. Whether such a single, grand meta-narrative is or is not best able to account for his thought is, to be sure, a methodological and philosophical issue that itself must be considered part of the thinker's ongoing legacy. I believe, at least as a historical principle, that the postmodernist insistence upon plurality and textuality is very beneficial, and in many ways my own conception of writing the history of the Nietzsche legacy has been shaped by the perception that Nietzsche has been read and has encouraged such reading in vitally heterogeneous ways.[49] In normative terms, this appropriation may even be richer than most others for it incorporates and thematizes Nietzschean complexity and multiplicity into its own reading. Nonetheless, such a reading must also be regarded as only part of an ongoing history: no more than a chapter of an unfinished Nietzsche legacy, a fact underlined and appreciated by the deconstructionist insistence upon the openness of texts to historical and future others. Like other interpretive constructions, its exponents, after all the necessary qualifications and exceptions have been inserted, have selectively molded what they take to be a "paradigmatically" postmodern Nietzsche.[50]

But if there is one constant in the history of Nietzsche-reception, it is the perception, variously and continuously reinterpreted, that Nietzsche was "paradigmatic." The notoriously vague and shifting meanings of terms like "modern," "modernism," and "postmodern" need not detain us here.[51] Suffice it to say that, for our purposes, these designations may themselves be regarded as landmarks of changing modes of historical self-understanding, and that Nietzsche—the man of multiple faces—has consistently been regarded as the very exemplification of these changing paradigmatic conditions and self-representations.

What accounts for this insistently continuous transnational fascination? In the final analysis, the answer must be sought in his almost uncanny ability to define—and embody—the furthest reaches of the general post-Enlightenment predicament and to encapsulate many of its enduring spiritual and intellectual tensions, contradictions, hopes, and possibilities. Admirers, opponents, and critics alike have always agreed that one did not simply read Nietzsche; rather, as Thomas Mann put it in 1918, one "experienced" him.[52] More than any other modern thinker Nietzsche has acted as a kind of seismometer of our spiritual and intellectual life, a personalized stamping ground and battlefield upon which our tensions, conflicts, contradictions, and possibilities have been played out.[53] From the 1890s through to the present, his life and thought have provided an acutely relevant prism through which to express and confront the changing meanings and problems of a fluid, always unclear, yet ultimate modernity most radically conceived, in the words of Leszek Kolakowski, as the belief "in the unlimited possibility of mankind's self-creation"[54] and characterized by the predicament of nihilism and its interconnected, transvaluative, liberating, and cataclysmic potential. Because he stands so close to the center of our ongoing concerns, Nietzsche has not been exhausted by, nor can he be reduced to, any particular political system or cultural movement or historical time frame.

While his paradigmatic status has not varied, perceptions as to the nature and content of the paradigm have changed in response to shifting intellectual, political, and generational circumstances. The dominant postmodernist Nietzsche has, for the moment, erased the overtly substantial and programmatic Nietzsche, so crucial to the political history of his reception and appropriations. But, whatever disputed conservative or radical political functions this indeterminate Nietzsche may serve, his "postmodern" guise may not be the last word.[55] While we cannot predict its future contours, the Nietzsche legacy will in all probability live on as a dynamic force and assume new forms, dangerous as well as potentially liberating, responding to the dilemmas and needs of changing times and integrated always into our own tentative self-definitions and representations. Because Nietzsche remains perhaps the most potent symbol of the variegated, continuously experimental, post-Enlightenment project, his legacy and its almost boundless capacity for renewal will persist, as will the opposition to it. Our relationship to him will thus surely continue to confirm Ernst Bertram's dictum that "great men are inevitably our creation, just as we are theirs."

Three

Against Social Science
Jewish Intellectuals, the Critique of Liberal-Bourgeois Modernity, and the (Ambiguous) Legacy of Radical Weimar Theory

> . . . the Social Sciences, an abominable discipline from every point of view.
> —Hannah Arendt to Mary McCarthy,
> 21 December 1968

W. H. Auden coined that delightful injunction: "Thou shall not commit social science."[1] But much of its animating spirit, its diverse theoretical articulations and various ideological impulses, seems to emanate from a number of Jewish thinkers whose intellectual worlds were molded in and by the Weimar Republic and whose biographies and subsequent thought were, in quite different ways, indelibly marked by the catastrophic experience of National Socialism. I want here to consider the genesis and the later, more nuanced elaborations of these varied critiques of social science. These constitute an important part of Weimar's ongoing and ambiguous legacy that, I would suggest, has become part of our own late-twentieth-century cultural sensibility. Under investigation here is a disparate group of thinkers whose intellectual stock has dramatically risen over the years and whose thought—each in its own very different fashion—is now regarded in some way as seminal or foundational. I am referring to the work and worlds of Hannah Arendt, Leo Strauss, and what has become known as the Frankfurt School (especially Theodor Adorno, Max Horkheimer, and Herbert Marcuse).

At first glance the differences seem more glaring than any commonalities. Leo Strauss has come to embody, perhaps misleadingly so, a militantly elitist neo-conservatism;[2] Adorno, Horkheimer, and Marcuse are recognized as crucial formulators of what is now termed "Western Marxism," albeit of a highly refined culturally and philosophically re-tuned variety;[3] and Hannah Arendt is today regarded above all as a determinedly post-traditional, anti-ideological political thinker.[4] The ideological differences between these thinkers are compounded, moreover, by a remarkable absence of reciprocal reference and public acknowledgement. Almost no statements of mutual recognition, let alone indebtedness, can be found.[5]

Indeed, there was often a nasty, profound dislike.[6] Thus Arendt not only rejected Strauss's attempt to court her when they met at the Prussian State Library, but acerbically criticized his conservative political views. As her biographer points out, the "bitterness lasted for decades . . . Strauss was haunted by the rather cruel way in which Hannah Arendt had judged his assessment of National Socialism: she had pointed out the irony of the fact that a political party advocating views Strauss appreciated could have no place for a Jew like him."[7] In return, Strauss openly agitated against Arendt upon the appearance of *Eichmann in Jerusalem* and encouraged students and acquaintances to pan it.[8] Arendt's dislike for Adorno was, if anything, even more intense. When he rejected her first husband's (Guenther Stern) musicological work on what Arendt took to be tendentious Marxist ideological grounds, she declared: "That man is not coming into our house!"[9] On the basis of the discovery of an obsequious 1934 piece Adorno wrote in a semi-official Nazi journal praising a song-cycle with words from Baldur von Schirach's poetry, Arendt declared that he was amongst those Jews who "would have gone along with Hitler if they had been allowed to."[10] (It is, perhaps, the crowning irony that recently Arendt herself has been berated similarly for her continuing loyalty to and defense of another apparently unrepentant Nazi, Martin Heidegger.)[11]

For all that, the similarities between these seemingly disparate figures are striking, all the more so for thus far having gone relatively unnoticed and unanalyzed.[12] All were acculturated German Jewish intellectuals, philosophers whose formative sensibilities were shaped in the Weimar Republic and whose personal biographies and subsequent worldviews were decisively stamped by Nazism and the experience of exile in the U.S. In one way or another they all experienced the travails described by Arendt in her "We Refugees."[13] (Their view of American society was exceedingly narrow, Walter Laqueur has observed laconically, because none of them had driving licenses!)[14] All in quite different—yet quintessentially Weimarian—ways were attracted to heterodox, radical, and even subversive modes of thought. They thus inhabited what can only be described as a post-Nietzschean universe,[15] and all of them, regardless of subsequent criticisms, came under the bewitching spell of Martin Heidegger.[16] Like so many of the Weimar intelligentsia, they were all critics of "mass soci-

ety," deeply suspicious of rationalist-technological modernity and liberal
bourgeois democracy. This is precisely what renders their legacy for us
an ambiguous one.[17] All of them formulated critiques of the social and
behavioral sciences and adumbrated overall political and cultural alternatives to the negative modernity they felt these social sciences embodied.
But there is still another important commonality. Given the circumstances
of the time, they were all confronted with and had to formulate responses
to what Strauss called the Jewish "theologico-political" predicament.[18]
As a consequence, all of them, albeit in varying degrees of commitment,
grew to acknowledge the symbolic and actual importance of Jewish matters and increasingly integrated these concerns into the marrow of their
work. Consciousness of the "Jewish Question" and their own Jewishness
informed, sometimes quite profoundly, both the critiques and the alternatives they posited.

We must also concede that in many ways their critique of technology
and liberal-leveling modernity was derived from the Weimar radical right.
Leo Strauss's turn to the medieval rationalist philosophy of Maimonides
as the antidote to the conceits of modern liberalism should thus perhaps
be read as the Jewish mirror-image of his erstwhile friend Carl Schmitt's
appeal to a unifying, saving Catholic rationalism.[19] In his 1933 critique
of Schmitt's "Concept of the Political," Strauss upbraided Schmitt for not
going far enough and for not executing the day's most "urgent task":
undermining liberalism at its very foundations. Schmitt's "critique of liberalism," he noted, "takes place within the horizon of liberalism; his illiberal tendencies are arrested by the as yet undefeated 'systematics of liberal
thinking.' The critique of liberalism that Schmitt has initiated can therefore be completed only when we succeed in gaining a horizon beyond
liberalism."[20] It is not surprising then to note that Strauss was almost
contemptuously critical of his *Doktorvater* Ernst Cassirer, who exemplified liberal thought and "the decrepit state of rational philosophy," especially when the comparison to Heidegger was in question.[21]

Yet, despite this palpable influence, none of these thinkers were content
with the moral and political conclusions drawn by the radical right.[22]
Strauss took offense at the Schmittian "adoration of animalist power"[23]
and defined politics (or, rather, political philosophy) not as a relentless
struggle between friend and foe but in the sublimated terms of the never-
consummated quest for the good and the noble;[24] Arendt turned not to a
Heideggerian being-toward-death but to natality and new beginnings as
the sources of human hope and creativity; and the Critical Theorists,
alarmed though they were by the grip of instrumental rationality, held on
however grimly to the universal emancipatory promise rather than submit
to a brutalized Juengerian type. Whether out of a sense of their own per-

ceived vulnerability, or a commitment to older Enlightenment humanizing traditions,[25] or even because of their own Jewish ideals, it is clear that these Jewish thinkers resisted both proto-Fascist notions of a resolute warrior-power society and the apocalyptic impulses of Weimar intellectual culture.[26] Their opposition to liberalism and bourgeois-capitalist modernity proceeded from within determinedly humanist frameworks, however elitist and idiosyncratic their biases may seem to have been. It was this spirit that animated their common antipathy for a positivist social science whose narrowing, reductionist preconceptions they regarded, in one way or another, as diminutions both of the actual and potential human condition.[27]

All these thinkers recognized the centrality of the social sciences in the intellectual economy of a modernity they viewed as sorely flawed and thus spent much time countering what they took to be its pernicious logic and implications. Social science was regarded as both a symptomatic reflection and agent of what, in their different ways, these thinkers took to be a fundamental pathology. At their hands the giants of "bourgeois" sociology—Auguste Comte, and, indeed, their own Weimar contemporaries, Karl Mannheim and Max Weber—underwent detailed scrutiny and critique.

Although Arendt and Strauss also took Auguste Comte to task,[28] it was the Marxist-oriented Frankfurt School that repeatedly damned him for the original sociological sin of positivism. The very term "sociology," Adorno and Horkheimer wrote, was a "malformation, half Latin, half Greek . . ."[29] and was, of course, coined by Comte. His "positivism," which by virtue of its revolt against metaphysics and Hegelian "negationism" prided itself on its empiricism, had created a static inductionism that wholly replaced the consciousness of the dynamic totality of society. Moreover, it was a vision shorn entirely of the critical impulse.

> From the very beginning of the new science the joy in progress was muted: its thought on society took pride in not transcending that which was. The impulse of philosophy to transform the Ought into the Is readily gave way to the sober acceptance of the Is as the Ought . . . sociology has remained "positive" not only because it desires to keep to the given . . . but also because it takes a positive stance toward that which exists. It has enjoined itself to refrain from treating that which exists critically.[30]

Marcuse, in his famous wartime investigation of the roots of Fascism, *Reason and Revolution*, went so far as to argue that Comteanism, which rapidly became transformed into the defense of middle-class society as it existed, bore the seeds of a later philosophic justification of authoritarianism and irrationalism. By equating the study of society with the study of

nature and its laws, by negating the very idea of a dialectic, "social practice" was effectively "throttled by the inexorable." This sociology was
charged with establishing the "general limits of all political action" and
preparing men for obedience and resignation to the existing order:

> The laws positivist science discovered and that distinguish it from empiri-
> cism, were positive also in the sense that they affirmed the prevailing order
> as a basis for denying the need to construct a new one. Not that they ex-
> cluded the idea of reform and change—on the contrary, the idea of prog-
> ress loomed large in the sociology of Comte—but the laws of progress
> were part of the machinery of the given order . . . the authority of natural
> laws in place of free action . . . The idea of order, so basic to Comte's posi-
> tivism, has a totalitarian content in its social as well as methodological
> meaning.[31]

The great sociologists of their own Weimar time came in for similar
treatment from our thinkers. The Critical theorists railed that Karl Mannheim's concept of "ideology' in effect reduced all knowledge to a kind of
"false consciousness."[32] And, indeed, Hannah Arendt's very first publication (in 1930) was devoted to a defense of the autonomy of philosophy
in the face of the reductionist threat posed by Mannheim's *Ideology and
Utopia* (published in 1929).[33] Sociology, the young philosopher indig-
nantly proclaimed, "denies reality to thought as a matter of principle . . .
Everything in the mental or intellectual realm is regarded as ideology or
utopia." In effect, Arendt adopted a technique which many years later
(1969) Peter L. Berger described as "relativizing the relativizers."[34] It was
not *thought* but sociology's (and psychoanalysis') *"mistrust* of the mind,"
she wrote, that was suspect and in need of explanation. The discipline
had to be understood as a product of the homeless condition induced
by a bourgeois economistic modernity and the breakdown of tradition.
"Sociology itself," she wrote,

> is bound to a historical moment without which it could not have arisen
> in the first place, the moment when a justified mistrust of the mind was
> awakened through its homelessness. . . . The interpretation of mental life
> purely in terms of reducing it to ideology or utopia is justified only when
> the economic component has gained such predominance in life that
> thought in fact can and must become "ideological superstructure.". . .
> Only when people no longer see their existence in community as given,
> only when, as by means of economic advancement, the individual sud-
> denly finds himself belonging to a completely different community . . .
> does the question of *meaning* arise.[35]

On the surface, Leo Strauss does not appear to share this hostility.[36]
Quite the contrary, actually, he once (quite disingenuously, I think) de-

clared that "my specialty is . . . social science"[37] and formulated his "sociology of philosophy" in explicitly Mannheimian terms, describing it as "a legitimate subdivision of sociology of knowledge."[38] Yet this "sociology of philosophy" contains a frontal attack upon the assumptions of the sociology of knowledge and, furthermore, is designed to grasp and preserve what that science, according to Strauss, grossly denies: the privileged, irreducible role of the philosopher in society.

> Sociology of knowledge emerged in a society which took for granted the essential harmony between thought and society . . . It did not see a grave practical problem in that fundamental relation. It tended to see in the different philosophies exponents of different societies or classes or ethnic spirits. It failed to consider the possibility that all philosophers form a class by themselves, or what unites all genuine philosophers is more important than what unites a given philosopher with a particular group of nonphilosophers.[39]

For Strauss, perhaps somewhat melodramatically, the practice of philosophy was a definitionally precarious one. Even in the apparent safety of a liberal-democratic society, he argued, one should not be blinded to "the existence of a danger which, however much its forms may vary, is coeval with philosophy." Radically subverting both the intent and structure of the traditional sociology of knowledge, Strauss pronounced that "the understanding of this danger and of the various forms which it has taken, and which it may take, is the foremost task, and indeed the sole task, of the sociology of philosophy."[40]

Even more significantly, Strauss, Arendt, and the Critical Theorists were all compelled, in more or less complex ways and from varying perspectives, to engage the sociological colossus Max Weber. Perhaps most bluntly, and crudely, the Frankfurt School regarded him as essentially a continuation of the conservative-bourgeois positivist tradition in sociology, a thinker whose formalistic dualism of facts and values acted in service of the status quo.[41] The Critical Theorists could, no doubt, sympathize with Weber's tragic awareness of the victory of the technocratic-instrumental realm and bureaucratic rationality as part of the "disenchantment of the world," since this was not all that far from their conception of the "dialectic of enlightenment." But they rejected Weber's contention that capitalism was the highest form of socioeconomic rationality: witness, for instance, Marcuse's famous presentation at the 1964 *Soziologentag* in Heidelberg where he attacked Weber as an outright apologist for capitalism.[42] As Marxists, they held that unplanned economies without socialized means of production were bound to be irrational.[43]

Hannah Arendt's relationship to Weber, on the other hand, is more complicated and requires some exegesis. Certain key aspects of her thought, such as the concepts of "world alienation" and "homelessness," conjure up (and perhaps derive from) Weber's notion of the "disenchantment of the world."[44] Indeed, she usually referred to the master with great respect and, when critical, attributed attendant weaknesses to the vulgarizations of his followers.[45] But this is only part of the story. Peter Baehr has recently suggested that Arendt's negative judgements are often coded or deflected, prompted by her desire not to hurt the feelings of her great friend and mentor, Karl Jaspers, whose admiration for Weber was virtually unbounded.[46] Whatever the case, as Baehr notes, in many ways it may be useful to view Arendt's philosophy as presenting a rather comprehensive alternative to Weber's politico-sociological outlook. Arendt certainly disapproved of the functionalist and instrumental bias attendant upon his kind of sociology.[47] But her deeper dissensions, although seldom overtly declared, revolve around their radically opposed conceptions of "action." The notion of "action" is pivotal to Arendt's philosophical reconfigurations and is diametrically opposed to that of the social sciences, especially the dominant Weberian kind, as Baehr has argued.

> In contrast to theories that posit action teleologically as a means-end relationship or as a "system," Arendt understands it as the ability to initiate a new course of events. . . . Action, in Arendt's account, is a category of politics, not of sociology . . . it is not primarily the result of a "motive" (Max Weber) or of a "project" (Alfred Schutz) but instead a corollary of [what she called] "natality". . . Moreover a categorical feature of action is its indeterminacy and irreversibility. For no person ever knows exactly what they have initiated, and the "meaning" of their action is less a force that impels them on, and more a retrospective judgment by the spectator . . . who weaves the strands of many actions into a story which as "history" or remembrance, preserves the actor's words and deeds.[48]

Arendt opposed these notions of action within social science because ultimately, she argued, they rested upon the reductive metaphorics of "fabrication" and instrumentality. She sought to strip action of its Weberian means-ends nexus and render it instead as revelatory of the human capacity for freedom. Action indicated the capacity to initiate, the ability to start something new and unpredictable.[49] Because action is freedom and thus the political characteristic par excellence, Arendt at least implicitly challenged the Weberian conception of politics as modes of rulership and domination and placed in its stead the normative (albeit idiosyncratic and to many even bizarre) proposition of politics as public spaces for the expression of freedom and individual self-disclosure, shorn of any particular or sectional "material" interests. This is far removed indeed from

Weber's conception of politics and state power as the capacity to monopo-
lize the means of violence; and it is utterly opposed to Schmitt's dichoto-
mous friend-foe conception of politics. Instead, power is conceived as a
positive form of energy deriving from a rather idealized notion of voluntary collective action.[50] For Arendt, Weberian domination cannot be political because it imposes a monopoly on speech and action, a monopoly
that destroys plurality, the very basis of the human condition.[51] The dissension from notions of politics as rule and domination is radical; freedom is to exist in a state neither of rule or being ruled. Arendt also never
endorsed the "competitive elitist" of liberal democracy supported by Weber and in its stead proposed the revitalization of the lost revolutionary
tradition of councils.[52]

If Arendt's dialogue with Weber was largely indirect and implicit, such
was not the case for Leo Strauss. Strauss too respected Weber, and regarded him as the intellectual giant with whom open engagement and
argument was crucial if the "modern" project was to be both understood
and "overcome."[53] As he put it in *Natural Right and History*: "No one
since Weber has devoted a comparable amount of intelligence, assiduity,
and almost fanatical devotion to the basic problems of the social sciences.
Whatever may have been his errors, he is the greatest social scientist of
our century."[54] Strauss's engagement with Weber was, of course, part of
his larger critique of modern historicism and social science—and thus
of liberal democracy—as destructive of conceptions of "natural right" (I
shall return to this later). But it was precisely because of Weber's eminence
and sophistication that Strauss singled him out for confrontation and
analysis.[55]

Weber's distinction between facts and values and his insistence upon
the ethically neutral character of social science, Strauss disapprovingly
noted, derived from his belief that no genuine knowledge of the Ought
was possible. A plurality of values existed in the universe "whose demands conflict with one another, and whose conflict cannot be solved by
human reason . . . Weber's thesis necessarily leads to nihilism or to the
view that every preference, however evil, base or insane, has to be judged
before the tribunal of reason to be legitimate as any other preference."[56]
The Weberian categorical imperative thus took on a kind of existential
hue of authentic resoluteness: to be base is to be lukewarm. "Follow God
or the Devil as you will, but, whichever choice you make, make it with
all your heart, with all your soul, and with all your power."[57]

In numerous complex, sometimes sophistic forays, Strauss questioned
whether Weber's basic premise of an unresolvable conflict between human
values, had "really been demonstrated, or whether it has merely been pos-
tulated under the impulse of a specific moral preference."[58] Strauss's proj-

ect, after all, his return to the verities of pre-modern philosophy and its assumptions, was based upon the search for universals denied by the postulates of Weberian social science and its associated historicist assumptions.[59]

But, of course, all these individual confrontations were really parts of broader critiques against social science itself, and these in turn were reflections of the wider alternative philosophies and politics respectively being adumbrated. Strauss, the Critical Theorists, and Arendt not only regarded social science as essentially "instrumental," but also as a reflection and reinforcement of a technico-reductionist mentality characteristic of liberal-capitalist modernity.[60] One need not elaborate on this for the Critical Theorists, for if the Frankfurt School is famous for anything it is for its enduring, multifaceted efforts to demonstrate the pernicious permutations and domination of "instrumental"—as opposed to substantive—reason in modern society.[61] Indeed, it is precisely its rather undifferentiated critique, its tendency in this regard to collapse distinctions between liberal-bourgeois and Fascist regimes or between mass murder and the Hollywood culture industry, that has aroused much of the criticism against it.[62] In their reading, bourgeois sociology becomes the very incarnation of this kind of instrumental reason, defined as a form of false consciousness. Bourgeois sociology, they argued, assumed an unproblematic unity between individual and society by, as it were, abolishing social antagonisms and the idea of a dialectical totality that would allow for genuine radical criticism.[63] It treated "society, potentially the self-determining subject, as if it were an object, and could be determined from outside . . . Such a substitution of society as object for subject constitutes the reified consciousness of sociology."[64] Indeed, it was in order to construct a kind of dialectical anti-positivist counter-sociology, which they dubbed "Critical Theory," that their alternative Institute for Social Research was founded in 1923.

While the Frankfurt School rejected positivistic sociology on the redemptive (albeit fragile) grounds of an as yet historically unrealized emancipatory dialectic, Leo Strauss dismissed it in favor of a resurrected pre-modern notion of enduring rationality and natural right. The positivist assumption that modern science represented the highest form of knowledge, he noted, inevitably deprecated an always existent and necessary pre-scientific knowledge. It was precisely these pre-scientific assumptions—for instance, the presupposition that social science can tell human beings from other beings—that not only remained valid but were the essential precondition for all later "scientific" operations.[65]

But this logical matter was not primary. Time and again, as with his analysis of Weber, Strauss returned to positivism's prescriptive inabilities and its paralyzing or trivializing effects. Serious issues become evaded, he bemoaned, "by the simple device of passing them off as value problems."[66] Even more bitingly, he wrote: "Moral obtuseness is the necessary condition for scientific analysis . . . The more serious we are as social scientists, the more completely we develop within ourselves a state . . . which may be called nihilism."[67] But of course, for Strauss, the distinction between facts and values itself (so foundational to modern social science) was fallacious, its inner contradictions legion. The social scientist resisted all values, he wrote, in the name of truth. "But according to his principles, truth is not a value which it is necessary to choose . . . Social science cannot pronounce on the question of whether social science itself is good," he wrote in quintessential Nietzschean fashion.[68]

For Strauss, neither social science nor historicism could be compatible with political philosophy since the latter unashamedly concerned itself with the search for the good,[69] while political "scientists" simply absolutized the given political order by remaining "within a horizon which is defined by the given political order and its opposite."[70] In quite Heideggerian manner, Strauss posited a conflict between "thinking about Being" and the purely external, relative, "objective" method practiced by the behavioral sciences.[71]

By contrast, Arendt's general judgments on the social and behavioral sciences, its functionalizing biases apart, always concentrated on their reductive and what she took to be their essentially demeaning method. I will come back to this point soon but here it is worth noting that, if anything, her comments on psychology and psychoanalysis were even more scathing than those concerning sociology.[72] This is somewhat surprising, especially given Arendt's own penchant for flashing psychological insights scattered throughout her work, though these were admittedly more of the intuitive than the theoretical and systematic kind.[73] While both disciplines were reductive, refusing to accept anything at face value, sociology—if, admittedly, in misguided fashion—at least attended to the historical dimension, while psychological analysis entirely ignored it.[74] Ironically, Arendt herself hardly ever took anything at face value; on the contrary, she almost willfully sought to make commonsense seem obscure, and obscurity commonsensical. At any rate, I would argue, the deeper source of both her unwillingness to abide psychoanalytical method and her overall disdain for social-scientific methods sprang from her performative emphasis, the notion that selves disclosed themselves and took on significance in the public realm. Thus she ideologically opposed the emphasis on unconscious motives, even on interiority (*Innerlichkeit*) itself, as antithetical to that which counted politically: the manifest world of action.

Arendt, Strauss, and the Critical Theorists alike historicized the social sciences as functional handmaidens of mass modernity. They variously argued that the very notion of "the social" and the accompanying "sciences" that proceeded in its name were both a reflection of the development of this particular kind of society. For the Critical Theorists, "society" was a bourgeois idea that contained both emerging, progressive, and later regressive moments: "The concept of society, itself," Adorno and Horkheimer proclaimed, ". . . was formulated only in the course of the rise of the modern bourgeoisie as 'society' proper in contrast to the court. It is a concept of the Third Estate." They hastened to point out, of course, that consciousness of "sociation" was of ancient provenance. But there it "had the character of something that existed for itself, something substantial and unproblematic, something predominating in relation to . . . the life process of mankind." Only in the age of the fully developed bourgeosie, "when the oppositions between the institutions of Feudal absolutism and that stratum which already controlled the material life process of society became strikingly evident, did the concept of society again become more fluid." Only then did its oppositional stance to existing institutions, such as the state, become actual.[75]

This was an essentially dynamic conception, they wrote, that also changed its character in accord with the changing plight of its articulators: "The concept of society, which is specifically bourgeois and antifeudal, implies the notion of an association of free and independent human subjects for the sake of a better life and, consequently, the critique of natural societal relations. The hardening of Bourgeois society into something impenetrably and inevitably natural is its immanent regression."[76]

In Hannah Arendt's work, there are also numerous meanings attributed to the terms "social" and "society," and these and their different uses have already been thoroughly analyzed elsewhere.[77] What must be stressed here, however, is that Arendt also "historicized" both its development and located the very possibility of the discipline of social science within this horizon: "Sociology itself, then, is bound to a historical moment without which it could not have arisen in the first place, the moment . . . when the economic component has gained such predominance in life that thought in fact can and must become 'ideological superstructure.' The primacy of the 'economic power structure' in reality has its own history and is part of the history of modern thought . . . ."[78] For Arendt, the notion of the "social" was "a product of the modern market economy, the concomitant transformation of fixed property into mobile, exchangeable, monetarized 'wealth', and of mass culture."[79]

All this is most explicitly worked out in *The Human Condition* where she declares that "the emergence of the social realm . . . is a relatively new phenomenon whose origin coincided with the emergence of the modern age and which found its political form in the nation-state."[80] Essentially a kind of bastard hybrid—neither genuinely private nor public—it is akin to the realm of the household, to consumption, necessity, and the "life-process." We view "the body of peoples and political communities in the image of a family whose everyday affairs have to be taken care of by a gigantic nationwide administration of housekeeping."[81] It was this uncontrolled modern process of leakage of the household to all other realms that ate away at the possibilities of politics, freedom, and action,[82] and indicated that the *animal laborans*—Marx's "socialized humanity"—had become the virtual reality, the archetype of contemporary existence.[83] Society here, she writes, becomes "the form in which the fact of mutual dependence for the sake of life and nothing else assumes public significance and where the activities connected with sheer survival are permitted to appear in public."[84]

Such a mode of organization, Arendt argued, rapidly generates its own appropriate norms and disciplines. There is a Foucaultian ring to all this: Society "expects from each of its members a certain kind of behavior, imposing innumerable and various rules, all of which tend to 'normalize' its members, to make them behave, to exclude spontaneous action or achievement." This is a negative definition rendering "society" as that form of human organization that serves only sheer survival, one in which "behavior" replaces—indeed excludes—action.[85]

Most relevant to us is the fact that for Arendt the "social sciences" represent the cognitive expression of this very development. Sociology was "no isolated phenomenon occurring in some ivory tower of scholarly thought. It is closely connected with the growing functionalization of our society, or rather with the fact that modern man has increasingly become a mere function of society."[86] "Under the concerted assault of the modern debunking 'sciences', psychology and sociology," she wrote in *On Revolution*, "nothing indeed has seemed to be more safely buried than the concept of freedom."[87]

There was an ominous history and logic of the development of the social sciences:

> It is the same conformism, the assumption that men behave and do not act with respect to each other, that lies at the root of the modern science of economics, whose birth coincided with the rise of society and which, together with its chief technical tool, statistics, became the social science par excellence. Economics—until the modern age a not too important part of ethics and politics and based on the assumption that men act with respect to their economic activities as they act in every other respect—could

achieve a scientific character only when men had become social beings
and unanimously followed certain patterns of behavior, so that those who
did not keep the rules could be considered to be asocial or abnormal.[88]

The precondition for the very possibility of the discipline called statis-
tics was

> great numbers . . . behaviorism and automatism in human affairs . . . The
> unfortunate truth about behaviorism and the validity of its "laws" is that
> the more people there are, the more likely they are to behave and the less
> likely to tolerate non-behavior . . . Statistical uniformity is by no means a
> harmless scientific ideal; it is the no longer secret political ideal of a soci-
> ety which, entirely submerged in the routine of everyday living, is at peace
> with the scientific outlook inherent in its very existence.[89]

Like "society" itself, the "social sciences" carry a totalizing, enveloping
logic.

> To gauge the extent of society's victory in the modern age, its early substi-
> tution of behavior for action and its eventual substitution of bureaucracy
> . . . it may be well to recall that its initial science of economics, which
> substitutes patterns of behavior only in this rather limited field of human
> activity, was finally followed by the all-comprehensive pretension of the
> social sciences which, as "behavioral sciences," aim to reduce man as a
> whole, in all his activities, to the level of a conditioned and behaving ani-
> mal. If economics is the science of society in its early stages, when it could
> impose its rules of behavior only on sections of the population and on
> parts of their activities, the rise of the "behavioural sciences" indicates
> clearly the final stage of this development, when mass society has de-
> voured all strata of the nation and "social behavior" has become the stan-
> dard for all regions of life.[90]

Arendt also critiqued notions of "scientific" historiography. She not
only entirely dismissed all teleological systems but held causality itself to
be "an altogether alien and falsifying category . . . Not only does the actual meaning of every event always transcend any number of past 'causes'
which we may assign to it . . . but this past itself comes into being with
the event itself. Only when something irrevocable has happened can we
even try to trace its history backward. The event illuminates its own past;
it can never be deduced from it."[91] Like her comments on social science,
this critique was closely linked to the Arendtian reaffirmation of action,
and the redemptive capacity for new beginnings. For historians, she insisted, causality constituted a denial of their own subject-matter for
"within the framework of preconceived categories, the crudest of which
is causality, events in the sense of something irrevocably new can never

happen . . . each event in human history reveals an unexpected landscape of human deeds, sufferings and new possibilities which together transcend the sum total of all willed intentions and the significance of all origins."[92]

Arendt distinguished "information" and "scientific knowledge" from "understanding," that complex, unceasing activity never able to produce unequivocal results and which, necessarily, preceded and succeeded knowledge. The task of the historian was thus to detect these *novelties* and analyze and articulate their implications and significance. Such novelties consisted of disclosive stories that had many beginnings but no end. "Ends" were actually always new beginnings. Indeed, precisely this capacity for new beginnings represented a (perhaps faint) hope that ultimately the nightmare fabricated by social science could be foiled. "No matter what sociology, psychology and anthropology will tell us about the 'social animal', men persist in making, fabricating and building although these facilities are more and more restricted to the abilities of the artists, so that the concomitant experiences of worldliness escape more and more the range of ordinary human experience."[93]

Let us now recover our bearings somewhat. That all these figures formulated critiques of social science should by now be obvious. Less obvious, perhaps, and precisely because they were all engaged in one way or another with social analysis, is the fact that they all proposed "alternative" social sciences. The Critical Theorists, after all, are virtually defined by this. Their "Institute of Social Research," founded in 1923 with the express intention of developing an anti-positivist counter-sociology and built upon conceptions of totality and dialectics and untapped social potentialities, is the most obvious example of this.[94] But, more modestly and subversively, Arendt's sociology of "mass society" and Strauss's "sociology of philosophy" sought similarly dissenting routes that would buttress their own larger worldviews and sense of the political.[95] Theirs was a quintessential Weimarian radicalism infused by the search for definitively non-liberal, non-bourgeois forms. This constitutes part of the attraction as well as the disturbing ambiguity of their legacy.

All not only articulated in various ways the discontents of modernity and liberalism but also drank rather deeply from the Heideggeran well. As Steven Smith has recently suggested, such an Heideggerianism provided a critical perspective on "modernity" not available to those operating within a more standard liberal democratic framework.[96] (Is it not this peculiar combination that still lends a peculiarly exciting and dangerous air to what we today term Weimar intellectual culture?) Yet their various critiques of liberalism went in quite different directions from that of, say, Ernst Juenger, Carl Schmitt, and Heidegger himself, all exponents of what today we regard as the radical, and rather brutalized, Weimar intellectual right.

Perhaps it is here that their Jewish and "marginal" status becomes of relevance. All sought anti-reductionist, humanizing, and redeeming possibilities rather than forms of hardness and domination. As Strauss put it: "Whatever the significance of modern natural science may be, it cannot affect our understanding of what is human in man. To understand man in the light of the whole means for modern natural science to understand man in the light of the sub-human. But in that light man is wholly unintelligible." For Strauss, it was classical political philosophy that "viewed man in a different light,"[97] whereas for the Frankfurt School, with its emphasis on dialectics and potentiality, it was, as Martin Jay demonstrates, a subtle defense of theory as itself a form of non-resigned practice.[98] For Arendt this entailed a thorough rereading of the Western tradition, pressing for a valorized understanding of politics and reconceptualizing freedom as action instead of some kind of internalized, apolitical "will." This common sensitivity and resistance to the reductive, reifying ingredients of social science characterized the (Jewish) Weimarians analyzed here, and prompted them to redirect their critique of liberal modernity in more "humanizing" ways and directions.

Inferring the ways in which such ill-defined psychological sensibilities and commitments as "Jewishness" enter the thought and values of thinkers is, of course, a notoriously difficult and subtle, perhaps even dangerous, matter, especially given that the nature and degree of Jewishness manifested itself in quite different ways amongst these thinkers. Thus, only Strauss immersed himself in, and placed integral value upon, Jewish texts and tradition itself. After all he began his career as a research fellow in Jewish philosophy at the Academy for the Science of Judaism in Berlin from 1925–1932 and immersed himself in and wrote about Maimonides, Spinoza, Isaac Husik, Moses Mendelssohn, and Hermann Cohen. The problem of Athens versus Jerusalem stood at the center of his thought. Arendt too explicitly placed issues and questions of Jewish politics, sensibility, and identity at the center of her life and thought but, unlike Strauss, paid almost no attention to the substance of the tradition and its content except to document its breakdown and the consequences flowing from it.[99] For the Frankfurt School, Jewishness was a far more problematic and subliminal matter—despite the fact that scholars have begun to underline more strongly the Jewish component.[100] Gershom Scholem, for instance, defined it as one of the most remarkable "Jewish sects" produced by German Jewry; perhaps for this reason non-Jewish members like Paul Massing and Karl Wittfogel felt somewhat marginal.[101] Yet one could argue that much of the Critical Theorists' growing interest in Jewishness and

Judaism had purely negative, external roots, and was simply a response to Weimar anti-Semitism and its later murderous Nazi incarnation, even if the evolution of their deepening attempts to grasp it indicates a rather far-reaching change in attitude. Witness, for example, Horkheimer's early and mechanical reduction of the "Jewish problem" to capitalism[102]—"he who does not wish to speak of capitalism, should also be silent about fascism"[103]—as well as the use of conventional empirical methods in the famous 1950 study of *The Authoritarian Personality* through Adorno and Horkheimer's far more subtle philosophical ruminations on Auschwitz and its implications.[104]

Still, here we want to examine whether the peculiar resistance to social science of these thinkers can in any other "more positive" way be linked to their Jewish predicament and (variously understood) sensibility. There are a number of possible approaches to this question. If a common thread is to be found perhaps it lies in the peculiar German tradition of *Bildung* which, in the context of a protracted struggle for emancipation, George Mosse has argued, ironically became integral to German Jewish intellectual identity itself. With its emphasis on the primacy of culture, the goal of an individual emancipation beyond religion and nationality, and its insistence upon personalized, humanizing modes, the *Bildung's* ideal became an almost automatic part of German Jewry's cultural and intellectual radar. Mosse even argues that it was with the Frankfurt School— the least explicitly Jewish of those considered here—that this peculiarly German Jewish identity reached its climax![105]

For the Frankfurt School, this may help illuminate the connections between their awareness of anti-Semitism and the Holocaust, the resistance to positivist reductionism, and the still glimmering hope for some kind of transcendence, a hope which animated their project to the end. While they sought to expose the murderous dialectic of the Enlightenment and the falsity of the present, they nevertheless did cling to an admittedly more blurred, ever more abstracted utopian ideal of universal human emancipation, which in the post-Holocaust era they defined as the paradoxical desire for the saving of the hopeless.[106] Martin Jay has suggested that in all this a clearly Jewish ingredient can be found. In the "cardinal tenet of Critical Theory: the prohibition of premature positivity," he writes, ". . . the Jews became the metaphoric equivalent of that remnant of society preserving negation and the nonidentical . . . underlying the Frankfurt School's refusal to describe the utopian alternative to the present society was the traditional Jewish taboo on naming God or picturing paradise."[107] At the same time, Anson Rabinbach has recently suggested, Adorno traced the origins of anti-Semitism to this Jewish *Bildverbot*. The enforcement of this taboo fostered enormous hatred and resentment. In this way a false, mythologizing mimesis became linked to the murderous hatred and extermination of the Jews.[108]

For all that, if the Jewish dimension did become increasingly central for the Critical Theorists, they never "essentialized" it—rather, they made it part of a greater problematic.[109] This also applied, in many ways, to Strauss and Arendt even though they were far more explicit about their Jewish loyalties and identifications. Their work as German Jewish intellectuals cannot be understood outside of a situation and consciousness of ambivalence, multiple loyalties, fissures, breakdowns, and partial reconstitutions. I would even argue that much of their acuity and creativity derived from an internalization and negotiation of these tensions, especially as they manifested themselves in the productive turbulence of the Weimar Republic. Would it be too far-fetched to suggest that their senses of complexity and vulnerability alerted them very early on to a profound distrust of reductionism in all its varieties?

In Strauss's case it is important to note that from his early Weimar days, he regarded with great skepticism the modern rationalist and social scientific critique of orthodoxy and revelation. By remaining within the horizons of the present order, "science" elided primary or fundamental questions.[110] Already in the 1920s his highly *normative conception of science and philosophy* (in contrast to what he took to be the debilitating Weberian distinction between facts and values) was stated in relationship to, and informed by, Judaism: "The norm of any science of Judaism," he wrote in 1929 in an essay on Franz Rosenzweig, was "the vindication of our existence as Jews."[111]

Jewish thought, like ancient philosophy and medieval religious rationalism, constituted not only a form of necessary opposition to conventional opinion, but preserved truth in an insidious world deformed by both historicism and social science.[112] It is interesting to note the way in which Strauss, the conservative, employs what can only be described as a kind of postmodernist, post-colonialist Nietzsche to couch his most radical dismissal of social science and thereby achieve a vantage point to uphold Jewish tradition. "Nietzsche," he wrote,

> has a deeper reverence than any other beholder for the sacred tables of the Hebrews as well of the other nations in question. Yet since he is only a beholder of these tables . . . he is not subject to the commandments of any. This is true also and especially of the tables, or "values," of Western culture. But according to him, all scientific-concepts, and hence in particular the concept of culture is an outgrowth of nineteenth-century Western culture; its application to 'cultures' of other ages and climates is an act stemming from the spiritual imperialism of that culture. There is then a glaring contradiction between the claimed objectivity of the science of cultures and the radical subjectivity of that culture.[113]

It is of some relevance to note that it was, pointedly, in a talk entitled "Why We Remain Jews" that Strauss insisted that sociology and psychology were "superficial and thoughtless": in no fundamental way did, or could, they reflect upon themselves. Science was poised against Jewish faith and history. "It is surely," he wrote, "nobler to be a victim of the most noble dream than to profit from a sordid reality and to wallow in it." That noble dream (which could "not be denied even by the unbelieving Jew of our age") was "the perception of the ultimate mystery, of the truth of the ultimate mystery—the truth that there is an ultimate mystery, that being is radically mysterious. . . ."[114] Jewish history, Jewish existence itself, was in this conservative, anti-scientist view, proof of the permanently unredeemed condition of the "noble vision."

While the experience of Nazism was central to all these thinkers' lives and reflections, Strauss responded in the most sublimated manner. Arguably his attack upon liberalism became more muted and refined as a result of Nazism and the emigration.[115] Still, even in the midst of concrete problems, as his tortuous, autobiographical comments on the "theologico-political predicament" indicate, his always abstract thought tended to spiritualize the political.[116] His aim throughout, as Alfons Söllner puts it, was to "rehabilitate the tradition that had—wrongly, in his opinion—been discredited by modernity."[117]

Arendt's Jewishness did, of course, relate much more explicitly to concrete political and personal questions. Her attitudes to Jewishness were peculiarly complex and here we must limit ourselves to the ways in which this was linked to her critique of social science and modernity and the alternative worldview that she espoused.[118] We should not forget that she undertook her first analysis of the "social" (beginning during the Weimar period) in the context of her Zionist-inspired "Jewish" book on Rahel Varnhagen. There, in apparent contrast to the rest of her work, the arena of the Berlin salon provides the "social"—or at least "sociability"—with an unexpected positive valence. But this would be a misperception, for her point was that the salons provided a social area outside of respectable bourgeois society and were characterized by the anomalous condition of the strata they brought together ("impoverished" nobility, actors, and Jewish women).[119] Their importance lay in the fact that they *suspended* normal social conventions. Jews and "society" stood somehow in a relation of antagonism. This assumption, of course, animates Arendt's emphases on the modern Jew as pariah and parvenu, as an outsider of a particular kind.[120]

Arendt's awareness of Jewish marginality and difference and her sensitivity to the duplicities and machinations entailed in the assimilation process, I would suggest, have some bearing upon the formulation and content of her conceptions of "the social"—and its accompanying be-

havioral sciences—as equivalent to a process of flattening and homogenization, the draining and loss of distinctive collective and individual identity. The anti-plural nature of "the social" leaves no room for Jews (or,
for that matter, other minorities).[121]

To be sure, the fear of social leveling and homogenization was an overall Weimarian concern, characteristic especially of the intellectual radical
right. But here Arendt's consciously Jewish concerns and traumatic experiences did perhaps make a decisive difference. Schmitt reduced plurality
to factional, selfish interests, and Heidegger subsumed it under the sense-
less chatter of "the public." For him the political realm was essentially
inauthentic, "fallen."[122] In response to Heidegger, I would argue, Arendt
radically reclaimed the authenticity and centrality of the political—which
she defined quite differently from Schmitt's friend-foe conception. Politics
is envisaged as autonomous, no longer subservient to the "social" but
conceived as its crucial antidote. Moreover, uniquely in her time, Arendt
rendered plurality and difference as intrinsic, central values. Natality, not
being-toward-death, is placed at the center.

One should never reduce thought, as Arendt herself insisted, to its biographical roots. Yet it is difficult to sever these emerging emphases from
Arendt's experiences in the Weimar Republic, her own trauma under Nazism and her analysis of it, and her self-consciousness as a Jew. Arguably,
her classical work on totalitarianism is, among other things, a record of
the obliteration of individual and collective identities and differences, of
the triumph of the homogenizing social over humanity itself. After all,
she regarded the nation-state as the political form of the "social." The
moment it reneged on its promises of political equality for all its citizens
and embarked upon policies of ethnic exclusion, it brought about the
mass twentieth-century predicament of "Statelessness" that effectively
ended the Rights of Man and ushered in the age of refugees, totalitarianism, human superfluity, and total extermination.[123] Much of her later
work was spent working out the implications of these insights, both
within a Jewish and a general context. Her Zionism, as well as her critique of it,[124] was based upon these commitments to politics, plurality,
and the right of distinctive identities to have rights.[125]

Already in *The Origins of Totalitarianism* not all was darkness. It was
there that Arendt began formulating her positive counter-vision. As its
poetic ending indicates, the triumph of the social could not be complete:
"But there remains also the truth that every end in history necessarily
contains a new beginning; this beginning is the promise, the only 'message' which the end can ever produce. Beginning, before it becomes a
political event, is the supreme capacity of man; politically, it is identical
with man's freedom. . . . [It] is guaranteed by each new birth; it is indeed
every man."[126]

How, finally, can we place these thinkers into historical perspective and assess their concerns and contributions? The inability, combined with the lack of desire, to give liberalism its due no doubt constituted a continuing and grave blind spot in their intellectual arsenal. Their condemnations and fears of "modernity" as such (never properly distinguished from its totalitarian variants) may appear today as overheated, melodramatic. These biases, built into the fabric of Weimar radical theory, do indeed render that legacy an ambiguous one. Yet, surely, the fact that these and other Weimar intellectuals continue to generate excitement and maintain their varied, yet foundational, relevance at the end of the twentieth century should give us some pause. Perhaps their ideas and sensibilities still speak to us because the unease with "modernity" (however understood) and its characteristic cognitive modes has never really been fully alleviated and because these (Jewish) thinkers, imbued with humanizing impulses, provide redemptive clues to understanding—and perhaps transcending—a still homogenizing and reductive age.

Four

Nazism and the Holocaust in Contemporary Culture

Within Western sensibility, Nazism and the atrocities committed in its name have over the years become endowed with a peculiarly powerful and distinctive status. Since World War II, Treblinka and Auschwitz (and, I would add, Hitler and Himmler) have evolved into what Jean Amery has called "symbolic code words."[1] They have come to function as a kind of outermost metaphysical norm, as tangible shorthand incarnating the culture's conception of "radical evil,"[2] encoded into consciousness as *the* measure of absolute inhumanity.[3] There are of course good and obvious reasons for this but, I would argue, the special sense of shock and outrage is generated above all by the acute discomfort occasioned by the penetration of the barbarous into the allegedly cultured, the transgression of basic taboos within the framework (and by the means) of advanced industrial civilization. The enduring fascination with National Socialism and the especially deep need to account for it and its atrocities—the rich multiplicity of ruminations it has produced as well as the accompanying and growing attempts to relativize or neutralize or elide and displace its significance and impact—resides precisely in this rather ethnocentric sense of scandal and riddle, the abiding astonishment that a so-called enlightened and modern *Kulturnation* could thus deport itself.[4] I shall later come back to this Eurocentric issue.

In a quite distinctive way, then, "Nazism" has developed into a dense, available paradigm, an emotionally charged limit-case serving manifold purposes of discourse, a figural commodity with powerful, putatively "absolute" associations. Twenty years ago Greil Marcus phrased it rather quaintly: Nazism was a kind of supreme "bogeyman," a mythology with which children scared themselves, "the single commonality onto which one could project fantasies of hatred without the slightest feeling of guilt."[5] Yet these absolute associations have always and necessarily interacted with, and at the same time been transformed by, changing modes of self-understanding; so too have they been mobilized and manipulated by divergent political and psychological needs and interests. There is a dynamic at work here, I suggest, that simply will not allow inscriptions of Nazism to be carved into canonic, normative monoliths of meaning. The cultural developments and academic debates of the 1980s and 1990s and, indeed, the resurgence of mass murder and genocide as a part of contemporary actuality, have made it increasingly clear that this is highly contested terrain and that the impulse to conceive of Nazism in "Orthodox" manner, in absolute and moralistic terms which insulate it from ongoing political conflicts, cultural shifts, and wider historical processes, will be rendered increasingly difficult, if not quite impossible.[6] The paradigm's peculiar location and loading—the central metaphorical and symbolic functions it has come to assume (especially as it relates to German and Jewish identity)—has always generated certain tensions. More than ever, however, it is presently beset by pressures toward redefinition, challenges to its status, and quite striking processes of ironic self-subversion.

Here I can point to only a few divergent examples of the tensions induced by this potent symbolism and the resulting drive to exploit, problematize, or undermine it. In the first place, I would suggest that one way of understanding the recent controversy amongst German historians, the *Historikerstreit*, is through this peculiar absolute emplacement of Nazism.[7] The demand to "historicize" the narrative around National Socialism and its defining atrocities aroused such indignation and heated debate to a large degree because of the *metahistorical* dimensions with which it has been so regularly endowed. As Dan Diner puts it: Auschwitz "is a no-man's land of understanding, a black box of explanation, a vacuum of extrahistorical singificance, which sucks in attempts at historiographic interpretation . . . As the ultimate extreme case, and thus as an absolute standard of history, this event can hardly be historicized."[8]

But, by training, historians "historicize," and with most other historical events (the French Revolution, the decline of the British Empire, and so on), they do so as a matter of course. Historians operate on the assumption that historical events and phenomena are, by definition, unique—thereby rendering insistence on "uniqueness" as relatively superfluous—while at the same time possessing both general and distinguishing features. To a large extent, the singularity of any particular event becomes assertable and comprehensible only within a comparative historical perspective. In this respect, the *Historikerstreit* did not raise a genuinely historical question but it did highlight the moral functions and extra-historical nature of the discourse of National Socialism and its genocidal impulses within various national moral economies and identities. Its genuinely pernicious ingredient was not the question of historicization or singularity, but rather Ernst Nolte's depiction of the Holocaust as an act of anticipatory self-defense in which the Nazis took preventive action against their Jewish Bolshevik enemies because "they regarded themselves and their ilk as potential or real victims of an 'Asiatic' deed."[9]

To take another example, it is largely within the terms of this paradigm—and the need to somehow weaken, if not entirely unravel it—that the very phenomenon of Holocaust denial should be understood.[10] On the surface, this is an almost incomprehensible project.[11] It begins to be a little more understandable (though no more legitimate) if one grasps that, because the extermination of European Jewry acts as a kind of morally negative absolute within post-World War II sensibility, any attempt to relegitimize either anti-Semitism or a fascist agenda within Western society will have to seek to undermine and subvert that code at its very core.

Moreover, in the broadest terms, and although there is clearly no direct link between them, this kind of so-called "revisionism" is nourished by the intellectual atmosphere attendant upon elements of a postmodernist sensibility and its perception of the essentially self-referential (well-nigh arbitrary) nature and equal validity of almost all competing historical narratives. As the recent volume edited by Saul Friedlander demonstrates, postmodernism has radically problematized the very possibility of accurately "representing" the Holocaust; in fact, for some, the crisis and consciousness of the sharp limits of representation itself derives from the experience of Nazism and the impossibility of getting "inside" the Shoah.[12] At the very least, postmodernism's ironic sensibility—that severs moral judgement, aesthetic norms, and intellectual analysis—has undermined the monumental-didactic mode most suited to the code's moral tone.

In addition, Martin Jay has recently pointed out that the current obsession with problems of narration, history, and memory has made it practically impossible to ignore the "constructive" moment in our reconstruction of these events. Self-conscious "second- or even third-order reflection" on the meaning of it all has become impossible to avoid. To make matters more complicated, the fluidity and mingling of competing and changing narratives and perspectives render any "pure" version, any separate framing of the event in contemporary consciousness, less persuasive.[13] This overall problematization of the discourse is, on the one hand, profoundly disturbing, yet it may also contain within it some positive possibilities. It may, in the long run, perforce, constitute the only way of keeping the issues raised by National Socialism alive.

In Germany and Israel, for obvious historical reasons, the fluid inscriptions of both Nazism and the Final Solution have always been integrally linked to core questions of national identity and negotiated in some way or another into the respective prevailing national ideologies and self-definitions. If there were obvious and enormous differences in the German and Jewish and Israeli situations and interpretations—involving nothing less than the distinction between the perpetrators and victims of genocide—there were, nevertheless, certain structural parallels at work. Both sides were immediately confronted with perplexing questions of comprehension and remembrance. In both cases there were clearly discernible, and significant, distinctions between public and private responses. Furthermore, until the mid-1960s—albeit for entirely different reasons—the respective *public* commemorations and explanations in both Germany and Israel assumed a rather formulaic character, inserted into compensatory, meaning-bestowing narratives that conformed to the prevailing ideologies of the time.

It is true that in the Germany of the Adenauer years, in many respects at least, a veil was drawn over the past: de-Nazification and war-crimes trials ceased; there was considerable continuity with past regimes in the personnel of the civil service, judiciary, and universities. Yet, for all that, all the leading politicians publicly committed themselves to democracy (even if "democracy" was to be achieved at the expense of "justice"), forcefully disavowed National Socialism, and drew the appropriate "lessons" from it, lessons that always dovetailed with and reinforced their own particular political philosophies.[14] Moreover, Adenauer's policy of reparations meant that, at least on the public level, as part of its formal identity and "official" collective memory, there was a rather unique willingness of a nation to incorporate recognition of and responsibility for the horrendous crimes it had committed.[15] But from the beginning official recognition of German criminality carried with it built-in tensions and resistances: if the nation had been diabolically criminal, what would constitute acceptable self-definitions? If ritual enactment at Bitburg[16] explicitly revealed a certain sense of resentment and longing for "normalization," these underlying emotions long predated that particular event. What is known of the less formalized, private responses tends to support the notion that serious confrontation with the past, genuine *Trauerarbeit*, was very much the exception than the rule, a fact upon which the generational revolt of 1968 played. As Alexander and Margarete Mitscherlich have demonstrated, the impossibility of mourning the death of one's own de-legitimized leaders produced a series of projective and denial mechanisms rendering comprehension of the evil and destruction Nazism had wrought as remote indeed.[17] Empathy for the victims was the exception, not the rule. But in our context what needs to be stressed is that the very "need" to mobilize these psychological mechanisms was generated by repeated internal and external allegations concerning an unprecedented personal and collective German evil and guilt.

As a result, the discourse on Nazism and the Shoah very early on high-lighted the general question of the limits and possibilities of empathy, an issue that with Bosnia and Rwanda has again become searingly relevant. It also produced, and quite quickly so, the unfortunate syndrome of "comparative victimization." Already in 1945 there was a German tendency either to blame or claim parity with (or, indeed, even greater suffering than) the classic victims of Nazism. No less a member of the exiled German resistance than Volkmar von Zuehlsdorff announced in 1946 that "Today the Jews and Poles are not the victims, but the Germans irrespective of their political persuasions."[18] "The ovens of Auschwitz," he wrote later, "have become the glowing fires of Hamburg and Dresden, of Berlin, Leipzig, Cologne, Essen, Dortmund . . . ."[19]

Since then, this "competition" as to who constitutes the most "authentic" victim has become one of the great hallmarks of contemporary political discourse not only within Germany and Israel but far beyond; American culture, for example, is rife with a kind of cult of the victim. The point here is that the rapid and deep enshrinement of paradigmatic status upon Nazism ensured that its uses and applications would reach far beyond its original historical circumstances.

On the one hand, given its symbolic-emotive force as a guiding moral metaphor, the "Holocaust" and the language of genocide have been used to characterize any number of historical and contemporary persecutions and atrocities, ranging from the medieval witch craze through black slavery to Vietnam. The differences in origin, scope, and consequences were usually rather significant and the analogies did not necessarily illuminate either the Shoah or the comparative historical case in question. On the other hand, over the years the insistence upon the uniqueness of the Holocaust assumed the form of an extra-historical and political vested interest, becoming a crucial means of defining the particularity of Jewish identity. The rhetoric—and elevation—of singular Jewish victimization (in itself not inaccurate when viewed in its purely historical context) inevitably produced a certain resentment and initiated a kind of fruitless competition in both historical and ongoing victimization that informs, for instance, even current tensions between Black and Jewish people. Michael Bernstein has elegantly formulated the problem: "once victimhood is understood to endow one with special claims and rights, the scramble to attain that designation for one's own interest group is heated as any other for legitimacy and power."[20]

The radical singularity, the "uniqueness" that is built into this paradigm of "absolute evil"—one that from its beginnings has satisfied multiple "extra-historical" cultural and political functions—has thus itself become a site of conflict. The Holocaust was certainly singular, unique, but, given the fact that historical events are such by definition, the status of such a categorization is far from clear. As David Biale has pointed out,

> the very discourse of uniqueness is . . . meaningful only either when history is invoked in political debate (as in the German historians controversy) or in theological speculation; for historians concerned with understanding the past for its own sake, "uniqueness" is either trivial, meaningless or a code word for an extra-historical agenda . . . the best medicine for the vulgar exercise of comparative victimization is not the copious assertion of Jewish uniqueness, but an end to the fruitless debate between the uniqueness and universality of suffering in the first place.[21]

In an acute and unresolved way the legacy of the catastrophe has opened up ultimate questions relating to the possibilities and limits of human empathy, solidarity, and the ability to block out or recognize the suffering of others. It has raised the delicate problem of balancing historically meaningful distinctions between atrocities with the commonalities of experience that allow for some kind of common ground and solidarity.

The centrality of the Nazi trauma within Israeli life needs little elaboration.[22] But there too its inscriptive meanderings have been complicated, dynamic, and ambiguous. There too, at least in the initial stages, a deep divide pertained between public commemoration and private experience; the mute pervasiveness of this within private experience is most poignantly captured in David Grossman's remarkable novel, *See under Love.*"[23]

In the early years of Statehood, the *Churban* (destruction), as it was initially called, was made publicly manageable by incorporating it—as the extreme edge, to be sure—into the traditional, Zionist narrative of the transition from a powerless Diaspora to potent sovereignty, a saga that moved from exile and catastrophe to resistance and, ultimately, collective national deliverance. But because this version more or less locked the event into conventional ideological categories of martyrdom and redemption (laden as it also always was with the equalizing heroic motifs taken from the uprising of the Warsaw Ghetto), this somehow lessened the need for a differentiated, direct confrontation with the horrific specificities of the event. It possessed, rather, a kind of shadowy mythic status, an event from a remote world populated more by archetypes than real people. This was certainly true for the way in which the Kastner trial of the 1950s was conducted, and the televised re-staging of the trial in 1994 was distinguished precisely by a nuanced, differentiated psychological and political understanding of the complexities involved. Moreover, the opposition to reparations headed by Menachem Begin, though powerful, could still not be articulated in a framework that transcended the concrete issue itself.

Beginning in 1961 with the Eichmann trial and accelerating during and after the high point of June 1967, a particular constellation of events produced paradigmatic shifts in Israeli (and general Jewish) representations of the catastrophe and placed what had been latent at the very defining center of consciousness. The outlines of these developments are familiar enough. In the days and weeks immediately preceding the Six-Day War a feeling of utter isolation and vulnerability, indeed, the fear of possible extermination, permeated the country. As the most obvious available existential and historical analogy, the Shoah suddenly assumed a central experiential relevance. No longer remote exilic history but a perceived imminent prospect, its meaning and salience underwent dramatic transformation. The prevailing wisdom and governing ideology were transformed. The predicament of the Jewish state and the powerless Diaspora were now no longer regarded as antithetical; Jewish fate was existentially and politically one. The uniqueness of Jewish continuity, fate, and victimhood—with the Holocaust as its measure and standard— was now, more than ever, underlined. While Diaspora Jewish self-definition was more and more tied to identification with the Holocaust, Israeli political culture increasingly invoked it as the crucial legitimizing force behind the state's existence.

Despite the insistence of many uncomfortable intellectuals at the time that Jerusalem was not Auschwitz, that the fact of sovereignty made all the difference, and that the structure of the Arab-Israel conflict was not analogical to the anti-Semitic Nazi project,[24] the Shoah was continually invoked as part of a continuing Jewish historical isolation—as expressed in the popular song, "the whole world was and is against us"—*and made into the governing metaphor of the Arab-Israel conflict*. Menachem Begin's famous reference to Yassir Arafat in Beirut during the Lebanon war as "Hitler in his bunker" is only the most well known of an ongoing tendency. (Note, however, that such rhetoric of extermination was not originally limited to the right: Abba Eban described the pre-1967 map of Israel as "Auschwitz lines.") The contemporary Israeli radical right derives its sustenance from this perception and takes it to an extreme. The world is depicted in terms of the murderous enemies and destroyers of the Jewish people and the Arabs portrayed as a mix of the Nazi and Amalek metaphors. The general phenomenon of Kahanism—and indeed the particular act of Baruch Goldstein and his multiple murder of Arabs at the tomb of the Fathers in Hebron in 1994—is incomprehensible outside of this mindset.

It was, then, in the late 1960s that the Shoah exploded into public consciousness in Israel and the Diaspora alike. Since that time it has insistently occupied a defining central role in political discourse. Placing the

Shoah at the center of events, making it an explanatory key and moral arbiter of Jewish identity, made it "respectable" and brought it out of the dark, vaguely obscene recesses that it had inhabited before. Previously quite unintegrable, unamenable to conventional frameworks, it was now able to find eloquent, unashamed, and even triumphalist public relevance and expression by speaking to, no doubt, a compelling need in the collective psyche. Given the staggering enormity of the event and its imprint on the victims, some kind of transformation in official collective memory was bound to occur. In numerous ways, this assumed the form of a secular religion. At the deepest level, precisely because they were the locus of desecration, of violations of basic taboos, the sites of obscenity came to possess an aura of sanctity: Auschwitz and Treblinka took on the aura of "holy" places, and Yad Vashem increasingly became its shrine, a visit to which has been obligatory for all foreign dignitaries until very recently.

Ironically, perhaps, this first serious engagement with the past was inextricably tied to ideologically and politically dubious premises. Moreover, if the 1967 war produced this new ideology, the political conditions it brought about almost immediately threatened its consensual possibilities. For the unleashing of Holocaust rhetoric (that most immediately accessible emotional shorthand), the incessant appeal to the Shoah (that most resonantly evocative, but variously interpretable, absolute metaphor) entailed its inevitable engagement in the political and cultural conflicts that have characterized the country since then. Mobilized and brandished as a weapon in the ongoing political divide for and against the occupation and annexation of the territories acquired during the June war, no side developed a discourse in which the Holocaust was or could be left honorably above and beyond the battle. The imperative to invoke the analogies (or lack of them) and draw the appropriate, if always problematic and ideologically loaded, "lessons" became irresistible. Far from being statically and uniformly inscribed, the catastrophe has been constantly reapplied and reworked to become, in the words of Sidra de Koven-Ezrachi, a dynamic "prism of the ambiguities and contradictions that inhere in the society itself."[25]

For many years now, for instance, certain sectors of the Israeli liberal left have criticized what they take to be the politically manipulative functions of this "secular religion." In so doing it has sought to departicularize and universalize the "lessons" of the Holocaust. Insisting that dehumanization and murder were not peculiarly German but universal human possibilities, they invoked the most sensitive point of the code, challenging its most ultimate premise: that Jews—as ultimate victims—could never be victimizers and were indeed incapable of oppression and cruelty. Some argued that the very enormity and uniqueness of the Shoah was being employed as a pretext, a means of soothing the conscience for those perpetrating present, if obviously lesser, injustices and wrongdoing. Instead of justifying a cult of military might, the Jewish experience of ultimate victimization, they argued, should act as a spur towards the fully realized recognition of the humanity of the Palestinian "Other." The fact that IDF soliders were often the children of Holocaust victims did not constitute a warrant for the continuing violation of Palestinian rights, they asserted. The Left's "imperative" posited that one's own historical experience could provide the necessary empathic qualities for a sympathetic imagination of the catastrophe of others, even, or perhaps especially, one's own victims (without fudging necessary and important distinctions).[26]

But such delicate comparative distinctions were not always possible. Precisely because of the Holocaust's status as a governing metaphor and symbol, for many years a staple of anti-Israel propaganda has been the Zionism-Nazism equation, a line even to be found in quite unexpected literary quarters. Thus George Steiner's 1981 *The Portage to San Cristobal of A. H.* intimated that the Jewish myth of the chosen people and its genocidal impulses ultimately produced an identical Nazi offspring.[27] Is it surprising then that many of those who see themselves as its victims depict Zionism as a genocidal force intent on systematically destroying the fabric of Palestinian society? The Shoah, far from constituting an obviously different, incomparable case, is seen here as a lesser one. Not only are the archetypes of the Nazi and the Israeli occupier melded but the fate of those under occupation is presented as worse than those who perished in Treblinka and Auschwitz, for, so the claim goes, while in the camps death was instant and the suffering over in one day, under occupation, the pain, suffering, and killing is unending.[28] This wisdom has now crossed the Atlantic. In a 1996 verdict a Quebec judge told a woman who had slit her husband's throat that such wanton cruelty could only have been performed by a woman and that her act was worse than those committed by the Nazis for at least the Jews killed in the gas chambers had not suffered.[29]

What this illustrates, among other things, is a process in which the unleashing of absolute Holocaust discourse, precisely because it has so pervasively penetrated the cultural and political marketplace, has increasingly assumed radical and anti-canonic forms. It has ricocheted in multifaceted, often contradictory directions and become unhinged from its official versions, transmuted, in de Koven-Ezrachi's words, into "radical and subversive symbols. The images themselves, the emblems of Nazism, now seem to be released from social taboo. . . ."[30]

In contemporary Israel, Western Europe, and the United States, pre-

cisely because of its immense emotive and symbolic power and its relevance as the governing metaphor of "evil," the accusation of or comparison with Nazism and Nazi-like behavior and intentions is employed by
virtually all sides of many political and cultural debates as a potent "la-
bel," the ultimate critique and form of political outlawing and an effective
means to either propel or still action. We in Israel tend to take for granted
both the depth of penetration of this discourse, its speed, and multiple
controversies: how many of us remember the outrage provoked by the
attempt to commemorate the Nazi murder of homosexuals and lesbians
at Yad Vashem, the invocation by the Sephardi "rebel" Uzi Meshulam of
the "Ashke-Nazi" analogy, accusations by the settlers during the Rabin-
Peres years that the army was behaving like Nazis, and the maverick religious dove Yeshayahu Leibowitz's recurring damnation of post-1967 Israel as Judeo-Nazi? In the period of just a few weeks in early 1995 there
occurred the scandal over the attempt to auction Holocaust "soap," the
debate over the visit to Israel of the converted survivor, Cardinal Lustiger
of Paris, and the outcry prompted by the historian Moshe Zimmermann's
portrayal of the attitudes of Hebron settlers as akin to that of the Hitler
youth. Most revelatory, and shocking, of course, was that infamous (indeed fatal) pictorial fabrication—of Yitzhak Rabin dressed in SS uni-
form—paraded so prominently at right-wing political rallies prior to the
assassination.

The intensity in Germany and Israel may be the greatest but the use of
the code as metaphor for ultimate evil and a mode of positioning one's
self and condemning one's enemies is exceedingly powerful and frequent
in American culture as well. Who has not heard abortion characterized
as Holocaust? The Gun Owners of America liken the FBI to the Gestapo,
while Minister Louis Farrakhan compares the condition of a deprived
Iraq's hospitals to those of the death camps. The examples are endless.

What does this all amount to? I am suggesting that National Socialism
and the atrocities its adherents committed will continue to play foundational roles but will increasingly do so not only in problematic but also
in consciously problematizing ways. More and more the subject will be
torn out of its known, predictable contexts and undergo critical "defami-
liarization." The controversies around its proper interpretation, appropriate lessons, and commemoration will generate its eventual cultural centrality and vitality.

While the future content of these discourses cannot be predicted, they
will certainly be affected by changing sociopolitical constellations. In
Germany, with its increased political and economic power, unification
and greater self-confidence will no doubt constitute a spur to reconsider
and rewrite a relatively "normalized" national history that mutes if not

represses the more problematic elements of its past. Germany, James Young has suggested, "will recall primarily its own martyrs and triumphs. These include civilian victims of Allied bombings, dutiful soldiers killed on the front, and members of the wartime resistance to Hitler."[31] The recent commemorations underlined the "equivalence" of German victimization and the indivisibility of the deaths of all victims. Nevertheless, I would suggest, the coded power and symbolism of the Nazi experience has not been expunged. The very tensions and ambiguities surrounding it will continue to serve as a means of somehow perpetuating it.

Indeed, as I write, a new cultural variation of this tension is being played out in Germany, adding yet another layer to the unresolved tenacity of such memories. On one hand, there is the rather strange and powerful affirmation among many German youths of Daniel Goldhagen's portrait of "ordinary Germans" as jovial and sadistic killers[32] while, on the other, an emerging image within German popular culture of the German as possible *savior* of the Jew—as evidenced by the mass sales of the diaries of the German Jewish survivor, Victor Klemperer, the extraordinary reception of *Schindler's List,* and Völker von Schlöndorff's film of Michel Tournier's *The Ogre,* in which the German hero is depicted, in classical mythic fashion, as rescuing the Jew and literally carrying him on his back through fire and ice.[33]

In Israel, to be sure, there is of course no prospect of the Jewish experience under National Socialism "disappearing" from memory. Still, well before the Oslo agreement was signed, Yitzhak Rabin insisted on challenging the old rhetoric, arguing that not victimization but prudent power and self-reliance were the significant achievements of Zionism. The horizons that the still highly uncertain peace process have opened up may point to it perhaps assuming different symbolic functions and occupying a less central mobilizing role in a more secure and maturing political culture whose future outlines are as yet unclear.

At a time of the recurrence of mass murder and genocide throughout the world, more and more observers are drawing our attention to some unexpected consequences of the invocation of this "absolutizing" discourse in relation to contemporary atrocities. As Scott Montgomery has recently pointed out, it may be a "closed system that does not aid us in posing new questions, continually offers a revue of shallow finalities and, still worse, promotes voyeurism . . . transformed from historical truth into icons both of the machine and of modern malevolence, the Nazis have been given a disturbing purity, a kind of sacred uniqueness. . . ." Could it be, he asks, "that recent atrocities in various parts of the world have not seemed to demand immediate attention intervention because . . . these events do not appear to sufficiently obey the requirements of a 'true

Holocaust'? . . . Is it perhaps conceivable that our political leaders would feel a greater . . . urgency to deal with genocidal acts . . . if these acts closely simulated those of fascism, mimicking more precisely the monstrousness of the Hitlerian regime?"[34] This, I should point out, is not merely an intellectual but a political distinction. International law requires intervention when genocide occurs, and in both Bosnia and Rwanda the reluctance to define either as such has already been keenly noticed. At the same time, the opposite case may also hold: the constant invocation of Auschwitz as a model, a metaphor, and an analogy may produce a reflexive sort of moral deadening and rhetorical numbing. As Montgomery goes on to argue, the enthronement of Nazis as ultimate demons and "the horror at Auschwitz by virtue of being fully modern, occurring in the very center of Europe" makes other horrors in Africa, Asia, and South America, "no matter how brutal or planned, somehow qualify as more primitive . . . In a strange twist of logic, the Holocaust is made to seem more sophisticated, more advanced than any other incident of its kind. The terrible irony here is that Nazism finally becomes, at this elevated symbolic height, a perverted reflection of Eurocentrism."[35] As Shiraz Dossa provocatively puts it, it is the classic instance of "cultured" perpetrators massacring "cultured" victims.[36]

The historically accurate perception of the radical, unique evil of Hitler's war on the Jews has brought about an insistence on the very strict definition of genocide. But this admirable desire to maintain proper distinctions may not necessarily make people more willing to take action when the real necessity arises. "Never again," goes the saying. Rather, as David Rieff has recently pointed out, such conceptions of ultimacy may drive people to even greater complacency as they dismiss the overwhelming number of crimes that do not correspond to the exacting definitions. Sharply, he writes: "In the matter of genocide, strictness of definition can have the same unfortunate effect as sloppiness of definition. Our sense of genocide must be as flexible and as inventive as the human capacity for evil."[37]

These are, to my way of thinking, powerful considerations. Yet the matter is far from decided and in certain recesses of my own mind the "purity" of the Nazi case remains not merely a part of contemporary mythology but a historically valid perception. Nazism presents us with a case in which—notwithstanding all attempts to blur, relativize, or paper over—the distinction between victims and perpetrators is surely as clear and as simple as it is possible to be in the realm of human affairs. In the new cases, even if, as I believe, one can establish genocide or genocide-like behavior in Bosnia and Rwanda, the moral clarity is simply not there. Both cases, horrifying as they are, are characterized by enormous complexity and by the unalterable (though clearly not mathematically symmetric) fact of massacres followed by counter-massacres. It thus appears that we must be on double-guard: not to allow the trivializing, shoddy use of the analogy while at the same time remaining open to the possibility that genocide (even if it does not approximate the Nazi case) can recur and may in fact be recurring at present.

The perhaps unfortunate but inevitable temptation to find ultimate "meanings" and draw alternative "lessons" will, of course, continue unabated as will its dubious place in political rhetoric. We all have our own meanings and lessons and will admire some more than others even if, like Martin Jay recently suggested, they are somewhat utopian. He writes,

> Only in Hollywood movies can the Holocaust be contained within the boundaries of an aesthetic frame; in real life, it spills out and mingles with the countless other narratives of our century. Its real horror, we might say, is not confined to the actual genocidal acts it has come to signify. Historicizing the Holocaust need not mean reducing it to the level of the "normal" massacres of the innocents that punctuate all of recorded history, but rather remembering those quickly forgotten and implicitly forgiven events with the same intransigent refusal to normalize that is the only justifiable response to the Holocaust itself.[38]

But whatever "lessons" are being proposed, would it be too much to hope that they will all encompass, as Primo Levi phrased it already in 1947, "the shame that the Germans never knew, the shame which the just man experiences when confronted by a crime committed by another, and he feels remorse because of its existence, because of its having been irrevocably introduced into the world of existing things, and because his will has proven nonexistent or feeble and was incapable of putting up a good defense"?[39]

Part II

(Con)Fusions of Identity—
Germans and Jews

Five

Excursus
Growing Up German Jewish in South Africa

I was born in South Africa, and it was in that shaping context, as a child of German Jewish refugees who had come to the shores of that country during the 1930s, that some of the sensibilities associated with the German Jewish legacy were transmitted to me.[1] Over the years, of course, my understanding of the meaning of that legacy changed and deepened as it became more conscious, and the task of this essay will be to delineate briefly that evolution. But from a child's emotional point of view, to the extent that one can distinguish the specifically German Jewish components from the general experience of growing up Jewish, it was initially a rather embarrassing inheritance.

It was, no doubt, my parents' German accent, at once comfortingly familiar yet clearly foreign, which first alerted me to the "alienness" of my background. To the outside world, or so I believed, the fact of *German* foreignness was especially unforgivable in the years following World War II. In the first few weeks of primary school, when asked where my parents came from, I murmured "Australia." How could a child, even around 1950, acknowledge German origins, admit that in some way *he* had been the mortal enemy? Of course, already at that age I intuited the difference well enough but it was well-nigh impossible to articulate that, no, my parents were not the enemy but victims, and that defining *them* as archetypal Germans was an obscene irony.

There was, in fact, a double bind in such a predicament. For if from a child's point of view being Jewish did not exempt one from the stigma of Germanness, very often in the eyes of our conventionally bigoted, lower-middle-class teachers, Germanness was little more than a synonym for Jewishness. This was brought traumatically home to me when a particularly sadistic manual-training teacher descended upon me and scolded me for crude behavior (what exactly I had done remains a mystery to this day). He was fully aware that I was Jewish—in South Africa a finely tuned ethnic radar is indispensable—and it was this animus which informed his question: "Where do your parents come from?" Upon hearing the answer he proclaimed loudly for all to hear: "That accounts for your manners."

At other times, the anti-Semitic intent was less veiled and the anti-German, anti-Jewish thrust explicitly fused. One day, in the middle of a science class, the teacher settled his gaze directly on me and asked why I believed World War II had been fought. Without waiting for a reply, he himself provided the enlightening answer: "Because of the Jews, Asch-heim, because of the Jews." Incidents like this pushed me ever deeper into the Zionist Youth Movement (in South Africa, unlike the United States, a vibrant "counter-institution" expressive of an oppositional Jewish youth culture) and at the same time into an increasingly critical stance toward the overall system of racial injustice in South Africa.

It has been suggested that this sensitivity was influenced by the culti-vated liberal-humanism of German Jewish *Bildung*. Does this hold? Only, I think, in subtle, perhaps even subliminal ways. For that legacy (forged during a century-long struggle for emancipation) was largely the product and ongoing activity of the Jewish intelligentsia, while people like my parents, the overwhelming majority of the approximately 6,000 German Jews who immigrated to South Africa in the 1930s, came from the ini-tially almost destitute, commercial, non-intellectual classes. Presumably the refugee German Jewish intellectual elite carried out a voluntary selec-tion process, rejecting even the possibility of going to what they probably conceived as the remote *kulturlos* jungles of Africa. The manifestations of German Jewish *Bildungsideologie* in South Africa accordingly bore little resemblance to the cultural and intellectual productivity or the moral and critical acuity which, according to the recent work of David Sorkin (*The Transformation of German Jewry, 1780–1840*, 1987) and George L. Mosse (*German Jews beyond Judaism*, 1985), marked the tradition at its best.

When *Bildung* did manifest itself in South Africa, it did so usually in other, more familiar ways: as the cultivating complement to successful commerce, the refining twin of Jewish *Besitz* (property). This is not meant disparagingly. As they rose up the economic ladder, some German Jews did indeed become pioneering patrons and practitioners of music, theater, and the fine arts, contributing to South Africa's cultural development, and here their European background doubtless stood them in good stead. But their numbers were not all that significant and, in any case, these kinds of activities, more often than not, served to tame and aestheticize the vaunted critical and moral edge of the *Bildung* legacy.

But the category of *Bildung* does not properly reflect the historical real-ity of the German Jewish relationship to South Africa. For it was, quite simply, *gratitude* which was the most characteristic and understandable response of these German Jewish immigrants to their adopted country. At a time when the gates of the world had been closed to them, South Africa had given them refuge. The warmth of the welcome and the gratitude they felt was reinforced by the professional and financial success many of them rapidly achieved in an expanding and industrializing economy: they too had acquired a vested interest in things as they were. This was a powerful combination limiting, if not entirely eliminating, any inclination to generalize from their own experience of racial injustice in Germany and protest against what was happening in South Africa.

For all that, I believe that this German Jewish background did play a conditioning role in the larger sensitizing processes of my life. In the first place, the imprint, brutality, and mystery of Nazism and the Holocaust have been with me ever since I can remember. These were topics that were never really analytically confronted, but they were nevertheless somehow omnipresent, palpably transmitted through my parents' revulsion for Germans and things German (my father adamantly refused reparation money), their reminiscences about the move from Germany to South Africa, and an unstated but quite unambivalent message about the fragility of the Jewish condition. Unlike my parents I was not beholden to South Africa as a refugee, and I could therefore translate this sense of vulnerability into quite different Jewish and general terms.

In the first place, Zionism seemed almost self-evident, the obvious solution to the Jewish plight of victimization, the basic precondition for the recovery of a constantly threatened dignity. At the same time, it naturally went hand in hand with a post-adolescent awakening to the fact that my own society was based upon an all-encompassing victimization of its nonwhite inhabitants. Not all children of German Jewish immigrants, by any means, saw things this way. But in my own case these sensitivities were, surely, colored by the cadences and emotional texture, if not the overt ideology, of a first-generation German Jewish home. This too presumably provided some of the affective background for a later awareness of the ironies of victimization implicit in my own chosen Zionist solution, an awareness made conscious in great part by discovering the writings of German Zionists like Robert Weltsch and Martin Buber—*Bildung* intellectuals who brought that critical humanizing tradition to bear on their own Zionism.

With all their distaste for Germany, my parents, like other new arrivals, carried Europe with them in a way that the Litvak majority of the South African Jewish community never did. This went beyond any ideological stance and reflected, quite simply, inherited reflexes and childhood habits revelatory of the cultural tastes and preferences of almost all German Jewish homes, and it was transmitted in a variety of ways. My father would, for instance, effortlessly and quite unselfconsciously, reel off reams of (to me, rather incomprehensible yet strangely attractive) poetry from the inevitable Goethe and Heine. Our house rang with the songs of Joseph Strauss, Richard Tauber, and Marcel Witrich, marvelous tenors whose 78–rpm records we possessed in abundance and which set the foundations, no doubt, for a later enduring passion for German classical music. There was a hidden, compounding irony here. I always took my father's "Germanness" for granted. His great warmth and humor seemed, indeed, to point to the fundamental inaccuracy of the "stiff Yekke" stereotype. It was only years after his death that I discovered he was born an "*Ostjude*," a Galizianer who had come to Kassel as a small boy and, like so many others, elegantly combined these two inheritances! The fact that he had chosen never to reveal those origins was made even more poignant by the fact that I learned all this as I was completing my dissertation on the problematic interdependencies between Eastern and Western Jewish identity.

My receptivity to German and German Jewish history and culture, then, springs from these domestic roots. I have never doubted that essentially biographical and existential impulses were behind my later scholarly interests: understanding the nature of the German catastrophe and the complexities of the German Jewish experience. The impulse to study the German world flowed from the dual desire to comprehend and in some way perhaps to perpetuate the lost reality from which my parents came, and at the same time, to grasp what had made Nazism and the Holocaust possible. To a young mind, part of the fascination of German culture lay in its compelling, although at that stage still quite incomprehensible, combination of the profound and the demonic (I only discovered Thomas Mann's explanation of the necessary connection between the two in his *Dr. Faustus* much later). Not yet able to penetrate the esoteric language in which they wrote, I found to my uninitiated, adolescent ears that names like Kant, Hegel, and Nietzsche possessed a kind of magic, an alluring and almost evil ring, resonant with the promise of dark and dangerous brilliance. The questions and fascination persist to this day.

But there is still another pertinent level. Since student days I had, quite unconsciously, equated what I valued most in German thought with what I later understood to be the legacy of German Jewish humanism. What was most attractive in German intellectual and moral life turned out, in most cases, to be linked, in one way or another, to its German Jewish component. Even if I had not really read them, the giants who in my mind at least were associated with this legacy—Marx, Freud, and Einstein—were heroic precisely because they were universal men, makers of modern secular thought and yet, in their different ways, quintessentially (or at least socio-psychologically) Jewish, embodiments of an always humanizing moral and rational impulse. In a sense this was to be expected—many educated Westerners' intellectual experiences surely included these figures. But a similar elective affinity applied also (and still does) to the endless other examples of German and Central European Jewish cultural and intellectual creativity, to the bewitching names and works of people as diverse as Gershom Scholem, Ernst Cassirer, Theodor Adorno, Franz Kafka, Franz Rosenzweig, and Georg Lukács, to name but a few from just the present century. These rather than French or British thinkers somehow acted as magnets, natural emulative models. Similarly, it was the work of post-World War II German Jewish or Central European exile-intellectuals such as Hannah Arendt, Jean Amery (originally Hans Meyer), George Steiner, Walter Laqueur, Raul Hilberg, Leo Strauss, George Mosse, Fritz Stern, Peter Gay, and others that seemed most relevant to me: in the post-Holocaust era they were as much the incarnation of the German Jewish spirit as they were chroniclers of its disappearance.

Rationally seeking the roots of irrationalism (only later did I begin to ponder the too-easy distinctions between the "rational" and the "irrational"), clinging onto the humanizing fragments of an always vulnerable culture: this is how George Mosse has, quite correctly, in my view, summed up the meaning and ultimate significance of this legacy.[2] To be sure, the totality of the German Jewish historical experience must not be romanticized. The distinction between "rationality" and "irrationality," for instance, needs to be more rigorously problematized. Thus German Jewish intellectual creativity was often fueled by diverse founts of "irrationalism," even by non- and anti-liberal streams of thought.[3] There was no "pure," undiluted German Jewish "spirit." Instead, that experience incorporated much that was human, all too human, and some things that were even mean and small-minded. But now that much of it has been physically extinguished—the present reassertion of Jewish life in Germany, I think, must be judged within a different frame—it is surely the legacy of this fragile, humanizing sensibility, independent of any particular time or space, that we should take care to preserve.

Six

Assimilation and Its Impossible Discontents
The Case of Moritz Goldstein

In March 1912, a young Zionist, Moritz Goldstein, published an explosive article, "The German-Jewish Parnassus." There he proclaimed that "We Jews are administering the spiritual property of a nation which denies our right and ability to do so."[1] Goldstein, it needs to be added, was himself a literary scholar, a Germanist, who, as he later ironically put it, was himself "by profession, an 'administrator' of the spiritual property of the German nation."[2] Jewish cultural domination, he argued, was multi-sphered and permeated the worlds of German literature, theater, journalism, and so on. Non-Jewish resentment over this state of affairs, Goldstein insisted, had to be acknowledged and its implications honestly confronted. Such a situation could be remedied, Goldstein wrote, only through a form of German Jewish cultural disengagement and the construction of a new, specifically "Jewish" culture in Germany.

Anti-Semites had long been espousing the view that over the course of the nineteenth century Jews had taken over the economics, culture, and, indeed, the very inner life of Germany. But no Jew—not even militant German Zionists ideologically predisposed to uncover the duplicities of assimilation—had openly pronounced this before. What made Goldstein's challenge to the tacit liberal agreement to pass over such sensitive matters in discreet public silence particularly provocative was the fact that this analysis appeared in the prestigious *Der Kunstwart* (The Art Guard), a cultural journal whose editor, Ferdinand Avenarius, was an avowed German nationalist and whose literary critic, Adolf Bartels, was a notorious anti-Semite. Previously, and for obvious reasons, Goldstein's piece had been rejected by the quintessentially liberal, and Jewish-owned, *Berliner Tageblatt*.

Goldstein, to be sure, castigated the *ressentiment* of anti-Jewish forces—those "German-Christian-Teutonic envy-ridden fools" who had brought about this state of affairs. But the "worse enemy," he insisted, were "those Jews who are completely unaware, who continue to take part in German cultural activities, who pretend and persuade themselves that they are not recognized" when, in effect, their cultural creations were widely viewed as un-German: instead of being fused with the spirit of *Deutschtum* (Germanness), non-Jewish Germans regarded them as being imbued with essentially foreign, "Asiatic," "Jewish" characteristics. Assertions of this kind predictably delighted anti-Semites. One of those, Ph. Stauff, contributed a vicious piece to *Der Kunstwart* and outraged liberals, especially Jewish liberals.[3] The two sides rendered inevitable a protracted and heated debate that spread well beyond the pages of *Der Kunstwart*.

There was, of course, nothing new in either the critique or the defense of assimilation. What was perhaps novel, apart from airing the issue in public, was Goldstein's advocacy of the creation of a separate Jewish culture on German soil—a recommendation that, like the article itself, was occasioned by the perception of a persisting anti-Jewish feeling in Germany and channeled by a radicalized "post-assimilationist" sensibility characteristic of second-generation German Zionists. Indeed, Goldstein's plea was comprehensible only in terms of a prior vaunted "Jewish renaissance" whose seeds were already planted at the fin-de-siècle. His thoughts were as much a product of that development as it was a call for its public recognition.

If this proposed radical cultural disjunction between Germans and Jews was unthinkable for Jewish liberals—the well-known critic Julius Bab dubbed the very attempt as a deliberate act of retrogression[4]—the same held for the first generation of German Zionists. In 1910, only two years before Goldstein dropped his bombshell, Franz Oppenheimer defined the original German Zionist relation to culture thus: "We are collectively German by culture . . . because we have the fortune to belong to cultural communities that stand in the forefront of nations. . . . We cannot be Jewish by culture (*Kulturjuden*) because the Jewish culture, as it has been preserved from the Middle Ages in the ghettos of the East, stands infinitely lower than modern cultures which our [Western] nations bear. We can neither regress nor do we want to."[5]

But for Goldstein and others the new culture, conceived upon essentially organic assumptions, would resolve a problem that liberals and older Zionists either denied or sidestepped: it would recreate a condition of authentic wholeness for essentially bifurcated, fragmented Jews. To be sure, the exact contours and nature of this "Jewish" culture were, as Goldstein himself admitted, exceedingly vague. What would constitute the framework and content for such a revival? Apart from the Zionists, other radical circles—such as the one associated with the journal *Der Freistaat*—joined the debate and proposed different solutions. Like the Zionists, they believed that the creative Jewish instincts were repressed under the dictates of a "foreign culture" and that authentic expression was possible only in a Jewish milieu suited to the structure of the Jewish soul. But they went beyond Zionism in arguing not for some vague, utopian Jewish culture of the future in Palestine but for the immediate union (*Anschluss*) of German Jewry with existing Eastern European Jewish culture. For these disaffected Zionists—most prominently Fritz Mordecai Kaufmann—the culture of *Ostjudentum* (Eastern European Jewry) was synonymous with Jewish culture itself.

More than its vagueness, Goldstein's posited solution, as well as his mode of diagnosis, revealed a kind of bewildered despair. It is here that the document retains its compelling historical interest. Perhaps, indeed, it should be read as a classic and pained restatement: a symptomatic expression of the ongoing and unresolved issue of the modalities and dualities of Jewish identity within German culture, a problem that both preceded and postdated his ruminations.

If the essay was informed by a Zionist sensibility, its tone was more confused than it was triumphalist. For Goldstein, the psycho-historical tragedy of acculturated Jews was to be found in their persistent condition of duality and fragmentation. The creation of a full Jewish, Hebrew-speaking culture was possible only in Zion, he wrote, but that was not really an option for the present generation of German Jews, those who had "left the ghetto, we lucky-unlucky beneficiaries of West European culture, we eternal-halves, we excluded and homeless." The cultural condition of German Jewry was thus part blessing, part curse. For although Goldstein proposed the creation of a distinct culture in which Jews would work unconditionally *as Jews*, it did not mean that the deeply ingrained German inheritance had to—or could or should—be simply jettisoned: "We cannot cast it off as one exchanges a garment. We do not want to give this all up; it means draining the blood of our life."[6] Ironically enough, some later radical Zionists were convinced that German Jews were so thoroughly acculturated, their German "spirit" so deep, that they were incapable of inhabiting a Jewish one. Thus, in 1917 a student Zionist, G. Wollstein, proposed that in order to prevent the "Berlinization" of the future Jewish state, German Jews should marry only Eastern European Jews and refrain from writing in Hebrew journals, for their contributions could consist only of Jewish words wrapped in the German spirit![7]

Forty-five years after the appearance of his *Kunstwart* piece, Goldstein reflected on the insolubility of the *Deutschtum-Judentum* nexus: his piece had been (mis)understood as "a programme for action whereas I merely wanted to free myself of a tormenting trouble by ventilating it."[8] There was, indeed, even something cloying in the cliche-ridden, romantic mode in which he described the relation of German Jews to German culture and their sense of being slighted by their exclusion from it: "The German spring is our spring, as the German winter is for us winter. . . . Were we not raised on German fairy tales? . . . Is not the German forest alive for us, are we not also allowed to behold its elves and gnomes, do we not understand the murmur of its streams and the song of its birds?"[9]

But of course his article was not received as a testament to German patriotism, nor even as an expressive document of cultural bewilderment. Ernst Lissauer (1882–1937), the Jewish author of the famous World War I "Hate Song Against England," insisted at the end of his indignant reply to Goldstein that the dualities over which Goldstein struggled could be straightforwardly resolved. A simple decision had to be made: either to "become German" or to leave the country.[10]

The polemics occasioned by this piece produced rather formulaic responses and have been thoroughly analyzed elsewhere. What has gone less remarked is the degree to which the discussion—indeed, the wider debate around *Deutschtum* and *Judentum*, the possibilities and limits of assimilation and of cultural creativity in general— employed a peculiar species of discourse that turned upon a hypostatized conception of "essences," of visible and hidden, external and internal characteristics taken to be profoundly determinative of "Jewishness." These characteristics were represented as both markers of a distinct identity and the "content" of such Jewishness, the inward and outward manifestations of an elusive but powerful Jewish being and "spirit," which assimilation in the last analysis could neither repress nor dissolve.

Goldstein, for instance, couched his arguments on the basis of what he regarded to be "inherited, ineradicable characteristics" of the Jews. Other participants in the debate spoke as if this were an unproblematic given of a constitutive Jewish "national substance."[11] It is significant that even the liberals, who were most obviously opposed to such essentialist thinking, were forced to construct their arguments within these terms, if only to dismiss the determinative role of such categories. Thus Lissauer, who categorically denied the existence of an inherent Jewish "national substance"—what one meant by that term, he argued, was simply the collectively acquired characteristics of ghetto life that were constitutive of East European Jews—noted that assimilation was a slow process and admitted that German Jews, already a quite distinct species from their East European branch, still exhibited some recognizable physical and mental signs of that past existence. But this was because they were still in a transitional phase. What one took to be inherent characteristics of the Jewish physique and psyche were simply products of their historical and sociological—and thus alterable—contexts. To speak of such an inborn substance, Lissauer exclaimed, was to speak in precisely those racial terms employed by enemies of the Jews.[12]

This underside of the debate, we should point out, merely refueled and underlined an intuition of an evasive yet palpable Jewish "otherness" that had been sensed and discussed throughout the period of modern German Jewish acculturation. This was a sentiment that was shared, even though it was evaluated and deployed in radically different terms, by Jews, non-Jews, and anti-Semites alike. Hannah Arendt has suggested that the dynamic governing the notion of an indistinct, yet powerfully felt, Jewish "spirit" or inner essence was embedded in the logic of emancipation, in the very terms of the assimilationist pact: "Instead of being defined by nationality or religion, Jews were being transformed into a social group whose members shared certain psychological attributes and reactions, the sum total of which was to constitute 'Jewishness.' In other words, Judaism became a psychological quality and the Jewish Question became an involved personal problem for every individual Jew."[13]

It was this hypostatization of some invisible but determinative inner essence that from the late-eighteenth century increasingly characterized both Jewish and non-Jewish perceptions. With the passing of time it became increasingly definitive of Jewish identity itself: as the overt signs of Jewish difference receded, this simultaneously elusive yet ultimately constitutive internality (whether viewed approvingly or with distaste) became of paramount importance. Heinrich Heine provided some of the earliest and most powerful expressions of both the positive and negative psychological valences of a "Jewishness" experienced both as a kind of mental defect—"Incurable deep ill! defying treatment. . . . Will Time, the eternal goddess, in compassion / Root out this dark calamity transmitted from sire to son?"—and as an expression of "the genuine, the ageless, the true": it was the "character of the Jewish people," he wrote, that was the "cause," the key agent in the moralization of the West.[14]

Goldstein's assertion of ineradicable inherited Jewish characteristics, then, was not simply a passing fancy, the mutterings of a whimsical eccentric, but part of a larger cluster of convictions that seemed if anything to become more pronounced during this period. As moderate a German Jewish journal as *Ost und West* announced in its 1901 opening statement that, apparent differences notwithstanding, all Jews "shared the same inherited characteristics."[15] Like others involved in the fin-de-siècle Jewish renaissance, it implied, rather remarkably, that genetics somehow doomed the politics and culture of assimilation.

Strikingly, the debate did not center on the issue of external characteristics. It focused instead on the question of internal content, of the corresponding Jewish "spirit," because there was, more or less, general agreement that Jews did in fact possess physically distinguishing features and mannerisms. Liberal Jews like Lissauer recognized that there were painfully obvious physical landmarks of Jewishness, but they asserted that these were hangovers from the ghetto and would disappear with the successful completion of the assimilation process. Similarly Ludwig Geiger, the editor of the *Allgemeine Zeitung des Judentums*, elsewhere admitted the existence of this external dimension, but he did not quite know what to do with such an awkward perception. Jews, he wrote, were easily identifiable by the way they moved, by the shape of their noses, and by other bodily cues, but he drew no cultural or sociological conclusions from these observations.[16] Still other liberal Jews of the time were often shocked by what appeared to be an "instinctive," physical recognition of kinship. Wrapped in a scarf so that only his eyes were visible, the playwright Richard Beer-Hoffmann was shocked when a caftan-clad *Ostjude* stopped him and said, "My good sir is one of us. . . . He will tell me how I can get to the Nollendorfplatz?"[17]

Many identifying German Jews claimed that they too possessed this instinctive capacity for mutual recognition. The radical anarchist Gustav Landauer, for instance, was convinced that he could identify fellow Jews merely by looking at them.[18] At the same time, for those interested in escaping their historical fate, Judaism could be regarded as a physiological defect. Thus, the famous linguist Fritz Mauthner experienced it as a kind of "duct" in the brain, a disease he was afraid to contract.[19]

Like Goldstein, it was yet another young Zionist and Germanist (perhaps such people most sharply and paradoxically experienced the tensions between *Deutschtum* and *Judentum*), Ludwig Strauss, who did most to radicalize and polarize the debate and who—on the basis of popular physiognomic and racial wisdom—sought to derive internal conclusions and content from these external characteristics, thereby providing a literal and unified psycho-physiological form to the notion of a Jewish "national substance." In Strauss's conception, Jewish identity was locatable by external signs that betrayed an inner life. "The obvious bodily differences between Jewish and non-Jewish Germans," he exclaimed, "is necessarily connected to an inner difference, a dissimilarity in national substance."[20]

Even if deployed for quite different, positive purposes, if such notions did not exactly mimic, they seemed at least to parallel a longstanding, anti-Jewish discourse that linked the external to the internal, the physiological to the spiritual and cultural. Richard Wagner's 1850 essay "Judaism in Music," for instance, explained the roots of an "instinctive," "involuntary repellence" to the Jew in terms that equally emphasized Jewish physical and spiritual structure and the interdependence between them.[21] The most extreme articulation, partly expressive and partly satirical, of this physio-cultural discourse was contained in Oskar Panizza's nightmarish short story "The Operated Jew" (1893).[22] Panizza's tale relates the desperate attempts of a stereotypical Jew, the culturally and physically deformed Itzig Faitel Stern, to alter his inner and outer nature and turn himself into a modern Aryan Christian. This physio-cultural transformation, which included a number of excruciating surgical procedures on the repellent Itzig's entire skeletal framework in order to bring about the required metamorphosis, ultimately fails. The grotesque denouement moves from his cultural regression—the lapse into his ugly Jewish accent and stereotypical mannerisms—to his quite literal reversion from normal to Jewish physiology: "Faitel's blond strands of hair began to curl. . . . Then the curly locks turned red, then dirty brown and finally blue-black. . . . His arms and legs which had been stretched and bent in numerous operations could no longer perform the newly learned movements. . . . A terrible smell spread in the room . . . [the surgeon] Klotz's work of art lay before him crumpled and quivering, a convoluted Asiatic image in wedding dress, a counterfeit of human flesh, Itzig Faitel Stern."[23] The assimilationist project was revealed in all its interrelated cultural and genetic absurdity.

In order to draw a similar conclusion but from a quite different source and for different purposes, Strauss explicitly employed the Buberian model of a Jewish essence that assimilation could perhaps hide and distort but never fully eradicate. This was a notion that Martin Buber developed in his influential 1909 "Bar Kochba" lectures, in which he portrayed the "community of blood" as the profound core of Jewishness, "the deepest, most potent stratum of our being . . . our innermost thinking and our will are colored by it."[24] Buber drew upon the common racial coinage of his day, obviously not as a tool for domination of others, but as a potent—some would argue merely metaphorical—device to imagine or conjure up a concealed but still pulsating Jewish essence. Ultimately, he proclaimed, Jewish belonging would be decided in terms of this community of blood rather than by the external "community of experience," those spheres and fields of assimilation to which Jews only apparently and superficially belonged.

It was on such Buberian premises that Strauss proceeded to argue that the greater the attempt to integrate into an alien (*fremdartig*) mode, "the 'national substance' becomes increasingly deeply repressed and hidden inside." In a startling confirmation of anti-Semitic and racial theses and couched in a similar organic discourse, Strauss proposed that to the extent that the "foreign" mixed with the Jewish soul, it would be apprehended as alien and a generalized Jewish ethnic distinctiveness (*Stammeseigenart*) would so assert itself in the individual that the instinct of survival would push him back toward his own ethnic particularity.[25]

To be sure, Strauss emphasized, after such a long dispersion it was not simple to locate and identify this essence (Buber, some time before, had described assimilation as an ongoing form of Jewish self-alienation), but no matter how vague it was, the feeling of something substantial, essential (*wesentlich*) was sufficient. The content of this essence would be clarified through diligent work; this was the most urgent and binding Jewish obligation of the moment. Affirmation of Jewishness as the informing center of one's life, thought, and deeds would render bifurcated Jewish lives whole again.

But Strauss was extreme in his physio-psychic fusion of identity. The importance of the *Kunstwart* affair for certain Jewish intellectuals who were not affiliated with religious or official communal life, yet who felt in some vague yet deep way "Jewish," was that it brought out the conviction that there were, indeed, real limits to assimilation and that these had to be explained not merely in terms of external antagonisms but also by acknowledging the intangible but powerful inner sense of Jewishness. In a private correspondence with Strauss over the issue that Goldstein had raised, the young Walter Benjamin voiced his enthusiastic support for the idea of a new Jewish (German-language) journal that would encourage, as Strauss put it, "conscious Jews to delineate the nature of the Jewish spirit clearly and credibly." But although Strauss sought to formalize and channel this "Jewish spirit" into explicitly Jewish frames, for Benjamin its value consisted in the absence of formal definition. The essence of Jewish, or Western European Jewish, identity was contained in this peculiar "sensibility" and should in no way, therefore, be harnessed to any fixed framework.[26]

For Eastern European Jewry, Benjamin declared, Zionism provided a solution of sorts—whereas for Western European Jews it was an irrelevance. Strauss's suggestion of creating an autonomous center of Jewish culture in Germany linked to the spiritual center that would arise in Palestine was objectionable because Jews in the West were at the forefront of a larger process that transcended parochial boundaries and activities. They were at the forefront of such a project because their ethnic-national bonds created a kind of shared spiritual and mental sensibility—never an end in itself—that rendered Jews an "elite in the party of intellectuals," "the most eminent bearer and representative of matters spiritual and intellectual."[27] Strauss also proposed an inner essence, but at the same time programmatically advocated what Paul Mendes-Flohr has called an "exoteric" conception of Zionism and Judaism, the formation of explicitly

Jewish cultural forms and the conscious practice of Jewish deeds. For Benjamin, Judaism was an "esoteric" matter: its power derived from the fact that it was both ill-defined and yet self-understood.[28] He was certainly not alone. For many intellectual Jews, the importance of Jewishness lay in its implicit nature; it was not a formal commitment or series of obligations but a hidden sensibility that powerfully informed one's spiritual and mental life.

In the years following the *Kunstwart* affair there were, nevertheless, numerous positive, "exoteric" developments in the direction that Goldstein had advocated. World War I and the years of the Weimar Republic witnessed the appearance of divergent, self-affirming "Jewish" journals of high intellectual quality, such as Martin Buber's *Der Jude* and the Centralverein's *Der Morgen* (under the editorship of Julius Goldstein); a virtual cult of the "Ostjuden" (or at least a serious reassessment of the East-West Jewish relation among various circles of German Jewry);[29] an outburst of "Weimar" Jewish intellectual and theological creativity that blossomed in diverse directions[30] and included the work and thought of Hermann Cohen, Franz Rosenzweig, and Gershom Scholem (and even the "esoteric" Walter Benjamin).[31]

But of course the tensions, ambiguities, and casuistic definitions concerning *Deutschtum* and *Judentum* continued unresolved. They were definitive, perhaps the source of much that was creative in German Jewry through 1933. Beneath all these exoteric re-definitions there remained a persistent, positively evaluated experience (indeed, an ideology) of an elusive, indefinable, yet radically determinative inner Jewish essence. Jewishness, as Franz Rosenzweig put it, was "no entity, no subject among other subjects, no one sphere of life among other spheres of life; it is not what the century of emancipation with its cultural mania wanted to reduce it to. It is something inside the individual that makes him a Jew, something infinitesimally small yet immeasurably large, his most impenetrable secret, yet evident in every gesture and every word—especially in the most spontaneous of them."[32]

Sigmund Freud, too, regarded Jewishness and its "many dark emotional powers" as "all the more powerful the less they could be expressed in words," and as "the clear consciousness of an inner identity, the familiarity of the same psychological structure."[33] This insistence on a Jewishness that resists definition, or as Yosef Hayim Yerushalmi has put it, the intuition of a distinct sensibility, essence, or character deprived of any particular content,[34] did not only play an important role for intellectual German Jews. We may also dub it a prevailing ideology of our own times, a way in which countless contemporary secular Jews approach articulating their own persistent but difficult to locate sense of a "Jewish self."

Seven

Hannah Arendt in Jerusalem

In the intellectual discourse of our day, Hannah Arendt has become something of an icon. The climate of postmodernism and identity politics, and
the search for a non-ideological, post-totalitarian posture, has endowed
her work with renewed relevance and vitality. In Western Europe, the
United States, and even in Eastern Europe, her work has become the subject of intense, often celebratory, interest and analysis.[1] In Israel this engagement has been conspicuously lacking. This may tell us as much about
our own cultural self-understanding and biases as it will about the nature
of Arendt's person and thought. In Israel—beginning prior to, but certainly coming to a climax with, the appearance in 1963 of her deeply
controversial, explosive book on Eichmann[2] —Arendt has, to all intents
and purposes, been relegated to the status of an adversary, an "enemy"
tainted by "self-hating," even anti-Semitic impulses, one condemned as a
thinker whose tone and work violated some of the society's most basic
taboos.[3] The experience of reading Arendt, I have been told by a number
of sophisticated Israeli intellectuals, still evokes a visceral sense of physical
revulsion! This is a distaste that has been marked, moreover, not so much
by overt confrontation and refutation as by stark collective silence and
implicit communal excommunication.[4]

It is a quite remarkable but telling fact that *none* of Hannah Arendt's
work was translated into Hebrew before the year 2000—it was only then,
after much politicking, that *Eichmann in Jerusalem* appeared.[5] It will not
do to claim, as some have, that other major thinkers of the Cold War
period (such as Karl Popper and Friedrich Hayek) went similarly untrans-
lated. For, quite unlike these authors, Arendt's life and thought were pas-
sionately linked to core predicaments of the modern Jewish experience.
Furthermore, her work often analyzed in pioneering and provocative
fashion almost all the great issues—the complex dynamics of emancipation and assimilation, the tortuous binds of Western Jewish identity
and its "psychologized" forms, the phenomenon of nineteenth- and
twentieth-century Jewish intellectual and cultural creativity, the nature
of anti-Semitism and totalitarianism, Jewish politics and Zionism, and

73

above all the genocidal eruption of Nazism and the Holocaust.[6] It was precisely her *involvement* in these matters, her troubling relevance, that rendered her so threatening. In Israel, in a still-developing, insecure, and highly ideological culture wary of partial identifications and provisional commitments, Arendt's critiques (especially in the ironic mode, often made in an offhand, arrogant manner) could not easily be absorbed.

Today, in a later, quite different climate, there are signs—as the conference for which this paper was prepared perhaps attests—of a new generational openness, a willingness to receive and read Arendt somewhat differently, perhaps even to appropriate selected aspects of her thought.[7] But to understand the history and nature of Arendt's reception in Jerusalem to date, we must also examine the closely interrelated ways in which Arendt herself engaged and imagined Jerusalem—both actually and metaphorically. In order to do this satisfactorily, it is necessary to place Arendt within the relevant historical context.

Like the figures she vividly brought to life—Rahel Varnhagen, Heinrich Heine, Franz Kafka, Hermann Broch, and many others—Hannah Arendt's achievements and biases, her creativity, and inner conflicts must all be seen as part of the quite extraordinary history of post-emancipation German Jewish intellectuals and their wider engagement with the imperatives of German culture and its later great breakdown. Arendt was not only a keen analyst of that experience but was herself a central expression of it.[8] Much of her acuity derived from the fact that she embodied the tensions and contradictions that fueled so much of its creativity, especially as they manifested themselves in the productive turbulence of the Weimar Republic in which she spent her formative years. Her Weimar friends, lovers, and adversaries—ranging from Karl Jaspers and Martin Heidegger to Kurt Blumenfeld, Theodor Adorno, Gershom Scholem, and Walter Benjamin—were all lightning rods of this history, incarnations of its manifold yet related sensibilities.

Arendt was both an explicator and a living example of what Dan Diner, in another context, has termed the "Western" Jewish narrative.[9] Unlike its East European counterpart—constructed upon the basis of collective national experience and a relatively singular self-understanding—this narrative takes as its starting point the individual and the rupture with community and tradition, as well as the engagement with manifold cultural worlds and political affiliations. It highlights ambivalence, multiple loyalties, fissures, breakdowns, and partial reconstitutions. One could argue that perhaps one source of difficulty of absorbing Arendt within Jerusalem was that such a model of fracture and conflict did not sit easily with more organic national narratives, cut out of more unified, heroic materials.

But, of course, the situation is more complicated than this. Events around Arendt pushed this classic *Bildungs* intellectual[10] to turn sharply away from that tradition's unworldly, apolitical cultivation of individual interiority.[11] In reaction to the duplicities of Western Jewish social assimilation (which she critiqued as acutely as she diagnosed them) and the rise of the Nazis and her own experience as a refugee, we should not forget that she advocated what amounted to an activist Zionist solution: a worldly, affirmative politics of collective Jewish existence and national Jewish rights. Witness her militant call for the formation of a Jewish army during World War II.[12] Throughout the 1930s and 1940s she entirely devoted herself, not just intellectually, but also practically and professionally, to Jewish and Zionist commitments.[13] None other than her later nemesis, Gershom Scholem, in 1941 described her as "a wonderful woman and an extraordinary Zionist."[14]

If later she rather controversially opposed statehood and wrote highly critical articles about Zionism, she did not question the need for a Jewish homeland, and her historiography of modern Jewish life and anti-Semitism was laden with Zionist assumptions. And, even after the great disputes around the Eichmann book, which she described as "the war between me and the Jews,"[15] she wrote to Mary McCarthy concerning the 1967 war: "Any real catastrophe in Israel would affect me more deeply than anything else."[16] In the wake of that war, even *her* critical judgment was momentarily suspended, overtaken by the prevalent euphoria of the time. She wrote to Jaspers:

> Israel: In many respects, in most actually, very encouraging. It's really
> quite wonderful that an entire nation reacts to a victory like that not by
> bellowing hurrah but with a real orgy of tourism—everybody has to go to
> have a look at the newly conquered territory. I was in all the formerly
> Arab territories and never noticed any conqueror behavior in the stream
> of Israeli tourists. The Arab population was more hostile than I expected
> . . . as far as the country itself is concerned, one can clearly see from what
> great fear it has suddenly been freed. That contributes significantly to im-
> proving the national character.[17]

It is precisely because of the complexity of her commitments, her partial "insider" status, and the difficulties of classifying her that Arendt was so inassimilable, baffling to Jewish establishments both within and without Israel.[18] After all, it is far easier to pigeonhole and dismiss classic disaffected intellectuals or what Isaac Deutscher called universalist non-Jewish Jews. They fit a pattern. Arendt was something else.[19] She is best understood in terms of Michael Walzer's portrait of "connected critics,"[20] those figures whose life and thought are characterized not by detachment but rather by passionate, yet essentially ambiguous, engagement. It is precisely this relationship that rendered her challenges and the responses to them particularly charged, emotionally over-determined. Moreover, Arendt's insistence upon what she termed "thinking without bannisters," upon critical judgment and non-ideological categories—peppered by what critics both in Israel and elsewhere regarded as an almost perverse desire for originality and a penchant for extreme and arrogant, even at times bizarre, declarations[21]—made her even more anomalous.

On the one hand, the fact of her Jewishness and her strident affirmation of it was never in question. "I belong to [the Jews]," she wrote, "beyond dispute or agreement."[22] "One does not escape Jewishness," reads the title of the last chapter of her most revealingly personal book on Rahel Varnhagen, a work that, as Arendt herself put it "was written from the perspective of a Zionist critique of assimilation"[23] and which was well received in Jerusalem.[24] Interestingly, her friend Karl Jaspers objected to the book precisely *because* of this proto-Zionist bias. In working through her own issues of identity, he argued, Arendt had presented Varnhagen entirely one-dimensionally: "you force everything under the rubric of being a Jew."[25] She had, he complained, ideologically flattened Varnhagen's "unconditional" humanity and, in her antipathy to the Enlightenment, reduced the full force of her own individual personality.

But, of course, Arendt's determined identification was by no means absolute. It was most clear and decisive under conditions of persecution where, as she put it in her 1959 Lessing Prize address, one had to "resist only in terms of the identity that is under attack."[26] "Politically," she declared in 1946, "I will speak only in the name of the Jews," but she immediately qualified this by adding "whenever circumstances force me to give my nationality."[27] Ultimately, though, she resisted all totalizing definitions, insisting that no single or homogenous identities and identifications adequately accounted for the disclosive complexities of selfhood. When asked by Jaspers whether she was a German or a Jew she replied: "To be perfectly honest, it doesn't matter to me in the least on the personal and individual level."[28] This problem of group versus individual loyalties formed an essential part of the tension between Arendt and Jerusalem. It was expressed in Arendt's famous response to Scholem's 1963 admonition that she lacked *Ahavat Israel*. "Love," Arendt insisted, was not a collective matter: "I indeed love 'only' my friends and the only kind of love I know of and believe in is the love of persons."[29]

At the same time, then, as she unabashedly confirmed her Jewishness and tried to provide it with political shape and expression, Arendt continued to challenge the non-reflexive, self-celebratory nature of group affiliations.[30] She took great pride in the complex, even subversive, nature of her own intertwined commitments: her second husband, Heinrich

Bluecher, was not only a non-Jew; he was, to boot, a proletarian and so non-conformist a German Marxist that as an adolescent he joined the Zionist group, the Blau Weiss![31] As Arendt put it in 1946: "If I had wanted to become respectable I would either have had to give up my interest in Jewish affairs or not marry a non-Jewish man, either option equally inhuman and in a sense crazy."[32] The intimate, sometimes highly erotic, correspondence between Bluecher and Arendt documents these unorthodox predilections in critically prejudiced and humorously self-conscious ways. Writing to Heinrich in 1936 about a meeting to found the World Jewish Congress, Arendt comments that the proceedings were partly conducted in Hebrew, "which after all my dismal attempts to learn it, is no language, but a national misfortune! So, my love, don't let yourself be circumcised."[33] Yet her letters to her friend, the great novelist Hermann Broch,[34] and to Bluecher were literally peppered with affectionate Yiddishisms. "I am the only German Jewess anywhere that has learned Yiddish," she declared to Bluecher, whom she addresses as my "beloved wonder-rabbi"![35]

These multiple loyalties clearly colored Arendt's dialogue with Jerusalem. In 1955 she wrote to Blumenfeld concerning Scholem: "I cannot tolerate this nationalist chatter that isn't really seriously intended and that springs from a quite understandable anxiety. And this gossip about the goyim gets pretty much on my nerves. I should have mentioned that I actually am married to such a 'Goy' and that one should feel as little free in my company to talk about this, as one should talk absolutely 'freely' about the Jews in Heinrich's presence."[36]

It is precisely this dual moment, this insider-outsider tension, and the personal and narrative clashes emerging from deep bonds and commonalities that constitute the complexities of Arendt in Jerusalem. I would suggest that the source of her achievements, conflicts, and limitations lay in the fact that in her great engagement with the wider world (especially that of German culture) she exemplified the bifurcated Western Jew that she so acutely diagnosed and critiqued. "The behavior patterns of assimilated Jews," she wrote in *The Origins of Totalitarianism*,

> determined by this continuous concentrated effort to distinguish themselves, created a Jewish type that is recognizable everywhere. Instead of being defined by nationality or religion, Jews were being transformed into a social group whose members shared certain psychological attributes and reactions, the sum total of which was to constitute "Jewishness." In other words, Judaism became a psychological quality and the Jewish question became an involved personal problem for every individual Jew.[37]

Arendt's really interesting insights—which both reflected, and were transformed into, her larger philosophical vision—concentrated upon both the "Jewish" and general aspects of Western and Central European cultural fragmentations, breakdowns, and attempted recoveries. These, of course, were particularly acutely felt and analyzed during the Weimar Republic.[38] Little wonder, for instance, that Arendt was so enamored of Kafka.[39] Her insightful analysis of Benjamin and Scholem applies equally to her own thought in matters both Jewish and general:

> Benjamin's choice, baroque in a double sense, has an exact counterpart in Scholem's strange decision to approach Judaism via the Cabala, that is, that part of Hebrew literature which is untransmitted and untransmissible in terms of Jewish tradition, in which it has always had the odor of something downright disreputable. Nothing showed more clearly—so one is inclined to say today—that there was no such thing as a "return" to either the German or the European or the Jewish tradition than the choice of these fields of study. It was an implicit admission that the past spoke directly only through these things that had not been handed down, whose seeming closeness to the present was thus due precisely to their exotic character, which ruled out all claims to a binding authority.[40]

The most clear-sighted of these intellectuals, Arendt added, "were led by their personal [Jewish] conflicts to a much more general and radical problem, namely, to questioning the relevance of the Western tradition as a whole."[41] This, surely, was also meant autobiographically. What ultimately was Arendt's project but the attempt to rethink the Western political and philosophical tradition? It is worth noting that many establishment Jewish and Israeli intellectuals have remained stuck at the level of problems engendered by Arendt's Jewish narrative. This, at least until now, has constituted an obstacle to engaging her more general thought.

Of course, if Arendt's strengths and insights were rooted in this experience, so too were many of her weaknesses and limitations. This great critic of assimilationist, bourgeois German Jewry shared many of its most basic historical prejudices. She poured all of them into a few pungent sentences in a letter from Jerusalem when she came to report on the Eichmann trial:

> My first impression. On top, the judges, the best of German Jewry. Below them, the persecuting attorneys, Galicians, but still Europeans. Everything is organized by a police force that gives me the creeps, speaks only Hebrew and looks Arabic. Some downright brutal types among them. They would follow any order. And outside the doors, the oriental mob, as if one were in Istanbul or some other half-Asiatic country. In addition, and very visible in Jerusalem, the peies and caftan Jews, who make life impossible for all the reasonable people here.[42]

But these were, on the whole, private utterances that need not preoccupy us here. What does need attention in the present context was Arendt's willingness, indeed determination, to publicly challenge fundamental precepts of collective narrative and memory. While her defenders argue that she sought to do so as a matter of intellectual principle and honesty, her critics regard this as a kind of tactless perversity, the desire to damage the Jews at their most sensitive and vulnerable points. Here I want to try to capture the emotional undergrowth, the atmospheric resonances, and subtexts which, I think, provoked such outraged reactions.

It was, of course, over the Eichmann book (especially Arendt's by now very familiar depiction of the behavior of the Judenraete[43] and the portrait of Eichmann) and its seeming violation of what Richard Cohen has called "the power of the myth and the sacredness of the memory" that the issues were most intensely played out.[44] The key protagonists themselves were quite aware of the pre-intellectual, pre-rational nature of the issues it broached and the extreme emotions it evoked. They ranged from feelings of liberation, of having told the truth in the face of collective pressures, to accusations of self-hatred, betrayal, and of having "crossed over." Mary McCarthy wrote: "To me, *Eichmann in Jerusalem,* despite all the horrors in it, was morally exhilarating. I freely confess that it gave me joy and I too heard a pean in it—not a hate-paean to totalitarianism but a pean of transcendence, heavenly music, like that of the final chorus of *Figaro* or the *Messiah* . . . The reader 'rose above' the terrible material of the trial or was borne aloft to survey it with his intelligence."[45] And Arendt, though she thought McCarthy's comparisons a little excessive, told her: "You were the only reader to understand what otherwise I have never admitted—namely that I wrote this book in a curious state of euphoria. And that ever since I did it, I feel . . . light-hearted about the whole matter. Don't tell anybody; is it not proof positive that I have no 'soul'?"[46] And, on the other side of the fence, it was not only this apparent lightheartedness, what Scholem called her "heartless, frequently almost sneering and malicious tone . . . touching the very quick of our life" that grated, but the shock that such sentiments could be publicly expressed by someone whom he regarded, as he put it, "wholly as a daughter of our people, and in no other way."[47]

Karl Jaspers, though he thought the book was "magnificent," acutely recognized the relevant gut level of the matter when he curtly dismissed Arendt's theory that the hostility toward her was motivated by her belief that the Judenrat members she had criticized occupied positions of power in Israel and by fear of revelations about Zionist-Nazi cooperation during the War.[48] "If that were so," Jaspers correctly pointed out, "then people would have some knowledge of these things." Instead, he suggested: "What is revealed here is a deep-seated sense of having been struck a mortal blow . . . Something in 'Jewry' itself has been struck a blow."[49]

It is worth pointing out that, although it did not evoke anything like the same outcry, the same structural tensions applied to Arendt's October 1945 piece, *Zionism Reconsidered*.[50] Again, what mattered as much as the content of her arguments was the fact that they touched upon the question of solidarity and the limits of loyal, connected criticism. Once more, but this time in an unpublished letter, it was Scholem who angrily responded. He fashioned a well-wrought, piercing refutation but what underlies it is the pain and confusion engendered by the fact that this attack was written by a supposed friend. He registered surprise that her arguments were based "not on Zionist but rather extreme . . . anti-Zionist grounds." Given Arendt's explicit Zionist commitments at the time, Scholem had expected an immanent critique, one that took a position from "within," as it were. Instead, as he put it, he found an indiscriminate mix of arguments, stated scornfully and written from the viewpoint of a universalistic morality that existed in practice nowhere but in the heads of disaffected Jewish intellectuals.[51] Years later, in 1968, he wrote an embittered letter to Hans Paeschke in which he made it clear that it was Arendt's fickleness, her disloyalty to her vaunted ideological and group commitments that above all disturbed him: "I knew Hannah Arendt when she was a socialist or half-communist," (an assertion, by the way, always heatedly denied by Arendt, who consistently claimed that "If I can be said to 'have come from anywhere' it is from the tradition of German philosophy"),[52] "and I knew her when she was a Zionist. I am astounded by her ability to pronounce upon movements in which she was once so deeply engaged, in terms of a distance measured in light years and from such sovereign heights."[53]

Even in his original reply to Arendt's anti-Zionist polemic, Scholem made explicit the fact that this was a confrontation about the nature of ideological commitment: "I confess my guilt with the greatest calm to most of the sins that you have attributed to Zionism. I am a nationalist and fully unmoved by apparently progressive declarations against a view, that since my earliest youth has been repeatedly declared as superceded. . . . I am a 'sectarian' and have never been ashamed to present my conviction of sectarianism as decisive and positive."[54]

As the years went by the rift between the two became even greater. We should not, however, exaggerate this. Viewed in larger historical perspective, their differences and the intensity with which they expressed them were linked, I think, to a certain kind of kinship and flowed from some profound commonalities. Family quarrels, after all, are often the most strongly felt. Both exemplified the radical revolt against German Jewish bourgeois modes of assimilation. Both were classical German Jewish intellectuals, products of the European and Jewish traditions which they subjected to the most withering critiques (this, I think, in many ways accounts for the current fascination with them in Western intellectual circles).[55] Both, as David Suchoff points out, "created new models for the transmission of tradition and the relation between culture and political action. Their writing sought to confront, without repressing, the scandal that Jewish particularity posed to German culture in their period."[56]

Paradoxically, their negative personal evaluations of each other also looked like mirror images. Both regarded the other as megalomaniacally arrogant and self-obsessed.[57] Already in 1957, Arendt wrote that Scholem was "so self-preoccupied that he has no eyes (and not only that: no ears). Basically he believes: The midpoint of the world is Israel; the midpoint of Israel is Jerusalem; the midpoint of Jerusalem is the university and the midpoint of the university is Scholem. And the worst of it is that he really believes that the world has a central point."[58]

Yet, for all that, the differences are not insignificant. Arendt's critical narrative ultimately did depart from a more organic and totalizing national (and Zionist) version. The twentieth-century experience of forced statelessness rendered her suspicious of the logic of all homogenizing politics. Her evolving political thought revolved around, at least in part, the dynamic possibilities entailed in multiple new beginnings and on an open, disclosive performativity.[59] In works such as *The Human Condition* and *On Revolution*, she developed an alternative conception designed to enhance the public spaces and dimensions of freedom and the possibilities of action. This was politics in which plurality was placed at the center. Whatever else she may have shared with her lover and mentor Martin Heidegger (post-metaphysical thinking, the problematic conservative critique of instrumental modernity and mass society, and so on), Arendt's emphasis on the primacy of the political realm and the intrinsic value of plurality decidedly separated her from him.[60] As recent readings have emphasized, she held that "a political community that constitutes itself on the basis of a prior, shared, and stable identity threatens to close the spaces of politics, to homogenize or repress the plurality and multiplicity that political action postulates."[61]

It was these emphases and not meanness or "self-hatred" that lay behind Arendt's repeated and not unwarranted warnings[62] about chauvinist Zionist and Israeli attitudes towards the Arabs.[63] She did, one must point out, repeatedly recognize the element of fear that lay behind such egocentric attitudes but held that such fears only increased the dangers.[64] If at times she spoke warmly of certain Israeli achievements, she could also be extremely cutting.[65] Israel, she stated in a 1961 letter, was the "ghetto-mentality with tanks and military parades."[66] For her, clearly, the logic of the nation-state did not solve the problem that totalitarianism had raised most acutely; rather it both preceded and, to some degree, reproduced it. "The troublesome majority-minority constellation," she wrote in May 1948, "is insoluble by definition."[67]

We need to examine a still more acute narrative tension between Arendt and Jerusalem and this in an even more sensitive area. In order to do so we must make a brief detour. Arendt, we should not forget, became famous above all for her work on Nazism and totalitarianism. We will be devoting a whole session of this conference to a reassessment of her *Origins of Totalitarianism,* that extraordinarily idiosyncratic book so patently wrong-minded in parts, so willfully peculiar in its historical method (or lack of it), yet so obviously punctuated by flashes of brilliance and original insight. What I want to stress here is that this work was animated by the conviction that Nazism and Auschwitz—far more than the Soviet experience—was the great transgressive moment in European history. This was certainly true for many of her essays throughout the 1940 and early 1950s.[68] Upon learning of Auschwitz in 1943 she later reported: "It was really as if an abyss had opened ... Something happened there to which we cannot reconcile ourselves. None of us ever can."[69] And as she wrote to Kurt Blumenfeld in 1947 (while composing the book): "You see, I cannot get over the extermination factories."[70] Arendt's classical "totalitarian" approach may have employed an essentially comparative method but, unlike the later *Historikerstreit* historians,[71] it never entailed a hint of relativization: implicitly, the Nazi case was the one really in need of explanation, the ultimate against which other crimes were measured.[72]

Despite all its shortcomings, the appearance in 1951 of *The Origins* satisfied an urgent need. Until then and for at least a decade after that, there were virtually no serious attempts to forge the theoretical, historical, and conceptual tools necessary to illuminate the great cataclysms of the twentieth century.[73] To this day even, historians find it difficult to persuasively and coherently integrate these events into the flow of this century's history. Arendt was seen to provide an account adequate to the enormity of the materials and problems at hand. To be sure, the term "Holocaust" had not yet crystallized and does not appear in the book. It may also be that the generalized notion of "totalitarianism" precluded any thoroughgoing, separate analysis of the "Final Solution" with a distinct motivational history. Later critics, like Saul Friedlander, did in fact argue that the "totalitarian framework is the means of destruction, not its basic explanation."[74] Nevertheless, for hungry contemporaries, the work was regarded as revelatory precisely because, as Alfred Kazin put it, it seemed to address itself "to the gas."[75]

What I want to highlight here, then, is Arendt's crucial role in the formulation and creation of the ubiquitous post-war "discourse of evil," one in which Nazism and Auschwitz have become emblematic of Western culture's conceptions of absolute inhumanity.[76] Already in 1945 she wrote: "The problem of evil will be the fundamental question of postwar intellectual life in Europe."[77] *The Origins* can thus be read as an attempt to try to answer the question, especially through her organizing idea of "radical evil," a notion that gave expression to her conception of the novelty of these events and the impulses that generated it. Here was an unprecedented evil, incomprehensible in terms of traditionally understandable, sinful human motives. She left the definition somewhat vague but concluded that "radical evil has emerged in connection with a system in which all men have become equally superfluous."[78]

Arendt's early awareness of Nazism's radical transgressiveness convinced her that entirely new (and often, very problematic) ways of thinking as well as new categories of analysis were required. Her espousal of a dubious model of mass society derived from conservative European social theory[79] and her total dismissal of German *Sonderweg* explanations— "Luther or Kant or Hegel or Nietzsche," she wrote, "have not the least responsibility for what is happening in the extermination camps"[80]—may have been extreme and somewhat misguided but I do not think were impelled, as has recently been suggested,[81] by her desire to exculpate a guilty culture to which she remained loyal. For her these conventional explanations were simply inadequate. "Nazism," she insisted, "is actually the breakdown of all German and European traditions, the good as well as the bad."[82] Continuity could not thus account for the emergence of an entirely new genocidal mentality. Rather, it was the breakdown of older frameworks, the emergence of new social and political structures and unprecedented expansionary drives, the urge to destroy all previous limits and to render everything possible that constituted the key.

But how does all this relate to the Arendt-Jerusalem relationship? If later there were doubts about placing Nazism and Stalinism under a single rubric, her emphasis on the link between the extermination factories and "radical evil" sat well in Jerusalem. So too, one presumes, did some of her general historiographic impulses. While her depiction of early modern Jewish power and its alliance with the absolutist state and economy raised eyebrows (she dismissed all scapegoat theories as painfully inadequate), her emphasis on situating Jews at the storm center of events and her desire to grasp anti-Semitism at its deadliest level flowed from her Zionist sensibilities: it is no accident that Arendt dedicated book 1 of the German version of *The Origins of Totalitarianism* to her Zionist mentor, Kurt Blumenfeld.[83]

But Arendt, to put it mildly, was not Daniel Goldhagen.[84] She was never happy to see these extreme events portrayed in terms of a simple dichotomy between wildly anti-Semitic German killers and Jewish victims.[85] From the beginning she was impelled by the conviction that the method and the nature of the killings went beyond essentialized anthropological distinctions and raised explanatory and moral issues of urgent universal concern.[86] She insisted that Jew-hatred was a necessary but not sufficient condition for genocide. "Neither the fate of European Jewry nor the establishment of death factories," she wrote, "can be fully explained and grasped in terms of anti-Semitism."[87] This jelled less easily with Zionist sensibilities, as did her repeated assertion that anti-Semitism was not an eternal, ahistorical given.[88] Moreover, her contempt for explanations that resorted to German national character or history did not (and perhaps still does not) sit comfortably with either popular or even some scholarly Israeli and Jewish archetypal images.[89]

In its stead, she insisted from the beginning upon general, rather than national, categories of historical and psychological analysis, viewing events in terms of universal processes and "human" capacities. Already in 1945 she stated: "The reality is that 'the Nazis are men like ourselves'; the nightmare is that they have . . . proven beyond doubt what man is capable of."[90] Whatever the validity or otherwise of this position, her later, much contested rendering of Eichmann in "ordinary" terms as a dull, essentially "thoughtless" bureaucrat flowed from these assumptions and deeply threatened the older, potentially more demonizing view that constituted, and perhaps still constitutes, the prevailing model. There are scholarly disputes as to whether or not there is continuity in Arendt's various imaginings of evil,[91] but clearly the apparent shift from its "radical" to "banal" expression was not well received, even as it was not always understood. In the eyes of many, Arendt was seen, quite mistakenly I believe, to slight the enormity of the event, to domesticate its monstrous unspeakability.

This was a real source of narrative tension. For, at the same time as she formulated this discourse of evil, Arendt also presciently problematized or, better put, sought to demystify it.[92] Indeed, in her treatment of the *Judenraete,* her apparent blurring of the almost sacrosanct distinction between perpetrators and victims seemed to violate fundamental sensibilities even though she contextualized this as part of a general moral collapse under the extreme conditions of totalitarian society. Moreover, very early on Arendt warned that the uniqueness of the atrocities could create a self-righteous cult of victimization, one that indeed has occurred. Witness, for instance, the absurd current competition in comparative victimization as a tool of identity politics. She wrote the following extremely harsh words in August 1946:

Human beings simply can't be as innocent as they all were in the face of the gas chambers (the most repulsive usurer was as innocent as the newborn child because no crime deserves such a punishment). We are simply not equipped to deal, on a human, political level, with a guilt that is beyond crime and an innocence that is beyond goodness or virtue . . . we Jews are burdened by millions of innocents, by reasons of which every Jew alive today can see himself as innocence personified.[93]

Arendt, then, was not prepared to insulate or grant absolute privilege to Jewish history and suffering despite her emphasis on the radical novelty of the exterminations. Even in the context of analyzing the murders she insisted on locating Zionism within a wider victimizing context. While she maintained that "the State of Israel . . . in no way arose exclusively from . . . necessity,"[94] she kept very much in mind the tragic price of that necessity. As she put it in *The Origins:*

After the war it turned out that the Jewish question, which was considered the only insoluble one, was indeed solved—namely, by means of a colonized and then conquered territory—but this solved neither the problem of the minorities nor the stateless. On the contrary, like virtually all other events of our century, the solution of the Jewish question merely produced a new category of refugees, the Arabs, thereby increasing the number of the stateless and rightless by another 700,000 to 800,000 people.[95]

Viewed historically it seems that Arendt was indeed inassimilable in Jerusalem, at least during the earlier years when the state and Israeli society were coming into being. Nation building encourages organic, heroic, homogenous narratives. It could not, I suggest, easily absorb her iconoclasms or afford her ambiguities, her blurring of boundaries. It may be, however, that now, in a more secure, mature, increasingly self-critical and self-ironizing intellectual culture—especially as it cohabits with an ever more intolerant and dogmatic polity—there can be greater receptivity not only to Arendt's insights into the modern Jewish experience and the Nazi genocide but also her general observations concerning the dangers of homogeneity and the importance of a free, plural political space.[96]

At any rate, we in Jerusalem need no longer demonize Arendt. Nor on the other hand must we canonize her. I am not suggesting that we name an express train in her honor or place her face on a postage stamp as was done in Germany.[97] And Karl Jaspers' 1963 prediction is certainly still premature. He wrote then to Arendt: "A time will come that you will not live to see, when the Jews will erect a monument to you in Israel. . . . and they will proudly claim you as their own."[98] As far as I know there is not yet even a sculpture. But, surely, the time for greater—critical and sympathetic— engagement is upon us.

Eight

German History and German Jewry
Junctions, Boundaries, and Interdependencies

I offer the following scattered reflections in the form of a quite unsystematic, indeed playful, *Denkschrift*.[1] It is intended as a means of generating and exploring ideas and examining new directions of thought and research, rather than as a polished, fixed product. In a sense it is a preliminary response to the symposium on "German-Jewish History" conducted in the Leo Baeck Institute Yearbook XLI (1996),[2] and a tentative attempt to go beyond the "dead end," to which Shulamit Volkov has drawn our attention, by providing some possible contours for the desired "new beginning."[3]

In order to begin this task we have to think through the ways in which "Jewish" and "European" history intersect beyond the familiar narratives of apologetic "contribution" history or even the more sophisticated emancipation-assimilation-integration model. Despite their obvious differences, both approaches assume a kind of one-way historical direction in which Jews are remade and absorbed (or not absorbed) into the given, normative external structures—the homogenizing, centralizing nation-state, market forms of economy, secularizing cultures, and so on. This, in many ways, has been the master narrative around which modern Jewish history, at least in Western and Central Europe, has been constructed. Historians have examined the complex ways in which such transformations have proceeded and analyzed the relative successes and failures of such integration.

I am not for a moment questioning either the obvious power and validity or the palpable and continuing fruitfulness of this model but am interested here in examining some of its usually unstated assumptions and suggesting some possible supplementary viewpoints. Whether written from a "liberal" or a "national-Zionist" point of view, this transformative, integrative, modernizing model, while certainly not a "passive" one, is almost always posited in unidirectional, "absorptive" terms in which Jews in one way or the other appropriate the majority normative culture.

Thus even David Sorkin's brilliant revisionist account of *The Transformation of German Jewry, 1780–1840,* which demonstrates the creative making of a modernized, new form of Jewish identity, paradoxically sees its origins in the drive to integration. This appropriative drive and the primary use of German cultural materials to affect this operation, Sorkin argues, rendered that sub-cultural identity, as a new basis for separation, invisible to its own makers![4]

How can we begin to think a little differently about these matters? How can we reconceptualize the relation between "normative" national and "minority" Jewish history? In which way, for instance, can the new "multicultural" sensitivity be brought to bear? Of late, some historians have suggested that its emphases may be helpful in challenging traditional conceptions of the centralized, homogenous nation-state. By rethinking the making of Europe "in unfamiliar terms such as diasporas, borderlands, and peripheries," John Gillis has recently argued, we will be able to rediscover the remarkably diverse (yet repressed) multicultural and multiethnic nature of that civilization.[5] Such an approach may help to significantly challenge and transform accepted perceptions and definitions. Among other things, it questions the given, static categories of center and periphery, and seriously problematizes notions of set "minority"-"majority" relations. The young scholar Till van Rahden has persuasively suggested that, in relation to both German and German Jewish history, a sensitivity to the multicultural dimension may lead us to question the "givenness" of a prior, normative German culture into which Jews and other groups were to be "fitted."

In this view assimilation is regarded less "as a process in which outsiders increasingly adapt to a stable core culture" than one in which so-called "'minorities' have a hand in defining and redefining 'majority' culture."[6] This holds out the somewhat mischievous possibility of not only reconceptualizing German Jewish but German history itself.[7] Instead of almost perplexedly registering the sometimes ambiguous "contributions" and adaptive presence of Jews within German life and analyzing their integration (or otherwise) into what are taken to be the pre-existent, static, normative structures of German "liberalism," market society, "socialism," intellectual culture, and the like would have to be viewed dynamically, as negotiated constructions in which, at critical points, the role of the Jews (whether or not they identified as such) is conceived not simply as contributory but well-nigh *co-constitutive.* As such, it puts into question any "essentializing" understandings of a fixed "German" or "Jewish" culture and identity, and it emphasizes the fact that such complex cultures and identities are contextually and interactively constructed. This is a point to which I will return.

These suggestions can be applied throughout Central and Western Europe but they may be most fruitful in terms of Germany where not only was the process of emancipation exceptionally protracted and contested, but so too were the virtually coincidental processes of nation building and constructing a modern culture. From the late-eighteenth century on, Jews were integrally associated with this (always bitterly contested) molding process. Ironically, liberal historians have either channeled this co-constitutive and negotiative role into the less threatening "contribution" paradigm or tended to deny it entirely because—translated into different terms—it more or less validates the claim of anti-Semites dissatisfied with the emergent, modernizing transformations of German society. For did not the persistent and peculiarly powerful notion of " *Verjudung*" ("Judaization" or "Jewification"), as it developed throughout the nineteenth century and through 1945, hold that Jews were increasingly wielding disproportionate influence and occupying pivotal positions of inordinate economic, political, and cultural power, and also that, most dangerously, the Jewish *Geist* was seeping (or had already seeped) through the spiritual pores of the nation to penetrate and undermine the German psyche itself?[8] This notion was not merely the province of hostile anti-Semites. Germans of many hues expressed such sentiments, to one degree or another. Indeed, the young Zionist Moritz Goldstein provoked a scandal among liberal Jews when, in 1912, he proclaimed that "We Jews are administering the spiritual property of a nation which denies our right and ability to do so."[9]

What do we do in the face of this dilemma? If we genuinely intend to pursue this co-constitutive foundational track, we will have to take heed of Jacob Katz's repeated observation that precisely because (unlike the liberals) they treated the Jewish dimension with deadly seriousness, anti-Semitic observations about Jews could at times be as revealing and insightful as their evaluations and intentions were repugnant.[10] In any case, it would not be wise for historians to be affected by either apologetic, liberal particularist blindness or anti-Semitic hostility. What they should do is rethink the question of the complex nature and structure of interactions and interdependencies. It would be well, for a moment, to examine the possibilities of this approach at a very late, critical moment of German history—the Weimar Republic. After all, many contemporary Germans and subsequent historians portrayed the Republic in significant, indeed constitutive, ways as "Jewish" and alien to Germans. In the more sublimated phrasing of Peter Gay, this was a society in which the outsider had become insider.[11] How can we determine the nature of Weimar's intertextual cultural interdependencies and tensions?

It goes without saying, I believe, that Weimar Jewish culture in all its affirmative expressions is unthinkable outside of general Weimar culture, whatever we may take that to be. In this sense the older "integrative" model retains its validity.[12] The question here, however, is whether the opposite applies: can one conceive of Weimar culture, that short era of explosive and astonishing creativity, without the Jewish presence?[13] If Jews (whether qua Jews or not) could co-found and thrive within its ambience, perhaps it is precisely because Weimar was characterized by freedoms and an openness unprecedented in German history. Indeed, this intensely experimental, avant-garde, and liberal atmosphere has come to define at least part of what we mean by "Weimar culture." "Without the Jews," Walter Laqueur writes, "there would have been no 'Weimar culture'—to this extent the claims of the antisemites, who detested that culture, were justified. They were in the forefront of every new, daring, revolutionary moment."[14]

Laqueur, of course, should have qualified this by mentioning that many non-Jews were also very much in the vanguard of this culture: the names of Brecht, Piscator, Ernst Ludwig Kirchner, Otto Dix, Emil Nolde, Hermann Hesse, Carl von Ossietzky, and many others spring immediately to mind. Moreover, it would be wise to mention that there were some important conservative Jewish intellectuals, men of the right such as Leo Strauss and Karl Wolfskehl or Ernst Kantorowicz and Friedrich Gundolf of the Stefan Georg circle. Peter Gay is undoubtedly correct when he says, "there were many modernists who were not Jews, many Jews who were not Modernists. And many of the Jews who were Modernists were so not because they were Jews."[15] I would also agree with his contention that viewing modernism from the vantage of the Jewish question "is sheer anti-semitic tendentiousness, or philo-semitic parochialism."[16]

But what I am suggesting here is something else: not that modernism, or more precisely Weimar culture, was "Jewish" but rather that it was jointly constructed by both Jewish and non-Jewish intellectuals who were not acting in their "Jewish" or "non-Jewish" capacities. I would argue instead that in this context the notion of co-constitutionality is not "multicultural" (at least in the usual sense of the term), but rather highlights the search for, and founding of, a new sensibility in which older ethnic and religious differences are either peripheral or play no role at all.

While the co-constitutive model helps us grasp modes of interaction, then, we must keep in mind that the dynamics and dialectics of Weimar society were characterized by an equally important negative reaction to this perceived co-constitutionality. It is this tension that defines the era. As Laqueur puts it: "The Jews gave greatness to this culture and at the same time helped to limit its appeal and make it politically impotent."[17] The "core of the current Jewish question," Walter Benjamin painfully observed in November 1923, was the fact that Jews endangered "even the best German cause for which they stand up *publicly,* because their public German expression is necessarily venal (in the deeper sense) . . . nowadays a salutary complicity obligates those individuals of noble character among both peoples to keep silent about their ties." [18]

It was precisely the widespread perception of Weimar as a *Judenrepublik,* as essentially alien, cosmopolitan, rootless, and denigrative of the German "spirit," [19] that was also the spur to creating a novel, radical, right-wing, genuinely "German" counter-cultural alternative. There is an intertextual irony here. One generally, and correctly, identifies the rise of modern, self-affirmative *Jewish* cultures (or sub-cultures) in connection with a felt need to counter a sense of debilitating dependency. The Weimar case is the strongest example I can think of that illustrates the opposite: the revolt of the putative core of normative culture, the assertion of a self-affirmative "German" alternative, to overcome what it took to be a debilitating "Jewish" hegemony. It was exactly against, and yet around, these points of co-constitutionality that countermodels of *Deutschtum* were constructed.

Given the preliminary nature of these remarks, let me suggest that in the—still insufficiently examined—area of intellectual confrontation, this ironic process most tantalizingly reveals itself. In one way or another, and at the very highest levels, these clashes—the titanic Heidegger-Cassirer 1929 Davos debate on Kant, the confrontations between Martin Buber and various Völkisch theologians, the subtle polemics between Carl Schmitt and Leo Strauss—whether in explicit or coded form revolved around this tension and the desire of the non-Jewish intellectuals to somehow reassert a threatened "German" spirit. [20] Perhaps inherent to the very act of co-constitutionality is this (Bloomian) "anxiety of influence," fueling the desire to proceed from perceived dependency to autonomy. It is a process in which the drive for separation unwittingly reveals a recognition of intimacy and the incapacity to abide it. Paradoxically, these quasi-Freudian categories beautifully capture the convoluted Freud-Jung relationship itself, a relationship that poignantly embodies the complex intertextual, interpersonal aspects of our story. The father-son, teacher-pupil relationship; Jung as the Christian outsider and Freud bending over backward to keep him within the fold and thus render analysis more respectable; and then the break, the revolt of the son, the parricide; and the end in which an angry Freud pinpoints and defines the difference by confiding to their common patient, Sabina Spielrein, "We are and remain Jews . . ." [21] while Jung insists that he has formulated a creative, healthy "Aryan" psychology as opposed to psychoanalysis which was sickly, destructive, and "Jewish." Freud, Jung proclaimed, "did not know the Teutonic soul."[22] Out of a previous intimacy, the differences are again constructed as "essentialized," incommensurable entities.

Of course, the co-constitutive approach definitionally puts into question any "essentializing" understandings of either "German" or "Jewish" culture and identity, and any development of its ideas will have to try to distinguish modes of "co-constitutionality" and identity formation from the traditional, familiar model of "assimilation."[23] It is a viewpoint in which, as Samuel Moyn has recently argued in a stimulatingly instructive paper, "*Deutschtum* and *Judentum* . . . deserve to be seen as constantly evolving and mutually implicated rather than ontologically fixed and polarized categories."[24] But there is a crucial disjunction here between our own historical understanding and preferences and the ways in which many nineteenth- and twentieth-century Germans either saw or wanted to shape their reality. In the first place, the "drive to uniformity" was an overall characteristic of the emergent, centralizing nation-state. "Essentialist" thinking may have been an inevitable part of this process in general but— given the extremely delayed, always precarious nature of German efforts first to create and then consolidate a unified national state and identity out of radically fragmented political, religious, regional, and class realities—such thinking was at a premium there. The novelty and insecurity of this identity rendered the quest for its realization ever more obsessive and exclusionary. The construction of the notion of "*Deutschtum*" and the evolving discourse around it increasingly assumed an essentialist nature precisely because liberalism continued to be regarded largely as a problem rather than a solution and heterogeneity a threat rather than an enrichment.

We should remember that the term *Deutschtum* emerges only during the Wars of Liberation[25] and that, as late as 1860, Grimm's *Wörterbuch* reports that its usage was mainly ironic.[26] Yet by the end of the century the discourse between these two contrasting hypostatizations—*Deutschtum* and *Judentum*—as warring and radically incommensurate principles, was already in place. German anti-Semitism is by now too familiar for it to be necessary to give examples of this. What is more interesting is that given the increasing power of the discourse, Jews too, willy-nilly, became enmeshed in its logic, forced to conduct the dialogue within this essentialist framework. As Jakob Wassermann put it in 1921: "The German and the Jew: I once dreamed an allegorical dream . . . I placed the surface of two mirrors together; and I felt as if the human images contained and preserved in the two mirrors would have to fight one another tooth and nail."[27] But this was only an extreme expression of a generalized, virtually unavoidable mode of thought. Not simply extreme assimilationists but Orthodox and liberal Jews and Zionists alike were increasingly forced to negotiate within its premises. In seeking to counter, re-code, or deflect it, or even send out an entirely different message, they automatically became involved in its inner logic. From that point on, one could argue, the German Jewish experience was defined by these essen-tialist categories. If these tensions and hypostatizations form part of the tragedy of German Jewry, they also prompted its unprecedented creativ-ity, its reshaping of various fields of Jewish, German, and general self-understanding and knowledge.

This is a very large subject but I must come back to the ways this im-pinges on our problematic here. For all those concerned, even those most unwilling to accept it, there was a lurking understanding that however incommensurable they were supposed to be, *Deutschtum* and *Judentum* were as deeply co-implicated as possibly could be. "German and Jew," Wal-ter Benjamin said, "stand opposite one another like related extremes."[28] This was true even—perhaps especially—for those who were most un-willing to accept this relationship. "Has it not struck you," Adolf Hitler is reported to have said in one of his rambling table conversations, "how the Jew is the exact opposite of the German in every single respect, and yet is as closely akin to him as a blood brother."[29] The discourse tried to cover up but nevertheless often unwittingly betrayed the perceived bond, the recognition of mutual co-implication as much as it generated identity and role confusions.

To be sure, this essentializing reduction of identity rendered more plau-sible the numerous "psychologized" definitions of Jewishness enunciated by any number of diverse people (including Freud, Buber, and Rosen-zweig) as something deeply internal, invisible yet infinitely powerful, transmitted by unconscious and little understood mysterious forces.[30] Further, given the illiberal, threatening framework in which the discourse operated, Jews more and more were forced to state the sense of mutuality and connectedness in tragic, continuingly essentialist ways that may well have been unthinkable to Jews in more obviously pluralist cultures. Ques-tioned about his relation to Germanness and Jewishness, Franz Rosen-zweig retorted that he refused to answer: "If life were at one stage to torment me and tear me into [these] two pieces . . . I would not be able to survive this operation. . . . I . . . ask . . . not to torment me with this truly life-threatening question, but to leave me whole."[31]

Nothing better illustrates the degree of German Jewish integration into German life than this and the later obsessive, horrible impulse to under-take that eradicative operation and make it truly life-destroying.

Nine

Archetypes and the German Jewish Dialogue
Reflections Occasioned by the Goldhagen Affair

We Israeli and German historians regularly assemble in Jerusalem to discuss matters of mutual concern.[1] These meetings are usually conducted in impeccably polite and scholarly, almost other-worldly tones—leaving largely untouched and unacknowledged the emotional and existential baggage we necessarily bring to such gatherings.[2] Whatever else it has done, Daniel Jonah Goldhagen's *Hitler's Willing Executioners: Ordinary Germans and the Holocaust* has brought this visceral underbrush to the fore.[3] How can it be avoided in the face of a thesis that, boiled down to its academically unfashionable core, views the Holocaust as essentially a "national project" explicable only in terms of a persistent and vicious hatred of the Jews by "the Germans" who, once given the chance, happily and enthusiastically proceeded to murder them? Defying the conventions of current scholarship, this is history written in the spirit of ontologically incommensurable archetypes, the narrative of a radically alien species unleashed. The "study of Germans and their anti-Semitism before and during the Nazi period," Goldhagen proclaims, "must be approached as an anthropologist would a previously unencountered preliterate people and their beliefs, leaving behind the preconception that Germans were in every ideational realm just like our ideal notion of ourselves."[4]

The book has been discussed and critiqued *ad nauseum*[5]—I myself have done this elsewhere and do not intend to repeat it here.[6] But its extraordinary reception, the extreme scholarly and popular passions it has aroused,[7] and its reassertion of an almost primordial German Jewish divide present us with an obligation to re-examine the complexities and dynamics of our own ongoing dialogue, to identify not only its hidden assumptions, implicit tensions and commonalities, mutual biases and

evasions, and tacit compromises—but also the fructifying possibilities—
that inform this relationship.

Exactly what kind of enterprise are we engaged in here? It is, of course,
a charged, rather unique affair. For it is a form of communication that
takes place, as Hannah Arendt noted in 1964, "precisely in the abyss of
Auschwitz,"[8] our culture's archetypal site of ultimate evil. But the scholarly encounter does not exist in a vacuum. It is part of the broader post-
World War II German Jewish meeting with its complex mix of reconnection, recrimination, mourning, evasion, guilt, and all the gyrations
summed up in that horrible term, "*wiedergutmachung*."[9] Clearly this is
an intellectual and emotional minefield. Because the representation of the
Holocaust is so acutely linked to central dimensions of German and Jewish identity, it will inevitably be marked by any number of transferences.[10]
In suitably altered forms it will satisfy complex, often contradictory sets
of present needs and interests. But it is precisely "the power of these
needs, often unrecognized and elusive,"[11] that provides the underlying dynamic of the dialogue.

Would it be unfair to suggest that when German and Jewish (especially
Israeli) intellectuals meet to discuss these matters, other emotions apart,
there is a certain eros, a mutual attraction, at work? This unspoken affinity, this powerful and problematic commonality, consists in the recognition that, albeit in radically different roles, "we"— and not any others—
are the most relevant actors in the story? Whatever alternative universalist
narratives we may construct, is there not a gut feeling that, however different our versions and vantage points may be, we are the primary "owners" of the story?

The umbilical chord may be a murderous one but it is, perhaps for
that very reason, both compelling and convoluted and reinforced by the
historic, and brutally betrayed, Jewish relationship to German culture. Is
not the dialogue an attempt, in some mutually placatory way, to resuscitate that relationship, and at the same time does it not stand as indicative
of a certain continued Jewish longing for reconnection and acceptance
into that culture? No one has written more biting poetic criticism of what
transpired than the survivor Paul Celan. Yet, as early as 1947–48, he was
hugely proud of his success in the German *Kulturbereich*. "God knows,"
he wrote, "I was happy when they told me I was the greatest poet in
Austria and—as far as they know—in Germany as well."[12] There may be
a grain of truth in Henryk Broder's sly and mischievous observation that
Goldhagen's project is less a product of "German-bashing" than the desire to be heard and taken note of by the German intellectual establishment, the attempt by the son to reestablish a connection lost by his father
50 years ago, even if such acceptance can be established only through

the Holocaust, "the end-point of German-Jewish history, but also the starting-point for common academic undertakings: the only thing that existentially binds Germans and Jews."[13]

Moreover, it should be admitted, there is a common fascination with its unspeakable dimensions: the atrocities and obscenities, the transgression of limits and taboos, the relations of victimizers to victims. It is at the level of these archetypal issues, images, and juxtapositions—in "high" as well as in "popular" culture—where much of the event is emotionally played out, and from where it receives the energy of its interpretive permutations. The astonishing resonance of Goldhagen's book—the intensity and range of emotions it has evoked—is related to the fact that he has tapped directly into these archetypal and stereotypical reservoirs. The answer to Goldhagen's own question concerning the success of his book ("Why are the pillars shaking?")[14] does not necessarily lie, as he would have it, in his successful challenge to what he takes to be an obfuscating and apologetic mainstream Holocaust scholarship, but rather in the fact that it overwhelmingly confirms everyday "commonsense" interpretations and perceptions. This may account for the peculiar divide in the reception of the book. The broad fault-line is not, as some commentators have suggested, between a defensive "German" response and a friendly American or even Jewish one[15]—though in some hostile, anti-Semitic reviews the latter two have been regarded as quite indistinguishable[16]—but rather between popular acclaim and scholarly derision.

The overall popular acclaim applies not just to the United States but also, emphatically, to Germany. There too, by and large, it was heralded by the public and castigated by the intellectual classes. The reasons for what one journalist described as Goldhagen's German "triumphal procession" are complex.[17] It derives, in part, from a widespread perception of unfairness: the brave graduate David persecuted by jealous professorial Goliaths. Still, this is not sufficient to account for the fact that a book condemned by the German political and academic establishment as little more than a restatement of the collective guilt thesis[18]—Germany as a nation of murderers—has been so warmly received. Why should so many—especially young—Germans hail it?[19] A major part of the explanation is related to a generational distance that enables the young to question the conventional distinction between "bad" Nazis and "ordinary" Germans and to upbraid their elders for fleeing from the concrete murderous acts of *their* parents by depicting the Holocaust as a kind of historical abstraction, a matter of impersonal industrial and bureaucratic processes, a mass killing operation shorn of flesh and blood killers.[20]

But there is, I would suggest, something else at work as well. The success of Goldhagen's book is reminiscent of the astonishing cult status attained in Germany after the war, also among the young, by Celan's un-endurably painful poem *"Todesfuge."* It gave the Germans, John Bayley writes, "a kind of enormous and magical relief, the equivalent in great art of the black joke current at the time: The Germans will never forgive the Jews for Auschwitz."[21] I do not intend, for one moment, to suggest similarities between the two projects. But Celan's categories, transmuted into aesthetic form, also belong squarely within the archetypal matrix: death, after all, is a blue-eyed master from Germany. The poetry comes astonishingly close to Goldhagen's portrait of jovial killers: "he whistles his hounds to come close / he whistles his Jews into rows has them shovel a grave in the ground / he commands us play up for the dance." Did not this indictment, Bayley asks, ironically lay "trouble to rest in the hearts and minds of many Germans, who could feel their guilt wonderfully, and painlessly, through its medium?"

Goldhagen, of course, has no aesthetics but he makes the guilt even less painful for subsequent generations by insisting that post–1945 Germans have purged themselves of murderous anti-Semitism. I would suggest that documents like these have served throughout as flagellant markers and ironic acknowledgements of a crucial but submerged dimension of German identity. What is new is that this emblematic proclamation is no longer seen as subversive or counter-cultural in nature. The contrary may be true. How else can one regard the sociologist Ulrich Beck's suggestion to view "Auschwitz *as* German identity"? Very recently, only half tongue-in-cheek, Maxim Biller, has described the obsession with the "Holocaust-Trauma as the mother of a finally found German national self-consciousness. . . ." For, he argues, only this event has finally brought forth the common experience, the key concept providing a previously quite unattainable unity to a hopelessly divided nation. That is why, Biller concludes (satirically or otherwise), "the Germans so love the Holocaust."[22]

The serious divide, then, has not been between German and Jewish intellectuals. Indeed, with a few exceptions, in both the Anglo-Saxon and Israeli academic world the critique has been devastating.[23] It can be summed up in the publicly circulated letter of the doyen of Holocaust studies, Raul Hilberg, who declared that he found "virtually nothing" of value in the book: "To me it is worthless."[24] The scholarly anger (to be sure, itself a complex mix of not always salutary motives) flows partly from the perception that the book's popular success is due to its simplistic monocausality, its uncritical resurrection of archetypes and stereotypes, and the pervading sense that somehow the national unit of analysis—the "Germans"—provides a satisfactory explanatory key.

Naturally, this does not mean that there are no tensions and fissures in the German Jewish/Israeli dialogue. It is *because* we both "own" the event that the interpretive custodianship is so much in dispute. This sometimes reaches absurd proportions. In response to Jewish objections concerning the nature of the proposed Berlin Holocaust memorial, Lea Rosh, the TV personality (who changed her name from Edith to the more Jewish Lea, presumably as an act of identification), sharply exclaimed: "It's the successors of the perpetrators who are building this memorial, not the Jews."[25]

The question of bias entailed in ownership forms part of the magnificent, and refreshingly honest, dialogue between Martin Broszat and Saul Friedlander. For Broszat "Jewish" historiography and memory must perforce be "mournful and acccusatory . . . a mythical form of remembrance"[26] rather than a scholarly and "scientific" enterprise, while for Friedlander, "the German context creates as many problems in the approach to the Nazi era as it does, differently, for the victims." "If we see things from your perspective," he admonishes Broszat, "why, in your opinion, would historians belonging to the group of perpetrators be able to distance themselves from their past, whereas those belonging to the group of victims would not?"[27] This is psychological tit for tat: Jewish historiography as mournful and mythical, German historiography as apologetic, or, at least, impelled into impersonal structures and processes, into modes of explanation that underplay individual agency and ideology and redirect compassion for the victim into forms of self-empathy.[28]

These differences, of course, have been sharply highlighted by Goldhagen, a fact that perforce will influence the dialogue. In effect, with his insistence upon the free, even enthusiastic choice of "ordinary" Germans to undertake the killings impelled by a peculiarly murderous anti-Semitism, he is offering a reactive mirror-opposite to the apologetic and simplified *Historikerstreit* histories of the 1980s, which relativized Auschwitz into the regular annals of human murderousness. He, so to speak, returns the Shoah to the Jews, in much the same way as some German scholars sought to rehabilitate German identity by "normalizing" it in the context of other twentieth-century genocides.[29] Given the *Historikerstreit* and a functionalist scholarship that, he believes, consistently underplays direct participation and complicity in crimes of the Third Reich, Goldhagen, whether consciously or unconsciously, may be construed as speaking for the victims and survivors. For a variety of reasons—the cruel workings of the passage of time; the notion that theirs is a "mythical" memory; the postmodernist problematization of witnessing and testimony[30]—they have undergone what amounts to a virtual academic de-legitimization. Goldhagen does not so much argue their case as seek to throw the moral and epistemological ball across the national net, to cast doubt upon the authenticity of current portraits of the perpetrators and present it from the immediate viewpoint of the victims.

I would suspect that for many survivors, Goldhagen is regarded as the historian who expresses the unbearable everyday cruelty of *their* experiences, who makes ineluctably clear the joy their tormentors took in inflicting such cruelty. It makes little difference that historians do not deny the reality of such experiences as much as they question the interpretive and explanatory framework in which Goldhagen locates them and are uncomfortable with what they take to be an almost pornographic, voyeuristic attention to gory detail that renders understanding more, rather than less, remote. From the point of view of such survivors, Goldhagen has succeeded in starkly representing their reality and thus the scholarly attack upon him may very well be experienced as an attack upon themselves.

The word "case" is apt for this is history written in the prosecutorial mode. Some German critics even view it as a kind of national provocation and have responded with rather revealing and thinly veiled threats. None other than Countess Marion Doenhoff, co-publisher of the liberal *Die Zeit,* a journal always sensitive to matters related to Jews and Nazism, asked whether the book would not "revive the anti-Semitism that has remained more or less dormant?"[31] And, in conversation, a prominent conservative German historian commented, quite unselfconsciously, that this work would help to strengthen traditional "anti-Western sentiments."[32]

It is precisely because of this confrontational dimension that we need to consider the book in the light of the ongoing post-war German Jewish conversation. At first glance, the work appears to be quintessentially anti-dialogical, a cutting off, a stifling, of that conversation. But that is to misconceive the nature and process of dialogue which occurs, in the first place, *because* there are different versions and positions. While ideally such conversations should assume a Buberian character of mutuality and openness, they originate in, and function through, discord. Defense and attack are crucial to its dynamic. To be sure, prosecutorial and archetypal history may be poor history—it certainly is not the kind of history that I seek to write—but it is decidedly very much part of the dialogue. It is precisely through his accusatory stance that Goldhagen has become central to it. Whether or not they like it, scholars will have to face this fact. For, even if he is not interested in listening to the position of the other or moderating his own and simply wants to extract a *mea culpa* from "the Germans," in effect, to change them, he ardently desires that they listen to his message. Nothing could be more indicative of the dialogical need than the act of translation and the publicity and personal appearances attending it.

If dialogical voices are definitionally non-identical, then the process of comprehending and writing history is less a dialogue than a "polyphony," a multiplicity of contesting voices generating a dynamic interplay of multiple meanings and interpretations ("polysemy").[33] The plurality of these continuously changing and revised perspectives are, willy-nilly, the lubricants of historiography: the more we can articulate the tensions, the more vital the history. In our own charged field, one could argue, the fact that divergent needs and interests are at play is not only inevitable but helps to shape and enliven our understanding. They are simultaneously the creative as well as the limiting ingredients of writing history.

Just as "history" and "collective memory" are not diametrical opposites but part of a continuum, a relationship that can oscillate from outright conflict through tension to mutual nurturing, becoming in the process what we call "historical consciousness,"[34] so too is it untenable to posit a hermetic separation between putatively "scientific" histories, on the one hand, and "archetypal" versions, on the other. Given the violently transgressive nature of the "Final Solution," archetypes form a constituent part of our moral, cultural, and historical imaginations, a kind of raw material that helps to animate our narrative reconstructions. In more or less subliminal or explicit, crude or sophisticated ways, archetypal antinomies often lie behind the models with which we work: good and evil; Germans and Jews; victimizers and victims; the banal and the monstrous, or demonic; the unique and the universal.[35] Of course, responsible scholarship will always have to view them critically, refining and deconstructing them even as we work with them.

These archetypal dimensions are related to the passionate, almost violent controversies that erupt from time to time within the inflammatory world of Shoah scholarship. Are not many of the scholarly (as well as the wider) debates and stakes related to the *rearranging, reassembling, problematizing, transvaluing, and questioning of these kinds of categories*? The Goldhagen affair is only the most recent example. Perhaps the best foil for comparison would be the equally raw nerves touched by Hannah Arendt in her 1963 work, *Eichmann in Jerusalem*. Was she not also indulging in a form of a threatening archetypal rearrangement when she quietly abandoned her nihilistic, demonic, ideological emphasis in *The Origins of Totalitarianism* and turned to an explanation of the essential thoughtlessness, the "banality" of the perpetrator?

Arendt's case also illustrates the fact that such archetypal schemes are not a matter of competitive national narrative identity, of monolithically motivated Jews challenging Germans or vice versa. On the contrary, the image of the destruction of European Jewry as an impersonal, industrial-bureaucratic process was articulated in the monumental 1961 work of the Jewish historian, Raul Hilberg. It was only later that the analyses of German functionalists like Hans Mommsen and Martin Broszat emerged.

Even more radically, though, Arendt caused major outrage when she rendered the Jewish leadership complicit in the destruction process and critically blurred the archetypally pure distinction between victim and victimizer. Hilberg, too, argued that inherited modes of submissive ghetto behavior served to smooth the wheels of destruction, and Bruno Bettelheim produced numerous biting critiques unmasking what he believed to be the self-duplicities of Jewish behavior.[36] Arendt, of course, throughout rejected the relevance of "Germanness" to any explanation of Nazism,[37] and it is worth noting that she and Hilberg and Bettelheim were all exiled products of a German culture with which, in complex ways, they continued to identify. This may have had something to do with the biases of their analyses, their downplaying of any *Sonderweg* explanations, and their views on complicitous Jewish behavior.[38]

We have come full circle. Goldhagen has again inflamed and re-energized the debate by revalidating and recirculating what was thought to be the discredited *Sonderspecies* archetype, the notion of "ordinary" Germans as anti-Semitic murderers impelled to kill exclusively in terms of this historically conditioned, fanatic belief. Scholars have criticized this (correctly, in my view) by arguing that individual genocidal acts can be better explained in terms of a complex cluster of motivational factors. These obviously include anti-Semitism as a central force but also include consideration of other ideological ingredients. Moreover, they recognize the weight of situational factors and take into account generalized psychological mechanisms, evidenced by the equally murderous activities of other national groups (both in the Shoah and elsewhere) that render more intelligible the qualitative leap from conventional everyday prejudice to radical genocidal action. These are the differences between Goldhagen's "ordinary Germans" and Christopher Browning's "ordinary men."

What must be made clear, however, is that the historical record never speaks unambiguously for itself: interpreting the nature, causes, and meaning of such motivations, whether in "simple" or "complex" ways,[39] is part of the ascriptive task of historians. This is true too for the general models that ground these motivational accounts. Goldhagen's explanation is based on an anthropological, even ontological, gulf between ourselves and the German murderers, while Browning's relies on an assumption of a commonality of possible experience and the desire to break down what he takes to be a comfortable and self-serving distance between ourselves and the perpetrators; yet both approaches are basically interpretive decisions, not matters of empirical observation. Both, in effect, are heuristic choices linked to the politics and values informing their diverging historical representations. Are these not archetypal choices: the genocide of the Jews as a paradigm of human potential? The exemplum of universal traits unleashed under certain conditions? Genocide as explicable in exceptional terms, the outcome of a singularly murderous anti-Jewish German polity and culture?[40]

So where does this leave us in terms of what brings us together—the German Jewish dialogue? It is clear from what I have said that we should welcome even as we heavily criticize the opposing positions and tensions that constitute it. Dynamic historical knowledge arises in the attempt to somehow negotiate these tensions. In so doing we redefine and refine our narratives. To be sure, it is only human to believe that our own positions are the most correct, the most persuasive, but we must also acknowledge their own historicity.

Still, if we cannot help but bring our collective and personal biographies and allegiances with us, we must, finally, insist upon rigorously honest, self-reflexive standards of scholarship that question, rather than simply reflect, one's own group affiliations and preconceptions. The dangers of history that understands itself as purely "German" or "Jewish" are too obvious to require discussion. Proper scholarly interchange demands the critical and refining qualities, the self-awareness of our mutual biases, so that we are better able to cope with them.

It is fitting then to conclude with the observation that the present moment is characterized in both German and Jewish historical memory by a kind of archetypal split consciousness. In Germany we have the paradoxical identity-affirming acceptance by many of Goldhagen's portrait of "the Germans." Simultaneously, as Frank Stern has recently pointed out, a new archetype, the myth of the good German—indeed, of the German as *savior* of the Jew—is emerging (evidenced by the mass sales of the diaries of the German-Jewish survivor, Victor Klemperer; the reception of *Schindler's List;* and Völker von Schlöndorff's recent film of Michael Tournier's *The Ogre* in which the hero rescues the Jew by carrying him on his back through fire and ice, in quintessentially mythical fashion.)[41] Can a more archetypal clash than this be imagined?

At the same time, within Jewish and Israeli circles the question as to the exceptional or paradigmatic nature of the Shoah remains open. It too is often couched in quasi-archetypal terms. Omer Bartov, in reaction to both Goldhagen and interested Israeli representations, has recently put it thus: "we must not consign Auschwitz to another planet nor perceive the perpetrators as different species. When we imagine the Holocaust we must imagine ourselves."[42] The marvelously unpredictable Hannah Arendt articulated the other side in her 1964 correspondence with Hans Magnus Enzensberger. When he wrote that "Fascism is not terrible because the Germans practiced it, but because it is possible everywhere," Arendt responded: "If all are guilty, then none are . . . This statement is even more problematic when it is advanced by a German for it says: not our parents, but mankind has brought about this catastrophe. This is simply not true."[43]

Our dialogue is destined to wrestle with these issues and, if we cannot arrive at ultimate truth, we can be sure that through the constant raising of such dilemmas and conflicts, through irresolution and problematization, the memory of this horrendous event and of those who perished in it will be most urgently preserved.

Part III

Understanding Nazism and the Holocaust: Competing Models and Radical Paradigms

Ten

Nazism, Normalcy, and the German Sonderweg

> For is it mere hypochondria to say to oneself that everything German, even the German mind and spirit, German thought, the German Word, is involved in this scandalous exposure and made subject to the same distrust?
> —Thomas Mann, *Doctor Faustus*

The atrocities committed by National Socialism have always called for special modes of explanation.[1] From the 1960s through the early 1980s the ruling conventional academic wisdom invoked, as almost self-evident, the thesis of an overall German exceptionalism to account for Nazism. Only an aberrant, perhaps pathological past, it was held, could spawn such a monstrous outgrowth. Nazism, in this view, was explicable only in terms of a hinterland of serious national deviance. This paradigm consisted of academic elaborations of much older popular and always stereotypical notions that somehow the "Germans"—their character, polity, culture, and society—were intrinsically different from the rest of the West. This always had two converse sides to it. Until 1945 many Germans proclaimed this to be their great *virtue:* it was these differences that constituted their separate, more exalted national identity. Cultivated inner *Bildung* confronted shallow external politics, deep *Kultur* was juxtaposed to mere *Zivilization*. And in the West, especially during World War I, the image of Germans as intrinsically militaristic, authoritarian, obedient, rapacious, murderous, and block-headed found a receptive, mass audience. These notions became immeasurably strengthened with the rise of Nazism and the outbreak of World War II. In all kinds of ways they have become an ongoing part of our everyday folklore. (Who has better captured this than John Cleese in his masterful *Fawlty Towers* episode "The Germans"?)

It was, however, only during the 1960s that the more respectable, sophisticated, and systematic academic elaborations of these—by now thoroughly negative—assessments by German, British, and American scholars appeared. During the 1950s, for instance, Western scholars placed a premium on models of totalitarianism. Hannah Arendt's classic work *The Origins of Totalitarianism,* for example, was virtually devoid of reflections on the specific nature (normal or otherwise) of the German mind and polity.[2] Nazism, instead, was conceived as one instance of a general, peculiarly modern, political project of total domination. Its genesis was not integrally bound to any particular historical culture. It incarnated a potential latent in the twentieth century itself. Its deadliness derived from its generality, not its nationality.

Marxists, too, had little time for national explanations. Nazism was merely a variant of fascism, which, in turn, had to be grasped as part of the dynamics of capitalism under pressure.[3] At the same time, conservative German historians[4] (such as Gerhard Ritter and Friedrich Meinecke)[5] similarly disavowed notions of any essential German historical abnormalcy. Unlike Arendt and the Marxists, of course, their perspectives remained doggedly national. But they regarded the course of German development as basically healthy. Its natural unfolding had been upset by the importation of alien and corrupting Western practices and ideologies. With the upheaval created by World War I and its disastrous aftermath, the fabric of German stability had been destroyed and the way to demagogic chaos in a mass age opened up.

All this was to change considerably in the 1960s when liberal historians began to apply sophisticated methods from the fields of intellectual and social history to the critical study of the German past. It was then that what we understand by the academic thesis of the German *Sonderweg*—the notion that the course of German historical development had been both peculiar and misshapen—was first systematically expounded.[6] In its bare outlines, the structural version of this theory claimed that the roots of Nazism had to be located in the distinctive and jagged mode of modernization that marked the German experience in the nineteenth and twentieth centuries. The German road to modernity, it was held, was quite different from that followed by the West, for it was characterized by a disjunction between economic development, on the one hand, and the social and political spheres, on the other. This lack of synchronization was of fundamental importance, for it pointed to the creation of a capitalist society in the economic sense of the term, but one that lacked the concomitant liberal values normally associated with such a transformation. Germany, in other words, never underwent a successful bourgeois revolution of the type that ensured liberal-democratic regimes in France, England, and the United States.

In Germany it was the Junker aristocracy, not the bourgeoisie, that set the tone. Instead of a nobility undergoing *embourgeoisement*, the middle classes were feudalized. The failure of the liberal revolution in 1848 and the Bismarckian mode of German unification, proponents of the *Sonderweg* thesis insisted, were the key events in a lasting historical pattern: Germany was fated to remain an obstinately authoritarian society dominated by pre-industrial elites. These elites, it was maintained, clung tenaciously to power, adjusting to a variety of changing circumstances. At the critical moment they became the chief agents propelling Hitler into power. Viewed from this perspective, Nazism was the extreme manifestation, the last fruits, of a foiled and distorted modernization process.

In what has by now become almost a classic work, two young British historians, David Blackbourn and Geoff Eley, issued a radical and sophisticated neo-Marxist challenge to this prevailing paradigm. First published in German in 1980 under the telling title *Mythen deutscher Geschichtsschreibung (Myths of German Historiography)*, the work was published in 1984 in English, together with an extensive introduction that detailed the heated debate their work had evoked up to that point.[7] Whatever the merits of their own alternative theories, a problem to which we shall presently return, their incisive critique of the *Sonderweg* model performed an invaluable service and has since that time rendered many of its positions untenable, forcing its proponents into more and more qualifications.[8] By and large, *Sonderweg* theories have subsequently gone into retreat though they still constitute a temptation of sorts and tend from time to time to reemerge in various guises. Paul Lawrence Rose's *Revolutionary Antisemitism in Germany from Kant to Wagner* (1990), Liah Greenfield's *Nationalism: Five Roads to Modernity* (1992), and Daniel Goldhagen's *Hitler's Willing Executioners: Ordinary Germans and the Holocaust* (1996) constitute representative examples of this genre. Blackbourn and Eley exposed assumptions that had already settled into the mold of an unexamined orthodoxy and opened up debate and possibilities concerning fresh directions in the study of German history.

The idea of a *Sonderweg*, they pointed out, presumes a norm, a series of suppositions and expectations as to what constitutes "proper" historical development.[9] "Proper" or healthy development is inevitably taken to be the Western liberal-democratic experience. Measured according to this yardstick, German history will always—and definitionally so—be found wanting. This normative exercise was regarded by Blackbourn and Eley as virtually worthless. They pointed to the fact that specialists in British and French history had long ago demolished the picture of bourgeois social transformation "of the kind that still seems to govern the categories in which German if-only history is constructed."[10] They argued that the elision of the bourgeoisie into liberalism and then popular democracy, a staple of the *Sonderweg* model, was simply historically inadmissible. Nowhere in Europe, they insisted, was the bourgeois revolution identical with political democracy. Its emergence in France and Britain postdated the bourgeois revolution and was always linked to "complex popular struggles against rather than for significant bourgeois interests. . . . The possibilities for democratic politics resulted from the contradictions of 'modernization' rather than its triumph, not as a condition of the bourgeoisie's success, but from the new antagonisms it created."[11]

The real bourgeois revolution, Blackbourn and Eley maintained, had to be located not in surface phenomena such as the presence or absence of constitutional government but rather in long-term structural transformations. Dominant classes, they wryly observed, are not always ruling classes, and aristocratic visibility did not necessarily mean preeminence (the authors preferred the Gramscian term "hegemony"). The "real power" of the bourgeoisie "was anchored in the capitalist mode of production and in civil society, in the spheres of property relations, the rule of law, associational life, and so on."[12] Viewed in this light, they argued, Germany did indeed undergo a highly successful bourgeois revolution, one that coincided with national unification.

Paradoxically, it was Bismarck who, in this view, orchestrated a

> classic instance of revolution from above, substituting military unification and political negotiation with the opposition for the far more confusing and volatile scenario of the English and French Revolutions. In some ways—the sharpness of the rupture with the past, the definitive character of the legal settlement, the commanding strength of capital in the new national economy—German unification was more specifically "bourgeois" in its effects than either the English or French Revolution had been, precisely because popular interventions failed to occur.[13]

In this rendering, Bismarck is metamorphosed into the bourgeois hero, delivering in a concentrated space of time through a radical process of political innovation "the legal and political conditions for a society in which the capitalist mode of production could be dominant."[14]

Seen thus, the modernization of Germany was in no way aberrant but rather exceedingly effective in securing the basic interests of the bourgeoisie. The Bismarckian state and an authoritarian mode of politics reflected a functional way of organizing capitalist relationships. These were perfectly "modern" responses to German conditions and not the vaunted machinations of supposedly pre-industrial groupings. German history in the nineteenth century, Blackbourn and Eley maintained, should be seen within this context of a burgeoning capitalism and the forms of politics required for its successful generation.

There is another salutary aspect of Blackbourn and Eley's work that merits our attention. This concerns their warnings as to the powerful dangers of teleology that especially attend the study of German history. The teleological temptation is one which, I believe, many teachers of German history in general and of Nazism and the Holocaust in particular find hard to resist. The inevitabilist, linear reading of the origins of Nazism deep in the recesses of the German past is a trap into which it is all too easy to fall. The catastrophes unleashed by National Socialism can in this sense "overwhelm" German history. How simple it is to portray that past as if it were the mere preparation, the prologue, of what was to come later! Blackbourn and Eley are correct when they point out that this makes for a highly undemanding form of history, one in which all sense of contingency is lost. Regardless of the temptations, German history should not be written as if 1933 were inscribed in every past event. Good historians, they remind us, are those who as far as possible do not reduce historical processes exclusively to their known results.

This rereading of German history, predictably enough, did not meet with unanimous approval. It was criticized on various grounds—and not solely by German historians with a vested interest in the concept of the *Sonderweg*.[15] Gordon Craig, for instance, questioned why Blackbourn and Eley omitted from their account such crucial comparative events as the Revolution of 1830 in France or the Great Reform Act and the repeal of the Corn Laws in England—"bourgeois" events that, according to Craig, simply had no parallel in the German experience.[16] And, as James Joll pungently asked, if Germany's bourgeois revolution from above was so successful, why was "the Bismarckian constitution . . . under strain from its inception, whereas British parliamentarians weathered many comparable storms?"[17]

These and other weaknesses in their model were certainly present. For all that, though, the emphasis on Germany as a modern and bourgeois society was a crucial corrective to the prevailing view; it faithfully captured critical features that were blurred or entirely filtered out by *Sonderweg* spectacles. Yet, had Blackbourn and Eley been more receptive to cultural and intellectual history, they would have discovered that contemporary work in these fields closely mirrored the same modern and bourgeois realities that they emphasized. Unfortunately, their neo-Marxist bias rendered them indifferent to, at times even contemptuous of, the role that a differentiated cultural-intellectual history can play in understanding German history in general and Nazism in particular. The methods of intellectual history are generally dismissed as "Nazi pedigree-hunting in the realm of ideas, with its habitual unwillingness to specify, sometimes even to recognize as a problem, who was influenced by what ideas, when, and to what effect."[18] Some examples of this genre, Blackbourn and Eley conceded, were better than others. Nonetheless, they argued, as a rule these works tended to dissect a disembodied "German Mind" and proved to be intellectually slack and unhistorical. It is a method that, as Eley put it, typically has "meant reconstructing the intellectual pursuits of an earlier epoch in the image of Nazi ideology. . . . All these ideas are described as in some way distinctively German and all are traced back to the eighteenth century as aspects of an unbroken linear continuity. . . . This is surely a fruitless exercise, the worst kind of intellectual history, which makes its connections by lifting ideas from their sensible context.[19]

This approach, indeed, captured some of the earlier attempts at intellectual history, as well as some of the popular ones still being written today. Eley singled out Butler's *The Roots of National Socialism* (1941) for its simplistic ideational reductionism. "The Nazis," wrote Butler, "say that might is right; Spengler said it; Bernhardi said it; Nietzsche said it; Treitschke had said as much; so had Haller before him; so had Novalis."[20] He could just as easily have mentioned Peter Viereck's study[21] of the same year where Wagner was indicted as a direct forerunner to, and a clear manifestation of, Nazi mentality, or Crane Brinton's similar treatment of Nietzsche, also written in 1941.[22] Simplistic cultural history of this kind is not confined exclusively to liberals. Perhaps the worst offender in this regard was Georg Lukács's *The Destruction of Reason.*[23] His Marxist treatise identified an unbroken and undifferentiated line of German irrationalism leading inexorably to fascism. Here the rejection of reason simply reflected the needs of an ever more expansionist and aggressive imperialist bourgeoisie, a class that in the post-Hegelian period had exhausted its progressive potential. Like Brinton, Lukács placed Nietzsche at the center of these developments, his open, "mythological" philosophy at once an anticipation and a foreshadowing of the fascist future.

Good intellectual history is no longer conducted in this fashion. Recent work is, by and large, infused with the sense of context. It concentrates on polyvalent modes of reception and appropriation, on the complex ways in which ideas, ideologies, myths, and stereotypes are diffused and absorbed, often among radically divergent political circles and institutions. It demonstrates that intellectual currents and movements commonly associated with proto-fascist or Nazi mentalities were adaptable to a wide variety of political positions and, furthermore, were used to buttress not only numerous shadings on the right but also the center and, surprisingly often, progressive and left positions.[24] Many of these movements were not specifically German phenomena but spanned the Continent. Currents like racism, eugenics, and anti-Semitism may have been strong in Germany, but they were also present (sometimes powerfully so) in most countries of Europe. These were ideologies that, in many ways, were flexible systems easily fitted into a wide variety of molds.[25] Strikingly, contemporary studies emphasize that this was also the case with peculiarly homegrown Germanic products that, as we have seen, earlier historians treated as almost synonymous with Nazism. Wagnerism[26] and Nietzscheanism[27] became European influences, attracting large and divergent publics and fusing with a range of political postures, including decidedly "progressive" ones. Neither possessed an inherent political personality. Of crucial importance in their dynamic development were selective modes of mediation and reception. In this way both heritages became part and parcel of numerous—in fact, often opposed—ideologies.

Reception studies of this kind sensitize us to the complexity of the role of ideas and make for nuanced distinctions previously overlooked. Not all racists were anti-Semites, nor for that matter were all anti-Semites necessarily racist. And, as Alfred Kelly has recently demonstrated, the popularization of Darwin often resulted in biologistic thinking that was quite compatible with humanitarian values.[28] The path from Darwinism, Wagnerism, Nietzscheanism, and even racism and anti-Semitism to Nazism, it is clear, was never simple or direct. Different roads did, of course, lead in different directions. Nevertheless, twisted though it may have been, one did, in point of fact, lead to Auschwitz. However great the perils of teleology, they should not blunt our determination to understand the processes and impulses that, at least in one instance, led to this destination. The fear of complexity is a poor reason, I believe, to abandon cultural history.

The central problem with which we are concerned in this essay, however, remains unresolved. How is the course of German history best understood—as somehow distinct and separate or as part of the spectrum of "normal" European experience? We have already seen that many of the materials from which the Nazis later constructed their own particular worldview were linked to a broader sense of a "crisis of civilization" that was common throughout Europe from the 1880s, a period of unprecedented social change and corresponding anxieties. It was then that a variety of ideological responses emerged, responses that numerous commentators have designated as proto-fascist.[29] Common to all these reactions was a highly "modern" conception of mass politics and a dynamic ideology that, with its promises of rejuvenation and the creation of a New Man, was quite different from conventional conservative and authoritarian politics. It was a mode of political ideology that tended to blur orthodox left-right distinctions and create a new, coherent, alternative form of identification. German intellectuals and activists partook in these activities. In that sense the German experience was "normal." It shared the same fears and problems and was part of the larger search for novel solutions that characterized important segments of the bourgeoisie through-out fin-de-siècle Europe.

There is, though, another sense in which the notion of "normalcy" is gradually becoming relevant to the study and explanation of Nazism. This concerns the modalities by which bourgeois society created its own codes of conformity, constructing notions of "respectability" in the fields of manners and morals. It was a process that succeeded in creating very distinct norms of behavior throughout modern Europe. In his new work, *Nationalism and Sexuality: Respectability and Abnormal Sexuality in Modern Europe,*[30] George Mosse places nineteenth-century as well as Nazi Germany firmly within the context of this overall *embourgeoisement* of morality. Germany is by no means separated from this experience. On the contrary, the German *Sonderweg* lies paradoxically in its fanatical pursuit of the general logic of bourgeois *Sittlichkeit* (morality). How are we to understand this unexpected coupling?

The defining characteristic of the nineteenth century, Mosse argues, was the powerful alliance between nationalism and middle-class morality. Together they defined modern standards of respectability in such a way that an ever-tightening distinction between "normality" and "abnormality" was created and enforced. Those who were perceived as lacking in the characteristics designated as normal were increasingly consigned to "abnormal" (outsider) status. This alliance, in Mosse's view, became increasingly comprehensive, insistent on assigning everyone a fixed place: man and woman, sane and insane, Jew and non-Jew, native and foreigner. An ordered and safe "inside" could be created and maintained only by extending the net of exclusion. A rigid ethic of *Sittlichkeit* was invoked to control the reality that the alliance itself had created.

From this point of view, bourgeois morality becomes a kind of autonomous historical villain, an ethic whose constrictive and intolerant moral sense gradually radicalized to the point that, in its Nazi version, it became an essential ingredient of genocidal motivation. "The new German man," Mosse tells us, "was the ideal bourgeois."[31] Auschwitz is comprehended here in a shocking new light, far removed from Rauschning's Nazi nihilists breaking all limits in a kind of Nietzschean ecstasy or from Ernst Nolte's portrayal of Nazism as the ultimate naturalist revolt against bourgeois transcendence or from Thomas Mann's Faustian and thoroughly Germanic covenant with the demonic.[32] Mosse's Nazi is none of these nor is he the reincarnation of a pre-industrial authoritarian world. He is rather the most extreme and corrupted expression of the alliance between nationalism and middle-class morality. At least in part, this Nazi is a bourgeois intent on preserving and cleansing his world against what he perceives to be the ubiquitous forces of degeneration. The paradigm of degeneration, as a new volume of essays edited by Chamberlin and Gilman reminds us, was always linked to bourgeois fears of losing control.[33] It became locked into the definition of the "abnormal," part of the strategy of labeling any relevant Other perceived to be a threat to the bourgeois status quo. It also provided the dynamic for theories of social regeneration and, correspondingly, classified and circumscribed populations "who would not or could not progress."[34]

Nazism emerges here as the most radical actualization of a more general movement toward the classification and denigration of the Other. The euthanasia program against the physically and mentally handicapped, the insane, and the criminal; the persecution and murder of homosexuals, Communists, and Gypsies; and the Final Solution itself—all of these represent not a challenge to, nor the antithesis of, the bourgeois project, but rather an actualization of one final corrupted version of it. Nazi ideology depicted middle-class men as men striving to maintain the values of orderliness and cleanliness, "honesty," hard work, and family life against "unnatural" groups that seemed to desecrate morally and aesthetically the basic tenets of national and middle-class respectability.

The Holocaust is now located directly within the larger context of the dynamics of European bourgeois society. Mosse's view coincides precisely with Eley's plea to view the Jewish fate in relation to other victimized groups and to relate the Jewish predicament to "specific historical conjunctures" instead of seeing it as in some way "timeless and universal."[35] Within this schema, of course, basic distinctions are still necessary. Some victims were more despised and more vulnerable than others. The destruction was most fatal to Jews and Gypsies because they were considered separate-people races, whereas, at least in Germany, other "abnormals" were partial insiders (asocials and mentally and physically handicapped non-Jewish German citizens) or deemed in principle capable of undoing their degeneration (homosexuals). In the case of the Jews, the longstanding tradition of anti-Semitism fundamentally reinforced all of this. Locked in by racism and quite incapable of overcoming their degeneration, they stood at the very center of this process. There was, clearly, a great irony in this. Although Jews aspired to bourgeois status, indeed, created themselves in this middle-class image, a counter-tradition insisted on reading them out of that bourgeois world.

This is truly a suggestive reading of bourgeois morality, but it requires further fleshing out. If National Socialism represented a "corruption" and "radicalization" of middle-class values, it would be useful to specify the nature of these processes—especially their transformative effects. For while bourgeois *Sittlichkeit* was often illiberal, it was never typically genocidal. The conditions and quality of this metamorphosis are in need of more precise elucidation. Such an analysis would highlight an important dual impulse within Nazism itself: its uneasy combination of both bourgeois and anti-bourgeois elements. For Nazism inherited older, common materials and attitudes but went well beyond their previously established limits. In its unique fusion of the conventional and the radical, Nazism succeeded in transcending middle-class morality at the same time that it paradoxically embodied it.

It is true that this kind of cultural history does not always establish in sufficiently concrete detail the connecting links between ideology and policy or the mechanisms facilitating the translation of ideas into action, but there is at least a growing awareness of the need to make such a connection. A similar sensitivity is often lacking in the work of the fashionable "functionalist" school. Their treatment of Nazism and the Holocaust pays lip service to the broader background, to the larger ideational structures that provided actions with form and content.[36] But functionalist analyses typically stress the non-ideational, polycratic, even chaotic nature of the Nazi regime, thereby rendering largely irrelevant the broader question of continuity. To be sure, many of these studies are useful additions, enlarging our understanding of the dynamics of Nazi power and decision-making at all levels. Even within these parameters, however, the historians are divided. For some, the "Final Solution" was the result of irrational bureaucratic procedures, the almost accidental outcome of lowly placed functionaries undergoing radicalization and responding to immediate field problems and, often, uncertain signals from above. For others, it was the relentless, systematic product of rational bureaucratic procedures from above.

Still, these explanations do not take any (or at least, sufficient) account of the fact that bureaucrats and decision-makers never operate in a void. They reflect and seek to shape the societies of which they are a part. Overemphasis on the structures of decision making and on bureaucratic mechanisms contains the danger of reducing fundamental processes to the level of technical problems. The admittedly complex question of motivation becomes increasingly remote. Although we are left with a highly differentiated analysis of the Nazi machine (and the machinery of destruction) at work, we are left uninformed as to why it was activated in the first place, and no more enlightened about the broader context that shaped the choices made and created the atmosphere in which the machine operated.

The debate over the German *Sonderweg,* of course, is concerned with precisely these broader problems, with the nature of the larger historical canvas, and it is to these questions that we now return. If Mosse integrates the German experience into the wider issue of nationalism and bourgeois respectability, Jeffrey Herf's important work stresses once again the uniqueness of Germany—but in a strikingly new light.[37] The distinctiveness of German history, according to Herf, lies not in its refusal to become "modern," but in its peculiar way of doing it. As against the *Sonderweg* model, Herf does not simply collapse modernity into, and equate it with, its liberal-rational version. He argues, instead, that Germany forged its own mode of modernity, at least from the late-nineteenth century. "Reactionary modernism" (as he terms it) embraced "the most obvious manifestation of means-end rationality," that is, "modern technology," at the same time that it rejected the heritage of rationalism and the Enlightenment. The overriding aspiration was to "liberate" technology from the fetters of Western *Zivilisation* and convert it into an organic part of German *Kultur*. The modernization of the right meant transforming a conservative, backward-looking pastoralism into support for a united, technologically advanced, post-capitalist nation. This was a worldview, Herf argues, that was born in (of all places) the German technical universities around the turn of the century. Propagated in Weimar by both conservative revolutionaries and prominent engineering circles, it was integrated into Nazi ideology in the 1920s and made into a pillar of the theory and practice of the Third Reich. Herf here proposes a path to modernity that consciously espoused the fusion of political irrationalism with industrial rationalization, what Goebbels called "steel-like romanticism."

Like Blackbourn and Eley, Herf also questions the extent to which Germany remained locked in "premodernity." Beyond this, however, his work represents a kind of mirror-opposite to their neo-Marxist approach.[38] For he has written a *Sonderweg* of German modernization that emphasizes the centrality of ideas and traditions within this process.[39] The social background of this ideology, Herf contends, was the unique combination of intense and rapid industrialization together with a weak liberal tradition. He thus dismisses those who argue that Nazism and "modernity" are somehow irreconcilable, while at the same time refuting the view that developments in Germany merely exemplified "a generalized sickness inherent in modern industrial societies."[40]

Of course, this fusion of an industrial-technological outlook with the rejection of liberalism and Enlightenment rationality was not limited to Germany. It was also a posture characteristic of numerous European avant-garde intellectuals of the right. Marinetti and the Italian Futurists, Wyndham Lewis and Ezra Pound, as well as George Sorel, Drieu La Rochelle, and Charles Maurras in France were all attracted to one version or another of this aesthetic. Here was a masculine ethic, a vitalistic romanticism infused with the rhetoric of the will to power. Its technological imagery derived from the *Kriegserlebnis,* the formative experience of World War I, from the community forged under fire in the trenches, an

image far removed from an effeminate early-nineteenth-century romanticism with its visions of an idyllic pre-industrial landscape. These, to
be sure, were themes common in non-German modernist circles. But,
according to Herf, what in the rest of Europe was a sporadic mood, a
tendency limited to certain intellectuals, became in Germany wedded to
numerous professional groupings and whole political and cultural movements. A fad elsewhere, in Germany it gradually became part of national
self-representation woven into a tradition that reached back to the nineteenth century.

Reactionary modernism, Herf insists, was not the inevitable product
of "capitalism" or "modernity" in general. It represented, rather, the particular form that modernity assumed in Germany. Acceptance of technology could go hand in hand with anti-liberalism. Its modernity went this
way for nowhere else in Europe "was the protest against the Enlightenment a constituent element in the formation of national identity as it had
been in Germany from the early nineteenth century up through Weimar."
In a rebuff of both the *Sonderweg* theorists (who stress the failure of modernization) and the Marxists, Herf proclaims "reactionary modernism to
be the specifically German response to the universal dilemma of societies
facing the consequences of the Industrial and French revolutions."[41]

Had the Nazis been committed Luddites or *völkisch* pastoralists, Herf
notes, they would never have been able to regard "trains as the embodiments of the will to power" or see "the racial soul expressed in the
Autobahnen."[42] Nor, for that matter, would they have been able to re-arm
Germany and start World War II. But that is where, precisely, the double-
edged character of reactionary modernism becomes apparent. In Herf's
view it was the explicit irrationalist component in Nazism that created
insuperable barriers to technical innovation and performance. Tragically
enough, Nazi technology was sufficient for genocide. It was not, however,
up to the challenge of war. Notions of the Nordic soul and the triumph
of the will were of little use when it came to scientific research and rational, military industrial production. The "will" could not compensate for
lagging tank production or a shortage of laboratories. In this sense reactionary modernism simultaneously provided the dynamic of the regime
and the cause of its downfall.

The alternative account Blackbourn and Eley propose for the rise of
fascism, their own interpretation of the nature of Nazism, is, of course,
quite different from these kinds of explanations, despite agreement as to
the "bourgeois" and "modern" nature of these phenomena. The long-
term origins of Nazism, they argue, lie in a profound metamorphosis of
the German Right between 1870–1920, in the expansion of its social
base, and in the growing radicalization of its style and ideology. They

stress not the manipulative activity of authoritarian pre-industrial elites from above, but pressure from interest groups from below. This, they argue, provided the real motive power for German political development. "If we wish," Eley writes, "to identify the sources of change in the forms of conservative politics . . . it is at the points of friction between the political parties and the pressure groups, the real mass organizations of the Wilhelmine Germany, that we must look."[43] In this friction, Eley argues, the forms of proto-fascism were born. Once this theory is grasped, their account becomes almost self-evident, culminating in a description of the Weimar crisis: the fragmentation of the bourgeois middle, a generalized hostility of middle-class parties to the Left, and the impossibility both before and after 1914 of creating a reformist bloc on the model of Gladstonian liberalism—all in conjunction, of course, with the disastrous effects of war and revolution.

These conditions rendered the traditional elite increasingly ineffective. As a result Hitler was needed to exert a radical, populist appeal against the liberal and left-wing elements of the system. This was something the older elites could do only partially and rather implausibly. They sought to ride a tiger that was becoming more and more radicalized and less open to control. Blackbourn and Eley summarize this process, "[I]f we see prewar and postwar demagogy as an increasingly reckless process of attempted political containment, rather than as accomplished political manipulation by one particular and narrow elite, then the Nemesis of Nazism becomes more readily explicable."[44]

Few historians nowadays would contest the argument that Nazism was the outcome of a radicalized political right whose leadership and policies in many ways reflected the rise of a constituency different in sociology and mentality from the traditional classes. Their analysis, moreover, provides an indispensable structural component to our understanding of Nazism. The major difficulty that renders their interpretation strangely incomplete is their reluctance to take seriously the cultural and ideological dimensions of German history in general and Nazism in particular.

Even when they deal with attitudes, as in David Blackbourn's discussion of the role of German "cultural pessimism,"[45] ideas tend to be treated as if their content is exhausted by, and exclusively explicable in terms of, their class function. Cultural pessimism, Blackbourn maintains, with its characteristic anti-rationalism, its organicism and celebration of *Kultur* over *Zivilisation,* was not peculiar to Germany but was instead a fin-de-siècle mood prevailing in a number of European countries. Far from being a product of the disembodied German "mind," cultural pessimism was a reflection of the ambiguities of modernity as such, the response of the bourgeoisie to its fluctuating fortunes in a time of great economic instability and political anxiety. Cultural pessimism was never an ideology that floated "above class perceptions." It existed within a particular socioeconomic context. Never a worldview in its own right, it was merely the opposite side of the bourgeois coin of optimism and material progress.

Blackbourn's insistence on the European-wide mood of cultural pessimism has some merit but in certain ways it blurs some German particularities. The distinction between *Kultur* and *Zivilisation was* originally and peculiarly German, one born not in the 1870s but a century earlier, as Norbert Elias has definitively established.[46] At first a conceptual tool of the *Bildungsbürgertum,* the educated bourgeoisie, against the aristocracy and the absolutist court, the distinction was later transposed onto the national level when it became a distinguishing mark of German identity against the rationalistic French Revolution and the ensuing Napoleonic invasion. German history, to be sure, does not consist of a single, linear tradition of anti-Enlightenment and anti-Western impulses.[47] But to entirely disregard this ongoing tendency may produce a certain historical colorblindness. Whatever its merits as an objective tool of historical analysis, many Germans repeatedly asserted a species of the *Sonderweg* thesis to describe—and celebrate—their own condition. In that sense the *Sonderweg* must at least be considered as a primary datum of German subjective historical consciousness from the eighteenth century onward.

Yet even if we limit ourselves to Blackbourn's periodization, his discussion remains misleading. For cultural pessimism went far beyond civic quietism and indifference. Indeed, it became a crucial political factor when it became linked to a view infused with its own positive dynamic and content, when it became associated with a new form of German nationalism: *völkisch* ideology. This *Weltanschauung*—with its metaphysic of national rootedness; its symbolism of blood, soil, and will; its anti-urban, anti-liberal bias—was widely diffused in many middle-class German institutions from the 1880s on. Like the anti-Semitism with which it so often joined forces, *völkisch* influences with varying degrees of success entered the political realm. Neither of these trends receives the independent treatment it deserves from Eley and Blackbourn. Had they considered them more carefully, they would have seen (as George Mosse's classic study of the subject clearly demonstrated) that in this guise such tendencies went well beyond mere pessimism and assumed a life of their own.[48] Activist conceptions of national regeneration stood at the center of a politics that transcended previous conservative ideas.

To argue that cultural pessimism was merely the opposite side of cultural optimism obscures the positive thrust that transformed its purported initial impulse. Degeneration, like cultural pessimism, was the obverse side of the notion of progress. Its significance, however, lay in the fact that as its mirror-opposite, it took on a more chilling and independent meaning. As Chamberlin and Gilman put it: "[T]he negative model . . . of degeneration was a particularly powerful one, caught as it was between its own negative power as the opposite of progress, and a positive energy which gave the model a fascinating appeal on its own, an appeal not manageable by any dialectic. It lurked in the nature of the Other . . . as it lurked within those who generated it."[49] Mirror-opposites are apt, at times, to be more than mere reflections. Consequently, when cultural pessimism was wedded to *völkisch* ideology, it promised nothing less than the ultimate Germanic revolution.

The Nazis radicalized this revolution, moving it from its original national-cultural basis to a racial-biological one. This racial-biological thrust was the driving force behind the Third Reich, an impulse before which the competing power cliques and bureaucratic and financial interests usually had to bow. With their rationalistic model of class interests, Blackbourn and Eley, like other Marxists before them, are simply unable to explain or even confront a central aspect of Nazi reality: the regular primacy of ideological against other considerations. Moreover, there is no attempt to examine the content of the cultural and ideological world of the Right and the degree to which it had a coherence, plausibility, and resonance of its own. Regardless of how the Nazis transformed these materials, they were its inheritors, deriving much of their legitimacy from this perceived continuity. Blackbourn and Eley consistently reduce right-wing ideology to a manipulative "demagogic process," a form of serving specific class interests and of containing others. Nazism is related to "the particular options open to German capital in the circumstances of the late Weimar Republic" and, in the last analysis, is not much more than a variant of facism.[50]

Despite the claims to the contrary, this approach does not go significantly beyond the limits of traditional Marxist analysis.[51] The authors' unwillingness to examine the content of the ideas and traditions that we have discussed in this essay obscures the resonance and specific character National Socialism possessed. In this respect Eley has turned the matter precisely upside down. Nazism's peculiarly irrationalist and extreme character, he tells us, can be largely explained by the absence of a popular German radical-nationalist tradition. It was thus constrained somehow to create such an ideology with its "recourse to new synthetic solutions (antisemitism, the race-mission in the East, 'national socialism'). . . ."[52] It is very unclear why any of these factors, casually placed in parentheses, should be regarded as "new synthetic solutions." In what possible way could anti-Semitism be so designated? There is no need to enter into a discussion of the role and resonance of a millennial tradition of European

Christian Jew-hatred (although, whatever its disputed weight, it is surely worth mention and consideration). When analyzing the rise of Nazism and the problem of continuity, though, it is necessary at the very least to deal with the admittedly complex links between that ideology and the rise of an explicitly political anti-Semitism in the nineteenth century. There was nothing new, either, about the notion of *Lebensraum*. The idea of annexing land in Eastern Europe, as Woodruff Smith has recently shown, can be traced to a mid-nineteenth-century migrationist colonialism linked to landholding interests and intent on saving Germans—and especially peasants—from the ravages of uncontrolled modernization. From then on such ideas maintained their currency in Germany and gradually became linked with notions of "race-mission" (themselves an integral part of racist ideology that was not born in Weimar but was articulated and diffused from the mid-nineteenth century on). And, of course, the idea of a "national socialism"—the fusing of these two concepts in some form or other—had been part of the rhetoric of the emergent European Right from the 1880s, and can in no way be regarded simply as a new, synthetic solution.[53]

What is needed is a comparative analysis of the way in which various national traditions shaped the character of later right-wing regimes. Blackbourn and Eley are naturally reluctant to place too much emphasis on this factor. When they do venture into this area, the solution is still not satisfactory. As we have already mentioned, Eley argues that Germany developed a more radical form of fascism because, unlike Italy, it lacked a strong tradition of popular radical nationalism. This, too, is extremely unclear. Germany certainly does possess a tradition of nationalism. Why it is somehow neither popular nor radical requires explanation, not mere assertion. In any case, what is most germane to the comparative issue is the fact that Italian Fascism took the course that it did because, unlike Germany, Italy did not possess a deeply rooted tradition of racism or anti-Semitism.

No analysis of Nazism that omits the centrality of the biological revolution and the key place assigned therein to the Jew (and, with varying degrees of animus, to other outsiders) will be able to capture its major impulse. Utilitarian conceptions of ideology as a function of class are simply unable to account for the ideological irrationalism that stood at the heart of the regime. The most sophisticated Marxist attempt to grasp Nazism, Franz Neumann's *Behemoth,* illustrates the difficulty. In 1942 he wrote, "the internal political value of antisemitism will never allow a complete extermination of the Jews. The foe cannot and must not disappear; he must always be held in readiness for all the evils originating in the socio-political system."[54] Neumann wrote his work while the war was still on. The horrible realities of Nazism had not yet been revealed. Today, of course, we know differently and that knowledge should compel us to abandon simple functionalist conceptions and to explain what Herf calls "the triumph of ideology in the Third Reich."[55] Neumann was quite correct when he argued that rationality demanded a break with a two-front world war and a policy of genocide. But that break never came precisely because the imperatives of racial revolution and genocide took precedence over everyday rational economic and strategic interests. Hitler's Third Reich, Herf emphasizes, was not moved by common sense or interest-group politics. "The utopia of a biologically superior master-race, not the defense of German capitalism, was the core of Hitler's worldview."[56] Capitalist interests were, in the last resort, subordinate to the fulfillment of this irrationalist racial utopia. Given this perspective it is not so much 1933 that needs explaining but Auschwitz.[57]

German conservative revolutionaries, political anti-Semites, *völkisch* ideologues, *Lebensphilosophie* irrationalists, and even avowed racists cannot simply be equated with Nazism's radicalized implementation of racism and genocide. But the impulse did not come from nowhere. The materials from which the Nazis constructed their vision, they fully believed, were rooted in, and faithful to, an authentic German past and tradition. When the time of testing came, the lack of a powerful liberal tradition became critical. Unlike France—similarly beset with racist, proto-fascist, and anti-Semitic forces—Germany possessed little in the way of significant countervailing influences. France had antibodies: a normative revolutionary tradition and a powerful heritage of Cartesian individualism.[58] The activation and counter-activation of these traditions remains a crucial part of the story.

The experience of Germany was indeed "normal" in the sense that it was exposed, more or less, to the same stresses and problems that confronted the other modern, bourgeois nations of Europe. At a certain level at least, history is obviously about uniqueness, distinctiveness, and yet diverse *Sonderwege*. And, of course, there were distinctive circumstances that applied in Germany as well as—perhaps most tellingly—the specific modes of action developed in response to them. But in addition, German "reality" was shaped, in no small measure, by its own perceptions, myths, stereotypes, and ideologies. People everywhere create their reality as much as they respond to it. If it has any meaning at all, perhaps the notion of a German *Sonderweg* ultimately comes down to the desire of a perverted elite to turn reality into myth and finally to transform that myth into a new, horribly deformed reality.

Eleven

Nazism, Culture, and The Origins of Totalitarianism
Hannah Arendt and the Discourse of Evil

The intense intellectual and emotional impact exerted by Hannah Arendt's *The Origins of Totalitarianism*[1] upon a whole generation of readers
during the 1950s and through the 1960s has been well documented and
is in no need of rehearsal here.[2] Any re-reading of the work, any appreciation of its cultural significance and the role it has played, will have to
seek the reasons for this. Its appearance satisfied a number of real, indeed
urgent, though often unarticulated and perhaps even unconscious, needs.
It would thus be wise to recall that in 1951, and for at least a decade after
that, there were painfully few serious attempts to forge the theoretical,
historical, and conceptual tools necessary to illuminate and explain the
great cataclysms of the twentieth century.[3] To this day, in fact, it is difficult
to find satisfactory accounts able to coherently and persuasively integrate
these events into the flow of this century's history. In its sweep, tone, and
content Arendt's seemed, at last, to provide an account adequate to the
enormity of the materials and problems at hand.[4] As Alfred Kazin recalls:
Hannah Arendt "became vital to my life . . . it was for the direction of
her thinking that I loved her, for the personal insistencies she gained from
her comprehension of the European catastrophe."[5]

At the time, to be sure, most readings of Arendt were relatively naive,
innocent of the personal and philosophical baggage and the political and
existential predilections that shaped and guided her analyses.[6] Yet even
then it was obvious that neither in method nor aim was this a conventional work of history. Even if one did not possess the term, it was clear
that this was a highly sophisticated *Kulturkritik* animated by the attempt
to comprehend, and in some way overcome, "the burden of our times"
(the title of the more appropriately named British edition).

The work, I must hasten to point out, was not only a guide to the

Jewish perplexed. Dwight MacDonald, for instance, hailed the book as the greatest advance in social thought since Marx[7] and, early in her friendship with Arendt (April 1951), Mary McCarthy proclaimed that she had been reading *The Origins* "and the marvel of its construction," "in the bathtub, riding in the car, waiting in line in the grocery store. It seems to me a truly extraordinary piece of work, an advance in human thought of, at the very least, a decade. . . ."[8] The work evoked such a response from many intellectuals because in an overarching way the "meaning"—and perhaps the still remaining, if fragile, promise—of the century seemed somehow to be laid bare. As one perceptive critic had it, the book was itself "a myth useful to the very time it analyzes."[9]

Arendt, it bears repeating, was not interested in the ordinary writing of history: "The representation of the past through the chronological arrangement of all the available evidence struck her as trivial. She had no interest in explaining how something came to be, step by step."[10] Rather, she pursued a kind of didacticism,[11] a Heideggerian concern, in Michael Marrus' words, "to present events as mere surface phenomena, reflecting deeper, subterranean currents of meaning."[12] It is, I would suggest, this overall meaning-endowing propensity that partly accounts for Arendt's current almost auratic status in our culture—Martin Jay, by no means a slavish follower, recently characterized her as a "charismatic legitimater"[13]—and the subsequent attempt by various camps to appropriate her thought.[14]

General though her appeal was, it was particularly powerful for many of her Jewish readers. Her capacity to remove the Jewish experience from parochial settings, to lift it from a "ghettoized" frame and integrate it into the marrow of world—or for her what was virtually synonymous, European or Western—history, indeed, to make the former virtually constitutive of the latter, provided a kind of dignity and importance to an existence that had come perilously close to extinction. The emphasis on situating the Jews at the storm center of events, combined with the desire to grasp anti-Semitism at its deadliest level, made *The Origins* particularly beguiling and attractive.[15] Irving Howe relates how, after reading Arendt, his generation "could no longer escape the conviction that, blessing or curse, Jewishness was an integral part of our life."[16]

To be sure, naive readers may have been a little puzzled, if not disconcerted, by her insistence on the absolute centrality of the Jews in the creation and maintenance of the modern state and economy, their instinctive alliances with ruling elites and concomitant deep alienation from "society" and the implication—as yet not explicitly spelled out—that the Jews bore some responsibility for their predicament, that indeed their actions and roles were not disconnected from the emergence of modern anti-

Semitism.[17] It was, of course, only later in 1963, when *Eichmann in Jeru-salem* appeared, that this thesis was radicalized, and the Jewish leadership indicted as an indispensable, complicit factor in the *"Endlösung."* Only then was the outraged attention of critics—in search of the genealogy of these views—drawn to this submerged theme in *The Origins*. Within the context of the ideological war triggered by the Eichmann book, Arendt's most virulent opponents went so far as to claim that her views echoed those aired in *Mein Kampf*, that her portrait of the determinative cen-trality of the Jew within the State simply repeated the Nazi view.[18]

The debate has not ceased since that time, and I thus shall not belabor it here.[19] Personalized accusations as to her "self-hate" apart, Arendt's opponents dismiss the analysis as essentially an exercise in blaming the victim. Leon Wieseltier has most recently stated this view. The sources of anti-Semitism, he argues, are

> to be found in certain aspects of German history, and French history, and Russian history. Not in Jewish money but in German industry . . . not in Jewish achievement, but in the pitiful inability of certain political cultures to tolerate it; not in the Jewish insistence upon difference, but in the non-Jewish insistence upon sameness. Study the goyim, in short, not the Jews . . . There is something morally quite simple about totalitarianism . . . the victims were, in these systems of slavery and murder, simply powerless.[20]

Whatever the merits and demerits of the debate, in the early years few pointed out the rather delicious irony that Arendt's critique of Jewish elites and leadership was a direct expression of her post-assimilationist Weimar Zionism, and of a consistently espoused, anti-apologetic view-point already present in 1929 as she undertook her work on Rahel Varnhagen.[21]

As with her analysis of anti-Semitism, so too with the rest of the book. Only much later retrospective interpretations have been able to demon-strate that the concepts employed to understand totalitarianism were in-formed by Arendt's broader ideational arsenal and a unique—and for some, rather bizarre—political worldview.[22] Such readings—as for ex-ample the argument that in Arendt's overall scheme of things totalitarian-ism is conceived as the ultimate form of false, world-less politics, the antithesis to her positive worldly ontology of freedom, plurality, action, and the public realm—became possible only with the later, full *oeuvre* in sight. Certainly, the Heideggerian influence and turn of thought were hardly perceived at the time, and the debate as to the extent of Arendt's debt to her teacher and the harmful or beneficial effects is only now really unfolding.[23]

At any rate, upon its appearance and ever since then, it was apparent both to the book's admirers and its many detractors that in aim, scope, construction, and conception *The Origins* was a quite extraordinary and at the same time a very curious, even eccentric book. It bears constant renewed scavengings and reveals a mind capable of flashes of brilliance and original insight. To be sure, there has never been unanimity and some views have been archly, even contemptuously, critical.[24] Still, I believe, Phillip Rieff's 1951 assessment reflected a more general view: applying Burckhardt's maxim on Machiavelli to *The Origins*—"Even if every line were demonstrated to be false, the whole would still present an indispensable truth"—Rieff declared that if the work "should, in some important parts, be an error, it is, by its sweep and passion a creative error . . . It will make public opinion as much as it tries to understand it."[25] Arendt's galvanizing intellectual energy, her knack for perceiving unexpected relationships and making almost recklessly large generalizations in novel, indeed subversive, ways rendered her always an exciting, almost "shocking" thinker, capable, on later reflection perhaps, of widely missing the mark but also of rare illumination. Even her sternest critics granted this.

Her still revelatory comments upon the structure of assimilation and the "psychologized" nature of modern Jewish identity;[26] her instructive analysis of the general disenfranchisement of minorities and its potentially genocidal implications attendant upon what she called forced "statelessness, the newest mass phenomenon in history";[27] her shrewd and still very pertinent identification of human with civic or political status and the almost poetic concluding pages on human plurality and the recuperative powers of natality and beginnings[28]—all these can still be read with profit. Above all, Arendt's phenomenological exposition of the transgressive impulse behind the camps—"the laboratories in which the fundamental belief of totalitarianism that everything is possible is being verified"[29]—retains its evocative power. One irritated scholar admonished that while useful in familiar situations and when applied to established concepts, the phenomenological method has no value when extended "to a new phenomenon and a new idea such as totalitarianism . . . It then has a kind of inherent and inescapable arbitrariness: whatever you put into the bag, you can also pull out."[30] Despite this, Arendt, certainly no postmodernist believer in the non-representability of things, yet aware of the difficulties, nevertheless can always be read as attempting to confront her subject directly, seeking to somehow imaginatively enter the abyss and render it comprehensible.

At the same time, the glaring inadequacies and weaknesses—both of the parts and of the book as a whole—have by now surely become crystal clear. Criticisms of the work abound and it is not my task here to engage them in detail nor to consider the obvious problems inherent in the very notion of totalitarianism[31]—not to mention Arendt's own view, about which one critic caustically and presciently noted, "the totalitarian essence did not arise mysteriously, fully armed out of the mind of History or of the mind of Stalin. Certain circumstances favored its emergence, and others will foster its disappearance."[32] I have already mentioned some of the numerous objections to her treatment of anti-Semitism. Let me just touch on a few other basic issues.

In the first place, Arendt's notion of totalitarianism as both the cause and the result of the political dynamics of uprooting, atomization, and loneliness rests upon a clearly flawed, and by now almost universally rejected, socio-psychological model of mass society derived from conservative European social theory.[33] Given Arendt's hostility to social science her reliance on it is somewhat curious. But while most historians object to the ahistorical deficiencies of this model, it may be worth pointing out parenthetically that other commentators, like Lyotard, find her account disappointing precisely *because*, as he puts it, her "description is essentially an external one, from a historico-political point of view." Indeed, he argues that Arendt subverted her own deepest insight into the matter— "The *need* for terror is born out of the fear that with the birth of each human being a new beginning might raise and make heard its voice in the world"—when she failed to elaborate upon it.[34] Arendt's recognition of the resistant function of the onion-like organizational structure of totalitarianism to "the shock by which it is threatened by the factuality of the real world" was a genuine psychological insight. For Lyotard it is here that Arendt actually locates "the origin of totalitarianism"—as a psycho-ontological rather than a historical reality—but only fleetingly, only soon to abandon it.

Not even the most sympathetic reader will be able to clearly grasp the way in which the book's three parts cohere. Karl Jaspers tried, not altogether persuasively, to explain it thus: "Hannah never claimed that English imperialism produced Hitler and Stalin, nor did she claim that there was any intellectual identity anywhere among them. But the analogies in the phenomena, which ultimately made the whole disaster possible, would still be there even if there were no causal relationships at all."[35] Arendt herself subsequently wrote that the book "does not really deal with the 'origins' of totalitarianism—as its title unfortunately claims—but gives a historical account of the elements [into] which [it] crystallized."[36] Yet even the most kindly disposed have noted how frequently there is a reliance on flashing paradox where "factual evidence is slight or balky."[37] There is no point rehearsing the critiques in detail but, consonant with her view of mass society, the rise of totalitarianism is linked to a very unclear account of the decline and collapse of the nation-state and the class system. Even if one accepts the dubious premise that such a decay took place, it is not at all apparent why particular societies rather than others became totalitarian. Moreover, as Margaret Canovan has noted, Arendt "writes about the downfall of the nation-state in terms that might give one the impression that Europe had consisted of such states until the coming of imperialism. When one considers, however, that most of Europe, and particularly the German and Austro-Hungarian parts of it, with which she is most concerned, had belonged to states that could not possibly be thought of as national, it is difficult to tell what she is talking about."[38]

These are all, however, familiar criticisms. I must therefore return to the main theme of this essay and argue that it is Nazism and Auschwitz—far more than the Soviet experience—that animates *The Origins*.[39] It is this great transgressive moment in European history and the prior creation of a genocidal mentality that obsesses Arendt and drives her analysis.[40] "You see," she confided to her friend Kurt Blumenfeld in July 1947, "I cannot get over the extermination factories."[41] Upon learning of Auschwitz in 1943 she later reported: "It was really as if an abyss had opened . . . *This ought not to have happened.* And I don't mean just the number of victims. I mean the method, the fabrication of corpses and so on . . . Something happened there to which we cannot reconcile ourselves. None of us ever can."[42] This concern, I believe, similarly explains the special attraction of *The Origins*. As one contemporary noted, "the life of the mind was of no use unless it addressed itself to the gas," and it was precisely this that Hannah Arendt did.[43]

What, in the light of this question, does *The Origins* propose? Most striking perhaps is what it does *not* say, what it rejects by loud omission. There is not a hint of the German *Sonderweg* here, no consideration of the role and weight of the peculiarities of German political and social development. It is not continuity but rather radical and nihilistic rupture that is indicted. "The real trouble," she wrote already in 1945, "lies not in the German national character but rather in the disintegration of this character."[44] Moreover, in a sharp departure from the conventional wisdom (of, say, Thomas Mann, Georg Lukács, Adorno, and Horkheimer), Arendt explicitly, even extremely, exculpated "culture" from the catastrophe.[45] Very early on, she dismissed any notion of the complicity not only of German but also European culture and tradition in what had transpired. She insisted,

> Nazism owes nothing to any part of the Western tradition, be it German or not, Catholic or Protestant, Christian, Greek or Roman. Whether we

like Thomas Aquinas or Machiavelli or Luther or Kant or Hegel or Nietz-sche—the list may be prolonged indefinitely as even a cursory glance at the literature of the "German problem" will reveal—they have not the least responsibility for what is happening in the extermination camps. Ideologi-cally speaking, Nazism begins with no traditional basis at all . . . only the experts with their fondness for the spoken or written word and incompre-hension of political realities have taken these utterances of the Nazis at face value and interpreted them as the consequence of certain German or European traditions. On the contrary, Nazism is actually the breakdown of all German and European traditions, the good as well as the bad.[46]

She later explained: "one compelling reason why I took such trouble to isolate the elements of totalitarian governments was to show that the Western tradition from Plato up to and including Nietzsche is above any such suspicion."[47]

It was partly this consideration that induced her to locate the alterna-tive "disintegrative" model in mass society. The roots of barbarism lay exclusively in the processes of uprooting and atomization, spearheaded by an imperialist bourgeois politics and economics of expansion for its own sake, rendering not only the nation-state, but culture and tradition, superfluous. Indeed, Arendt regards the totalitarian loss of limits itself—where "everything becomes possible"—as a bourgeois invention. It is sur-plus capital that produces the precondition for genocide: surplus people. *The Origins*, thus, idiosyncratically fuses the conservative theory of mass society with an exceedingly radical and insufficiently remarked Marxist analysis of imperialism.[48] It elaborates what Young-Bruehl has called a "frontal assault" on the European nineteenth-century bourgeoisie, con-ceived as the agent, rather than the victim, of unprecedented breakdown and nihilistic expansion.[49] This is a far cry from the 1960s scholarship of other German Jewish refugees such as George Mosse and Fritz Stern who firmly located Nazism within an ongoing anti-liberal, anti-bourgeois Ger-man cultural tradition.[50]

Ernest Gellner has commented that given Arendt's background and ed-ucation, she was perfectly placed to provide a much-needed historical ac-count of the German—especially the cultural—roots of the catastrophe and that her adamant refusal to do so must be regarded as both strange and significant. Her picture of a mass society controlled by terror, he cor-rectly notes, obscures the fact "that Hitler's New Order was indeed an Order, which as long as it was victorious, was acceptable to many, with-out the sanction of terror, and which could be justified in terms of themes that had long been present,"[51] that were a recognizable part of the nor-mative (rather than subterranean) historical European inheritance. This "strange refusal" to speak or to confront and indict culture, Gellner claims, arises from the fact that Arendt was raised in and remained wedded to some of the intellectual traditions taken up by Nazism (such as romanticism) and thus sought to give such traditions a clean bill of health. Her "dæmonic" picture of totalitarianism, the over-dramatic presentation, he argues, "is itself very much in the romantic tradition even if here, ironically, it is used to exculpate romanticism and philosophy from having fathered the allegedly alien evil." [52]

Gellner's comments need careful unpacking, [53] but at least his critique has the merit of not stooping as low as some recent highly personalized attacks on Arendt linking her exculpation of mind and culture from Nazism with her renewed 1950 defense of her ex-lover Martin Heidegger, who in her mind is held to be "the embodiment" of such a culture. [54] This is both a chronological and conceptual distortion. Arendt's refusal to indict culture and the specificities of German life in the catastrophe may well be idiosyncratic, even dubious, history, but as we have already shown, it far predated her purported 1950 Heideggerian *Kehre*. And as I hope this essay will make clear, reducing the complexity of Arendt's engagement with the Nazi experience to her amorous rationalizations is cheap at best.

The refusal to engage culture is, of course, problematic but Gellner is quite wrong to claim that through distancing it from the catastrophe she sought to represent totalitarianism as so novel and alien that it was "not really after all very much concerned with *us*." [55] He mistakenly conflates novelty with alienness. There is no doubt that Arendt believed she was dealing with radically unprecedented phenomena and was groping for the intellectual equipment and conceptual vocabulary adequate to the task, and she was doing this, to be sure, to some extent with the inherited and problematic tools of romanticism and existentialism, for what else did she have? But she rejected the *Sonderweg* approach in part *because* she was impelled by the conviction that the issues raised transcended "Germans" and "Jews" [56] and far from being alien were a matter of urgent universal concern. Already in 1945, and this was programmatic of what she defined as her future task, she declared: "The reality is that 'the Nazis are men like ourselves'; the nightmare is that they have shown, have proven beyond doubt what man is capable of." [57]

It may very well be that Arendt's dismissal of peculiarly German factors, the continuity of its political and social history, was too extreme, perhaps even misguided. [58] But while conventional historical explanations may be able to account for novel occurrences they may also require entirely new, alternative ways of thinking even if some of them, like the idea of mass society, turn out to be markedly inadequate and flawed. Hannah Arendt, Alfred Kazin writes, saw totalitarianism "Biblically as a great fall." The break with tradition was her very *definition* of totalitarianism, and rightly or wrongly, she regarded it as her task to radically and thus controversially think through this novum, this "law unto itself."[59] There was nothing, contra Gellner, suspicious or covert about this: Arendt explicitly critiqued interpretations of Nazism that tended to rely on past experiences or that employed older interpretational systems which, in her view, were rather tortuously transposed onto what she regarded as a quite different, novel sort of phenomenon.[60] She consciously sought to repair this predicament of *Begriffslogiskeit*, the lack of relevant master-models, and to provide the missing ethical and cognitive equipment she deemed necessary for the task.

Gellner, moreover, picks up on what many other commentators have observed: her propensity for "operatic, metaphysical" description and overblown analysis. There is very little in Arendt about the humdrum, everyday world of politics; the quotidian workings of representative liberal democracy hardly excite her interest.[61] The Arendtian world revolves around ultimate existentialist moments—the totalitarian abyss or the ecstasy of the revolutionary moment or of *disinterested* and high-minded decision making in the polis. Very early on, friends and critics alike were aware of this "ecstatic" predisposition. In 1954 Raymond Aron shrewdly observed of the book that "one sees the world as the totalitarians present it, and one risks feeling mysteriously attracted by the horror and the absurdity that is described. I am not sure that Mme. Arendt herself is not in some way fascinated by the monsters she takes from reality but which her logical imagination, in some respects comparable to the imagination of the ideologues she denounces, brings to the point of perfection."[62]

Aron did not mention the word but it was this predilection for a kind of "dæmonic" discourse that her always sympathetic friend Karl Jaspers detected as early as August 1946 when she wrote to him that one could not think through the Nazi experience within familiar categories of crime, guilt, and responsibility as Jaspers' *Die Schuldfrage* had sought to do.[63] "The Nazi crimes," she wrote, "explode the limits of the law; and that is precisely what constitutes their monstrousness . . . this guilt, in contrast to all criminal guilt, oversteps and shatters any and all legal systems . . . We are simply not equipped to deal, on a human, political level, with a guilt that is beyond crime and an innocence that is beyond goodness or virtue. This is the abyss that opened before us as early as 1933 (much earlier, actually, with the onset of imperialistic politics) . . . ."[64]

Jaspers retorted: "You say that what the Nazis did cannot be comprehended as 'crime'— I'm not altogether comfortable with your view, because a guilt that goes beyond all criminal guilt inevitably takes on a streak of 'greatness'—of satanic greatness—which is, for me, as inappropriate for the Nazis as all the talk about the 'demonic' element in Hitler and so forth." Anticipating a theme Arendt would pick up 17 years later, he wrote,

> It seems to me that we have to see things in their total banality, in their prosaic triviality, because that's what truly characterizes them. Bacteria can cause epidemics that wipe out nations, but they remain merely bacteria. I regard any hint of myth and legend with horror, and everything unspecific is just such a hint . . . The way you express it, you've almost taken the path of poetry. And a Shakespeare would never be able to give adequate form to this material—his instinctive aesthetic sense would lead to falsification of it—and that's why he couldn't attempt it. There is no idea and no essence here. Nazi crime is properly a subject for psychology and sociology, for psychopathology and jurisprudence only.[65]

Arendt was aware of this issue even before Jaspers raised it. In 1945 she had already noted that such demonization was a "flight from reality . . . evading the responsibility of man for his deeds."[66] I believe that this ongoing problem—finding a mode of representation adequate to the transgressive nature of the phenomenon which, at the same time, does not fall into mystification—is endemic to the material and perhaps unresolvable."[67] To Jaspers she confessed the dilemma and admitted that she was groping for the correct formulation:

> I realize completely that in the way I've expressed this up to now I come dangerously close to that "satanic greatness" that I, like you, totally reject. But still, there is a difference between a man who sets out to murder his old aunt and people, who without considering the economic usefulness of their actions at all (the deportations were very damaging to the war effort) built factories to produce corpses. One thing is certain: we have to combat all impulses to mythologize the horrible, and to the extent that I can't avoid such formulations, I haven't understood what actually went on. Perhaps what is behind it is only that individual human beings did not kill other individual human beings for human reasons, but that an organized attempt was made to eradicate the concept of the human being.[68]

This kind of thinking was crucial to the Arendtian project, which we must now try to locate within its larger cultural and historical context. To be sure, Arendt wrote in an age before the term "Holocaust" had become common currency. The term does not appear in the book. Moreover, viewing matters through the generalized prism of "totalitarianism" precluded any thoroughgoing analysis of the specificities of the war against the Jews (this Arendt was to do twelve years later in *Eichmann in Jerusalem*). Nevertheless, she fitted into and played a crucial role in the creation and formulation of an ongoing and increasingly contested post-World

War II "discourse of evil" in which Nazism and Auschwitz have become symbolic code words, emblematic of our culture's conceptions of absolute inhumanity.[69] She did this, above all, through her organizing idea of "radical evil" that expressed and animated her notion of novelty. "The problem of evil," she already insisted in a 1945 piece, "will be the fundamental question of postwar intellectual life in Europe—as death became the fundamental problem after the last war."[70] Positing matters in this way, to be sure, entailed patently extra-historical, perhaps even quasi-theological formulations. Arendt admitted the vagueness of the term but insisted upon its necessity in coming to terms with what had transpired. "Evil," she wrote in a letter to Jaspers,

> has proved to be more radical than expected. In objective terms, modern crimes are not provided for in the Ten Commandments. Or: the Western tradition is suffering from the preconception that the most evil things humans can do arise from the vice of selfishness. Yet we know that the greatest evils or radical evil has nothing to do anymore with such humanly understandable, sinful motives. What radical evil really is I don't know, but it seems to me it somehow has to do with . . . making human beings as human beings superfluous . . . This happens as soon as all unpredictability—which, in human beings, is the equivalent of spontaneity—is eliminated.

This, Arendt added, was a function of the delusion of omnipotence that differed from the Nietzschean will to power that "wants simply to become more powerful and so remains within the comparative, which still respects the limits of human existence and does not push on to the madness of the superlative."[71]

She put it thus in *The Origins*:

> Until now the totalitarian belief that everything is possible seems to have proved only that everything can be destroyed. Yet, in their effort to prove that everything is possible, totalitarian regimes have discovered without knowing it that there are crimes which men can neither punish nor forgive. When the impossible was made possible it became the unpunishable, unforgivable absolute evil which could no longer be understood by the evil motives of self-interest, greed, covetousness, resentment, lust for power, and cowardice; and which therefore anger could not revenge, love could not endure, friendship could not forgive. Just as the victims in the death factories or the holes of oblivion are no longer 'human' in the eyes of their executioners, so this newest species of criminals is beyond the pale even of solidarity in human sinfulness.
>
> It is inherent in our entire philosophical tradition that we cannot conceive of a "radical evil." And this is true both for Christian theology, which conceded even to the Devil himself a celestial origin, as well as for Kant, the only philosopher who, in the word he coined for it, at least must have

suspected the existence of this evil even though he immediately rational-
ized it in the concept of a "perverted ill will" that could be explained by
comprehensible motives. Therefore, we actually have nothing to fall back
on in order to understand a phenomenon that nevertheless confronts us
with its overpowering reality and breaks down all the standards we know.
There is only one thing that seems to be discernible: we may say that radical evil has emerged in connection with a system in which all men have become equally superfluous.[72]

We must touch now on some of the problematics of this general discourse and Arendt's particular role within it. I have elsewhere recently
noted that under the very many relatively immediate post-war attempts
to comprehend the experience and atrocities of National Socialism, there
lay a common denominator. Whether one approached it as in some way
an outgrowth of or standing in dialectical relation to "history" and "culture" or, like Arendt, denied any such normative connections, all these
theories were occasioned by essentially the same sense of outrage, the
shock that such events could issue from within a modern, civilized society,
and in particular be perpetrated by what many of these theoreticians had
taken to be *the* most enlightened *Kulturnation*.[73] I am convinced that the
enduring fascination with and the deep need to account for National Socialism and the atrocities it committed—the rich multiplicity of ruminations it has produced and its cumulative imprint on political and intellectual discourse, as well as the accompanying, increasingly ubiquitous
attempts to elide or neutralize and displace its significance and impact—
resides in this rather ethnocentric sense of scandal and riddle, the abiding
astonishment that a modern, allegedly cultured society could thus deport
itself. Arendt's importance and enduring attraction lies in helping to create this paradigm.[74]

It is a paradigm that has never been problem-free nor has it gone un-
challenged. Arendt herself presciently anticipated some of its problems.
She understood, for instance, that the uniqueness of the atrocities could
potentially create a self-righteous cult of victimization, bringing in its
turn the absurd current competition in comparative victimization as the
site of group-identity confrontation. She already noted, in August 1946,
and to her readers then this must have appeared as strange at best, that
"Human beings simply can't be as innocent as they all were in the face of
the gas chambers (the most repulsive usurer was as innocent as the newborn child because no crime deserves such a punishment). We are simply
not equipped to deal, on a human, political level, with a guilt that is beyond crime and an innocence that is beyond goodness or virtue . . . we
Jews are burdened by millions of innocents, by reason of which every Jew
alive today can see himself as innocence personified."[75]

But beyond this, we must at least raise the delicate problem of Eurocentricism. If I am correct in saying that the abiding scandal resides in the fact that it is advanced European, especially German, civilization that perpetrated these atrocities, the very shock implies both a certain superiority as well as a much-needed self-critical posture.[76] By extension, if and when atrocities occur in places removed from the European center—such as Rwanda or, a little more threateningly, in "half-Asian" Slavic places like Yugoslavia—one is tragically less likely to be appalled, less able to empathically connect. Of late, critics have increasingly drawn our attention to and questioned this Eurocentric bias, both as it affects the "discourse of evil" in general[77] and the work of Arendt in particular.[78]

In Book 2 of *The Origins*, Arendt directly treats the genocidal imperialist past in Africa and the inhuman treatment and massacres of its native population as the prelude to later events, the site where the genocidal mindset is born. She certainly does not elide these happenings but the critics correctly point out that the same sense of shock, outrage, and scandal is missing, the analysis of a different order. This is at least in part because, as Arendt herself correctly and repeatedly pointed out, the factory-like method of Nazi exterminations, the systematic gassings, in fact went beyond anything previously known. Still, within its own terms her framework of analysis is not altogether innocent. She emphasizes the "ahistoricity," the "naturalness" of African life:

> What made them different from other human beings was not at all the color of their skin but the fact that they behaved like a part of nature, that they treated nature as their undisputed master, that they had not created a human world . . . They were, as it were, "natural" human beings who lacked the specifically human character, the specifically human reality, so that when European men massacred them they somehow were not aware that they had committed murder . . . Moreover, the senseless massacre of native tribes on the Dark Continent was quite in keeping with the traditions of these tribes themselves.[79]

To argue, as some of her critics have done, that Arendt was racist is, I think, quite absurd given her fundamental belief in plurality—in the "undetermined infinity of forms of human living-together"[80]—but it is true that, as Anne Norton has pointed out, the African viewpoint, unlike that of the Boers, is not even considered. They are not given a voice.[81] Another critic, Shiraz Dossa, has put it even more extremely: with Arendt, he writes, the enormity of totalitarian atrocities and the Holocaust consists in "the murder of eminently 'civilized' victims by equally 'civilized' killers." For her, "the issue becomes a profoundly moral one in this context when 'unnatural' human beings are both reduced to and murdered as pathetically 'natural' beings, as if they knew neither a history, a tradition, nor a past of human achievement. For the European Jews, unlike the African, were unmistakably human."[82] Only with their transformation from political beings to "natural creatures" bereft of rights and legal claims could they be, literally, expelled from humanity.

This perception of Nazism as a kind of absolute "bogeyman" (the phrase comes from Greil Marcus), the most radical embodiment of evil— "the single commonality onto which one could project fantasies of hatred without the slightest feeling of guilt"[83]—may act as a kind of psychological safety valve, as a belief that such evil has now been wiped out. It may also function as a form of political justification for inaction concerning present injustices that can in no way be compared to the ultimate case. In the words of Scott Montgomery, here is a "closed system that does not aid us in posing new questions, continually offers a revue of shallow finalities and, still worse, promotes voyeurism . . . Transformed from historical truth into icons both of the machine and of modern malevolence, the Nazis have been given a disturbing purity, a kind of sacred uniqueness, even a mystifying grandeur of depravity that finally gives back to them certain qualities of myth they sought for themselves." Could it be, he asks, "that recent atrocities in various parts of the world have not seemed to demand immediate attention intervention because . . . these events do not appear to sufficiently obey the requirements of a 'true' Holocaust?" . . . "Is it perhaps conceivable that our political leaders would feel a greater . . . urgency to deal with genocidal acts . . . if these acts closely simulated those of fascism, mimicking more precisely the monstrousness of the Hitlerian regime?"[84] At the same time, the opposite case also holds— that the constant invocation of Auschwitz as a model, a metaphor, and an analogy produces a reflexive sort of moral deadening and rhetorical numbing. As Montgomery argues, the enthronement of Nazis as ultimate demons, "the horror at Auschwitz [as] supreme by virtue of being fully modern, occurring in the very center of Europe," makes other horrors in Africa, Asia, and South America, "no matter how brutal or planned, somehow qualify as more primitive . . . In a strange twist of logic, the Holocaust is made to seem more sophisticated, more advanced than any other incident of its kind. The terrible irony here is that Nazism finally becomes, at this elevated symbolic height, a perverted reflection of Eurocentrism."[85]

These are problems and dangers that inhere in any discourse that insistently, indeed obsessively, presses the case for its "uniqueness."[86] It is a code word that invariably contains an extra-historical agenda. At the very least, it raises the delicate problem of balancing historically meaningful distinctions between atrocities with the commonalities of experience that allow for some kind of common ground and solidarity.[87] I must note parenthetically, however, that this vulgar exercise in comparative victimization works both ways. As Alain Finkielkraut has pointed out, the opposite bias can be cynically and obscenely manipulated.[88] Thus the defense at Klaus Barbie's trial contended that the genocide of the Jews "offended only the consciousness of white people." As merely a moment in the history of the oppressors, "there was no reason for humanity (and those in charge of its progress) to mourn its victims. And since the Third World is the herald of progress, those perceived as its enemies are the logical successors of Nazism: the Americans in Vietnam, the French in Algeria, the Israelis in the West Bank."[89] The Holocaust, Jewish pain, thus becomes a means by which to obscure and obstruct world memory of the great colonial and other slaughters.

It is inevitable that, once mobilized and unleashed, Holocaust rhetoric (that most immediately accessible emotional shorthand) and the incessant appeal to the Shoah as the most resonantly evocative, but variously interpretable, absolute metaphor, would entail engagement in political and cultural conflicts and be brandished as a weapon in ongoing political divides. The imperative to invoke the analogies (or lack of them) and draw the appropriate, but always problematic and ideologically loaded "lessons" became irresistible.

How, within this larger picture, may Arendt be located and assessed? Despite all its drawbacks, it was necessary—indeed, quite unavoidable— to formulate a discourse that sought to capture something that *was*, after all, without precedent and that required modes of conceptualization adequate to it. If the rhetoric was overblown and excessive, the material was beyond the conventional pale of historical representation. The proper mode in which to render it remains to this day a heatedly contested matter.[90] In a secular society self-consciously lacking the tools to do so, she sought to provide a rational vocabulary and explanation of this evil in its radical or "banal" guise. In many ways this was not successful, but who can deny the validity and fascination of her search?

Twelve

Post-Holocaust Jewish Mirrorings of Germany

Hannah Arendt and Daniel Goldhagen

Since 1945 the image of Germany has been inextricably linked to that of Nazism and the Shoah.[1] Tied as they are to core questions of national self-definition, of personal and collective identity, latter-day representations of Germans and Germany have perforce become particularly charged matters in which the ethical, psychic, and cultural stakes remain enormously high. This is true as much for the scholarly as it is for the popular and political realms and applies with equal force to both "German" and "Jewish" narratives. We are only now beginning to explicitly acknowledge the role and force of these inevitable emotional loads and confront the ways in which trauma is grasped and reworked in historiography.[2]

In this essay I am going to deal with Hannah Arendt and Daniel Jonah Goldhagen who have constructed perhaps the most extreme, mirror-opposite, post-war Jewish scholarly paradigms of Germany, Nazism, and the Holocaust. But first let me make it clear that I am not claiming any kind of substantial equivalence between these two figures. The difference is not only a temporal one. Arendt does indeed remain controversial but, as her present cult status demonstrates,[3] her place as a thinker of substance, complexity, and originality is surely assured, an assertion that can hardly be applied to Goldhagen.[4] Here I am interested in a comparative juxtaposition only to the extent that both have articulated antithetical archetypal narratives of the National Socialist catastrophe.[5] Since both, in their very different ways, touched raw nerves, achieved fame and notoriety, and elicited highly emotive support and vitriolic attack, we may be better placed to understand the underlying needs which such radically opposed mirrorings of Germany seek to satisfy by examining the genesis, substance, and stormy reception of their formulations.

If Auschwitz has rendered both plausible and widespread the post-war image of Germany as quintessentially tainted, a murderous and criminal nation, then the degree to which in her manifold analyses of National Socialism Hannah Arendt consistently exculpated peculiarly German factors—its history, politics, character, and culture—from responsibility or involvement is striking indeed. Arendt explicitly reacted to and consistently negated the long tradition of scholarly and popular stereotyping, the demonizing of Germans and Germany. In both *The Origins of Totalitarianism* and *Eichmann in Jerusalem* (very different works) she dismissed as virtually worthless the notion of the *Sonderweg*. There was, she claimed, no relation at all between German or even European culture and what transpired under National Socialism. Already in 1945 she wrote:

> Nazism owes nothing to any part of the Western tradition, be it German or not, Catholic or Protestant, Christian, Greek, or Roman. Whether we like Thomas Aquinas or Machiavelli or Luther or Kant or Hegel or Nietzsche—the list may be prolonged indefinitely as the literature of the "German problem" will reveal—they have not the least responsibility for what is happening in the extermination camps. Ideologically speaking, Nazism begins with no traditional basis at all . . . [It] is actually the breakdown of all German and European traditions, the good as well as the bad.[6]

While Arendt opposed the very idea of a national essence or an ingrained national character (her correspondence with Karl Jaspers, who insisted upon a kind of integral liberal German "Wesen," makes this point crystal clear),[7] with regard to Nazism she went so far as to rhetorically exclaim: "The real trouble lies not in the German national character but, rather in the disintegration of this character."[8] This total dismissal of the relevance of any peculiarly German factors, of anything relating to the continuity of its political, social, or cultural history as complicit in Nazism and its atrocities, was no doubt extreme and certainly idiosyncratic. Indeed, it has prompted some critical commentators to regard these omissions as in some way ominous, strange, and significant. Given her background and education, it is suggested, who was better equipped than Arendt to provide what at that stage was still a very much needed cultural-historical account of the German catastrophe? Her picture of a mass society controlled by terror, Ernest Gellner has correctly pointed out, obscured the fact that the regime *was* acceptable to many and was so precisely because it replicated themes that had long been present and which were a recognizable part of the normative—not just the subterranean—historical German and European inheritance. This "strange refusal" to indict culture, to consider continuity, Gellner argues, arises from the fact that Arendt was herself raised in and remained wedded to some of the intellectual traditions taken up by Nazism—most notably romanticism—and thus sought to give such traditions a clean bill of health.[9]

Germany and Germans as such are then more or less absent from Arendt's narrative emphases. Indeed, in *The Origins* it is France (the Dreyfus
Affair) and England (Cecil Rhodes and British imperialism) that figure
most centrally in the making of a genocidal mentality. Replacing the
Sonderweg is the definitively supra-national notion of totalitarianism just
as, in radical contrast to Goldhagen's later portrait, anti-Semitism is characterized by its cross-national, rather than peculiarly German, character.[10]
It is not continuity but rather radical and nihilistic rupture that is indicted. Not the tradition but the disintegrative model of mass society lies
at the source of the evil. Totalitarianism— and the camps that incarnated
its essence—was such a radical *novum,* Arendt argued, that the emergence of the Nazi type, actually "has replaced *the German.*" Such a
type—who decides to turn himself into a destroying force—was "not
confined to Germany alone" but was the result of "the vacuum resulting
from an almost simultaneous breakdown of Europe's social and political
structures."[11] The roots of barbarism are to be found in processes of uprooting and atomization, spearheaded by an imperialist bourgeois politics and economics of expansion for its own sake that render not only the
nation-state, but also culture and tradition, superfluous.

Moreover, by the time *Eichmann in Jerusalem* was written (it was published in 1963), even the earlier generalized emphasis on anti-Semitism is
muted or entirely reconceived. Eichmann is not at all viewed within the
ongoing history of Jew-hatred, but as quintessentially non-ideological,
his crime the outcome of a perverted Kantian sense of duty and bureaucratic thoughtlessness. Most problematically and shockingly, Arendt goes
further than this depiction and insists upon a new kind of criminal who
"never realized what he was doing" (her italics).[12]

We must leave aside here whether or not Arendt's ongoing personal
connectedness to Germany is linked to this stance, though we should note
parenthetically that she was not alone in such emphases. Other Jewish
scholars such as Raul Hilberg and Bruno Bettelheim were also exiled
products of a German culture that shaped their thought and with which,
in complex ways, they continued to identify. As Dan Diner has suggested,
this may have had something to do with the bias of their analyses, with
their downplaying of any *Sonderweg* explanations and their highly critical views on complicitous Jewish behavior.[13]

But we should not make things too reductively easy for ourselves. If
some of Arendt's elisions of peculiarly German factors seem somewhat
idiosyncratic, very early on she perceptively and presciently concluded
that conventional historical explanations were inadequate to account for
these unprecedented events. Novel occurrences, she insisted, required alternative ways of thinking. To her great credit, this is what the Arendtian
project thereafter became: the effort to think these catastrophes anew and

to ever-greater depth. She explicitly critiqued interpretations of Nazism that tended to rely on past experiences or that employed older categories which, in her view, were rather tortuously transposed onto what she regarded as a quite different, novel sort of phenomenon. She keenly sought tools for dealing with the radical magnitude of these phenomena, groping for the novel intellectual equipment and conceptual vocabulary adequate to the task. This was as true for her forays into philosophical speculation and political theory as it was for the more historically oriented works. Indeed, she rejected the *Sonderweg* approach in part because she was impelled by the conviction that the issues raised transcended "Germans" and "Jews." These were not, she insisted, exotic or alien phenomena but matters of urgent universal concern. Already by the end of the war, she declared: "The reality is that 'the Nazis are men like ourselves'; the nightmare is that they have shown, have proved beyond doubt what man is capable of."[14]

It is interesting to note that when Arendt started writing she was doing so more or less as a pioneer project, groping in the dark, aware of a complexity that went beyond standard modes of thinking and explanation. Daniel Jonah Goldhagen's work[15] is set in a quite different context. He quite openly presents his case as a *reaction* to precisely this kind of explanatory complexity whose historical function, he believes, has been, above all, to obscure and rationalize. "Simple explanations," he writes in his rebuttal to his critics, "are not to be rejected merely because they are simple . . . The call for complexity is sometimes the refuge of those who find certain conclusions unpalatable."[16] The explanation that he does provide is indeed simple and, as many of his critics argue, simpleminded. It posits the mirror-opposite of Arendt's narrative: if, for her, the category of "the Germans" disappears, for Goldhagen the term is omnipresent, its constant invocation ultimately transformed into what he takes to be the explanation itself! If national characteristics and historical continuity, the *Sonderweg*, is dismissed in Arendt, its singular, venomous eliminatory and exterminationist anti-Semitism is the key to Goldhagen's analysis, the motor of the special cruelty that characterized the killings— and the basis of his refusal to make any meaningful distinction between committed Nazis and "ordinary Germans." Moreover, the killers are depicted in diametrically opposite ways: the portrait of thorough but thoughtless bureaucrats is replaced by jovial ideological killers enthusiastically intent on carrying out what amounts to a historically grounded, consensual national project. As opposed to the convolutions and probings of Arendt, Goldhagen's thesis can be summed up in one stark proposition: "the Germans" always hated the Jews and once given the opportunity they killed them—with zest.

This is not the place to go into the rights and wrongs of the thesis, since by now this has been done ad nauseum,[17] but to compare it with its extreme Arendtian mirror opposite. For Goldhagen the Nazis are in no way "like ourselves": indeed, there is a vast ontological gap between "us" and them. "The study of Germans and their anti-Semitism before and during the Nazi period must be approached as an anthropologist would a previously unencountered preliterate people and their beliefs, leaving behind especially the preconception that Germans were in every ideational realm just like ourselves."[18] He restores the portrait of the German perpetrator almost as a distinct alien species.

In addition, it is clear that Goldhagen is also reacting to a perceived ongoing academic de-legitimization of the victims and their viewpoint.[19] For many, this tendency began in *Eichmann in Jerusalem* where Arendt not only "humanized" the image of the perpetrator through his alleged "normality" and "banality," but also rendered the Jewish leadership complicit in the destruction process. This critically blurred what until then had been regarded as a pure moral and conceptual distinction: that between victims and victimizers, Nazis (or Germans) and Jews. Goldhagen reestablishes the purity and starkness of the distinction. His is not a narrative from the perspective of "bureaucrats" or "the system." Even though the book presents itself as a work about the perpetrators, it is in effect Holocaust history from the viewpoint of its victims.

It should thus come as no surprise that many survivors regard Goldhagen as the historian who most accurately conveys the unbearable everyday cruelty and reality of their experiences and the joy their tormentors took in inflicting such cruelty. It makes little difference that other historians do not at all deny the reality of these experiences even as they question the interpretive and explanatory framework in which Goldhagen locates them and are uncomfortable with what they take to be an almost pornographic, voyeuristic attention to detail that renders understanding more, rather than less, remote. From the viewpoint of such survivors, Goldhagen has succeeded in capturing their reality, and this is why the various scholarly attacks upon him are, quite erroneously of course, experienced by the victims as attacks upon themselves.

How, within the framework of this conference's theme, do we place all this into some kind of conceptual and contextual perspective? Because Arendt and Goldhagen represent two opposed, extreme, even archetypal, paradigms of Nazism and the Holocaust, they mirror Germany in radically antithetical ways. In the one version Germans are exculpated; in the other they are indicted: while the one entirely dismisses the generalized framework of national units as valid or relevant categories of explanation, the other places it at its ontological center. If Arendt's work can be viewed, at least in part, as a reaction to the negative stereotyping of Germany, then, in turn, Goldhagen's "Germans" must be regarded, to some extent, as a reaction to this perceived rehabilitation, to undoing what he takes to be the apologetics entailed in the division between "ordinary Germans" and Nazis. But it goes much further than this. In larger terms his work should be read as a protest against a much broader tendency to, as it were, "universalize" the Shoah, a tendency associated with but not at all limited to Arendt.

Such a universalist model holds that genocide, far from being a distinctive German act, was in many ways inherent in the modern bureaucratic, and especially totalitarian, state and a crime perpetrated not so much by a *Sonderspecies* of Germans as by Christopher Browning's "ordinary men," not particularly impelled by malevolent or anti-Semitic motives but a variety of socio-psychological and ideational pressures and forces. For Goldhagen these are all flights into abstractions. Explanations that privilege an impersonal bureaucratic "system" and the generalized role of psychological mechanisms (such as obedience to authority, peer pressure, and so on), he argues, mask the essential free choice, the fact of enthusiastic agency entailed in these murders and allow a convenient escape from personal responsibility for such actions. The perpetrators, contra Arendt, knew exactly what they were doing—indeed, far from being pressured, they reveled in it.

In an age of the universalization of the Holocaust, both in its historiographic and memorializing modes, Goldhagen, so to speak, returns the Shoah to the Jews.[20] The event is now restored to its primal, even archetypal, simplicity: "the Germans" enthusiastically murdered defenseless Jews in an orgy of a historically unique, continuous, and culturally conditioned anti-Semitic hate. The degree to which this cultural conditioning vitiates the issue of choice and agency, and the extent to which such a venomous Jew-hatred makes it appear that this national project was somehow a predetermined eventuality, is one that we will not address here.

In order to explain the differences between these two paradigms—the universalist versus the particular, the exemplum versus the exceptional—one could, I suppose, invoke Dan Diner's interesting distinction between "Western" and "Eastern" Jewish narratives and sensibilities to the work and divergent emphases of Arendt and Goldhagen.[21] But what I want to suggest here is that for all their differences there is also a hidden common denominator. Each, in its own diametrically opposed ways, resorts to stark, extraordinary forms and categories of explanation. What else is Goldhagen's Germany and German culture if not anthropological "Other" or Arendt's "totalitarianism" if not an entirely novel regime with laws unto itself? In that sense both, for entirely different reasons, cut the Nazi experience off from the mainstream of broader European culture. Such extraordinary explanations have their origins in, and are fueled by, a common tortured awareness of the deeply transgressive nature of the phenomenon in question. In a sense, both ultimately lean upon "archetypal" schemes: both in effect propose heuristic extra-scholarly models linked to the divergent needs, politics, and values that inform their different historical representations. Goldhagen's explanation— based on an assumed anthropological and civilizational gulf between ourselves and the German murderers—and Arendt's (and other universalizers') assumption of a commonality of experience and the desire to break down what they take to be a comfortable and self-serving distance between ourselves and the perpetrators thus remain interpretive decisions, not purely matters of empirical observation.

Both lack a certain balance and present their narratives too starkly, in simple either/or terms, rather than the complex gray with which most historians are comfortable. Nevertheless the extreme paradigms that they present remain the relevant ones for us. On the one hand, as Omer Bartov has recently put it: "We must not consign Auschwitz to another planet nor perceive the perpetrators as different species. When we imagine the Holocaust we must imagine ourselves."[22] And, in a more intimate, private moment it was none other than the delightfully complex and never fully consistent Hannah Arendt who, upon reading Hans Magnus Enzensberger's comment that Fascism is not terrible because the Germans practice it, but because it is possible everywhere, retorted: "If all are guilty then none are ... This statement is even more problematic when it is advanced by a German for it says: not our parents but mankind has brought about this catastrophe. This is simply not true."[23]

These two paradigms and the archetypes they represent may be extreme, undifferentiated, simplistic, and even unhistorical, yet to a large degree in their tension they provide the raw materials, and act as indispensable guides, to both help us think through and memorialize a still unthinkable episode in the history of human (or is it a peculiarly national?) cruelty.

Part IV

Historians, History, and the Holocaust

Thirteen

Reconceiving the Holocaust?
Daniel Goldhagen's *Hitler's Willing Executioners*

The study of the Holocaust is a visceral and cognitive minefield. Poised in our consciousness at the crossroads of history, myth, and memory, no matter how carefully and responsibly constructed the narrative, it elicits the most powerful emotions. Guilt and hate, sorrow, mourning, and resentment are never far from the surface. The *Shoah* raises awesome issues of criminal and moral culpability: it touches on subtle and complex psychological strategies for confronting or repressing an unbearable reality. As our culture's symbol of absolute evil it has become the site of multiple and contested appropriations, harnessed to rival versions of identity politics, the limit-case in a strange but pervasive cult of comparative victimization. Above all, German and Jewish existence, albeit in different ways, are inextricably defined by it. How the Holocaust is understood shapes, in essential ways, the very identities and self-definition of both groups.

This is the backdrop for the conception and extraordinary reception of Daniel Jonah Goldhagen's *Hitler's Willing Executioners: Ordinary Germans and the Holocaust*.[1] The lavish praise and popular acclaim as well as the hostility and unease it has evoked can be traced to the same source. For this avowed "reconceptualization" essentially confirms older stereotypical conceptions as to how and why the Holocaust occurred. It is presented—and possesses its appeal—as a kind of "common-sense" history that derides conventional scholarship as somehow naive, misled, and suspiciously self-serving. By viewing the Holocaust exclusively through the prism of a uniquely German anti-Semitism, as the unleashing of a long-brewing national project of "the Germans" and not just the Nazis, and by shearing it of what he regards as its recent scholarly reductions and evasions into universalizing abstractions ("bureaucratic murder," the "banality of evil," "obedience to authority," and so on), Goldhagen, so to speak, returns the Shoah to the Jews. In effect, he offers a reactive mirror-opposite to the disputed and simplified *Historikerstreit* histories of the 1980s that sought to relativize Auschwitz into the "normalized" annals of regular human murderousness. It bears careful scrutiny and criticism.

Goldhagen's "Final Solution" is the logical outcome of a peculiarly lethal and singularly German "eliminationist anti-Semitism" that, he argues, was deeply built into the country's political culture and its social and religious institutions. Already in the nineteenth century the overwhelming majority of Germans accepted this view as their "cognitive model" of the world. With the rise of Hitler, "eliminationist" anti-Semitism almost seamlessly melded into its racist, exterminationist form, and the overwhelming majority of Germans either "understood" or willingly engaged in the task of killing the Jews, usually in the most cruel and humiliating ways possible. For Goldhagen, the *Shoah* cannot be explained merely as the outcome of the policies of a dictatorial Nazi elite. Rather its roots are to be found within the deepest continuities of German history. As such it reflected the authentic underlying sentiments and the popular will of the majority of the German nation. Nazism and Hitler in effect merely provided the state-sanctioned legitimization for a popular desire awaiting its proper opportunity. With some, though never really significant, exceptions, "ordinary Germans" either supported or, indeed, became enthusiastic executioners of a "national project."

This is a teleologically reworked version of the *Sonderweg* thesis in which the peculiarity of German history, its mind, and polity is characterized not by the disjunction between advanced economic development and immature political institutions, not by its illiberalism and late national unification, but almost completely by the persisting, special character of its anti-Semitism. Goldhagen is able to reach these conclusions by leaning upon a vastly more refined and differentiated body of scholarship which he then either does not acknowledge or summarily dismisses.

That anti-Semitism disfigured, and was profoundly evident in, nineteenth- and twentieth-century Germany is beyond dispute; that it was deeply bound up—as a necessary if not sufficient condition—with the decision to exterminate the Jews is common coin. However, what is at issue here is not the existence of Jew-hatred but the question of its relative weight as a causal agent amidst a welter of other forces and factors. Goldhagen's rendering of anti-Semitism as a kind of disembodied, autonomous force determining the course of modern German history results in a grossly imbalanced portrait.

To depict Germany as united in its consensual anti-Semitism is to ignore its particularly conflict-ridden, fractious nature and the constant attacks upon Catholics, socialists, and liberals that were no less characteristic of this political culture. The generally pro-Jewish Social Democrats—already in Wilhelmian times, *the largest German political party*—are passed over in virtual silence. If German anti-Semitism was as unanimously popular and respectable as Goldhagen asserts, why were the Nazis constrained to *mute* their anti-Semitic rhetoric from 1929 to 1933? Numerous local studies suggest that ideological anti-Semitism was often the result of being won over to Nazism rather than the cause of the attraction.

To be sure, the conspicuous absence of protest over the measures that gradually excluded Jews from German society, the fear and compliance of life in a dictatorship notwithstanding, also indicates a measure of shameful assent. But why, one wonders, was the *"Endlösung"* kept secret? Even if, as Goldhagen asserts, it eventually became an "open" secret, the authorities continued to do everything possible to maintain complete secrecy. There is certainly no indication that the genocidal impulse proceeded from the bottom up, that it somehow represented the pent-up fury of an enraged citizenry. If Goldhagen's view is to be believed, the Nazi removal of restraints of violent action against the Jews imposed by various Imperial and Weimar governments should have resulted in spontaneous popular anti-Semitic eruptions, in roving bands carrying out Jewhunts on the streets of Germany. This never happened.

Most tellingly, Goldhagen never discusses the responses of German Jews to this purported omnipresent and monolithic anti-Semitic reality. Had he done so, he would have had to conclude that, from emancipation on, they were spectacularly blind to their surroundings, grandly deluded. It is true that German Jews often idealized German society, omitting many of its less pleasant dimensions. But such idealizations were rooted within a certain, albeit limited, social reality. Indeed, the whole point about the German Jewish experience, the source of its enduring fascination and unparalleled creativity, lies in its ambiguous nature, the tension between acceptance and rejection. The anti-Jewish impulse was certainly always there, sometimes very powerfully, but if this were all, it would be quite impossible to explain why Germany stood for East European Jews as the magnet, the symbol of enlightenment and emancipation so sorely lacking in their own societies.

German Jewish life was always negotiated in a social field of essentially mixed signals. Side by side with rejection, resentment, and hostility, there was cultural and economic success—and some significant social integration. In 1911, 13 percent of Jewish men and 10 percent of Jewish women had married non-Jews. The figures are more or less double that for the years between 1919 and 1933. This does not jell with the picture of a virtually unanimous society of Jew-haters. Even within the brutalized, post-War context of Weimar Germany, it was precisely these mixed signals that proved so confusing to German Jews. Right-wing political rantings and nationalist agitation proceeded together with unprecedented Jewish success and participation in virtually all areas of life. Moreover, for anti-Jewish forces, the problem consisted precisely in the fact that, as Peter Gay put it, the outsider had become an insider. It is the combination of integration and assimilation with rejection and hostility that constitutes the more dense reality. Even under the Nazis, as Eric Johnson points out in his work on the Gestapo, it was precisely the mixed messages of the authorities and a degree of *kindness and friendship* shown by various "ordinary Germans" that proved to be *a trap* for many German Jews.[2] History is strewn with complexities and ambiguities—Goldhagen will have none of them.

When Goldhagen analyzes the actual murders, he does have some useful things to say. There may be substance to the charge that historians have increasingly tended to marginalize complicity or even tacit support and sublimate it into forms of indifference and passivity. Certainly the degree to which the "Final Solution" was (or could have been) known seems to be far larger than recent literature suggests. Although Raul Hilberg already documented this in 1961, it is salutary to be reminded that many sectors and layers of German society either supported or were actively involved in the machinery and activity of destruction. Above all, Goldhagen's shift of focus, although not entirely original, is important. He correctly reminds us that millions of people were murdered outside of the death camps, and that the dominant image of depersonalized, bureaucratic-industrial murder tends to underplay the importance of the perpetrators themselves. Like Christopher Browning before him, he demonstrates that many of these atrocities were carried out not by trained, ideological SS fanatics but by "ordinary Germans"—men and women. They did so in numerous police battalions, in indescribably cruel work camps, and on the death marches where the killings persisted, despite Himmler's late orders to the contrary; and Goldhagen's description of the scope and scale of their activities is perhaps the most important contribution of the book. Had Goldhagen written a book emphasizing these aspects of the genocide and placing them within a different, more modest analytic and historical framework, this would have been a far more significant work of scholarship.

The interpretive problem, however, remains and revolves around the issue of motivation. Goldhagen's ordinary "Germans" are explicitly contrasted to Christopher Browning's ordinary "men." Browning posits the murderous willingness of the now infamous Hamburg Police Battalion

101 in situational and "human" terms. In his version anti-Jewish sentiment and stereotypes do play a role. For these murderers, he writes, the Jews "stood outside their circle of human obligation and responsibility." But Browning insists upon integrating this factor into a complex cluster of general situational pressures and dehumanizing mechanisms (group conformity, deference to authority, the dulling powers of alcohol, routinization, and rationalization) that together facilitated the killings.

For Goldhagen the issue is framed entirely within the confines of a "national" explanation. Germans believed their national cognitive model of the Jews and, sharpened by its racist elaboration under the Nazis, when given the right opportunity, they proceeded to act upon these beliefs. He mentions but never satisfactorily explains the especially vicious murderousness of non-German auxiliaries. In a work that proposes a peculiarly "German" exterminationist anti-Semitism, the lack of serious comparative analysis is particularly regrettable. But even if we stay with the German case the monocausal argument cannot be sustained. In the case of these individual field-killers we have no way of knowing whether their putative anti-Semitism operated as cause or rationalization of their actions. It was, after all, a posture officially encouraged in ever more brutalizing, war-time Nazi propaganda. Goldhagen acerbically dismisses the social psychological factors adduced by Browning as masking the elements of choice and agency entailed in the killings. But precisely because Goldhagen posits it as the single explanatory motivating force (as inaccessible to empirical demonstration as the approaches he criticizes), it is *his* unidimensional psychology that must be deemed mechanistic, less true to the vagaries of human complexity to which the historian must always be sensitive.

What, however, of Goldhagen's evidence that the killers went about their murderous work with voluntaristic gusto and enthusiasm? These men sent gloating, happy pictures home, brazenly advertising their activities; some even brought their wives along. The perpetrators committed genocide with essentially undisturbed consciences. But even if we accept that the murders were committed with relish, the issue of motivation remains unresolved. Saul Friedlander, never one to underestimate the power of anti-Semitism, has argued that the staggering dimensions of the mass murders were also facilitated by a quite non-ideological state of mind, a form of intoxication (*Rausch*). The perpetrators, he writes, were "seized by a compelling lust for killing on an immense scale, driven by some kind of extraordinary elation in repeating the killing of ever-huger masses of people."[3] There are simply too many instances of such "dionysian" mass murders in history for us to accept a peculiarly German genocidal anti-

Semitism as the singular motivating force. During the Spanish civil war, a distressed Simone Weil wrote incisively of the protagonists:

> I have never seen either among the Spaniards or among the French . . . any-one who expressed, even in private conversation, repugnance or disgust for, or even only disapproval of, unnecessary bloodshed. . . . Men . . . would relate with a warm, comradely smile how they had killed priests or "fascists". . . whenever a certain group of human beings is relegated, by some temporal or spiritual authority, beyond the pale of those whose life has a price, then one finds it perfectly natural to kill people. When one knows that one can kill without risk or punishment or blame, one kills; or, at least one smiles encouragingly at those who kill. If one happens to feel some revulsion, one hides it, one stifles it, fearing to be seen lacking in virility. There seems to be in this some impulse of intoxication which it is impossible to resist . . . I have not found it in anyone. On the contrary, I have seen sober Frenchmen who of their own accord would never have thought of killing anyone—plunging with obvious relish into that blood-soaked atmosphere.[4]

Goldhagen's monocausal "German anti-Semitism" not only fails at the level of the field-killers, it also ultimately narrows and distorts the larger historical context in which these Nazi horrors could become an option in the first place. It is, indeed, only within the setting-up of a new war-time framework and the unprecedented creation of an enabling killing-environment that the debate over ordinary "men" and ordinary "Germans" makes any sense at all. For the atrocities to occur, Nazism had to provide the warrant for genocide, to officially and radically loosen previously intact taboos (taboos that applied equally to Goldhagen's pre–1933 Germans). It is this great transgressive transformation that characterized Nazism, in effect rendering the "*Endlösung*" both a thinkable and practicable proposition. Historians agree that German and European racism and anti-Semitism, eugenics, and the discourse of degeneration and regeneration were part of the informing background, the building blocks of the Nazi vision. But they also recognize the force of the rupture with the past, which seriously weakens the force of conventional explanatory connections. In their unique ideological synthesis and fanatic determination to implement it, the Nazis created something *sui generis*.

Certainly demonological anti-Semitism was central to National Socialism; the Jews were consistently its most hated and ultimate victim. This is a pathology that will always require special emphasis. But it is the enabling context in which Jew-hatred was transformed into genocide that is also crucial and left unaddressed by Goldhagen. Nazism's imperial utopia, its propelling dynamic, flowed from its sustaining vision of a "positive" biological politics and a radical racial reorganization of the world, implemented through hitherto undreamed-of, large-scale eugenic and interrelated schemes of regeneration and destruction. Only the Jews were obsessively targeted for total extermination, but that operation occurred within a general eugenic framework of German "renewal" and resettlement coupled with exclusionary measures that included mass sterilizations, the killing and gassing of the German sick and insane, the mass murder of Gypsies, the virtual extermination of the Polish intelligentsia, the persecution and killing of homosexuals, and, between 1941 and 1944, the deaths of about seven million civilians in Russia. Goldhagen mentions some of these crimes but their significance is left unexplored; his explanatory scheme precludes him from setting them into proper context, as part of an ideological continuum of despised and victimized outsider groups. This is surprising for in a 1989 review he correctly castigated Arno Mayer for reducing all of Nazism to anti-Bolshevism and failing to integrate this catalog of crimes into *his* account![5] It was not the autonomous strength of Jew-hatred that impelled it to assume its entirely novel, systematically genocidal apotheosis, but rather its integration within the implementation of this total, eugenic vision of racial community. The Holocaust must be seen within the context of this continuum— of which it represented the ultimate, extreme edge.

In a laudatory review, Elie Wiesel comments that Goldhagen's work is "driven by the suffering of his people."[6] The graphic, painstakingly detailed descriptions of unspeakable horrors and atrocities do indeed evoke pain and focus our anger. The book powerfully taps into this emotional substructure. But Goldhagen should have more carefully consulted a new body of scholarly literature that seeks not to indulge but harness such feelings through a concerted and responsible exercise of self-reflexiveness. His never-doubting explanatory framework is fueled by a vilifying mystique of "the Germans." He repeatedly insists that "the study of Germans and their antisemitism before and during the Nazi period must be approached as an anthropologist would a previously unencountered preliterate people and their beliefs, leaving behind especially the preconception that Germans were in every ideational realm just like our ideal notion of ourselves."[7] This distancing comfortably relieves us from recognizing the implication of generally "human" (as well as uniquely German) propensities in the cruelties. But even more important, it signifies a failure to grasp the very heart of the issue: the glaringly obvious fact that Germany was *not* a preliterate or alien but rather a modern, supposedly cultured society fashioned in many ways after our own Judeo-Christian, Enlightenment-humanistic image. The enduring outrage and ongoing fascination, the scandal, and the riddle consists precisely in seeking to understand the penetration of the barbarous within the familiarly cultured, the transgression of basic taboos within the framework of advanced civilization.

Generations of scholars and thinkers, many of them Jewish and equally "driven by the suffering" of their people, have thought and continue to think deeply and painfully over this issue. They have not reached a consensus, other than the realization that in matters as dense and complex as these, humility is of the essence and that closure and certainty are probably unachievable. The refining task of scholarship is surely to call into question, rather than reinforce, stereotypical thinking and to encourage balanced and complex historical judgements *on all sides*. Goldhagen's book does not help in this endeavor. His "reconceptualization" of the Holocaust is as much a reflection of our own times as it is a history of the Germans and the crimes they perpetrated. This is the source of its success—and its failure.

Fourteen

George Mosse at 80
A Critical Laudatio

George Mosse's Europe has always been peopled by strange and powerful forces threatening to engulf its precious but fragile humanist heritage. His cultural history is animated by a complex but unabashed commitment to that heritage; his work over nearly the last 40 years has also made clear its radical precariousness.[1] The twentieth-century experience of totalitarianism and of genocide and the personal circumstance of becoming a refugee[2] intertwined with an emerging acknowledgment and consciousness of his own minority sexual status[3] have constrained Mosse to become perhaps *the* contemporary historian of the manifold strategies of inclusion and exclusion, of racism and stereotypes, outsiders and respectability, war, "irrationalism," and mass murderousness in the modern age. He has throughout concerned himself with the deeper roots of Nazism and its destruction of the Jews, always lifting this subject out of narrow, parochial contexts and linking it to wider—and usually unperceived—modalities of culture. Over the years the foci have become ever more broad, probing, and daring. Viewed in composite, his work—always evolving and covering different aspects of the European experience—represents an unfolding vision of, and ongoing concern with, that continent's dialectic of hope and hazard, liberalism and totalitarianism, breadth and narrowness, freedom and constriction.[4]

Any appreciation of Mosse's project requires brief mention of the particular approach he brings to the study of cultural and intellectual history. Here one is not limited to abstract and rational ideas that are somehow borne autonomously aloft through the historical process as was the practice with the traditional "history of ideas" school. Rather, we enter a far broader realm. Culture, Mosse declared very early on, is "a state or habit of mind which is apt to become a way of life intimately linked to the challenges and dilemmas of contemporary society."[5] We have entered, above all, the political and popular culture, the mental worlds, of an

155

industrializing nineteenth- and twentieth-century Europe—mass societies—in which the diffusion of consolatory and demonizing myths and
ideologies, symbols, and stereotypes becomes of paramount importance.
In effect, Mosse's project constitutes a history of mediated human perceptions, one that is concerned with the active constructions of meaning and
its consequences. Material factors, Mosse would acknowledge, are fundamental to historical life. But, as he notes in the introduction to *Masses
and Man:* "However much they may be limited by objective reality, men
and women do have choices to make. Indeed, that reality tends to be
shaped by the perceptions men and women have of it. . . . [They] act upon
reality as they perceive it, and thus they help to shape it as well."[6]

Today, even for historians, this notion of culture does not seem surprising but we should not forget that Mosse was years ahead of his times
when he formulated it and, indeed, shaped our revised conceptions of it.[7]
In 1966 his anthology "Nazi Culture" had already appeared.[8] For many
readers, schooled in older conceptions of the idea of "high" culture, the
title itself must have seemed shocking. Was not the very notion "Nazi
Culture" an oxymoron, a contradiction in terms? Who had not heard of
Goebbels' perhaps apocryphal (but nevertheless famous) declaration that
"every time I hear the word 'culture' I reach for my revolver?"[9] Documenting diverse aspects of everyday life under Hitler, it sought to discover
how "National Socialism" impinged on the consciousness of those who
lived under it and, in the process, sought to create an integrated racial
universe.

In all of Mosse's work this understanding of culture is never represented statically or unidimensionally. History becomes a kind of updated
Hegelian totality, a dialectic in which the political cannot be separated
from the religious, the scientific from the aesthetic, the rational from the
mythological. Although its outlines were already apparent in Mosse's
first, very successful career as an early modernist,[10] it becomes central to
his sustained, multi-pronged effort to come to grips with the later period,
especially his studies on European Fascism in general and Nazism in
particular.

His first foray into the field, *The Crisis of German Ideology: Intellectual Origins of the Third Reich* (1964), has become a classic and continues to shape our image of Nazism to this day.[11] This book took issue with
the conventional view in the 1950s of Nazism as totalitarianism. It denied
the notion that Nazism was simply the product of mass propaganda and
terror, the rule of an atomized and terrified population by a ruthless elite.
Nazism, rather, had to be conceived as an immanent tendency with its
roots in German sociopolitical development and popular culture. Mosse
did not, however, try to demonstrate this via the usual history-of-ideas

approach. Nor did he accept the crude argument that Nazism was some-how inherent in German national character and that the line from Luther to Hitler was a direct and irresistible one, as one reviewer charged when the book was published.[12]

What he sought to identify instead was one particular tradition: the emergence and crystallization of a habit of thought, feeling, and perception that he designated as *Völkisch* ideology. This ideology was a response generated by the perplexities and singularities of the German experience of modernization during the latter part of the nineteenth century and re-inforced and radicalized in the twentieth century. *The Crisis of German Ideology* treats us to an erudite and differentiated exposition of this semi-mystic, organic, nationalist *Weltanschauung*. The work demonstrates how it was absorbed into German popular culture and transformed into a cul-tural resource available for appropriate political tapping.

It was through *Völkisch* ideology, Mosse contended, that conceptions of German identity during this period became so critically linked with the "Jewish question." The central foil, the salient anti-type of *Völkisch* thought and imagery—with its metaphysic of national roots; its symbol-ism of blood, soil, and will; its anti-urban and anti-liberal bias— focused most naturally upon the Jew. Who better fit the requisite stereotype of rootlessness and foreignness and of liberalism and restless modernity than the Jew? For Mosse, therefore, the eventual development of Nazism into an "anti-Jewish revolution" became comprehensible largely within the wider context of *Völkisch* thinking, which had its beginnings long before the Weimar period.

If in many ways *The Crisis of German Ideology* departed from the conventional wisdom of the day, it did, nevertheless, contain a species of the *Sonderweg* thesis, a notion critically analyzed in chapter 10 of this volume. Mosse, to be sure, disdained simplistic conceptions of German national character. No historical determinism, no assertions of inherent murderousness are to be found in that tome. Yet, in the last analysis, *The Crisis of German Ideology* held that Nazism could be grasped only as a result of long-term historical differences between Germany and other nations. German Fascism, Mosse wrote, was different from Fascism else-where because it ultimately reflected "the difference between German thought and that of the other western European nations." Only there was the repudiation of the heritage of the European Enlightenment "planted so deep or for such a long time."[13]

Subsequently, these kinds of analyses have become considerably muted in his work and, if invoked at all, formulated more in terms of "absences" and deficiencies than pernicious presences. Thus, Mosse has repeatedly pointed out that prior to 1914 the most lethal proto-Fascist, racist, and anti-Semitic tendencies were to be found not in Germany, but in France.[14] There were no German equivalents of the Dreyfus Affair, the Panama Scandal, or the Third Republic. Nevertheless, as Mosse also emphasizes, France did possess vital countervailing tendencies. Unlike Germany, it did have a powerful and ongoing liberal, revolutionary tradition. When Germany was defeated in World War I and the crisis erupted, there were no similar effective and popular antidotes available.[15]

When viewing Mosse's work as a whole, we can discern an unfolding development, an emerging pattern woven onto his ever-broadening canvas. To be sure, the animus, the search for the deeper, underlying sources of Fascism and Nazism, remains a constant leitmotif of his work. "I have been accused, not without reason," he candidly writes, "of writing teleological history, that is to say history which always looked to the future, ending up in the fascist or Nazi embrace. However, fascism did provide the climax of many of the trends which have interested me. . . ."[16] But the *oeuvre* has become increasingly European-wide and not restricted to the German realm and linked integrally rather than exotically to the course of modern cultural and political developments, a part of normative and mainstream not subterranean history. For instance, in his pathbreaking work, *Fallen Soldiers* (1990),[17] it is the well-nigh universal twentieth-century experience of mass death that takes center stage. The unprecedented event of total world war—and the later militant, right-wing appropriation of its thematics into national political mythology and memory—becomes paramount. The brutalizing events of 1914–1918 were fundamental to the rise of Fascist politics throughout Europe, and only war and defeat were able to propel prior relatively marginal German trends such as *Völkisch* ideology into the center.

The Nationalization of the Masses (1975)—in Mosse's opinion, "the real breakthrough in putting my own stamp upon the analysis of cultural history" —delved into a different dimension of the problem.[18] In it, Mosse sought to uncover not so much the content as the form of what he identified as a new kind of an essentially sacralized politics. Its most sophisticated and radical expression was indeed to be found in Nazism but its origins were virtually co-extensive with modernity itself. Ultimately Fascism and Nazism were part of the broadest, defining political developments, incomprehensible outside this European backdrop of the fusion of democracy and nationalism and the creation of a new mobilizing, liturgical politics. Here we witness the rise of a visually oriented, participatory "counterpolitics" to liberal parliamentarianism. In this book Mosse still defined liberal and bourgeois modes as antithetical to Fascist and Nazi modes, a position which, as we shall see, he later rendered decidedly more problematic. Characteristically fusing nationalism with democracy, the new politics had a style which, Mosse argued, could not be subsumed under the canons of traditional theory.

In order to understand its driving impulse, one had to go beyond explanations such as that found in J. L. Talmon's *The Origins of Totalitarian Democracy* that sought to account for it in terms of the centrality of ideas and the continuity of political thought.[19] What Mosse proposed instead was the emergence of an extra-parliamentary, secular religion based not upon a coherent rational analysis of philosophical premises, but rather upon salient myths and symbols, concretizing its mystique through the creation of new ceremonial and liturgical forms. The origins of this were hardly German. It was the French Revolution, Mosse argues, which ushered in the new visual age of mass politics:

> Political movements now had to project themselves upon the largely illiterate or semi-educated masses, whose newly roused political consciousness had to be taken into account. They were moved by what they could see and touch, by politics as a drama which gave them a feeling of political participation. We witness a change, slow to be sure, from written to iconographical language.[20]

The Nationalization of the Masses demonstrates how mass meetings, national monuments and symbols, public festivals, and political aesthetics objectified— perhaps even created?—the conscious and unconscious wishes of the masses, canalizing their desires and harnessing an ever-present hunger for community into the nationalist framework. In the preparation of this work Mosse had, after all, conducted personal interviews with the great practitioner of this politics, Albert Speer. Yet, it seems, these talks only confirmed his almost instinctive understanding of the inner dynamics and emotions of this political religion. Few of his students will forget his classroom descriptions of the lure of its mass meetings, of its "fully furnished houses," its attempt to forge a political environment of totality in an era of "wobbles" and confusing alienation. For Mosse this alternative politics did indeed constitute a general temptation: the Left, he makes clear, also indulged in its modalities. But it was the Right that most successfully activated its liturgical political style and annexed it to its own needs. Unlike its liberal and Left opponents, the Right was not constrained by the tenets of Enlightenment rationalism and abstract theorizing.

George Mosse tends to conceive of culture and cultural process in terms of a dialectical relationship between center and periphery. The insider acquires identity and defines himself in terms of the outsider he creates. There can be no ideal types without anti-types: the victor cannot be understood apart from his victim. The concern with the outsider and the "abnormal"—with processes of exclusion and victimization—critically illuminates the "inside" and the "normal."

The earliest work that pointed both conceptually and methodologically in this direction was Mosse's *Toward the Final Solution: A History of European Racism* (1978).[21] In this text he analyzed perhaps the most lethal of all modes of exclusion by showing how Jews and, to a somewhat lesser extent, Blacks became its central victims. What distinguished Mosse's treatment of racism from other approaches was his emphasis on the centrality of visual stereotypes and his insights into the usually hidden but absolutely crucial role of aesthetics in the making of stereotypical judgements. Mosse's racism is bent on creating a divided world according to ideal types and anti-types. Its model, he argues, was based upon the deeply rooted ideal of Greek beauty. This aesthetic provided the basis for making judgments not only about external appearance but also concerning inner moral qualities. Classical beauty came to symbolize not only the perfect form, but also the form within which a "true soul" was bound to reside.

It was, inevitably, Christian Europeans who most closely corresponded to the ideal type and exemplified nobility of appearance and character. The obvious anti-types were the Blacks and the Jews. No one could claim a Greek heritage for the thick lips, flat nose, and crinkly hair of the Negro; nor was the hunched, ugly stereotype of the ghetto Jew any closer to the ideal. The "sciences" of physiognomy and phrenology buttressed this aesthetic, for they espoused notions in which external appearance was held to reflect internal moral, spiritual, and characterological qualities. Black deportment confirmed an essential inner violence and primitivism. Jewish looks validated an inherent criminality and manipulative nature.

Mosse made it quite clear that such "sciences" did not always necessarily have either racist or anti-Semitic intentions. Nor, he emphasized, was it possible to draw a straight line from eugenics to racial genocide. Nevertheless, these kinds of beliefs did feed into the worldview of those committed to racist positions, a worldview found in all European countries. Its adherents forged what Mosse strikingly termed a "scavenger ideology," one that annexed all the virtues of the modern age and condemned those regarded as deficient in such virtues as inferior and "degenerate," a category which fused the biological with the social and which attested to the ever-growing and influential medicalization of discourse.

Beyond this, however, racism, in Mosse's view, represented the most stark case of the modern inversion of the relationship between myth and reality. "The world racism created was realized because racism willed it so, despite the fact that it lacked any basis in historical, social, or political reality." In the concentration camps, the Nazis were able to create the outsiders of their own fantasies, to realize their myths about the Jew and other sub-races. Racism succeeded in transforming its stereotype into self-fulfilling prophecies. Systematic dehumanization turned the victim into the image that the victimizer desired. "Myth accepted as reality became the reality."[22]

Mosse has consistently argued for the centrality of the Jewish dimension in the unfolding of his historical inquiry. Indeed, he has gone considerably further than this and, in a remarkable statement that I shall attempt to unpack over the course of this essay, has stated: "All my books in one way or another have dealt with the Jewish catastrophe of my time which I have always regarded as no accident, structural fault or continuity of bureaucratic habits, but seemingly built into our society and attitudes towards life. Nothing in European history is a stranger to the holocaust."[23] The Mosseian project therefore, amounts to a cumulative examination of the manifold, yet always interrelated, components of that history. Fascism, Nazism, and the "Final Solution" come to be viewed as the culmination of deeper immanent trends, perceptions, and processes—albeit in their most radical and corrupted form. While always keeping in mind the special venom of Jewish victimization, Mosse has increasingly extended the scope of his inquiry and come to locate the issue within the frame of the general creation of "outsiders" and "insiders."

I will return to this point presently but here it is important to note that already in *The Crisis of German Ideology* Mosse's interpretation of anti-Semitism differed from the conventional view. Neither continuity nor the sustained influence of traditional Christian Jew-hatred within the modern world is emphasized. Mosse would not deny these as crucial background factors. Nevertheless, nineteenth- and twentieth-century manifestations of anti-Semitism assume qualitatively different forms and substance, comprehensible only within the specific configurations and crises of modernity that produced them. As the convenient foil for a host of ideologies—*Völkisch*, nationalist, and above all the racist variety—anti-Semitism had to be placed against the conditioning background of the dynamics of post-emancipation bourgeois society. Mosse's insistence on the historical contingency of anti-Semitism provides a salutary corrective to the tendency—still surprisingly widespread—to regard anti-Semitism as somehow above history, an eternal metaphysical phenomenon quite beyond contextual explanation or change. By linking Jewish fate to these central currents, Mosse reveals the previously obscure, if not entirely hidden, connections between realms normally compartmentalized.

This approach similarly animates his overall conception of modern Jewish history. Jewish existence is, as it were, de-ghettoized, and its relation to the surrounding society and the mutual interplay remain always paramount. Mosse's analyses of the appropriation of pietism and middle-class values into Jewish theology,[24] the Jewish internalization of Christian symbols (albeit in secularized form) attendant upon participation in the national state,[25] and the influence of *Völkisch* ideology on Jewish self-definition[26] define the connections in mischievously unorthodox, yet highly illuminating ways. At the same time, however, he calls attention to the unresolved contradictions of this experience and points to the positive re-appropriation of non-Jewish modes to maintain a distinctive Jewish identity along modern lines.

Nationalism and Sexuality (1985)[27] must be regarded as a landmark, a departure—most recently elaborated in *The Image of Man*[28]—in which the continuity of Mosse's concern is matched by a strikingly new perspective. The victimization of the Jew remains both central and unique, but the scope of analysis is considerably broadened: Jews as victims form part of a continuum and dynamic affecting other victims, and their status and stereotype becomes comprehensible only alongside other outsiders. "The Jewish stereotype is not unique," Mosse proclaimed in a revealing newspaper interview. "It's the same as the stereotype of all outsiders: sexual deviants, gypsies, the permanently insane, people who have hereditary diseases. They all look alike. They are all absolute lookalikes. And, of course these are all the people Hitler wanted to exterminate and whom he did exterminate. They all look the opposite of the middle-class, self-controlled idea of beauty, energy, all of this sort of thing."[29] The stage has not only become European-wide, but the central categories rendered appear far more a matter of class than of nation.

These works represent the fruits of Mosse's long-developing, critical reassessment of the role of the bourgeoisie and its all-pervasive ethic. As Arthur Mitzman has incisively observed, in *The Crisis of German Ideology* Mosse enunciated the prevailing liberal conventional wisdom that Nazism represented the pure, irrational antithesis of rational, liberal bourgeois modernity.[30] Over the course of time, his view of the role of the bourgeoisie and its worldview has been almost inverted: at least in some of its guises that class is now seen not so much as the mirror opposite, the victim of Nazi ideology, but rather as an essential expression of it.[31]

In which way is Mosse able to draw such conclusions? He argues that from the late-eighteenth century onward, nationalism and middle-class morality entered into a powerful alliance, together defining modern standards of respectability, both sexual and otherwise, in such a way that an ever-tightening distinction between normality and abnormality was created and enforced. Both *Nationalism and Sexuality* and *The Image of Man* are histories of manners and morals that, unlike many other contemporary studies of sexuality, do not enter the privacy of the bedroom but rather seek to grasp the collective dimensions of sexuality and unmask its hidden connections to public ideologies. According to Mosse, the markers of manliness and virility became essential parts of normal national and bourgeois self-definition. Anyone perceived as lacking in those characteristics was necessarily consigned to abnormal, outsider status. This alliance, Mosse holds, became increasingly totalized, insistent on assigning everyone a fixed place: healthy and degenerate, manly men and effeminate homosexuals, sane and insane, productive and lazy, native and foreigner. An ordered and safe "inside" could be created and maintained only by extending the net of exclusion. This rigid code, cloaked under the guise of respectablity and *Sittlichkeit,* was invoked to control the reality that the alliance had itself created. "Bourgeois society," Mosse contests, "needed its dialectical opposite in order to exist." [32]

These most recent books, with their hints of delicious subversion (so typical of Mosse's thinking), are themselves a challenge to the respectability they expose. In his insistence on illuminating our own condition, Mosse has always been the opposite of an antiquarian. The autobiographical impulses behind the study of Jewish history, anti-Semitism, and the Holocaust have always been clear. Similarly, we are now able to recognize that his present forays into the more generalized processes of exclusion, his unmasking of the pernicious functions of "respectability," and his insights into the making of the categories of normal and abnormal sexuality (i.e., homosexuality) have experiential roots. The personal dimension, Mosse writes, has decisively entered the concern with outsiderdom in general for "I have also addressed the specific outsiderdoms of which I have been a member." The fact that homosexuality only became explicitly addressed over the last 15 years or so must itself be regarded both as a testament to the power of—and an indictment against—that very "respectability" he has exposed. In the earlier years, his memoirs relate, "homosexuality could not be mentioned, and certainly not admitted, without paying the steep price of being driven out of one's profession (especially as a teacher) and expelled from normative society. . . . My preoccupation with the history of respectability . . . was driven by a sense of discovery and my own situation as a double outsider." [33]

This, then, is history fueled by autobiography and resonant with social criticism. It also constitutes part of Mosse's ongoing concern with the submersion of individuality and tolerance in an increasingly homogenized world. From this point of view, bourgeois morality becomes a historical villain whose constrictive and intolerant moral sense is gradually radicalized to the point that, in its Nazi version, it became an essential ingredient of genocidal motivation. The new man of National Socialism, Mosse tells us, "was the ideal bourgeois." [34] In terms of conventional historiography, this is perhaps the most startling of all of Mosse's theses: Nazism as the incarnation, the most extreme defender of bourgeois respectability.

This picture is far removed from Rauschning's Nazi nihilists breaking all limits in a kind of Nietzschean ecstasy or Thomas Mann's covenant with the demonic or Ernst Nolte's portrayal of Nazism as the ultimate naturalistic revolt against bourgeois transcendence.[35] Mosse's Nazi is a corrupted middle-class man intent on cleansing his world and preserving it against what he perceives to be anti-bourgeois forces of degeneration. The so-called euthanasia program against the handicapped, the insane, and the criminal; the persecution and murder of homosexuals, gypsies, and communists; and the "final solution"—all represent not so much a challenge to or the antithesis of the bourgeois experience, but rather an extreme, corrupted version of it. Here were middle-class men attempting to maintain the values of manliness, orderliness, cleanliness, honesty, hard work, and family life against those outsider groups who, in their eyes, seemed morally and aesthetically to desecrate the basic tenets of respectability.

During the Nazi period, that morality proved most fatal to the Jews and Gypsies precisely because, as separate peoples, they seemed radically different; all other categories of outsiders were at least partial insiders, deviants with some sort of a claim. Mosse would hold, however, that bourgeois morality in general is debilitating to outsiders—and potentially murderous. This thesis contains a suggestive insight,[36] but a more detailed discussion relating middle-class morality to murderous Nazi modes would be helpful. Bourgeois *Sittlichkeit*, after all, while often illiberal, was seldom genocidal, and it is surely in the processes of corruption and radicalization that such a transformation was engendered. It would be useful to flesh out further the nature of these processes.

Mosse has argued that the answer is to be found in the totalizing logic of racism. But unless one works out in very fine detail the exceedingly unique characteristics of its Nazi variety, "racism" as such may merely push the argument a step backward. For on its own, racism—while always pernicious—has to be made murderous, genocidal. This murderousness does not happen automatically. Historically and in principle, after all, it has coexisted with policies of emigration, separation, enslavement and domination, or even paternalism. Knowledge of perpetrator motivation is, of course, always very much a speculative affair but, at some level of consciousness, however remote, it seems to me, the conceivers and perpetrators of the Holocaust and associated atrocities were aware of the transgressive, taboo-breaking—that is, the highly "unbourgeois"— nature of their acts.[37] The analysis of these corrupting and transformative processes, these transgressive impulses, would bring out, I believe, the dual moment within Nazism itself: its combination of bourgeois and radical anti-bourgeois elements. Mosse himself brilliantly demonstrated these in *The Crisis of German Ideology*. Precisely in the combination of and tension between these elements, in the fusion of the conventional and the extraordinary, could Nazism transcend middle-class morality at the same time that it embodied it. Whatever future research will bring, however, Mosse has performed a valuable service in alerting us to these important middle-class dimensions of the Nazi experience.

Indeed, in more general terms would it be going too far to suggest that he has cumulatively woven a conceptual and historical critique of the very notion of "normalcy" and our own complicity within it? In a typically provocative and offhand remark he once commented to me that "everything normal is boring"! But, of course, it goes deeper than that for he has demonstrated that such stifling discourses of normative conformity are also potentially murderous—and rendered effective and dangerous precisely because they come disguised in the redemptive vocabulary of nation, race, health, and respectability.

These are the insights of an historian, the product of deep reflection. One will search in vain for a set of ideological or politically correct positions. If Mosse has focused on problems of his own outsidership—as a Jew and homosexual—he also has clearly stated, "I do not belong to a more recent generation where victimization is a badge of pride rather than a frustration or a test of character."[38] An unflagging honesty informs his work; there is no confusion of his own preferences with the historical reality he analyzes. This sobriety is very much in evidence in the way he ultimately frames his overall analysis of respectability. Its normative manners and morals are essential, he insists, "for the cohesion and functioning of society itself."[39] If the gist of *Nationalism and Sexuality* was critical—bourgeois morality as intolerant of outsiders and indeed potentially murderous—the last paragraph of that book hinted at the profundity of the dilemma, at the conviction that "respectability" was, indeed, built into the very structure of our societies. "What began as bourgeois morality in the eighteenth century," Mosse concluded, "in the end became everyone's morality."[40] That being so, Mosse has defined his task as producing a critical recognition—not a fundamental subversion—of this reality. As he puts it, "I like to provoke, to break taboos, but purely theoretically . . . to get people to think—not in the practice of daily life."[41] Once in conversation he perplexedly wondered if it were at all possible to imagine a world, a society, run along lines qualitatively different from those enshrined in this normative bourgeois morality. After a short silence, he concluded, sadly but firmly, that it was not.

There *are* of course affirmations in Mosse's thought, and a positive vision *is* to be found in his work—one that is in fact related to another side of the very "bourgeoisie" he criticizes. I shall shortly attend to this. But before moving on we should pause to elaborate on the nature and logic of the tapestry he has woven from the 1960s through to the present for it may help to reveal a perhaps previously unnoticed but crucial dimension of his work. I am referring to the tightly interrelated nature, the mutual implication, of the manifold and apparently separate building blocks and forces complicit in the process leading toward Nazism and Fascism. Mosse's work is informed and animated by a conceptual frame of ever-constricting incorporation. Nationalism, middle-class morality, notions of inclusion and exclusion, racism, mass politics, aesthetics, and stereotypes have different origins, pedigrees, and functions, but in this evolving portrait they come to coalesce. Mosse's writings are suffused with the language of alliance, annexation, penetration, and co-optation. Nationalism and bourgeois "respectability" stand in "alliance" together defining increasingly homogenizing standards of inclusion and exclusion; they "annex" aesthetics and a secular, sacralized mass politics into this lethal combination; and racism, that great "scavenger," as Mosse suggestively calls it, penetrates all these forces, driving them to new heights of exclusivity and radicalism and "locking" them, as he puts it, "securely in place." Viewed in composite, we can discern an unfolding development, an emerging pattern woven into an ever-broadening canvas, in which the Holocaust and its related barbarities are conceived finally not as some kind of aberration but as continuous with the normative and mainstream, rather than subterranean and deviant, dimensions of post-Enlightenment European society, politics, and culture.

George Mosse is a historian who analyzes phenomena that go against his grain—a humanist pushed into the study of the inhumane. But, like Benedetto Croce, who has greatly influenced Mosse,[42] he accepts the notion that this is an unavoidable task, for outside of history there is no reality. The only way, therefore, of confronting the reality is by coming to grips with history from the inside and in a committed, rather than a positivistic and descriptive, manner. History, for him, must be a passion, certainly not "a profession like any other."[43] Like Croce, Mosse insists that the mind of the historian is central to historical analysis; as a result, only history relevant to one's present situation is worthy of its name. Like Croce's work, too, Mosse's writings are animated by a commitment to individual liberty in a world threatened by the forces of mass irrationality and mass politics.

To be sure, over the years both the source and the very nature of this "irrationality" have undergone change and deepening in Mosse's work. Until *The Nationalization of the Masses,* he did indeed simply equate "irrationality" with those cultural, political, and ideological forces that stood opposed to a normative bourgeois liberal rationalism. Michael P. Steinberg may be correct in discerning in Mosse's work a kind of "fortress rationality," a refusal to accept the complex mixture and intertwining of the rational with the irrational. This, he argues, is a result of firsthand experience of European fascism, leading Mosse "to abjure negotiation with cultural demons by adopting this strict posture."[44] Steinberg's characterization may, to some extent, capture the spirit of some of Mosse's earlier work. But over the years, he has increasingly stressed that some of the most problematic, even pernicious, properties themselves lurk in the fortress.

Still, in this troubled Europe Mosse sees not only points of darkness; muted potentials for redemption are always present. His legendary lectures at the University of Wisconsin on "The Culture of Western Europe" (presented in his textbook of the same name) presented many young American audiences with unknown, almost magical areas of European culture. Here were liberal, libertarian, Freudian, existentialist, Kantian socialist, and Hegelian Marxist answers to the contemporary dilemmas of European society. These answers, to be sure, failed in the inter-war period in Europe; yet long after the demise of Nazism and Fascism, in Mosse's presentation, they retained their vitality, their possibilities apparently far from exhausted. Of course, he has always kept a critical distance from these options. Nevertheless, as one student of his has pointed out, he retains a deep empathy for the ethical utopian impulse,[45] a hope that somehow a humanist fusion of liberalism with socialism would be possible. His writings and lectures unfailingly both encourage and critically examine these unorthodox alternatives.

There is, however, another source that, I believe, gets us closer to the core of Mosse's positive commitments. In order to grasp this, we must first examine his analysis of the ideal of *Bildung*. For, as Mosse puts it, if *Sittlichkeit*, or respectability, represents bourgeois constrictiveness or the contraction of tolerance and human expression, then the German Enlightenment and of course mainly middle-class ideal of *Bildung* embodies the ideal of the expansion of human possibilities and stands for tolerance, cultured self-cultivation, and the primacy of individual autonomy.[46] To be sure, this view goes well beyond a naive liberal Enlightenment position. Over the years Mosse *has* become increasingly sensitive to the darker side of *Aufklärung*.[47] More specifically, he has recently spelled out an important critique of the liberalism to which he himself is attached. Liberalism, he argues, has always equated liberty as such only or mainly with political freedom. As a result, it also sanctioned the rigid rules of personal behavior as laid down by the precepts of respectability, and legitimized the restrictions upon the individual by society, if not by parliaments. His critique of bourgeois morality (of *Sittlichkeit* as opposed to *Bildung*) is, in the last resort, a plea "to extend the liberal definition of freedom even to those moral and behavioural restraints which liberalism has sanctioned."[48]

In his recently published *German Jews beyond Judaism,* Mosse brilliantly analyzes the historical process whereby German Jewry slowly, but irrevocably, became virtually the sole carrier of that humanizing *Bildung* sensibility, and witnesses to the gradual desertion by the non-Jewish German educated middle class of a doctrine that they had originally shared with their emancipated Jewish co-citizens; German nationalism, he has constantly maintained, did not have to take the course it ultimately did.[49] For him, the German Jewish heritage ultimately becomes the heritage of *Bildung,* which becomes transformed into a kind of new Jewish tradition. Indeed, it becomes the defining ingredient of post-emancipation Jewish identity.[50] For traditionalists, of course, there is something profoundly shocking, even subversive, in the notion that nineteenth- and twentieth-century intellectual Jewishness is synonymous with a particular strand of German culture, even if albeit its most tolerant, progressive side. They would likely not join Walter Benjamin in praise of the statement by Ludwig Strauss that "in a study of Goethe one finds one's Jewish substance."[51]

Mosse demonstrates that the internalization of the ethos of *Bildung* derived from the specific historical circumstances of the struggle for Jewish emancipation in Germany. For a community emerging from the ghetto and seeking integration within German life, the prevalent ideal of *Bildung* seemed tailor-made "because it transcended all differences of nationality and religion through the unfolding of the individual personality."[52] Thus, Mosse holds, cultural humanism became integrally interwoven into the fabric of modern German Jewish being. He is characteristically critical of much of this internalization. He argues, for instance, that *Bildung* modes of thought encouraged an almost automatic belief in the primacy of culture over politics, which tended to distort contemporary perceptions and blind one to the imperatives of an ever-strengthened mass politics. *Bildung* Jews engaged in the politics of delusion, projecting their ideals of a tolerant Germany onto a quite different, far more brutal reality. Jews clung to a heritage that by 1933 was overwhelmed and rendered irrelevant.

For all that, Mosse insists, the heritage lives on. It was kept alive originally by liberal and left-wing intellectuals in exile and later "by new generations eager to take up a heritage thought long dead and forgotten." It is in this heritage, indeed, that Mosse the man and his work most profoundly meet. Here Mosse himself closely resembles the Jewish intellectuals, ranging from Sigmund Freud to Stefan Zweig and the Frankfurt School he describes. In them, as he put it, Jewishness became a metaphor for the critical, unmasking, yet always humanizing and autonomous mind. It is as much a plea and statement of hope as it is historical analysis.

German Jews beyond Judaism, then, presents Mosse's creed. It is, he admits, "certainly my most personal book, almost a confession of faith."[53] Mosse is a historian whose essential task has been that of a critic of culture, ideology, and politics, opposed to mindless conformities and stultifying orthodoxies of any kind. Yet there is a complexity here that we should not overlook. We have already demonstrated that Mosse is aware of the necessity, even the desirability, of order in society, that he recognizes that the conflicting demands between cohesion and tolerance require a delicate balance. He is aware, too, that criticism without the act of positive building, devoid of constructive vision, has historically led to both impotence and alienation.[54] Moreover, and most intriguingly, he often has a certain sympathy for some of the myths and symbols he studies; they answer deep needs for human community and meaning and will not be wished away in terms of mindless negation.

This certainly applies to Mosse's Zionism, his identification with the very nationalist myths and symbols he has done so much to demystify. This, indeed, has been a source of puzzlement to many. How are we to explain it? At a certain intellectual level, of course, the case can be made that there is no built-in inconsistency. For Mosse has gone out of his way to recover the liberal, *Bildung* legacy of the early German-speaking Zionists, ranging from Robert Weltsch, Kurt Blumenfeld, and Martin Buber[55] through Gershom Scholem,[56] insisting upon the originally humanist face of an essentially tolerant liberal experiment which could have avoided going the way of conventional nationalism.[57]

Yet the matter is surely more complicated than this. For someone as acutely aware of the Nazi experience and the destruction of European Jewry as Mosse is, his Zionist affirmation may well have as one of its sources a largely unstated appreciation of the need for force and collective self-defense in a very imperfect, uncultured world: a corrective to the blind-spot of the *Bildungs* intellectuals who habitually misdiagnosed the harsh political realities that directly confronted them. How ironic, one wonders, was his constant invocation of Max Nordau's contemptuous juxtaposition of "coffee-house" with "muscle Jews"?[58]

Mosse himself disarmingly notes that "I was far from consistent. My own engagement in Israel told of the need for a more concrete embodiment of my Jewish identity; my accelerated heartbeat when I witnessed the swearing-in of Israeli paratroopers on Massada—Israel's Holy Mountain—reveals the attraction of an emotional commitment even for one who prides himself on the use of his reason. . . . once again, ideal and reality differ even within my own person."[59] Later in his memoirs, in relating his reactions to the Israeli experience, Mosse puts it even more candidly: "I remember vividly my joy on my first visit when I saw sturdy, self-confident Jews, and though this was, once again, a stereotype, I was only conscious of the contrast between the present and the humiliating past. I knew full well that this 'new Jew' represented a normalization, an assimilation to general middle-class ideals which otherwise I professed to dislike. But I could not help myself; faced with this Zionist ideal my reason and historical knowledge were overcome."[60]

For all his wariness as an exile of passports, his dislike of conformity and homogenization, his suspicion of labels and stereotypes, and his uniquely individual personality, Mosse may have found Zionism attractive simply because it provided him with a "sense of belonging."[61] Yet, even though Mosse regards this as the defeat of his reason by his emotion, I think he does himself an injustice. For he has indeed intelligibly integrated these forces of collective identification within his larger intellectual vision. Because nationalism, religion, Marxism, bourgeois respectability, and any number of other ideologies correspond to real human desires and are built into the modern experience, the crucial question for Mosse is not how to abolish and dismantle these structures, but how to humanize them. The challenge for him is to maintain the values of Enlightenment-*Bildung*—of autonomy, reason, tolerance, and the free play of mind and human action—in a world of conformity, mass politics, and mass brutalization. Mosse does not accept total solutions. His is rather a meliorating response based always on the compassionate, personalizing mode.

It is no accident that among the values he most admires in both the Enlightenment and German Jewish heritage is that of friendship, the attempt at all times to personalize relationships.[62] This is deeply embodied both in his work and in his caring, scintillating person. The task he sets before us is to reassert the positive potentials within these forms of community, to make us aware of the dangers inherent in conformity and homogenization, and to alert us to the primacy of humanization and solidarity over domination and superiority. His is truly a personal and historical sensibility for all seasons.

Fifteen

On Saul Friedlander

There are few arenas of Western cultural and intellectual life where the ethical, interpretive, and political stakes are more charged than in the ongoing analyses and debates concerning the nature and implications of Nazism and the Holocaust. In this powerfully contested field of Shoah historiography and commemoration, Saul Friedlander constitutes a distinctive, always stylish, and sophisticated presence, a peculiarly authoritative custodial voice.[1] It is this sense of protective custodianship, the eloquent assertion and defense of the historical and moral centrality, as well as the ultimate inexplicability, of the Holocaust that animates Friedlander's project and provides unity to his work. At the same time, it is the haunting awareness of the fragility of this centrality that informs his sensitivity to, identification of, and polemic with those multiple forces constantly operating to undermine, elide, or even eradicate its normative standing.

This sensitivity and authority derives from a unique combination of personal and intellectual qualities and biographical circumstances. That this event has indelibly shaped his life, demanding ever-greater reflection and moral and intellectual probity, will be clear to anyone familiar with Friedlander's poignant, elegantly written 1979 memoir *When Memory Comes*.[2] There he portrays, in fragmented form and with almost unbearable restraint, his tale of survival under the Nazis and its effects on his dismembered life:[3] the pain of a Czech Jewish child "abandoned" by parents intent on saving his life by placing him in French Catholic hands for care; the nature of terror and its regressive effects ("and every morning I was sopping wet with urine when I woke up"); the confusion of identity and the consolatory move to Catholicism (in devotion to the Virgin "I rediscovered something of the presence of a mother"); the secret shame ("of having passed over to the compact, invincible majority, of no longer belonging to the camp of the persecuted but, potentially at least, to that of the persecutors"); learning from a compassionate priest of his parents' death and of Auschwitz ("to hear him speak of the lot of the Jews with so much emotion and respect must have been an important encourage-

171

ment for me"); the rediscovery of his Jewishness (with its immediate, albeit confused, "sensation of absolute loyalty") and the ongoing complexities inherent in the move from Pavel to Sha'ul, from Paul to Saul.[4]

For all that, Friedlander is seldom associated with those—like Elie Wiesel, Primo Levi, and Jean Amery—whose fame revolves almost exclusively around the questions and problematics of survivorship.[5] He somewhat self-deprecatingly describes his choice of career—"to adopt the gaze of the historian"—as a "way out for me to attach myself to the necessary order, the inescapable simplification forced upon one by the passage of time. . . ."[6] Yet his accomplishment rests upon a rare sublimative capacity to both integrate and yet surmount the fact of his personal experience into subtle historical and cultural scholarship. He is alert as few others are to the nuances separating and joining the personal and the objective realms, childhood memory ("For me . . . Hitler's Reich is always summed up, in one first instant, by two motionless sentinels: not faces but two helmets"), dispassionate history, and both the tactile-experiential ("The smell of their leather overcoats!") and analytic dimensions.[7] Indeed, these sensitivities have helped to define his role within the culture: as a kind of seismometer consistently identifying and opening for discussion emergent interpretive questions and meta-issues surrounding the historiography of the Holocaust.

I would suggest then that the distinctiveness of Saul Friedlander's work lies in the close monitoring of changing cultural and political currents and the rigorous examination of their moral, philosophical, and psychological implications for the representation of the Shoah within Western ethical and intellectual discourse.[8] This does not mean, of course, that he has neglected the craft of regular narrative history.[9] His first book, a revised version of his dissertation published in 1963, was a closely documented study of Nazi policies toward and perceptions of the United States.[10] As the reviewer in *The Christian Science Monitor* stressed, Friedlander "practices the self-effacing zeal of the scholar in letting the facts and documents speak for themselves . . . All is related carefully and dispassionately. Perhaps the most eloquent tribute one can pay to the author is that unless the reader were told, he would never guess from the book that Saul Friedlander's father and mother were caught by the Nazis in 1942 and killed in Auschwitz."[11]

Indeed, in his second book on Pius XII and the Third Reich, tellingly subtitled, *A Documentation,* Friedlander insists that in the face of bewilderingly opposed positions regarding the relationship of the Catholic Church to the Nazis, the only possibility of honest investigation was "to adhere as far as possible, *to the documents.*" After a thorough examination of the available evidence, Friedlander concluded with positivistic caution that: "At the end of this study, which claims to be nothing more than an analysis of documents, I cannot make any definite answer to the questions raised by the wartime policies of the Holy See toward the Third Reich because I only have incomplete documents at my disposal."[12] For all that, the thrust of the work is painfully—if implicitly—accusatory.[13] It pointedly noted the continuing predilection of the Pope for the Germans even when he was aware of the deadly nature of the Hitler regime— and raised a moral issue always central to Friedlander's concern: how by the end of 1943 could the Church (even given its anti-Bolshevist impulses) continue to wish for victorious resistance in the East "and therefore seemingly accepted by implication the maintenance, however temporary, of the Nazi extermination machine?"[14]

There was only one clue in the book that pointed to Friedlander's personal odyssey—the telling dedication: To the Memory of My Parents Killed at Auschwitz. Only a retrospective reading of the work informed by knowledge of Friedlander's own saving engagement with Catholicism enables one to grasp the pain and poignancy, the caution and restraint, indeed, the ongoing desire for some kind of future redeeming explanation: "The historian, while noting the lacunae, is reduced to the hope that the essential documents he lacks, and particularly the documents of the Vatican archives, soon will be published so that the events and personages can be brought into proper perspective."[15]

It is, however, less for his conventional historical work that Friedlander is well known. He has always been particularly alert to the accompanying moral and psychological complexities that accompanied the exterminations, a sensitivity whose origins may well lie in the complexities of his own personal experience. It is especially telling today that, as early as 1967, Friedlander chose a quite "extra-ordinary" German, Kurt Gerstein, as the subject of his only biographical study—a "brutally deadpan historical essay," as one reviewer put it[16]—of what he termed "the ambiguity of good."[17] In a rare act of moral conscience and heroic anticonformity, Gerstein joined the SS in order to try to *impede* and inform the world of the "Final Solution." The story, as Friedlander relates it, is rent with paradoxes and tragic ambiguities: Gerstein shipped more liquid prussic acid than he was able to destroy; he risked his life informing all and sundry about the exterminations but his warnings were ignored; instead of being celebrated as a hero in 1945 he was incarcerated by the French and committed suicide; and in his posthumous Tübingen trial in 1950, the court acknowledged his actions and exonerated him from criminality but condemned him for his ineffectuality, and labeled him as "tainted."

Gerstein, Friedlander concluded, was condemned

. . . in effect, for the *uselessness of his efforts . . .* punished, in a way, for not having behaved like the great majority of "good" Germans and waited quietly until all the Jews were dead; paradoxically, the "innocence" of such Germans is contrasted with the "guilt" of a man who was obliged in some degree to accommodate to the crime in order to resist it. This paradox is inherent in any opposition carried on from within against a system such as Nazism, to the extent that it enforces participation in its crimes as a condition of being able to act against them. Under totalitarianism, right must at times seem indistinguishable from wrong, good from evil, the resister from the executioner . . . what lends Gerstein's tragic fate its unique character and its full magnitude is the complete passivity of the "others." Had there been in Germany thousands or even hundreds of Gersteins . . . then hundreds of thousands of victims undoubtedly would have been saved by these same "official" accomplices of the regime. If these things had happened, all of these Gersteins would have been acknowledged heroes.[18]

In effect, until this piece, Friedlander's historical writings had taken on issues that in some way or another related to the question of the Nazi extermination of the Jews but had not yet quite touched its causal core: the issue of perpetrator motivation. Throughout, he has stressed that the ultimate singularity of the event lay in its fundamentally transgressive and taboo-breaking nature, in the fact that those who embarked upon and implemented this project went beyond all thinkable limits. Quoting from Hannah Arendt to the effect that the Nazis tried to "determine who should and who should not inhabit the world," Friedlander comments that this

is something no other regime, whatever its criminality, has attempted to do. In that sense, the Nazi regime attained what is, in my view, some sort of theoretical outer limit: one may envision an even larger number of victims and a technologically more efficient way of killing, but once a regime decides that groups, whatever the criteria may be, should be annihilated there and then and never be allowed to live on Earth, the ultimate has been achieved. This limit, from my perspective, was reached only once in modern history: by the Nazis. It goes without saying that one may try to compare Nazi annihilations to other annihilationist policies, that one may look for any number of comparable elements; all this does not exclude the identification of some differences. The aspect just mentioned is what gives the Nazi regime its specificity.[19]

For Friedlander, such murderous extremity renders "conventional" histories and methodologies unable to grasp the deep structures and motivations of the event. Thus in the 1970s, when such theories were more or less in vogue,[20] Friedlander was powerfully drawn to psychoanalysis and psychohistory as the proper means of addressing and answering these questions. The fruits of this approach are to be found in the (never translated) French work, *Nazi Anti-Semitism: History of a Collective Psychosis*.[21] The burden of his thesis was that Hitler and his genocidal followers shared a collective unconscious fantasy: the Jews constituted a germ and thus had to be eradicated.

It was this fantasy, Friedlander argued, that led to a behavior of identification and purification (similar to the structure of many individual obsessions) that would take the ultimate form of the physical extermination of the Jews. We need not pause too long to point out the by now familiar difficulties inherent in psychohistory in general and of the Nazi genocide in particular[22]—the entirely speculative nature of the inferences concerning the content and dynamics of the unconscious not only of dead individuals but of entire groups[23]—because Friedlander himself very soon realized their shortcomings[24] and, with a candor rare among scholars, later wrote regarding the deficiencies of psychohistory: "My own study of Nazi anti-Semitism poses the same problems."[25]

Though psychohistory was quietly abandoned, Friedlander nevertheless continues to insist upon "an independent psychological residue" as the appropriate level of explanation (unavailable to most conventional approaches), a crucial component for understanding the unprecedented nature of the exterminations. Moreover, he continues to chide historians for regarding the psychological dimension as "a kind of riddle" which they then subsume under—and reduce to—other explanatory categories such as ideological motives or institutional dynamics.[26] His writings thus continue to be steeped in an illuminating psychological sensibility. Most recently, on the basis of his reading of Himmler's famous speech to high-ranking SS officers in Posen on 4 October 1943, Friedlander has invoked the notion of *Rausch*, a kind of intoxication, as the psychological clue behind the radically transgressive, morality-defying behavior of the perpetrators:

> Could one of the components of *Rausch* itself, as far as killing and exterminations of others are concerned, not be the effect of a growing elation stemming from *repetition*, from the ever-larger numbers of the killed others? . . . the perpetrators do not appear anymore as bureaucratic automata, but rather as beings seized by a compelling lust for killing on an enormous scale, driven by some kind of extraordinary elation in repeating the killing of ever-huger masses of people.[27]

But theorizing about the inner motivations of the perpetrators—a necessarily speculative area[28]—does not take up the bulk of Friedlander's present psychological interests. His focus has shifted from the subjects of history to those who perforce must commemorate, culturally re-imagine, and write it. Those who come after, he insists, will necessarily be encircled within a structure of "trauma and "transference." The insights thus garnered, it seems to me, are both less speculative and immensely fruitful and, indeed, applied not only to the work of other researchers in the field but also to his own writings. "The extreme character of the events and the indeterminacy surrounding their historical significance create even for the professional historian a field of projections, of unconscious shapings and reshapings, of an authentic transferential situation."[29] *All* approaches to this subject, Friedlander insists, possess a built-in subjective dimension, and are at least in part existentially and transferentially determined.

These kinds of insights formed an integral part of the dazzling correspondence Friedlander conducted with the German historian, Martin Broszat. In this, perhaps *the* exemplary document of a tough, entirely candid, post-Shoah German Jewish dialogue (of which more later), there arose the question of bias entailed in the respective "German" and "Jewish" national and scholarly representations of the Holocaust. As Friedlander put it there: "This issue . . . has not been openly dealt with up to now and it is important for all that it be brought to the surface and clarified."[30] Broszat had argued that, given its victim status and background, "Jewish" historiography and memory must perforce be "mournful and accusatory . . . a mythical form of remembrance" that had little to do with the rational, scholarly, "scientific" enterprise.[31] It is interesting that in his reply Friedlander did not point out the dubiousness of relating to scholarship in terms of its national background, as "German" or "Jewish." Instead, while accepting the likelihood of some Jewish bias, he generalized his transferential insight. "Wouldn't you agree," he pointedly asked Broszat, "that this German context creates as many problems in the approach to the Nazi era as it does, differently, for the victims? . . . If we see things from your perspective, why, in your opinion, would historians belonging to the group of the perpetrators be able to distance themselves from their past, whereas those belonging to the group of the victims would not?"[32] "For us," he concluded, "a kind of purely scientific distancing from the past, that is, a passage from the realm of knowledge strongly influenced by personal memory to that of some kind of 'detached history', remains, in my opinion, a psychological and epistemological illusion."[33]

Over the years, Friedlander has become a master of the manifold psychological ploys and techniques by which scholarly narratives and collective memory (always carefully differentiated into its victim, perpetrator, and other components) seeks to selectively confront—or evade—this essentially "unmastered"(and perhaps unmasterable) past.[34] He has identified and analyzed the diverse currents within both "high" and "low" culture that in some usually unrecognized way tend to abuse, trivialize, undermine, or, to use a ubiquitous term in his lexicon, "neutralize" the scandalous centrality of Nazism and its atrocities.

In his most famous book-length essay on developments within popular culture, on "Kitsch and Death," Friedlander charted the signs of what he took to be not forgetfulness but rather an essential transvaluation of the memory of National Socialism: "At the end of the war, Nazism was the damned part of Western civilization, the symbol of evil. Everything the Nazis had done was condemned, whatever they touched defiled; a seemingly indelible stain darkened the German past . . . . By the end of the Sixties, however, the Nazi image in the West had begun to change." In an exercise of decoding Friedlander set out out to "understand the logic of this transformation, this reelaboration."[35] Not surprisingly, he emphasized that the key to grasping the new discourse lay in the "autonomous psychological dimension."[36] The attraction to Nazism not only in the past but in its present reflections "lay less in any explicit ideology than in the power of emotions, images and phantasms."[37] What attracted contemporaries to the new discourse, with its juxtaposition as well as ultimate fusion of kitsch and death,[38] Friedlander argued, was important not only in itself (as an expression both of continued fears and mute yearnings) but because its profound logic revealed the logic of National Socialism, the grip Nazism had exerted in its own day: "a deep structure based on the coexistence of the adoration of power with a dream of final explosion—the annulment of all power . . . a particular kind of bondage nourished by the simultaneous desires for absolute submission and total freedom."[39]

For Friedlander the new discourse replicated precisely those elements that had formed the basis of attraction to Nazism itself and in so doing crossed a vital barrier of post-Nazi Western sensibility: "Attention has gradually shifted from the reevocation of Nazism as such, from the horror and pain—even if muted by time and transformed into subdued grief and endless meditation—to voluptuous anguish and ravishing images, images one would like to see going on forever. It . . . is tuned to the wrong key. . . . Some kind of limit has been overstepped and uneasiness appears."[40]

It is, indeed, this very uneasiness that over the years has informed Friedlander's wide-ranging watch over cultural developments ("the massive change," as he puts it, "in the production of the imaginary in Western societies") and the ways in which this has affected emergent representations of Nazism and the Holocaust.[41] Whether applied to general interpretive models of National Socialism, the functionalist-intentionalist controversy, the infamous *Historikerstreit* of the 1980s, the debate over the

ramifications of the historicization of National Socialism, or the challenge of postmodernism to historical narrative, Friedlander has always
been at the forefront, examining their assumptions and identifying the
challenges they pose to the normative notion of Nazism as the transgressive absolute, Auschwitz as "the indelible reference point of the Western imagination."[42]

It is this absolute nature of the exterminations, the singularity of the
total drive against the Jews, that for Friedlander has consistently constituted the moral and historical bedrock, a datum which, as he put it in
1976, "makes it impossible to integrate . . . not only within the general
framework of Nazi persecutions, but also within the wider aspects of
contemporary ideological-political behaviour such as fascism, totalitarianism, economic exploitation and so forth."[43] The validity of the main
global interpretations of National Socialism is undermined, according to
Friedlander, precisely in relationship to Nazi anti-Semitism and Nazi policies against the Jews, by their inability to incorporate the singularity of
the exterminations within their overall explanatory schemes.

In the first place, Friedlander argues, the "functional" accounts that
they all invoke in order to explain anti-Semitism breaks down in the face
of genocide. How could the Jews be "functional" enemies when the drive
to utterly destroy them was secret, hidden as far as possible from the public eye? "For the Nazis, the extermination of the Jews was a fundamental
urge and a sacred mission, not a means to other objectives." Moreover, in
his differentiated analysis regarding levels of explanation and the distinction between means and motivations, Friedlander demonstrates both the
uses and, more critically, the limits of generalized "totalitarian" explanations thus:

> This is not to say that the Nazi action against the Jews did not utilize the
> extreme forms of bureaucratic manipulation and domination which are
> typical of totalitarian regimes—and on a more diffuse level—of modern
> society in general. Nor does it mean that the complete disregard for hu-
> man life and for the value of the individual, so often demonstrated in our
> century, did not make the Nazi task easier. But these are circumstances
> which facilitated the exterminatory drive: they do not explain its chief
> characteristic—its absolutely uncompromising nature.[44]

As he tersely observed elsewhere *"the totalitarian framework is the means
of destruction, not its basic explanation."*[45] Works like Hannah Arendt's
on totalitarianism and (the early) Ernst Nolte on fascism, while "aware
of the centrality and the specificity of the Jewish question within Nazi
ideology and practice . . . nevertheless built a general theory which, instead of attempting to explain this specificity, disregarded all its main as-

pects."[46] Friedlander later sharpened the point thus: "the point is not that such concepts as 'totalitarianism' or 'fascism' seem inadequate for the contextualization of the 'Final Solution', but, obversely, that these concepts fit much better the particular phenomenon they deal with, once the 'Final Solution' is *not* included."[47]

It is worthwhile noting that Friedlander has never resorted to simple or monocausal explanations of perpetrator motivations; rather, he has always carefully differentiated between the driving ideological, pathological core, the implementing bureaucratic and field functionaries of murder, and the outer rim of more or less complicit bystanders. Nor will one find simplistic generalizations as to a murderous national culture or an anti-Semitic character. Extreme racial anti-Semitism, Friedlander wrote well over a decade ago, "certainly fed Hitler's ideology and that of the 'true believer's' within the NSDAP, but it offered latent rather than active support to the policies against the Jews . . . as far as its prevalence among the general population is concerned." In his account no enthusiastic national executionary drive can be found: "public opinion was not particularly enthusiastic about the anti-Jewish persecutions."[48] And in his new book he writes that "the majority of Germans, although undoubtedly influenced by various forms of traditional anti-Semitism and easily accepting the segregation of the Jews, shied away from widespread violence against them, urging neither their expulsion from the Reich nor their physical annihilation."[49]

Indeed, the very relevance of historical continuity as an explanatory factor undergoes critical scrutiny. While Friedlander would agree that Nazi anti-Semitism is explicable only within some kind of German national purview, he specifically points to the difficulties that lie "in assessing the significance of those roots, the relative importance of the *völkisch* ideology, and the place of anti-Semitic themes and attitudes within German society, be it during the Wilhelmine period or under the Weimar Republic." To be sure, no general interpretation could afford not to include, in some way or another, the factor of national continuity, but "the importance of that background is often difficult to assess."[50] Most crucially, Friedlander is critical even of those narratives that place anti-Jewish impulses at its explanatory center. "The only global historical interpretation which seems to 'fit'," he writes, "is the most traditional one: the incremental effect of an ever-more radical anti-Semitic factor. But even those historians who still remain close to this view have to admit that because of the very nature of Nazi anti-Semitism and the 'Final Solution', 'the question of continuity becomes problematic.'"[51]

Friedlander's custodial insistence upon what constitutes the important as opposed to the side issues has never been in doubt. This certainly informs his leading role in the debates over "functionalist" interpretations of Nazism and the Shoah that raged in the 1980s. These harshly severed the ties between the intentional ideological impulses and the political practice of the Nazis. It was not in the preordained ideological aims of Hitler and the Third Reich, the exponents of functionalism held, that the genesis and disposition of its genocidal policies were to be found but rather but in its non-monolithic, polycratic structure, its structurally built-in infighting with its struggle for power and resultant "cumulative radicalism."

The details of the intentionalist-functionalist debate are too well known to require rehearsal here. At the time of this writing, a kind of unspoken compromise, a sort of integration between the two, characterizes most current approaches. Here we need simply note that Friedlander's "intentionalist" defense was, in the first place, characterized by a fair and judicious analysis of the functionalist position. The functionalist analysis, he wrote, fitted "better within the mainstream of modern historiography" and its proponents could "claim, quite correctly, that their position implies a much broader spread of responsibility for the crimes committed than that recognized by the opposite position which considers Hitler as the prime mover and the key authority." Nevertheless, Friedlander hastened to spell out the moral and historiographical implications attendant upon this interpretation: "The image it offers of Nazism is more 'normal', easier to explain: any group can stumble haphazardly, step by step, into the most extreme criminal behavior . . . functionalism confronts us, implicitly, with Hannah Arendt's thesis of the 'banality of evil.'" Functionalism, too, thus assumed for Friedlander a neutralizing impulse, one that overlooked or even denied "that it is Nazi anti-Semitism and the anti-Jewish policies of the Third Reich that gave Nazism an essential part of its *sui generis* character."[52]

Friedlander's sensitivity to these kinds of elisions was very much in evidence in his prominent role in, and analyses of, the by now infamous *Historikerstreit* of the 1980s. There is no need to repeat here the nature of the debate, the ways in which the work of historians like Andreas Hillgruber and, more notoriously, Ernst Nolte, seemed to mirror larger political and cultural desires in Germany to somehow "normalize" German identity by placing the Nazi past within more relative, comparative, and easily empathic frameworks.[53]

While Friedlander acutely dissected the historiographical content and biases of these works, his most distinctive contribution came from an analysis of the implications entailed in this shift of perspective. Given the historically unprecedented nature of the crimes, he argued, the ultimate question—of concern to all approaches to National Socialism—was the issue of responsibility. For all their differences, Friedlander noted, the traditional *Sonderweg* (the special path of German history) and "totalitarian" narratives were "liberal" in nature, viewing Hitler, the Nazi party, the SS, and its bureaucratic instruments as essentially responsible, while the bystanders (most of German society) had at least some partial knowledge of crimes committed and were thus guilty of sustained indifference and passivity. He wrote,

> In terms of self-perception within contemporary West German society, this narrative implies the recognition of a *basic historical responsibility* both anchored in the pre-Hitler past and having found its expression in the events which occurred during the Third Reich. The overall background for the events may well be found in various trends in European history, but the immediate supporting system is firmly rooted in German soil. After the war, this representation shaped official German memory, as well as Western memory in general.[54]

Moreover, he argued, even if the structuralist-functionalist account ended up "with a somewhat paradoxical image of mass murder of a totally unprecedented kind being enacted without any clear representation of a primary *locus* of responsibility," like the older liberal narratives it was still very much concerned with the issue. All focused "on the fundamental responsibility of the perpetrators *as a German group within a system, the roots of which were to be found within German society*." Whatever had divided the older approaches, Friedlander acutely noted, "some kind of implicit moral stand suffused the representation of the past and the criminality of the system was perceived from the viewpoint of the victims."[55]

To be sure, like the *Historikerstreit* historians, the classical "totalitarian" approach employed an essentially comparative method but it did not, Friedlander insisted, entail relativization because, as he correctly identified its informing tacit assumption, it *"ultimately maintained the Nazi case as the nec plus ultra, in relation to which the other crimes were measured."* All the traditional approaches had—at least implicitly—set the criminal dimensions at center stage. That did not mean that their history was written from the known outcome backwards. Nevertheless, the authors as well as their readers agreed that "the sense of those twelve years was to be found in its catastrophic dimension."[56] All, explicitly or implicitly, distanced themselves from the object of study and there was no hint of relativizing Nazi crimes in any way. A moral consensus had obtained.

Now, Friedlander argued, conservative German historians like Nolte, Hillgruber, and Joachim Fest had fundamentally shifted the established forms of reference and questioned "the specificity of Nazi crimes in order, essentially, to contextualize the problem of historical responsibility and thereby to solve the issue of German identity within a traditional national mode."[57] In Nolte's ascription of the Holocaust to "a reaction born out of the anxiety of the annihilating consequences of the Russian revolution," the "traditional perpetrator of the early narratives becomes a potential victim" and "the *source* of all evil is placed outside of the traditional framework for the representation of historical responsibility."[58]

Friedlander explicitly distinguished the challenge of historicization from the work of the above historians. Still, he argued, by its emphases on the importance of social transformations and on the continuities of daily life, it "challenges the traditional view of the Nazi epoch which mainly focuses, in the last instance, on the political sphere and on its criminal dimension." It seeks, he wrote in his earliest article on the subject, to cancel

> the distance from the object of study which historians imposed upon themselves, quite naturally, when studying Nazism; it aims at reinserting the Nazi phenomenon into normal historical narrative, that is, at relativizing what still makes it appear as singular . . . The main thrust of the arguments for historicization is . . . to do away with the black-and-white picture of the Nazi era . . . by focusing on the bravery of the Wehrmacht on the Eastern front instead of the murderous core of the system, by following diverse social processes rather than the already "well-known" decisions taken in Berlin, there is the possibility that the core be left empty and relegated to the area of antiquated questions, too obsessively studied in the past. The new focus substantially changes the landscape and something—possibly the essential—becomes blurred.[59]

The champions of historicization presented their revision as if they were transcending the traditional, moralistic, black and white, partly mythical historiography of National Socialism and stepping into the domain of a supposed "objective" or "scientific" history. But this, Friedlander wrote, was naive. In effect, these historians were merely proposing an alternative narrative, dominated by a different agenda. The contending views could not be settled in historiographical terms, for they were determined by sets of *a priori* values.

Friedlander identified Martin Broszat as the main scholarly exemplar of this impulse and it was, indeed, in the wake of the *Historikerstreit* and Broszat's "A Plea for the Historicization of National Socialism," that their quite extraordinary correspondence took place.[60] It is a document that stands alone in the annals of the post-Shoah German Jewish dialogue. Most have either been sycophantic or, like the strained and defensive letters between Hermann Broch and Volkmar von Zuehlsdorff in the immediate post-war years, mutually uncomprehending, apologetic, and accusatory. The remarkable and prolonged exchange of views between Karl Jaspers and Hannah Arendt was not marred by such a lack of mutual empathy—as an early attempt to try to penetrate the depths of the Nazi evil it has no peer—but it was perhaps their very closeness, the proximity of views, that precluded it from having the productive tensions that illuminate the Broszat-Friedlander correspondence.[61] As Friedlander put it when the dialogue came to an end: "The inner tension, which, to various degrees, accompanied our exchange of letters, may have been, among other things, the expression of a fundamental commitment to the values which have prompted both of us to devote our entire professional lives to the study of the Nazi epoch. This tension does not stem from a divergence in basic values, but from differences in perspectives which, nevertheless, appear to us to be of major importance."[62]

The correspondence is characterized by a self-conscious understanding of the special, peculiarly charged nature of their post-Shoah conversation. Friedlander articulated it thus: "The fundamental difficulty of such a dialogue remains . . . and is compounded by the layers of ritualized behavior and gross interests which cover it. . . . Some measure of openness belongs to our 'experiment' and this openness, as you yourself noted, is the only possible basis for a true German-Jewish dialogue."[63] Refreshingly shorn of apologetics and with striking sophisticated candor, these two masters took up vital issues that until then had been submerged, outlawed as too sensitive for cross-national academic dialogue.

The letters dealt with numerous issues but at their animating center stood the question of the place of Auschwitz. Broszat explicitly acknowledged its crucial importance within the Western moral economy. "A point is reached in confronting the singular event of Auschwitz," he wrote, "where scientific comprehensibility and explicability doubtless are far outstripped by the sheer epochal significance of the event." But he also pointed out the historiographical danger that derived from this centrality, "an attempt to unfurl the entire history of the Third Reich in reverse fashion backwards starting from Auschwitz, instead of unfolding its development in a forward direction, in keeping with historical methodology." Moreover, he noted, the ease of the liquidations was made possible precisely because it was not in the limelight of events, because it was able to be concealed and kept quiet:

It is evident that the role of Auschwitz in the original historical context of action is one that is significantly different from its subsequent importance in terms of later historical perspective. The German historian too will certainly accept that Auschwitz—due to its singular significance—functions in retrospection as the central event of the Nazi period. Yet qua scientist and scholar, he cannot readily accept that Auschwitz also be made, after the fact, into the cardinal point, the hinge on which the entire factual complex of historical events of the Nazi period turns. He cannot simply accept without further ado that this entire complex of history be moved into the shadow of Auschwitz— yes, that Auschwitz even be made into the decisive measuring-rod for the historical perception of this period.[64]

Friedlander has never doubted that Auschwitz should indeed be made the measuring-rod of the period and his answers in this respect were tuned to that ongoing sensitivity:

> I agree with you that the historian, as historian, cannot consider the Nazi era from its catastrophic end only . . . we have to start at the beginning and follow the manifold paths as they present themselves, including numerous developments within German society which had little to do with Auschwitz, and this throughout the history of the era. But the historian *knows the end* . . . This knowledge should not hamper the exploration of all the possible avenues and interpretations, but it compels the historian to choose the central elements around which his unfolding narrative is implicitly built. In short, we come back to the problem of focus.[65]

Moreover, Friedlander insisted that "although the destruction of the Jews may have been a minor point in the perceptions and policies of the Allies during the war, it seems, more and more, that it loomed as a hidden but perceived fact in many German minds, during the war itself . . . indeed, normal life with the knowledge of ongoing massive crimes committed by one's own nation and one's own society is not so normal after all. . . ."[66] In his reply Broszat hastened to point out that his call for historicization of National Socialism was "a plea for normalization of the method, not of the evaluation."[67]

Friedlander later reflected "that the ultimate significance of [Broszat's] plea and of the debates that followed was, in the most general sense, about memory itself."[68] Indeed, a great deal of Friedlander's personal and professional life has been concerned with analyzing its mediated, complex dynamics.[69] He is a master of the commemorative inscriptions and the ways in which the "memory" of National Socialism continues to be molded and refashioned according to changing modes of collective and personal self-understanding, and mobilized and manipulated by divergent political interests and psychological needs.[70] No one has more acutely mapped the major strategies of its appropriation and canonization or the guiles and techniques of its repression, neutralization, and displacement.

Yet, given his sense of the complexities, his thought is torn between documenting National Socialism's irrepressible role "as a past that will not go away" and an anxiety that it will disappear from viable memory. There is an internal tension between his fear that with the passing of living personal memories the event will fade into a kind of ritualized oblivion, and the conviction that something "in the nature of the events themselves gives it some of its apparent irreducibility and therefore of its persistence."[71] He has chronicled the well-nigh universal recognition of Nazism as the great transgressive moment of Western civilization, yet noted that the catastrophe "has not been incorporated into any compelling framework of meaning in public consciousness."[72]

Friedlander is best in dissecting the ways in which this limit-event operates within various national moral economies, political ideologies, and collective identities.[73] Of course, this most critically applies to German and Jewish memory where, as Friedlander puts it, "the representation of this past has a present dimension of major importance."[74] While perhaps best known for his watchful eye over the developing gyrations of "perpetrator" memory ("For the last forty years, Germans belonging to at least two generations have been caught between the impossibility of remembering and the impossibility of forgetting"),[75] Friedlander has also cast a watchful eye over modes of Israeli commemoration.[76] He has written insightfully on the ideologically interested nature of Shoah inscriptions and its uses and abuses within Israeli society.[77] He has analyzed its "canonic" functions (the political appropriation of the Holocaust as a mobilizing, justifying myth bolstering an ultra-nationalist mystique) as well as its "subversive" uses (its employment as a "comparative" tool to criticize Israeli occupation policies). He has observed the close ties between the state of war and the centrality of the Shoah within national narration. He has strongly stated that it would be tragic if "the memory of catastrophes and particularly of the Holocaust will be so deeply ingrained in Jewish collective consciousness as to become an impediment to the progress toward peace."[78] Yet, perhaps because of his sense of national identification (complex and ironic though it may be) and an awareness that, regardless of its manipulations and abuses, these are nevertheless narratives of the victims, he has always tended to keep such critical remarks rather low-keyed, and his analytic attention and acuity focused elsewhere.

It will come as no surprise to learn that Friedlander has written far more intensively and anxiously about the question of German memory, as we already have had occasion to see. The reason for this is clear: "The representation of the Nazi epoch cannot be considered as already beyond the pale of relevant historical consciousness. It remains an imperative knowledge not only for its own sake or for understanding the scope of criminal human potentialities, but more directly in terms of present-day political responsibility."[79]

For all that, the most illuminating aspect of his ruminations on public memory and collective identity are those concerned with the subtle interdependencies between "perpetrators" and "victims": "On a symbolic level . . . one may speak of a Jewish memory of Auschwitz and of a German one. Although the incompatibility between these two memories may be growing, they are helplessly interwoven in what has been called a 'negative symbiosis'. . . . Any re-elaboration of one memory directly impinges on the other; any neutralization casts an overall shadow of oblivion. Neither Jews nor Germans can relate to their own memory without relating to the other's as well."[80] Friedlander is, of course, aware that this model is too simplistic and that no monolithic "German" or "Jewish" collective memory can be unequivocally located; differentiations and nuances are to be found on and between both sides. Still, was not this kind of tension and dynamic exemplified in the exchange with Broszat and does it not, to some degree or another, reverberate each time the fragile cultural, political, economic, and historiographical relationship between the two groups is called into question?

"Memory" is, of course, expressed in diverging and competing modes of representation and historical narration, and, given Friedlander's sensitivities and priorities, it should come as no great surprise that it was he who was instrumental in bringing to the fore and raising for discussion the manifold ways in which postmodernism[81] has affected discussion concerning the "Final Solution."[82] Postmodernism, with its rejection, as Friedlander puts it, "of the possibility of identifying some stable reality or truth beyond the constant polysemy and self-referentiality of linguistic constructs challenges the need to establish the truth and realities of the Holocaust."[83] He demonstrates how this decidedly ironic epistemological sensibility and its accompanying "disconnection between moral judgement, aesthetic norms, and intellectual analysis" tends to undermine what he tellingly describes as the natural "monumental-didactic" narrative structure of the prevalent paradigm and erodes the normative moral and symbolic status of Nazism within the culture.[84] He takes issue with a postmodernist positing of "reality" as essentially embodied in (if not entirely created by) narrative emplotments and rhetorical modes and choices. "*It is,*" he argues, "*the reality and significance of modern catastrophes that generate the search for a new voice and not the use of a specific voice which constructs the significance of these catastrophes.*"[85]

Yet if for Friedlander postmodernism problematizes the grounds of Holocaust historiography, it also renders it more critically self-conscious and, indeed, provides some subtle modes for its expansion and refinement. He notes some of its possible benefits and advantages thus: "the very openness of postmodernism to what cannot yet be formulated in decisive statements, but merely sensed, directly relates to whoever considers that even the most precise historical renditions of the Shoah contain an opaqueness at the core which confronts traditional historical narrative." [86] We should not be blind, then, to a certain affinity, an implicit sympathy, which Friedlander's stance evinces toward this approach. This is so because various aspects of this sensibility reinforce Friedlander's continuing insistence upon the limits of understanding, "the unease in interpretation," [87] the ultimate inaccessibility and inexplicability of this transgressive event. This emphasis on the essential opacity of the "Final Solution" demands critical attention for it stands at the core of much of his work.

Few people have written more suggestively or provided such rich insights into the structure of Nazism as Friedlander. Yet, unlike, for example, Raul Hilberg's "process and machinery of destruction," Hannah Arendt's "banality of evil," Christopher Browning's "ordinary men," or even Daniel Goldhagen's "ordinary Germans," he offers no unifying explanatory scheme nor, indeed, would he want his work to be subsumed into any general theoretical framework. This is a principled resistance. As we have seen, one of the motivating aspects of his thinking has been to demonstrate the ways in which the radical singularity of the event makes it impossible to persuasively integrate it into any global historiographical interpretation and, thus, render it less amenable to conventional explanation. The unknown, he writes, "is not being assimilated by the known; the unprecedented, although constantly drawing upon precedent motifs and images, is not transformed into new understanding; the imaginative leap has only partly succeeded; the mind is not at rest." [88]

It is true that Friedlander often claims that the extrication of a "rational historiography" is "ever necessary." He has written: "The extermination of the Jews of Europe is as accessible to both representation and interpretation as any other historical event." [89] Already in 1976, he was quite aware that the positing of a radical singularity laid it open to charges that it was ". . . an anomaly of history which may have the utmost significance on a theological or even philosophical level, but falls outside the scope of any historical interpretation. By trying to escape the banalization of the Holocaust through the use of inadequate generalizations or outright evasions, do we not fall into the other extreme, that of making the Holocaust an event so unique in human history that we cannot give it any signification whatsoever?" His answer, then, was that if the Shoah resisted these explanatory and contextual generalizations, it was "nevertheless the result of cumulative historical trends which, can, in part at least, be identified and explained."[90]

Of late—in ways that conform closely to a postmodernist sensibility and which satisfies the issues of historicization debated with Martin Broszat—he has even programmatically set out the ground rules for an improved, more sensitive historical narrative in which a certain critical self-awareness remains cardinal and in which the voice of the commentator is explicitly present:

> The commentary should disrupt the facile linear progression of the narration, introduce alternative interpretations, question any partial conclusion, withstand the need for closure. Because of the necessity of some form of narrative sequence . . . such commentary may introduce splintered or constantly recurring refractions of a traumatic past by using any number of vantage points. The dimension added by the commentary may allow for an integration of the so-called mythic memory of the victims within the overall representation of this past without its becoming an obstacle to rational historiography. For instance, whereas the historical narrative may have to stress the ordinary aspects of everyday life during most of the twelve years of the Nazi epoch, the "voice-over" of the victims' memories may puncture such normality, at least at the level of commentary.[91]

For all that, Friedlander's most distinctive efforts have been expended on demonstrating the difficulties, perhaps even the principled impossibilities, of this "ever-elusive goal" of rational historiography.[92] He goes so far as to say that "even if new forms of historical narrative were to develop, or new modes of representation, and even if literature and art were to probe the past from unexpected vantage points, the opaqueness of some 'deep memory' would probably not be dispelled."[93] For, as he repeatedly insists, "we are dealing with an event which tests our traditional conceptual and representational categories, an 'event at the limits.'"[94]

In effect, Friedlander's analyses of such opacity, the sources of this ultimate un-integrability and inexplicability, are numerous, even overdetermined. The basis of incomprehension derives, in the first place, from the nature of the event itself. For it broke "the most fundamental of all taboos: the Nazi perpetration of systematic, prolonged extermination of categories of human beings considered as non-human. Such behavior causes instinctive repulsion at the level of the species as well as that of the individual. The very disappearance of these psychological (or sociobiological) barriers concerning the 'scientific' mass killing of other human beings represents, it seems to me, the first and foremost issue for which our usual categories of interpretation are insufficient."[95]

It is not only the event itself, but the protective neutralizing responses to the event, that similarly reinforce and express the limits of understanding. Fifteen years ago Friedlander wrote that

> . . . systematic historical research, which uncovers the facts in their most precise and most meticulous interconnection also protects us from the past, thanks to the inevitable paralysis of language. That is the exorcism and *the involuntary evasion to which we are all subject* and whose mechanism has to be taken apart . . . In some ways the scholarly mind does not allow an emotional reaction. It is blocked and immediately replaced by a problem drawn from the text. . . . And paralysis of language aside, what is the fundamental characteristic of this exorcism? To put the past back into bearable dimensions, superimpose it upon the known and respected progress of human behavior, put it into the identifiable course of things, into the unmysterious march of ordinary history, into the reassuring world of the rules that are the basis of our society . . . There should be no misunderstanding about what I am trying to say: The historian cannot work in any other way, and historical studies have to be pursued along the accepted lines. The events described are what is unusual, not the historian's work. We have reached the limits of our means of expression. Others we do not possess.[96]

More recently, Friedlander has argued that the *"historian can analyze the phenomenon from the 'outside', but, in this case, his unease stems from the incongruence between intellectual probing, and the blocking of intuitive comprehension of events that happened more or less during his or her lifetime, within his or her society."*[97] Our understanding of the basic transgressive moving forces—such as the elation that animated the perpetrators and which was created by the very dimensions of the killing—is simply blocked at the level of self-awareness.

Indeed, perhaps most compellingly and controversially, Friedlander argues that the unease, the exorcisms, neutralizations, and interpretive rationalizations are not only post-facto responses but (as in the commitment to secrecy) were built into the event, practiced by the Nazis themselves. "It is a neutralization in which we all take part and which . . . began in a certain way at the heart of the Nazi phenomenon itself, even as the extermination was at its height."[98] In parallel fashion, our own "paralysis of comprehension" is a kind of mirror of the inability of bystanders and victims themselves to grasp what was transpiring.

I would suggest that Friedlander's emphasis upon this meta-level, what he calls the "undefined but clearly felt *limits to interpretation*," the need for "*a sense of self-restraint about the available repertoire*,"[99] derives less from methodological or even historiographical concerns than from essentially moral ones. Nothing disturbs him more than "the danger of breaking the barrier of the imagination that is Auschwitz."[100] His insistence upon radical singularity has entailed adopting a strategy of what can be dubbed (in almost Adornian terms) as a kind of "negative incommensurability," a built-in *resistance* to meaning and lesson-drawing. He underlines that there is nothing commensurable with the enormity of the event that this past can teach us. Despite the many tomes seeking to do so, it does not significantly instruct us about the nature of "industrial society" or "modernity": the "linkages are kept at such a level of generality that they are irrelevant or the contradictions become insuperable."[101] And while it is easy to draw a universally valid significance from the Shoah, the "difficulty appears when this statement is reversed. No universal lesson seems to require reference to the Shoah to be fully comprehended."[102]

"Paradoxically," Friedlander writes, the very exceptionality of the "Final Solution" makes it "inaccessible to all attempts at a significant representation and interpretation," perhaps rendering it "fundamentally irrelevant for the history of humanity and the understanding of the 'human condition.'"[103] Again, paradoxically, this incapacity to yield meaning—a judgment which Friedlander notes "applies also to my own work"[104]— flows either from a "blankness" or from what he terms "an excess," defined approvingly in Lyotardian terms as "'something [that] remains to be phrased which is not, something which is not determined.'"[105] When Friedlander quotes Maurice Blanchot to the effect that "working through" consists of the effort "to keep watch over absent meaning," he is, in effect, defining a crucial part of his own project.[106]

Given these kinds of pronouncements and a repeated emphasis on the opaque core of the matter, Friedlander's custodianship has been viewed by some critics as increasingly assuming the nature of a defensive "holding operation," an exercise in special pleading. As Martin Broszat put it in their exchange:

> I wonder whether your skepticism necessarily has to burden our discourse
> with such a high degree of suspicion, which I can repeatedly sense behind
> your comments and remarks. . . . Haven't you yourself staked out such
> definite positions in your suspicious distrust of possible tendencies toward
> trivialization and minimization in dealing with the Nazi period in the
> work of German historians . . . that you are no longer able to break free
> from and abandon these positions, even here in this exchange of letters?
> . . . haven't you also erected a fence around yourself, one which only per-
> mits you "some measure of openness"?[107]

For "bread-and-butter" historians, Friedlander's utterances regarding "absent meaning," "opaqueness at the core," and so on may well appear rather vague, too allusive (if not outright elusive), almost mystificatory.

To be sure, Friedlander's strictures on closure—consonant with postmodernism's suspicion of totalizing history—are unexceptionable, though one would want to ask whether, in any area of historical inquiry characterized by its dynamic nature, such closures ever actually occur. The Shoah was indeed a radically new occurrence characterized by a lack of comprehension and a stunned *Begriffslosigkeit* (lack of adequate concepts). But novelty is not equivalent to inexplicability. The unprecedented may simply require new and increasingly refined categories and tools of understanding and should not necessarily be regarded as in principle inaccessible. There are many historians who simply will not accept that this object of study must perforce remain "indeterminate, elusive, and opaque."[108]

Would it be unreasonable to argue that the "Final Solution" was a secular, human event that occurred at a particular, identifiable time and place and that—while always keeping the radical and unprecedented dimensions of the event clearly in mind—it should be equally amenable to the rules and methods that govern the increasingly refined and self-reflexive practice of historiography in general? To be sure, most historians would agree that no event can ever be fully grasped from "within" or that we can arrive at some form of "ultimate knowledge." By and large, the craft is animated by the conviction that comprehensibility is a finite, changing, and plural state rather than a single, final one. "In one sense," Michael Marrus writes, "the Holocaust will forever be . . .'unimaginable.' Yet . . . much the same could be said, mutatis mutandis, about many other things as well. . . . Historians are used to trampling over their fields while suspending judgements on the fundamental issues that are ultimately at stake. . . . We simply do the best we can, knowing that our efforts are necessarily imperfect, incomplete and inadequate."[109]

Moreover, given the inevitable dynamic, the built-in shifts in historical perspective that come naturally with time and changing contemporary experience and the imperatives of the historical profession, in a matter as complex, loaded, and dense as the Shoah, no theoretical or methodological Orthodoxy, no holding operation, can possibly be expected to pertain.[110] The matter will continue to be fluid and marked by a plurality of approaches and perspectives even if Friedlander is correct to write darkly that the sheer diversification, complexity, and multitude of studies of the Nazi era "tends to erase the sharp outlines of certain central issues, be they conceptual or ethical. Therefore, whether one wishes it or not, the very momentum of historiography may serve to neutralize the past."[111] One could argue against this position and claim that the problematization of the past and the vital debates thus generated will keep the memory most relevantly alive: "the surest engagement with memory," James Young has written, "lies in its perpetual irresolution."[112] At any rate, despite—or perhaps because of—its attendant difficulties, the very magnitude of Auschwitz has rendered inevitable a plethora of attempts at interpretive historical comprehension. "After fifty years," Arno Mayer writes, "the question is no longer whether or not to reappraise and historicize the Judeocide, but rather how to do so responsibly."[113]

Mayer's own attempt to contextualize the "Final Solution" within a larger global historical interpretation was, indeed, far from satisfactory.[114] But, it seems to me, attempts of this kind do not necessarily, as Friedlander suggests in various places, have to be doomed in principle. Could not one, for instance, persuasively relate it to the overall imperial vision of the racial Nazi State with its grandiose bio-eugenic policies of mass resettlement and enslavement, its interlinked measures combining philoregenerative "positive" programmes for the *Volksgemeinschaft* with a series of increasingly radical measures against "abnormal" and "unwanted" elements? The mass sterilizations, the euthanasia program, and the murder and persecutions of the Gypsies, the "asocials," and the homosexuals are only comprehensible within the informing framework of such a bio-eugenic framework. They also informed the massive repopulation programs. Himmler's *Generalplan Ost* envisaged shifting 31 million non-Germans across Eastern Europe not only in order to get rid of such "inferior" peoples but also to facilitate the resettlement of Germans and *Volksdeutsche*.[115] Indeed, in inextricable fashion, the murderous impulses of Auschwitz arose within the context of an overall plan to ethnically "purify," reconstruct, and re-Germanize the surrounding upper Silesian areas. Himmler viewed towns such as Auschwitz, Blachstadt, and Saybusch as relics of medieval German colonization and sought to convert these into model ecological, urban, and architectural centers.[116]

Many historians are currently arguing that it is within this informing bio-eugenic context that the extermination of the Jews needs to be located. To be sure, total extermination was reserved exclusively for the Jews—and Friedlander is correct always to emphasize the specificity of what he has recently called "redemptive" anti-Semitism, "this synthesis of a murderous rage and an idealistic goal, shared by the Fuehrer and the hard core of the party."[117] "The criminal dimension," he wrote in 1976, "is certainly the same in every case of genocide, be the victims Armenians, Jews or Tutsis; the attempt at total physical eradication may sometimes be identical, but the motivations are quite different; in that sense, the Nazi exterminatory drive against the Jew remains unmistakably singular."[118] But placing this drive within a more global context and theory does not necessarily weaken the claim; it may instead sharpen our understanding and explain the major enabling preconditions. Thus the imperial bio-eugenic framework may help to explain how such anti-Semitic impulses were able to take on precisely the character upon which Friedlander insists: its entirely novel, systematically genocidal form. In this view, killing the Jews was not something separate from but triggered by, and the outer edge of, this total, transgressive vision of racial community.

To be sure, Friedlander does write about, and is sensitive to, these overall brutalizing forces and the other victimizing programs of National Socialism. But he insists that they were in no way causally linked to the "Final Solution." Despite the fact that they were roughly simultaneous and parallel developments, they were quite separate policies, characterized by "different origins and different aims." [119] He does state that these ideological trends reinforced each other, that *"the separateness and compatibility of both the specific anti-Jewish and the general racial and eugenic trends were at the very center of the Nazi system."* [120] But this is a point of view which is simply suggested and which is never quite integrated into the fabric of his narrative. Friedlander's commitment to the totality and singularity of the drive against the Jews has resulted in a refusal to locate it within such an informing bio-eugenic framework, a framework that, while it contextualizes matters differently, in no way undermines the special pathology directed against the Jews. [121]

Wulf Kansteiner has recently pitted Friedlander's historiographic strategy of "exceptionality" against the backdrop of what he sees as an opposite, developing trend that regards Nazism and the Shoah as exemplifications of wider processes, integrable and explicable within larger contexts, comparable to other historical events, and able to illuminate a variety of theoretical and political issues. Friedlander's dictum concerning the inaccessibility of significant representation and interpretation, Kansteiner argues, his notion that the only truth of the "Final Solution" is its extraordinary resistance to rationalizations of any kind, necessarily results in a paradox. While the new contextualism "naturalizes" the event in order to circumvent the concept of the Holocaust's incomprehensibility, Friedlander takes up "an impossible task, the attempt to stabilize and defend an interpretive void." [122]

I shall come back to this matter in a moment but before doing so should note that even if for Friedlander the history of the Holocaust must ultimately remain opaque, he himself is nevertheless constantly engaged in the attempt to write it—as his powerful new narrative, replete with persuasive "positive" interpretations, amply demonstrates. This should not be regarded as a damning contradiction but rather as a productive tension in his work. There is no reason why his thought on meta-matters should always neatly dovetail with the narrative content of his concrete history. In fact, as we have seen, Friedlander has consistently applied his meta-critical observations to his own work.

Yet, beyond this, there is something about the nature of his custodianship, his detection of biases, the battles he wages, the level and focus of his analyses, and the values he upholds that constitutes a unique and indispensable cultural presence. It may or may not be that this "holding operation," "keeping watch over absent meaning" will prove to be a Sisyphean task. But its eloquent insistencies—morally sensitive, ethically tuned, yet never cloying, evasive, or self-righteousness—are nevertheless vital to the slippery interpretive processes whereby Western, German, and Jewish collectivities continuing to recall, contest, commemorate, and elide their catastrophic past. Saul Friedlander is a consummate analyst of these worlds—and a master of a discipline that should never have come to be.

Notes

Index

Notes

1. I have tried to map some of the key dimensions of this paradoxical link in my *Culture and Catastrophe: German and Jewish Confrontations with National Socialism and Other Crises* (New York: New York University Press, 1996).

CHAPTER I. FRIEDRICH NIETZSCHE, MAX NORDAU, AND *DEGENERATION*

Paper first published in *Journal of Contemporary History* 28, no. 4 (October 1993): 643–57. Reprinted by permission of Sage Publications.

1. This essay is based upon a presentation given at a conference sponsored by the University of Paris in July 1992 on *Max Nordau: Parisian Writer, German Philosopher, Zionist Activist*.

2. For a typical example of this, see the various mentions of Nordau in the collection of essays edited by J. Edward Chamberlin & Sander L.Gilman, *Degeneration: The Dark Side of Progress* (New York: Columbia University Press, 1985).

3. Daniel Pick, *Faces of Degeneration: A European Disorder, c. 1848–1918* (Cambridge: Cambridge University Press, 1989), 23.

4. See Max Nordau, *Degeneration*, introduction by George L. Mosse (New York: Howard Fertig, 1968), 551.

5. Ibid., 537.

6. Ibid., 415.

7. Ibid., 5.

8. Nordau differed in one important respect from Lombroso. He did not accept that geniuses were insane; rather, the fact that these artists were degenerate was an indication to him that they could not have been geniuses! Nevertheless, based on precisely this misunderstanding of his position, one of Nordau's degenerates, Oscar Wilde, produced a characteristic witticism: "I quite agree with Dr. Nordau's assertion that all men of genius are insane, but Dr. Nordau forgets that all sane men are idiots." See Richard Ellmann, *Oscar Wilde* (London: Penguin, 1988), 517.

9. Nordau, *Degeneration*, 17.

197

10. See Nordau's dedication to Professor Caesar Lombroso in *Degeneration*, esp. vii.

11. The best known rebuttal is by George Bernard Shaw, *The Sanity of Art: An Exposure of the Current Nonsense about Artists Being Degenerate* (London: New Age Press, 1908).

12. Dr. Hermann Tuerck described the way in which Nietzsche's mental condition was translated into his moral and philosophical system: "Thus, it may happen that an intellectual and highly gifted man, born with perverted instincts, and feeling as torment . . . the nonsatisfaction of instinct, will hit upon the idea of justifying the passion for murder, the extremest egoism . . . as something good, beautiful, and according to Nature, and to characterize as morbid aberration the better opposing moral instincts . . . ." See Hermann Tuerck, *Friedrich Nietzsche und seine philosophische Irrwege* (Dresden: Gloess, 1891), 7. Nordau liberally quoted this work. See also the stamp of medical-professional authority given to these notions in Paul Julius Moebius, *Ueber das Pathologische bei Nietzsche* (Wiesbaden: J. F. Bergmann, 1902).

13. Nordau, *Degeneration*, 416.

14. Gilman's incisive essay, "The Nietzsche Murder Case; or, What Makes Dangerous Philosophies Dangerous," appears in his *Difference and Pathology: Stereotypes of Sexuality, Race, and Madness* (Ithaca, N.Y.: Cornell University Press, 1985). See esp. 59.

15. Whole books—pro and con—were written about the phenomenon of Nietzsche cults. For examples and an analysis of the cultural significance of this new influence, see Steven Aschheim, *The Nietzsche Legacy in Germany, 1890– 1990* (Berkeley & Los Angeles: University of California Press, 1992), esp. chap. 2.

16. Nordau, *Degeneration*, 453.

17. For a good outline of Nordau's system of thinking, see George L. Mosse's introduction to Nordau, *Degeneration*, esp. xxi.

18. Nordau, *Degeneration*, 243.

19. Ibid., 540.

20. Ibid., 560.

21. For some examples of such treatments, see David B. Allison, *The New Nietzsche: Contemporary Styles of Interpretation* (Cambridge, Mass.: MIT Press, 1985); Nancy S. Love, *Marx, Nietzsche, and Modernity* (New York: Columbia University Press, 1986); Clayton Koelb, ed., *Nietzsche as Postmodernist: Essays Pro and Contra* (Albany: State University of New York Press, 1990).

22. Friedrich Nietzsche, *The Gay Science*, book 1, trans. Walter Kaufmann (New York: Random House, 1974), 79.

23. Nordau, *Degeneration*, 55–56. "The consciousness of a healthy, strong-minded, and consequently attentive man," Nordau wrote, "resembles a room in the full light of day, in which the eye sees all objects distinctly, in which all outlines are sharp, and wherein no indefinite shadows are floating."

24. See Friedrich Nietzsche, *The Will to Power*, ed. Walter Kaufmann (New York: Random House, 1968), 293.

25. Nietzsche, *Will to Power*, 330.

26. Friedrich Nietzsche, "On Truth and Lie in an Extra-Moral Sense"

(1873), a fragment published posthumously. This piece can be found in *The Portable Nietzsche*, ed. Walter Kaufmann (New York: Viking Press, 1968), 46–47.

27. Nietzsche, *Will to Power*, 535.

28. Nordau, *Degeneration*, 458.

29. Friedrich Nietzsche, *The Birth of Tragedy*, trans. Walter Kaufmann (New York: Random House, 1967), Section 1: 37.

30. Nordau, *Degeneration*, 64.

31. Ibid., 543.

32. For some interesting comments on Nordau's views on art, see P. M. Baldwin, "Liberalism, Nationalism, and Degeneration: The Case of Max Nordau," in *Central European History* 12:2 (June 1980): 102.

33. Nordau, *Degeneration*, 543.

34. Ibid., 541.

35. The most systematic analysis of the nature and wide dissemination of this discourse is to be found in Pick, *Faces of Degeneration*.

36. "On the Gift-giving Virtue" 1, "Thus Spoke Zarathustra" in Nietzsche, *Portable Nietzsche*, 187. Italics in original.

37. Nietzsche, *Will to Power*, 142.

38. Nordau, *Degeneration*, 551.

39. Ibid., 557.

40. See Max Nordau, *The Conventional Lies of Mankind* (Chicago: L. Schick, 1884), 51.

41. Magnus Hirschfeld, *Geschlechtskunde III. Band. Einblicke und Ausblicke* (Stuttgart: Julius Puettmann, 1930), 257.

42. The entire thrust of my book *The Nietzsche Legacy in Germany, 1890–1990* is to establish the multiple, often contradictory nature of Nietzsche's influence and the impossibility of reducing it to an "essential" political direction or position. Clearly, this should be kept in mind here but little would be served by rehearsing all this again. This essay, obviously, deals with only *one* strand of influence.

43. For instance, he wrote: "Good nature is in a woman a form of degeneration." The degree of metaphor, irony, and literality in such statements are clearly open to interpretation. Friedrich Nietzsche, "Why I Write Such Good Books," in *Ecce Homo*, ed. Walter Kaufmann (New York: Random House, 1969), Section 5: 266.

44. Ibid., "The Birth of Tragedy," Section 4: 274. My translation differs somewhat from Kaufmann's.

45. For various examples see chapters 8, 9, and the afterword of Aschheim, *The Nietzsche Legacy*. While there were always those who opposed this alliance, these forces were never decisive.

46. On this point see the generally informative article by Jens Malte Fischer, "'Entarte Kunst' Zur Geschichte eines Begriffs," *Merkur* 38:1 (January 1984).

47. All the differences between Nietzsche and Nazism notwithstanding, as Jacques Derrida has pointed out, there "is nothing absolutely contingent about the fact that the only political regimen to have *effectively* brandished his name as a major and official banner was Nazi." See Jacques Derrida, *The Ear of the Other*

(New York: Schocken, 1985), 31. And, as Martin Jay has written, "while it may be questionable to saddle Marx with responsibility for the Gulag Archipelago or blame Nietzsche for Auschwitz, it is nonetheless true that their writings could be misread as justifications for these horrors in a way that, say, those of John Stuart Mill or Alexis de Tocqueville could not." See Martin Jay, "Should Intellectual History Take a Linguistic Turn? Reflections on the Habermas-Gadamer Debate" in Martin Jay, *Fin-de-Siècle Socialism* (New York & London: Routledge, 1988), 33.

48. See George L. Mosse's paper for this conference, "Max Nordau, Liberalism, and the New Jew," *Journal of Contemporary History* 27:4 (October 1992): 565.

49. See Nordau, *The Conventional Lies of Mankind*, and also Max Nordau, *Paradoxes*, trans. J. R. McIlraith (London: William Heinemann, 1906).

50. Nordau, *Conventional Lies of Mankind*, 132–33.

51. See "Introduction," in Nordau, *Degeneration*, xix–xx. Mosse points out that this tough, disciplined liberalism was quite different from the open and permissive twentieth-century version.

52. Ibid., xxi. Nordau's conception of human solidarity was based upon his view of the interdependence of all living matter within a scientifically determined universe.

53. Nietzsche, *Will to Power*, 539.

54. Nordau, *Conventional Lies of Mankind*, 353.

55. Max Nordau, *Morals and the Evolution of Man* (Biologie der Ethik) (London & New York: Cassell & Company, Ltd., 1922), 82. The work was first published in 1916. See also 276 for an example of how Nordau's hero differs from the Nietzschean version: "heroism is the noblest victory of a thinking and volitional personality over selfishness; it is altruism which rises to self-sacrifice, the proud subjugation by Reason of the most primitive . . . of all instincts, . . . self-preservation . . . heroic conduct liberates [the hero] from the trammels of his individuality and enlarges this to represent a community, its longings, its resolutions."

56. Nietzsche, *Will to Power*, 61; Nordau, *Morals and the Evolution of Man*, 278.

CHAPTER 2. THINKING THE NIETZSCHE LEGACY TODAY

1. This essay is based upon a paper presented at the New York University International Conference on "Nietzsche Today" in October 1994.

2. I have explored this in detail for the German case in *The Nietzsche Legacy in Germany, 1890–1990* (Berkeley & Los Angeles: University of California Press, 1992).

3. Ernst Bertram, *Nietzsche: Versuch einer Mythologie* (Berlin: G. Bondi, 1918), 5.

4. See chapters 8, 9, and the afterword of Aschheim, *Nietzsche Legacy*.

5. Friedrich Nietzsche, *The Will to Power*, ed. Walter Kaufmann (New York: Vintage Books, 1968), 960; (1885–1886), 504.

6. See Georges Bataille, *On Nietzsche*, trans. Bruce Boone (New York: Paragon, 1992). On Bataille's politics and special brand of Nietzscheanism see Aschheim, *Nietzsche Legacy*, 229–30, 292–95.

7. There is no end of supporting contemporary examples of this. At the "higher" levels of discourse this was best illustrated by Heidegger who initially viewed Nazism (and Fascism) as essentially Nietzschean projects, the most radical attempts to overcome Western nihilism. "The two men," he proclaimed in his 1936 lectures on Schelling, "who each in his own ways, have introduced a counter-movement to nihilism—Mussolini and Hitler—have learned from Nietzsche, each in an essentially different way. But even with that, Nietzsche's authentic metaphysical domain has not yet come into its own." Quoted in Thomas Sheehan, "Heidegger and the Nazis," *New York Review of Books*, 16 June 1988.

8. Alain de Benoist was an early French exception to this statement. See his *Nietzsche: morale et grande politique* (Paris: n.p., 1973).

9. Georg Lukács, *The Destruction of Reason*, trans. Peter Palmer (Atlantic Highlands, N.J.: Humanities Press, 1981), 341. The work was completed in 1952 but based on essays written in the 1930s and 1940s.

10. Walter Kaufmann, *Nietzsche: Philosopher, Psychologist, Antichrist* (Princeton, N.J.: Princeton University Press, 1950).

11. Derrida has considered this question in detail in "Otobiographies: The Teaching of Nietzsche and the Politics of the Proper Name," in *The Ear of the Other: Otobiography Transference Translation*, ed. Christie V. McDonald, trans. Peggy Kamuf and Avital Ronell (New York: Schocken Books, 1985), see esp. 23–24, 30–31.

12. Our culture is awash with this Nietzsche. All the above-named authors' works should be consulted. For typical examples of this genre among many see Clayton Koelb, ed., *Nietzsche as Postmodernist: Essays Pro and Contra* (Albany: State University of New York, 1990), and David B. Allison, ed., *The New Nietzsche: Contemporary Styles of Interpretation* (Cambridge, Mass.: MIT Press, 1985).

13. On Kaufmann's denaturing of Nietzsche's power-political dimensions see Walter Sokel, "Political Uses and Abuses of Nietzsche in Walter Kaufmann's Image of Nietzsche," *Nietzsche-Studien* 12 (1983): 432–36.

14. See Ernst Behler, "Nietzsche jenseits der Dekonstruktion" in Josef Simon, ed., *Nietzsche in der Diskussion* (Würzburg: Königshausen & Neumann, 1985), 88–107.

15. For an interesting postmodernist exception, see Avital Ronell's application of Nietzschean immunological themes to current Californian problematics in "Hitting the Streets" in her *Finitude's Score: Essays for the End of the Millennium* (Lincoln: University of Nebraska Press, 1994), esp. 47–61.

16. See Jean-François Lyotard, *The Postmodern Condition: A Report on Knowledge* (Minneapolis: University of Minnesota Press, 1984).

17. Terry Eagleton, "Awakening from Modernity," *Times Literary Supplement*, 20 February 1987, 194.

18. In Germany more than elsewhere and for the mainstream intellectuals at least, the charged Nazi past endows the term Enlightenment with immediate

positive resonance and rich political connotations while the new Nietzscheans discussed in this essay harbor either a deep suspicion of or an active hostility towards it as an essential, manipulative tool of Western "metaphysics." See the interesting comments by Joachim Whaley, "Enlightenment and History in Germany," *The Historical Journal* 31 (1 March 1988): 195–99.

19. The most relevant text in this regard is Jürgen Habermas, *The Philosophical Discourse of Modernity*, trans. Frederick Lawrence (Cambridge, Mass.: MIT Press, 1987). Habermas declared prematurely in 1968 that Nietzsche was "no longer contagious" and has subsequently spent a considerable amount of time combating the epidemic! For his mistimed proclamation, see his "Zur Nietzsche Erkenntnistheorie" in Friedrich Nietzsche, *Erkenntnistheoretische Schriften* (Frankfurt: Suhrkamp, 1968).

20. The fact that Foucault and Habermas got on rather well does not alter the intellectual differences. See the excellent intellectual biography by James Miller (a work that I shall be drawing upon extensively in this essay) in *The Passion of Michel Foucault* (New York: Simon & Schuster, 1993), 337–38.

21. Terry Eagleton, for instance, relates this to the concrete French generational experience of 1968 and sees postmodernism as simultaneously a recognition of the failure and a displacement and recreation of the revolutionary moment. See "Marxism, Structuralism and Post-Structuralism" in *Against the Grain: Essays, 1975–1985* (London: Verso, 1986), 93. Eagleton, one of the shrewdest Marxist observers of postmodernism, puts it thus:

> Its profound pessimism (power is ubiquitous, the law inescapable, the ego impotent and derisory, truth and communication inconceivable, general theories of society terroristic, only marginal political activity feasible) is sure to be tracked to that source, as a later more theatrical version of Western Marxist melancholia. Similarly, the euphoria of post-structuralism—and its paradoxical other face—is at once displacement and recreation of the revolutionary moment: the orgasmic crisis of *jouissance,* the thrills and spills of the skidding signifier, the *éclat* of *écriture,* Lyotard's aging-hippie points of libidinal intensity.

See too James Miller, chap. 2, "Waiting for Godot," in *Passion of Michel Foucault* and Robert Young, chap. 1 in *White Mythologies: Writing History and the West* (London & New York: Routledge, 1990).

22. Koelb, ed., *Nietzsche as Postmodernist*, 5.

23. Of Foucault's *Madness and Civilization*, Derrida wrote, "The attempt to write the history of the decision, division, difference, runs the risk of construing the division of an event or a structure subsequent to the unity of an original presence, thereby confirming metaphysics in its fundamental operation." See Jacques Derrida, "Cogito and the History of Madness," in *Writing and Difference* (London: Routledge and Kegan Paul, 1981), 40.

24. Jacques Derrida, *Spurs/Nietzsche's Styles*, trans. Barbara Harlow (Chicago: University of Chicago Press, 1979), 75.

25. See the interesting volume edited by Richard Schacht, *Nietzsche, Genealogy, Morality: Essays on Nietzsche's Genealogy of Morals* (Berkeley & Los Angeles: University of California Press, 1994) and Gary Shapiro's essay "Translat-

ing, Repeating, Naming: Foucault, Derrida, and *The Genealogy of Morals*," in Koelb, ed., *Nietzsche as Postmodernist*.

26. Any number of examples of this genre would serve. For one, see Allison, *New Nietzsche*.

27. See his "Nietzsche: Nach Fünfzig Jahren," in Gottfried Benn, *Essays. Reden. Aufsätze* (Stuttgart: Ernst Klett, 1977), 488–93.

28. Here the French connection to Georges Bataille comes to mind. That early most radically transgressive Nietzschean, a man of the left who flirted with and was, for a time, attracted to the irrationalist Fascist thematic, displayed a radicalism and an attraction to the transgressive beyond that parallels Foucault. See note 6 of this essay.

29. I have summed up the scholarship from a number of sources. The biography by James Miller, *Passion of Michel Foucault* is basic here. See too Alexander Nehamas, "Subject and Abject: The Examined Life of Michel Foucault," *New Republic*, 15 February 1993, 27–36.

30. See Lilla's insightful remarks, "A Taste for Pain: Michel Foucault and the Outer Reaches of Human Experience," *Times Literary Supplement*, 26 March 1993, 3–4.

31. See Derrida, *Spurs/Nietzsche's Styles*, 101.

32. See the introduction to Paul Patton, ed., *Nietzsche, Feminism, & Political Theory* (London & New York: Routledge, 1993), xi.

33. See Diana Behler, "Nietzsche and Postfeminism," *Nietzsche-Studien* 22 (1993): 354–70. For another recent consideration of the issue see Peter Burgard, ed., *Nietzsche and the Feminine* (Charlottesville: University Press of Virginia, 1994).

34. Throughout the history of this legacy the appeal to any number of (left and right) political positions has been the radical Nietzschean promise—present but never clearly articulated; this after all, was the job of individual self-creation—of personal and collective transvaluation going beyond all previously thinkable forms. What parts of the feminist movement today regard as the necessary feminine transvaluations—the peace-loving, anti-war, nurturing feminine values—will not be easily reconciled with the kind of vitalist transvaluation Nietzsche so graphically outlined in many of his works.

35. See Aschheim, *Nietzsche Legacy*, 85–92.

36. See de Saint-Point's "Futurist Manifesto of Lust 1913" in Umbo Apollonio, *Futurist Manifestos* (London: Thames and Hudson, 1973), 70–74 and "Manifesto of the Futurist Woman" (1912) in *Futurism and Futurisms* (New York: Abbeville Press, 1986), 602–3. Italics in original.

37. Avital Ronell, "Hitting the Streets," in *Finitude's Score*, 69.

38. David Haar, "The Play of Nietzsche," in David Wood, ed., *Derrida: A Critical Reader* (Oxford: Blackwell, 1992), 57, 65.

39. See the essay by Maudemarie Clark, "Language and Deconstruction: Nietzsche, de Man, and Postmodernism" in Koelb, ed., *Nietzsche as Postmodernist*.

40. Ken Gemes, "Nietzsche's Critique of Truth," *Philosophy and Phenomenological Research* 52 (1992): 49.

41. See Ted Sadler, "The Postmodernist Politicization of Nietzsche," in Patton, ed., *Nietzsche, Feminism, & Political Theory.* See too Brian Leiter, "Perspectivism in Nietzsche's Genealogy of Morals," in Schacht, *Nietzsche, Genealogy, Morality,* 334–57.

42. See Walter Kaufmann, ed., *The Portable Nietzsche* (New York: Viking Press, 1954), 42–47.

43. Indeed, the assertion that Nietzsche would not recognize the very notion of "incorrect" readings has induced at least one critic to charge Paul de Man with "a grotesque misreading of a central passage about what might be called 'truth doing' in Nietzsche . . . he proceeds almost deliberately to distort the very different atmosphere of Nietzsche's late masterpieces." Richard H. Weisberg, "De Man Missing Nietzsche: *Hinzugedicthet* Revisited," in Koelb, ed., *Nietzsche as Postmodernist,* 111.

44. Daniel Conway, "Nietzsche Contra Nietzsche: The Deconstruction of Zarathustra," in Koelb, ed., *Nietzsche as Postmodernist,* 91.

45. Mark E. Warren, *Nietzsche and Political Thought* (Cambridge, Mass.: MIT Press, 1988), 157.

46. In an acute review of my work, John Toews commented that it would have been better had I revealed the ethical and value-laden contours of my own construction of the historic constructions of Nietzsche. These, I should have stressed, were clearly marked by my quest to understand the murderousness of the Nazis and a sense that—no matter how parodistically—Nietzsche was somehow implicated in this. At the same time, I also believe that his thought is too rich and complex to be simplistically reduced to this one historical outcome. See John E. Toews' review of Aschheim, *The Nietzsche Legacy,* in *Central European History* 26, no. 3 (1993): 353–55.

47. "The Antichrist," in Kaufmann, ed., *Portable Nietzsche,* 592–93.

48. See my paper "Nietzsche, Anti-Semitism, and the Holocaust" in Jacob Golomb, ed., *Nietzsche and Jewish Culture* (London: Routledge, 1997). See too Aschheim, *Nietzsche Legacy.*

49. This may be the place to situate myself within this problematic. As Terry Eagleton has pointed out (in *Against the Grain,* 85) both metaphysicians and "wild" deconstructionists believe that unless you have "the whole truth" you have none at all, specular images of each other in this as in much else. I would agree with Eagleton that radical contextualization for the historian does not mean the subversion of the truth but only adequate understanding of and tentative approach to it.

50. See the introduction in Koelb, ed., *Nietzsche as Postmodernist,* esp. 6–8.

51. On precisely this problem see the rather uneven collection of essays in Koelb, ed., *Nietzsche as Postmodernist.*

52. See his *Reflections of a Nonpolitical Man,* trans. Walter D. Morris (New York: F. Ungar, 1983), 13.

53. This has been recognized since Nietzsche-reception began. See Gerhard Hilbert, *Moderne Willensziele* (Leipzig: Deichert, 1911), 19. This was a very common theme adjusted to suit the proclivities of the particular commentator. Thus, as one put it, Nietzsche's struggle against his own time and the Christianity of his

age was "the anticipation of our own struggle, Nietzsche's inner tension, from which his spirit sprang, is our tension." See Theodor Odenwald, *Friedrich Nietzsche und das heutige Christentum* (Giessen: Alfred Töpelmann, 1926), 17, 23. Nietzsche, Thomas Mann wrote in a similar vein, was a kind of incarnation, "a personality of phenomenal cultural plenitude and complexity, summing up all that is essentially European." See his "Nietzsche's Philosophy in the Light of Contemporary Events" (1947) in *Thomas Mann's Address: Delivered at the Library of Congress 1942–1949* (Washington, D.C.: Library of Congress, 1963), 69. Most recently Ernst Nolte has revived this notion of Nietzsche as a personalized "battleground" (*Schlachtfeld*) in his *Nietzsche und der Nietzscheanismus* (Frankfurt/Main & Berlin: Propyläen, 1990). For a critical discussion of this work, see Aschheim, *Nietzsche Legacy*, chap. 9.

54. See "On the So-Called Crisis of Christianity," in Leszek Kolakowski, *Modernity on Endless Trial* (Chicago: University of Chicago Press, 1990), 90–91. See too his fascinating reflections on the complexity of Nietzsche's modernity in the opening essay (from which the book takes its title), esp. 8–9.

55. See the interesting, critical comments by Robert C. Solomon, "Nietzsche, Postmodernism and Resentment: A Genealogical Hypothesis," in Koelb, ed., *Nietzsche as Postmodernist*, esp. 291–93.

CHAPTER 3. AGAINST SOCIAL SCIENCE

This paper was prepared for an International Conference on "Jews and the Social and the Biological Sciences" held at the Oxford Centre for Hebrew and Jewish Studies, in August 1998.

1. "Under Which Lyre: A Reactionary Tract for the Times (Phi Beta Kappa Poem, Harvard, 1946)," reproduced in W. H. Auden, *Collected Poems*, ed. Edward Mendelson (New York: Random House, 1976), 259–63. The quote appears on 262. I would like to thank Stuart Pierson of St. John's Memorial University, Newfoundland, for drawing my attention to the source of this quote in October 1999. Auden composed the poem before he met Arendt but—in the light of such similar attitudes—it is not surprising that they later became friendly.

2. This is a commonplace. But for the most sustained and unqualified attack on Strauss as an active anti-liberal, anti-democrat see Luc Ferry, *Political Philosophy*, vol. 1, *Rights: The New Quarrel between the Ancients and the Moderns*, trans. Franklin Phillip (Chicago: University of Chicago Press, 1990).

3. For a sympathetic account, see Martin Jay, *The Dialectical Imagination: A History of the Frankfurt School and the Institute of Social Research, 1923–1950* (Boston: Little, Brown and Company, 1973). For a very skeptical account, see Leszek Kolakowski's magisterial *Main Currents of Marxism*, vol. 3, *The Breakdown*, trans. P. S. Falla (Oxford: Oxford University Press, 1978), esp. chap. 10.

4. For some major recent accounts, see Seyla Benhabib, *The Reluctant Modernism of Hannah Arendt* (London: Sage, 1996); Dana R. Villa, *Arendt and Heidegger: The Fate of the Political* (Princeton, N.J.: Princeton University Press, 1996); Richard J. Bernstein, *Hannah Arendt and the Jewish Question* (Cam-

bridge, Mass.: MIT Press, 1996); Phillip Hansen, *Hannah Arendt, Politics, History, and Citizenship* (Stanford, Calif.: Stanford University Press, 1993).

5. Arendt mentions Adorno's involvement with Walter Benjamin—see her essay, "Walter Benjamin: 1892–1940" in *Men in Dark Times* (New York: Harcourt Brace Jovanovich, 1968), 153–206. Other than that, as far as I can ascertain, there is no acknowledgment of each other's work in their published writings! Given the common background, contemporaneity, and similarity of interests of these figures, such omissions are in themselves noteworthy. In a private communication of 1 April 1998, Eugene Sheppard points out that given that Arendt and Strauss spent their lives contemporaneously within the same cities (Marburg, New York, Chicago) and institutions (and departments and disciplines within these institutions), this can only be interpreted as a "deafening silence."

6. For instance, Arendt wrote of Strauss to Karl Jaspers (Letter 159, 29 August 1954): "He is a convinced orthodox atheist. Very odd. A truly gifted intellect. I don't like him." See Hannah Arendt & Karl Jaspers, *Correspondence 1926–1969*, ed. Lotte Kohler & Hans Saner (New York: Harcourt Brace Jovanovich, 1992), 244.

7. See Elisabeth Young-Bruehl, *Hannah Arendt: For Love of the World* (New Haven, Conn.: Yale University Press, 1982), 98. Ironically, she later took Strauss to task for his stand that no Jews after the war should have anything to do with Germany (see 169). The ironies and ambivalences, it should be pointed out, existed on both sides. Precisely these render their respective biographies so compelling.

8. Letter 343 of Arendt to Jaspers, 23 November 1963, in Arendt & Jaspers, *Correspondence*, 535; pers. comm. Eugene Sheppard (presently writing a doctoral dissertation on Strauss), 2 March 1998.

9. Arendt & Jaspers, *Correspondence*, 80.

10. For details of Adorno's piece, the circumstances of its rediscovery, and Arendt's comments upon it see her letters (numbers 373 and 399) to Karl Jaspers in Arendt & Jaspers, *Correspondence*, esp. 592–93, 644. See also footnotes 2 and 3 to Letter 399 on 793–94.

11. For these rather scurrilous analyses see Elzbieta Ettinger, *Hannah Arendt/Martin Heidegger* (New Haven, Conn.: Yale University Press, 1995) and Richard Wolin, "Hannah and the Magician: An Affair to Remember," *New Republic*, 9 October 1995, 27–37.

12. Other than occasional ironic comments, like that of Walter Laqueur (quoted in footnote 14), some commentators, like David Biale, do mention these thinkers, citing them in common for their radicalism but not extending the analysis. See Biale's "Leo Strauss: The Philosopher as Weimar Jew" in Alan Udoff, ed., *Leo Strauss's Thought: Toward a Critical Engagement* (Boulder, Colo.: Lynne Rienner Publishers, 1991), 37. There is now a volume on Arendt and Strauss in America that surprisingly possesses virtually no serious comparative analysis. George Kateb's contribution, "The Questionable Influence of Arendt (and Strauss)," is a partial exception. Arendt and Strauss, he writes, were "two whose love of Greece, inflamed and mediated by German philosophy, set them against modern democracy" (12). See Peter Graf-Kielmansegg, et al., eds., *Hannah Arendt and Leo Strauss: German Émigrés and American Political Thought after*

World War II (Washington, D.C.: German Historical Institute & Cambridge University Press, 1995).

13. This is reproduced in Hannah Arendt, *The Jew as Pariah: Jewish Identity and Politics in the Modern Age*, ed. Ron H. Feldman (New York: Grove Press, 1978), 55–66.

14. See his "Hannah Arendt as Political Commentator" to appear in Steven E. Aschheim, ed., *Hannah Arendt in Jerusalem* (Berkeley & Los Angeles: University of California Press, 2001).

15. As is to be expected their attitudes to Nietzsche were complex but his formative centrality, his relevance to their various problematics, cannot be doubted. See, respectively, Laurence Lampert, *Leo Strauss and Nietzsche* (Chicago: University of Chicago Press, 1996); on the Frankfurt school and Nietzsche, see my *The Nietzsche Legacy in Germany, 1890–1990* (Berkeley & Los Angeles: University of California Press, 1992), 185–92, 289–92; on Arendt and Nietzsche see Villa, *Arendt and Heidegger*, chap. 3.

16. Strauss's admiration for—as well as departures from—Heidegger is documented in Steven B. Smith "*Destruktion* or Recovery? Leo Strauss's Critique of Heidegger," *Review of Metaphysics* LI, no.2 (December 1997): 345–78. Smith also lists the already large secondary literature on this topic. I thank Michael Morgan for this reference. The Frankfurt School eventually became known as great critics of Heidegger. See particularly Adorno's *The Jargon of Authenticity*, trans. K. Tarnowski and F. Will (London: Routledge & Kegan Paul, 1973). The work was originally published in 1964. Still, apart from the fact that Marcuse was a Heidegger student, Heidegger's radicalism and, especially, his rather undifferentiated critique of modernity proved to be very influential. See Aschheim, *Culture and Catastrophe: German and Jewish Confrontations with National Socialism and Other Crises* (New York: New York University Press, 1996), 6–8. Dana Villa, in *Arendt and Heidegger*, has written a whole book tracing the complex philosophical relationship between the two.

17. The Frankfurt School's residual Marxism, however diluted and moderated, and its constant critiques of instrumental rationality render further explanation unnecessary. Kateb argues that both Arendt and Strauss had in common an opposition to modern liberal, representative or constitutional democracy—albeit from different viewpoints. He views Strauss, far more of a cultural snob and pessimist than Arendt, as an "authoritarian anti-democrat" (39) while Arendt, from her participatory viewpoint, "reproaches modern democracy because it is not democratic, or not democratic enough." See his "The Questionable Influence," in Graf-Kielmansegg, et al. eds., *Hannah Arendt and Leo Strauss*. And as Albrecht Wellmer points out, Arendt castigated the liberal (indeed the entire Western philosophical) tradition for downgrading the "political" in favor of the "social" and the private. See his "On Revolution" in Aschheim, ed., *Hannah Arendt in Jerusalem*.

18. See Strauss's typically elliptic analysis of this question in the preface to the English translation of his *Spinoza's Critique of Religion*, trans. E. M. Sinclair (New York: Schocken Books, 1965). The work, significantly, was dedicated to Franz Rosenzweig.

19. On their relationship see Heinrich Meier, *Carl Schmitt and Leo Strauss:*

The Hidden Dialogue (Chicago: University of Chicago Press, 1995). On Schmitt see John P. McCormick's excellent *Carl Schmitt's Critique of Liberalism: Against Politics as Technology* (Cambridge: Cambridge University Press, 1997).

20. This was originally published in *Archiv für Sozialwissenschaft* 67, no. 6 and is reproduced as "Comments on *Der Begriff des Politischen* by Carl Schmitt" in Leo Strauss, *Spinoza's Critique of Religion*, 331–51. The quote appears on 351.

21. For the "decrepit" quote see Kenneth Hart Green's "Leo Strauss as a Modern Jewish Thinker" in Leo Strauss, *Jewish Philosophy and the Crisis of Modernity: Essays and Lectures in Modern Jewish Thought* (Albany: State University of New York Press, 1997), 60 (note 26). For the comments on Cassirer, see the essay "Kurt Riezler" in *What Is Political Philosophy? And Other Studies* (Glencoe, Ill.: Free Press, 1959), 246. In the same volume see too Strauss's review of Cassirer's *The Myth of the State*, 292–96.

22. The influence and the dissension, it seems to me, remained. Apart from the constant dialogue of Arendt and the Critical School with Heidegger, even in the 1940s—in a still unpublished lecture—Strauss could still evince the misguided but sincerely noble minds of Stefan George, Oswald Spengler, Martin Heidegger, Ernst Jünger, and Carl Schmitt. I thank Eugene Sheppard for this information, communicated on 4 March 1998.

23. This is noted in Alfons Söllner, "Leo Strauss: German Origin and American Impact," in Graf-Kielmansegg, et al. eds., *Hannah Arendt and Leo Strauss*, 123.

24. Eugene Sheppard, in a private communication, suggests that while Strauss's "German" writings contained foundational criticisms of liberalism, his post-emigration works were more ameliorative in attitude.

25. George Mosse has identified this humanizing, universalist *Bildung* propensity—beyond nationalism and religion—to be the defining ingredient of a new German Jewish identity. See his *German Jews beyond Judaism* (Bloomington: Indiana University Press, 1985). We will elaborate on this later.

26. I have elsewhere traced the similarities between the ahistorical or post-*Bildung* apocalyptic temper of the Weimar radical right and certain Jewish intellectuals—such as Gershom Scholem, Ernst Bloch, Franz Rosenzweig, and Walter Benjamin. See "German Jews beyond Bildung and Liberalism: The Radical Jewish Revival in the Weimar Republic" in Aschheim, *Culture and Catastrophe*. The thinkers considered here, despite their criticism of liberalism, it should be noted, were quite different. Even for the Frankfurt School, if redemption was to come, it was out of dialectically induced social—not messianic— developments. Arendt's politics produced constant processes of disclosure without any teleological or epiphanic end and, as Eugene Sheppard noted in a personal communication of 15 May 1998, Strauss dismissed as naive and misguided any holistic, totalized solutions to political problems. The astonishing intellectual creativity of the Weimar Republic and especially its Jewish intellectuals needs to take into account both these commonalities and the differences.

27. I owe some of these insights to a conversation with Antony Skinner.

28. Arendt criticized Comte—by linking him to Marx! See her "Religion and Politics," in Hannah Arendt, *Essays in Understanding 1930–1954*, ed. Jerome

Kohn (New York: Harcourt Brace & Company, 1994), 377. Leo Strauss too includes Comte in his severe and ongoing (though differently oriented) critique of positivism but does so in a more differentiated form:

> Positivism is no longer what it desired to be when August Comte originated it. It still agrees with Comte by maintaining that modern science is the highest form of knowledge, precisely because it aims no longer, as theology and metaphysics did, at absolute knowledge of the Why, but only at the relative knowledge of the How. But after having been modified by utilitarianism, evolutionism and neo-Kantianism, it has abandoned completely Comte's hope that a social science modeled on natural science would be able to overcome the intellectual anarchy of modern society.

See his "What Is Political Philosophy?" in *What Is Political Philosophy?* 18.

29. Max Horkheimer & Theodor Adorno, *Aspects of Sociology*, trans. John Viertel (London: Heinemann, 1973), 1. Based upon a series of radio talks given in 1953 and 1954 and designed for a large popular audience, these presentations are among the most accessible of the Frankfurt School's writings.

30. Ibid., 7. Note that this was a generalized indictment that flowed from Comte through to Max Weber, Emile Durkheim, and Vilfred Pareto.

31. See "The Positive Philosophy of Society: Auguste Comte" in Herbert Marcuse, *Reason and Revolution: Hegel and the Rise of Social Theory* (Boston: Beacon Press, 1960). The quotes have been culled from pp. 340–60. The work was originally published in 1941.

32. "Mannheim felt quite clearly that the concept of ideology was justified solely as that of a false consciousness, but was no longer capable of dealing with such a concept in terms of content, and therefore postulates it solely in a formal manner, as an allegedly epistemological possibility." See Horkheimer & Adorno, *Aspects of Sociology*, 197.

33. See her "Philosophie und Soziologie: Anlässlich Karl Mannheim, *Ideologie und Utopie*," *Die Gesellschaft* 7, no. 2 (1930): 163–76. Reprinted under the title "Philosophy and Sociology," in Arendt, *Essays in Understanding*, 28–43. All the quotes provided here are taken from this translation. As so often with Arendt there was an irony in the publishing history of this piece. Arendt's biographer, Elisabeth Young-Bruehl recounts it thus: *Die Gesellschaft* was a socialist journal. Its editor, Rudolf Hilferding "wanted a critical review, for he felt that Mannheim's work posed a threat to socialism. Hannah Arendt agreed to do the review, but she saw quite another threat in the work and wrote as a defender of the autonomy of philosophy." See Young-Bruehl, *Hannah Arendt: For Love of the World*, 83.

34. See Peter L. Berger, *A Rumour of Angels: Modern Society and the Rediscovery of the Supernatural* (Harmondsworth: Penguin Books, 1971). See esp. the chapter, "The Perspective of Sociology: Relativizing the Relativizers."

35. These quotes have been culled from Arendt, "Philosophy and Sociology," 41. Arendt did qualify her remark by stating that the "question of meaning is, however, older than capitalism because it goes back to an earlier experience of human insecurity in the world, that is, to Christianity." Ultimately, as in Arendt's use of the notion of "mass society" to explain totalitarianism—of which more

later—she leaned on the *psychological* experience of insecurity to ground her historicizing critique of sociology and psychoanalysis!

36. Strauss, of course, was famous for his principled distinction between esoteric and exoteric writings, between superficial and deeper meanings. For a very close analysis and attempt to view Strauss's essentially admiring attitude to Nietzsche despite the many (superficial) negative references, see Lampert, *Leo Strauss and Nietzsche.*

37. "Why We Remain Jews: Can Jewish Faith and History Speak to Us?" in Strauss, *Jewish Philosophy and the Crisis of Modernity,* 312.

38. "Introduction to *Persecution and the Art of Writing,*" reproduced in Strauss, *Jewish Philosophy and the Crisis of Modernity,* 428.

39. Ibid., 417.

40. Ibid., 428.

41. Max Horkheimer, "Traditionelle und kritische Theorie," *Zeitschfrift für Sozialforschung* 6, no. 2 (1937): 186. See too Jay, *Dialectical Imagination,* 81.

42. See O. Stammer, ed., *Max Weber und die Soziologie heute. Verhandlungen des 15.Deutschen Soziologentages* (Tübingen: Mohr, 1965). On Weber generally, see the excellent anthology edited by Wolfgang J. Mommsen and Jürgen Osterhammel, *Max Weber and His Contemporaries* (London: Unwin Hyman, 1987).

43. Martin Jay, *Dialectical Imagination,* 121. "Accordingly," Jay adds, "political authority in a capitalist society could not be rational in the substantive sense of reconciling particular and general interests."

44. I owe this insight to Jeffrey Andrew Barash in a conversation on 23 May 1998, Jerusalem.

45. A brief look at the mentions of Weber in the text and footnotes of *The Human Condition* (New York: Doubleday Anchor Books, 1959) establishes this point. 46.

See Peter Baehr, "The Grammar of Prudence: Arendt, Jaspers, and the Appraisal of Max Weber" in Aschheim, ed., *Hannah Arendt in Jerusalem.* 47.

Although even here, the weight of the criticism was deflected onto followers:

> Max Weber coined his ideal type of the "charismatic leader" after the model of Jesus of Nazareth; pupils of Karl Mannheim found no difficulty in applying the same category to Hitler. From the viewpoint of the social scientist, Hitler and Jesus were identical because they fulfilled the same function. It is obvious that such a conclusion is possible only for people who refuse to listen to what either Jesus or Hitler said.

See Arendt's 1953 piece "Religion and Politics," reproduced in Arendt, *Essays in Understanding,* 378. On page 388, note 24, Arendt explicitly qualifies her comments by adding: "I do not mean to imply that Max Weber himself could ever have been guilty of such monstrous identifications."

48. Peter Baehr, introduction to *The Portable Hannah Arendt,* ed. Peter Baehr, (New York: Penguin Books, 2000), 43 (of manuscript version).

49. See the admirable analysis by Villa, *Arendt and Heidegger,* 320–21.

50. "'All politics is a struggle for power; the ultimate kind of power is violence,' said C. Wright Mills, echoing, as it were, Max Weber's definition of the

state as the 'rule of men over men based on the means of legitimate, that is, alleg-edly legitimate, violence.'" See Arendt's *On Violence* (New York: Harcourt, Brace & World, 1969), esp. 35.

51. Villa, *Arendt and Heidegger*, 29.

52. Ibid., 66–67. For Arendt's most extended discussion of the councils, see her *On Revolution* (London: Faber & Faber, 1963).

53. Although the confrontation was repeated many times and in many ver-sions, the earliest is to be found in Leo Strauss, "The Social Science of Max We-ber," *Measure: A Critical Journal* 2, no. 2 (Spring 1951): 204–30.

54. See the famous chapter 2, "Natural Right and the Distinction between Facts and Values" in Strauss, *Natural Right and History* (Chicago: University of Chicago Press, 1953). The quote appears on 36.

55. Given Strauss's penchant for esoteric reading, it is not surprising that various theorists have argued that his hostility to many of the great thinkers is far more apparent than real and that, in effect, his engagement amounts to serious identification. For a thesis contending that "Strauss did not argue that Weber was a nihilist, but rather sought to determine why Weber was not," see Robert Eden, "Why Wasn't Weber a Nihilist," in Kenneth L. Deutsch & Walter Soffer, eds., *The Crisis of Liberal Democracy : A Straussian Perspective* (Albany: State University of New York Press, 1987), 212–42. The quote appears on 212. For another ex-ample see the very close reading of the complex Strauss-Nietzsche relationship (one that entirely contradicts Strauss's portrayal in various places of Nietzsche as nothing less than a dangerous philosophical criminal) in Lampert, *Leo Strauss and Nietzsche*.

56. Strauss, *Natural Right and History*, 42. Weber, Strauss added, concealed from himself the nihilistic consequences of his doctrine of values. Strauss added that, in examining the process by which Weber reached these conclusions, "we shall inevitably reach a point beyond which the scene is darkened by the shadow of Hitler. Unfortunately, it does not go without saying that in our examination we must avoid the fallacy that in the last decades has frequently been used as a substitute for the *reductio ad absurdum*: the *reductio ad Hitlerum*. A view is not refuted by the fact that it happens to have been shared by Hitler" (42–43).

57. Ibid., 45.

58. Ibid., 64.

59. Weber, Strauss wrote,

> was inclined to believe that twentieth century man has eaten of the fruit of the tree of knowledge, or can be free from the delusions which blinded all earlier men: we see the situation of man without delusions; we are disenchanted. But under the in-fluence of historicism, he became doubtful whether one can speak of the situation of man as man or, if one can, whether this situation is not seen differently in differ-ent ages in such a manner that, in principle, the view of any age is as legitimate or illegitimate as that of any other. . . . Hence what originally appeared as freedom from delusions presented itself eventually as hardly more than the questionable premise of our age or as an attitude that will be superseded, in due time, by an attitude that will be in conformity with the next epoch.

(*Natural Right and History*, 73).

60. "Our social science," Strauss wrote, "may make us very wise or clever as regards the means for any objectives we might choose. It admits being unable to help us in discriminating between legitimate and illegitimate. Such a science is instrumental and nothing but instrumental: it is born to be the handmaid of any powers or any interests that be" (*Natural Right and History*, 3–4).

61. The examples are endless here. See, for instance, Max Horkheimer & Theodor W. Adorno, *Dialectic of Enlightenment*, trans. John Cumming (New York: Seabury Press, 1972). The work originally appeared in 1944. See too Max Horkheimer, *Eclipse of Reason* (New York: Oxford University Press, 1947). Much of the great success of Herbert Marcuse's *One Dimensional Man: Studies in the Ideology of Advanced Industrial Society* (Boston: Beacon Press, 1964) is attributable to this emphasis. A still excellent introduction to these thinkers is Jay, *Dialectical Imagination*.

62. On this point see Aschheim, *Culture and Catastrophe*, 6–8.

63. See Adorno's introduction to his *The Positivist Dispute in Sociology* (London: Heinemann, 1976), 19–20: "Scientism becomes false with regard to central states of affairs by engaging itself one-sidedly in favour of the unified moment of individual and society for the sake of logical systematics, and by devaluing as an epiphenomenon the antagonist moment which cannot be incorporated into such logical systematics."

64. Ibid., 33.

65. Strauss, "What Is Political Philosophy?" 23.

66. Ibid., 23. Note, too, that this almost foundationalist document defining Strauss's creed was, tellingly, presented in Jerusalem.

67. Ibid., 18–19. As was his wont, Strauss qualified his own statement a little further on. In fact, he wrote, social scientists were inevitably people of integrity. "I have never met any scientific social scientist who apart from being devoted to truth and integrity was not also wholeheartedly devoted to democracy." This was not so much nihilism "than an alibi for thoughtlessness and vulgarity; by saying that democracy and truth are values, he says in effect that one does not have to think about the reasons why these things are good. . . . Social science positivism fosters not so much nihilism as conformism and philistinism" (20). This, of course, represented a typical "conservative" position on the issue.

68. Ibid., 19.

69. Ibid., 14.

70. Ibid., 24.

71. See Strauss on "Kurt Riezler" in *What Is Political Philosophy?*:

> The most fundamental proposition of all thought is what one may call the decision as to what it means "to be." For instance, modern science may be said to identify "to be" with "to be observably by everyone" or "to be a possible object" or "to belong to the spatial-temporal order." "To be" thus understood is relative to the observer, to any observer, to the anonymous observer. But we divine somehow that "to be" means above all "to be in itself" and not merely "to be relative . . ."; "to be" means, above all and primarily, to be a subject and not an object. . . . More generally and more cautiously, the fundamental question concerns not this or that being, not the totality of beings, but beingness. (249)

See too the critical comments in his *The City and Man* (Chicago: University of Chicago Press, 1964), introduction and chap. 1.

72. To be sure there was a prior history to the tension between philosophy and psychology which Arendt reflected. See Martin Jay, "Modernism and the Specter of Psychologism" in his *Cultural Semantics: Keywords of Our Time* (Amherst: University of Massachusetts, 1998).

73. Her essays on particular individuals contained in *Men in Dark Times* are packed with such penetrating observations. Moreover, in his introduction to *The Portable Arendt*, Peter Baehr notes that Arendt ignored her own strictures: "Ostensibly committed to eschewing the psychologizing mode, Arendt showed little hesitancy in deciphering Rahel's dream life to a degree that would make the hardened pyschoanalyst gasp" (8).

74. Arendt, "Philosophy and Sociology," 33–34.

75. This summary and the quotes therein are drawn from the chapter "Society" in Adorno & Horkheimer, *Aspects of Sociology*, 16–36, and Adorno's introduction to *The Positivist Dispute*.

76. See the introduction to *The Positivist Dispute*, 25. The quote goes on thus:

> Something of the opposing intention was expressed in the social contract theories. No matter how little these theories were historically correct, they penetratingly remind society of the concept of the unity of individuals, whose conscious[ness] ultimately postulates their reason, freedom and equality. In a grand manner, the unity of the critique of scientific and meta-scientific sense is revealed in the work of Marx.

77. Hanna Fenichel Pitkin, in "Conformism, Housekeeping, and the Attack of the Blob: The Origins of Hannah Arendt's Concept of the Social," in Bonnie Honig, ed., *Feminist Interpretations of Hannah Arendt* (University Park: Pennsylvania State University Press, 1995), 51–81, has well analyzed and clarified these various meanings, although the explanatory and pychoanalytical framework into which she places this—Arendt's conception of society as "the facsimile of one superhuman family" derived from her own biographical experience—is dubious and, as she herself admits, goes against the grain of Arendt's own warnings in the preface to *Rahel Varnhagen*—to avoid "that modern form of indiscretion in which the writer attempts to penetrate his subject's tricks and aspires to know more than the subject knew about or was willing to reveal; what I would call the pseudo-scientific apparatuses of depth-psychology, psychoanalysis, graphology, etc., fall into this category of curiosity-seeking" (xviii). Even if, as we have noted, Arendt never hesitated to provide pyschological explanations when she deemed them necessary, her principled unwillingness to employ *psychoanalytical* method and theory—quite apart from her overall disdain of social science in general—derives from her performative emphasis, the notion that selves disclose themselves in the public realm. Indeed, she opposed the emphasis on "interiority" as antithetical to that which counted politically—the world of action.

78. Arendt, "Philosophy and Sociology," 41.

79. Peter Baehr, *Portable Hannah Arendt*, 57.

80. Arendt, *Human Condition*, 27.

81. Ibid., 28.

82. *The Human Condition* formulates these views most systematically. *On Revolution* develops the crucial distinction between the "social" and the "political" within revolutionary contexts. See too the essay "The Crisis in Culture: Its Social and Its Political Significance" in the important collection by Hannah Arendt, *Between Past and Future: Six Exercises in Political Thought* (Cleveland & New York: Meridian Books, 1961). The nuances and development of Arendt's ideas on the "social" are too complex for us to do them justice here. For a brilliant exposition of this component and Arendt's thought in general, see the indispensable work by Villa, *Arendt and Heidegger*.

83. Clearly, Arendt knew that means-ends relationships and fabrication were a necessary and even desirable part of the human condition. But, as she wrote in *The Human Condition*, 137: "The issue at stake is, of course, not instrumentality, the use of means to achieve ends, as such, but rather the generalization of the fabrication experience in which usefulness and utility are established as the ultimate standards." One should also note, as Baehr points out, that Arendt's notion of the "social" was not always negative. Arendt approved of salon sociability and in her article, "Reflections on Little Rock," she argued that the "social" was well worth protecting. If the principle of the public realm is equality and the private exclusivity, that of the social is "discrimination": the ability to choose with whom to mix. It is thus not "society" as such that she feared but "mass society" which blurs lines of such discrimination and levels group distinctions. Perhaps here too we can detect a Jewish chord being struck?

84. Arendt, *Human Condition*, 46. Elsewhere she writes: "Socialized mankind is that state of society where only one interest rules, and the subject of this interest is either classes or man-kind, but neither man nor men. The point is that now even the last trace of action in what men were doing, the motive implied in self-interest disappeared. What was left was a 'natural force', the force of the life process itself, to which all men and all human activities were equally submitted . . ." (ibid., 293).

85. Arendt, *Human Condition*, 43.

86. Arendt, "Religion and Politics," in *Essays in Understanding*, 379.

87. Arendt, *On Revolution*, 1. And as she put it elsewhere: "That politics is nothing but a function of society, that action, speech and thought are primarily superstructures upon social thought, is not a discovery of Karl Marx but on the contrary is among the axiomatic assumptions Marx accepted uncritically from the political economists of the modern age" (Arendt, *Human Condition*, 31).

88. Arendt, *Human Condition*, 38–39.

89. Ibid., 40.

90. Ibid. See also, on page 295: "The trouble with modern theories of behaviorism," she added ominously, "is not that they are wrong but that they could become true, and that they actually are the best possible conceptualization of certain obvious trends in modern society." The same quote elaborates a clearly Heideggerian theme combined with Jungerian metaphors. It "at once becomes manifest that all his [man's] activities, watched from a sufficiently removed vantage point in the universe, would appear not as activities of any kind but as pro-

cesses, so that . . . modern motorization would appear like a process of biological mutation in which human bodies gradually begin to be covered by shells of steel."

91. Arendt, "Understanding and Politics," in *Essays in Understanding*, 319.

92. Ibid., 319–20.

93. Arendt, *Human Condition*, 296.

94. For an analysis of the alternative conception developed by the Frankfurt School (despite their forays into quite ordinary empirical social science such as Adorno's *Authoritarian Personality*), see Helmut Dubiel, *Theory and Politics: Studies in the Development of Critical Theory*, trans. Benjamin Gregg, (Cambridge, Mass.: MIT Press, 1985), and Theodor Adorno, *The Authoritarian Personality* (New York: Harper, 1950).

95. It would take a monograph to develop these differences with any seriousness. One could, I think, get to a crucial difference in terms of their respective attitudes to foundations. Strauss views classical political philosophy as the basis for any valid normative conception of the good life and society, whereas Arendt views politics—very much in a non-foundationalist, post-traditional way—as performative action, the open-ended sphere best designed for the human condition of plurality and self-disclosive activity. For Arendt, the "social" is equivalent to the "natural," that is, part of the realm of necessity, pre-political and thus to a degree not yet fully disclosive of real human potentiality; for Strauss classical rationalism is to be taken seriously because it is there that one discovers "things which are by nature just" (Strauss, *City and Man*, 5). As he said of Aristotle: "Political philosophy is primarily the quest for that political order which is best, according to nature everywhere and, we may add, always. This quest will not come into its own as long as men are entirely immersed in political life . . . The first political philosopher will then be the first man not engaged in political life who attempted to speak about the best political order" (ibid., 17). Arendt, of course, would take quite a different, activist tack.

96. Smith, "*Destruktion* or Recovery?"

97. Strauss, "What Is Political Philosophy?" 38.

98. See the chapter "Theodor W. Adorno and the Collapse of the Lukácsian Concept of Totality," in Martin Jay's *Marxism and Totality: The Adventures of a Concept from Lukács to Habermas* (Berkeley & Los Angeles: University of California Press, 1984), 241–75.

99. A recent reviewer, Irwin M. Wall, has correctly noted that the Jewish *content* of her ideas was minimal—her intellectual world was clearly not grounded in Judaic sources as was Buber or Rosenzweig or Scholem—or, indeed, Strauss. Rather, what needs to be noted are the ways in which her Jewish life-experiences shaped, and interacted with, the development of her thought. See his review of Richard J. Bernstein, *Hannah Arendt and the Jewish Question* in *Central European History* 30, no. 3 (1997): 467.

100. See Jack Jacob's "A 'most remarkable' 'Jewish sect'? The *Institut's* Early History," an unpublished paper presented at a conference of The Institute for German History, Tel Aviv University, 7–8 June 1998, on "Critical Theory in Contexts."

101. Gershom Scholem, *From Berlin to Jerusalem: Memories of My Youth*,

trans. Harry Zohn (New York: Schocken Books, 1980), 131. Scholem's connection to the Frankfurt School was, of course, above all through Walter Benjamin. Apart from Scholem's indignation at the Horkheimer piece quoted below, he commented to Adorno that anti-Semitism was a matter for metaphysicians and could not be understood by sociologists. This was somewhat ironic. Scholem addressed Adorno as a social scientist although ultimately he is far more properly classified as a kind of metaphysician: "As an old historian, sadly, I can no longer believe that the social sciences have anything relevant to contribute to this theme." See Gershom Scholem to Adorno, Letter 122, 28 October 1943, *Briefe Band I, 1914–1947* (Munich: C. H. Beck, 1994), 291.

102. On this see Jack Jacobs, "1939 Max Horkheimer's 'Die Juden und Europa'" in Sander L. Gilman & Jack Zipes, eds., *Yale Companion to Jewish Writing and Thought in German Culture, 1096–1996* (New Haven, Conn.: Yale University Press, 1997), 571–76.

103. "Die Juden und Europa," *Zeitschrift für Sozialforschung* 8, nos. 1/2 (1939): 115.

104. See the nuanced analysis of the complexities involved in Anson Rabinbach's essay "The Cunning of Unreason: Mimesis and the Construction of Anti-Semitism in Horkheimer and Adorno's *Dialectic of Enlightenment*" in his *In the Shadow of Catastrophe: German Intellectuals between Apocalypse and Enlightenment* (Berkeley & Los Angeles: University of California Press, 1997). See also Adorno, *Authoritarian Personality*.

105. On the *Bildungs* thesis generally, see George L. Mosse, *German Jews beyond Judaism*; on the Frankfurt School in particular, see chapter 4, "A Left-Wing Identity."

106. Reinhart Maurer, "Nietzsche und die Kritische Theorie," *Nietzsche-Studien* 10/11 (1981–1982): 41–42.

107. Martin Jay, "The Jews and the Frankfurt School: Critical Theory's Analysis of Anti-Semitism" in his *Permanent Exiles: Essays on the Intellectual Migration from Germany to America* (New York: Columbia University Press, 1986), 100. Jay adds that as the School "moved away from the traditional Marxist belief in the proletariat as the agent of positive totalization and more toward the conclusion that the best that could be hoped for in the present world was the preservation of enclaves of negation . . . attention . . . to the Jewish question increased . . . anti-Semitism became a model of the totalistic liquidation of nonidentity in the one-dimensional world" (100).

108. Rabinbach, "The Cunning of Unreason," 186.

109. Thus in the (ironic?) memorandum Adorno sent to Horkheimer in 1944 he suggested that since "not all the recurring objections against the Jews are of an entirely spurious, projective, paranoid character," a "manual for distribution among Jews" be prepared that listed such traits and suggestions as to how to overcome them. See Rabinbach, "The Cunning of Unreason," 194. These kinds of suggestions were, incidentally, an ongoing part of German history. See for instance, the suggestions during the mid-19th century to create special schools to overcome such traits in my *Brothers and Strangers: The East European Jew in German and German-Jewish Consciousness* (Madison: University of Wisconsin Press, 1982), 10.

110. Strauss, "What Is Political Philosophy?" 24.

111. "Franz Rosenzweig und die Akademie für die Wissenschaft des Judentums," in *Jüdische Wochenzeitung für Kassel, Hessen und Waldeck*, 13 December
1929, 2. Quoted in Udoff, "On Leo Strauss," in *Leo Strauss's Thought*, 13–14.

112. David Biale, "Leo Strauss," in Udoff, *Leo Strauss's Thought*, 32.

113. "Jerusalem and Athens," in Strauss, *Jewish Philosophy and the Crisis
of Modernity*, 378–79. This meant that "however much the science of all cultures
may protest its innocence of all preferences or evaluations, it fosters a specific
moral posture . . . by asserting, if only implicitly, the rightness of pluralism, it
asserts that pluralism is *the* right way; it asserts the monism of universal tolerance
and respect for diversity; for by virtue of being an ism, pluralism is a monism."

114. See "Why We Remain Jews: Can Jewish Faith and History Still Speak to
Us?" in Strauss, *Jewish Philosophy and the Crisis of Modernity*, 328–29. Strauss
was able to jump from social analysis—regarding the difficulties of Jewish existence
in liberal, secularizing Christian society—to theological pronouncement: "From
every point of view it looks as if the Jewish people were the chosen people, at
least in the sense that the Jewish problem is the most manifest symbol of the
human problem insofar as it is a social or political problem." See also Strauss,
Liberalism Ancient and Modern (New York & London: Basic Books, 1968), 230.

115. Eugene Sheppard (in a communication to me of 15 May 1998) writes
concerning Strauss: "The common denominator throughout his 'German' writings is a scathing assault upon the foundations of liberalism or more broadly
'liberalism as a system': liberal culture, religion, and politics. It is only after the
Weimar republic had dissolved that Strauss supplemented the uprooting of liberalism with the search for alternative systems and then more pragmatic ways to ame-
liorate the inherent deficiencies in modern liberal regimes."

116. This small-print piece is typically given a quite noncommittal title,
"Preface to the English Edition" to his *Spinoza's Critique of Religion* (New York:
Schocken Books, 1965), 1–31.

117. Söllner, "Leo Strauss: German Origin and American Impact," 123.

118. I have tried to analyze her attitudes toward Jewishness in "Hannah
Arendt in Jerusalem," reproduced in chapter 7 of this volume.

119. "The Jewish salon . . . was the product of a chance constellation in an
era of social transition. The Jews became stopgaps between a declining and an as
yet unstabilized social group: the nobility and the actors; both stood outside of
bourgeois society—like the Jews . . . ." See Hannah Arendt, *Rahel Varnhagen:
The Life of a Jewish Woman*, trans. Richard & Clara Winston (New York: Harcourt Brace Jovanovich, 1974), 57.

120. On the whole, it would seem, Arendt regarded this as a normatively
positive development that also had consequences for the remarkable feats of modern German Jewish intellectuals. It should be noted, however, that in *Origins of
Totalitarianism*, she argued (in my view, rather problematically) that anti-
Semitism was closely related to the alienation of Jews from society and their alliance with ruling State elites.

121. "The Jewish salons united the two features—social 'outsidedness' and
theatricality— that Arendt deemed essential in her reappropriation of the Aristo-
telian concept of the polis." Thus argues an unnamed author in a paper entitled

"Hannah Arendt, Rahel Varnhagen, and the Origins of Arendtian Political Philosophy" submitted to *The Journal of Jewish Thought and Philosophy*, 19.

122. See Villa, *Arendt and Heidegger*, esp. 137. On Schmitt see John P. McCormick's excellent *Carl Schmitt's Critique of Liberalism: Against Politics as Technology* (Cambridge: Cambridge University Press, 1997).

123. See the brilliant chapter entitled "The Decline of the Nation-State and the End of the Rights of Man," in Arendt, *Origins of Totalitarianism* (New York: Meridian Books, 1958).

124. On her Zionism see my "Hannah Arendt in Jerusalem." It is instructive to note that Arendt employed this critique consistently and applied it not only to Zionism but also to its victims. As she put it in *Origins of Totalitarianism*,

> Hitler's solution of the Jewish problem, first to reduce the German Jews to a nonrecognized minority in Germany, then to drive them as a stateless people across the borders, and finally to gather them back from everywhere in order to ship them back to extermination camps, was an eloquent demonstration to the rest of the world how really to "liquidate" all problems concerning minorities and stateless. After the war, it turned out that the Jewish question, which was considered the only insoluble one, was indeed solved—namely, by means of a colonized and then conquered territory—but this solved neither the problem of the minorities nor the stateless. On the contrary, like virtually all other events of our century, the solution of the Jewish question merely produced a new category of refugees, the Arabs, thereby increasing the number of the stateless and rightless by another 700,000 to 800,000 people. And what happened in Palestine within the smallest territory and in terms of hundreds of thousands was then repeated in India on a large scale involving many millions of people. Since the Peace Treaties of 1919 and 1920 the refugees and the stateless have attached themselves like a curse to all the newly-established states on earth which were created in the image of the nation-state (290).

125. This has to do with Arendt's conception of political community. For Arendt, as Bonnie Honig argues, "a political community that constitutes itself on the basis of a prior, shared, and stable identity threatens to close the spaces of politics, to homogenize or repress the plurality and multiplicity that political action postulates." See her "Toward an Agonist Feminism," in Honig, *Feminist Interpretations*, 149.

126. Arendt, *Origins of Totalitarianism*, 478–79.

CHAPTER 4. NAZISM AND THE HOLOCAUST
IN CONTEMPORARY CULTURE

1. Amery is himself a key contributor to this kind of discourse. See his quite remarkable *At the Mind's Limits: Contemplations by a Survivor on Auschwitz and Its Realities*, trans. Sidney Rosenfeld & Stella P. Rosenfeld (Bloomington: Indiana University Press, 1980), vii.

2. This generally felt intuition was provided with intellectual coherence in

relation to Nazism above all in the work of Hannah Arendt. See her *The Origins of Totalitarianism* (New York: Meridian Books, 1958), 443, 459.

3. For suggestive analyses of this, see Yehuda Bauer, "Conclusion: The Significance of the Final Solution" in David Cesarani, ed., *The Final Solution: Origins and Implementation* (London & New York: Routledge, 1994), 300–309, and Saul Friedlander, "The Shoah in Present Historical Consciousness," in *Memory, History, and the Extermination of the Jews of Europe* (Bloomington: Indiana University Press, 1993), esp. 50.

4. I have addressed some of these issues at greater length in chapter 1 of my *Culture and Catastrophe: German and Jewish Confrontations with National Socialism and Other Crises* (London & New York: New York University Press, 1996).

5. See his "Götterdämmerung after Twenty Years" (1976), reprinted in his *The Dustbin of History* (Cambridge, Mass.: Harvard University Press, 1995), 52–69. The quotes appear on 52–53.

6. In a sense this is what the famous "Controversy about the Historicization of National Socialism" between Martin Broszat and Saul Friedländer is all about. See this in *Yad Vashem Studies* 19 (1988): 1–47.

7. For a good contextual review of the *Historikerstreit*, see Charles S. Maier, *The Unmasterable Past: History, Holocaust, and German National Identity* (Cambridge, Mass.: Harvard University Press, 1988). The main polemic documents are to be found in *Yad Vashem Studies* 19 (1998).

8. "Between Aporia and Apology: On the Limits of Historicizing National Socialism," in Peter Baldwin, ed., *Reworking the Past: Hitler, the Holocaust, and the Historian's Debate* (Boston: Beacon Press, 1990), 144.

9. See his "Vergangenheit, die nicht vergehen will" in *"Historikerstreit": Die Dokumentation der Kontroverse um die Einzigartigkeit der national-sozialistischen Judenvernichtung* (Munich: Piper, 1987), 45. The *Historikerstreit* actually began with Nolte's infamous article, "Between Myth and Revisionism? The Third Reich in the Perspective if the 1980s." This first appeared in English in H. W. Koch, ed., *Aspects of the Third Reich* (New York: St. Martin's Press, 1985), 17–38.

10. See Pierre Vidal-Naquet, *Assassins of Memory: Essays on the Denial of the Holocaust*, trans. Jeffrey Mehlman (New York: Columbia University Press, 1992) and Deborah Lipstadt, *Denying the Holocaust: The Growing Assault on Truth and Memory* (New York: Free Press, 1993).

11. The phenomenon, distasteful as it is, actually does have contemporary parallels. How else can one characterize the obtuse and long-lasting denial of countless liberal and left Western intellectuals concerning the very existence of, let alone crimes perpetrated in, the Soviet Gulags? On this see T. Todorov, "The Touvier Trial," *Salmagundi* 106–107 (Spring-Summer 1995): 3–13. See esp. 11–12.

12. Saul Friedlander, *Probing the Limits of Representation: Nazism and the "Final Solution"* (Cambridge, Mass.: Harvard University Press, 1992).

13. Martin Jay, "The Manacles of Gavrilo Princip," *Salmagundi* 106–107 (Spring-Summer 1995): 14–21. See esp. 18.

14. For a succinct and excellent account of these issues, see Peter Pulzer,

German Politics 1945–1955 (New York: Oxford University Press, 1995) and Jeffrey Herf, *Divided Memory: The Nazi Past in the Two Germanys* (Cambridge, Mass.: Harvard University Press, 1997).

15. This rather unusual acknowledgment of guilt (whatever its underlying sources and motivations) has been ably documented, and compared to Japan's quite different record, by Ian Buruma in *The Wages of Guilt: Memories of War in Germany and Japan* (London: Farrar, Straus & Giroux, 1994).

16. For an overview of primary and secondary materials relating to this, see Geoffrey Hartman, ed., *Bitburg in Moral and Political Perspective* (Bloomington: Indiana University Press, 1986).

17. Alexander and Margarete Mitscherlich, *The Inability to Mourn: Principles of Collective Behavior*, trans. Beverley R. Placzek, preface by Robert Jay Lifton (New York: Grove Press, 1975). The German original appeared in 1967.

18. See "The German-Jewish Dialogue at its Limits: The Case of Hermann Broch and Volkmar von Zuehlsdorff," in Aschheim, *Culture and Catastrophe*, 91.

19. Ibid., 94.

20. See "Backshadowing and the Rhetoric of Victimization" in Michael Bernstein, *Foregone Conclusions: Against Apocalyptic History* (Berkeley & Los Angeles: University of California Press, 1994), 85.

21. See Biale's comments in a review of Steven T. Katz, *The Holocaust in Historical Context*, in *Tikkun* 10, no. 1 (January-February 1995): 79–80, 88.

22. The most recent popular and highly controversial treatment of this question is to be found in Tom Segev, *The Seventh Million: The Israelis and the Holocaust*, trans. Haim Watzman (New York: Hill & Wang, 1993).

23. Grossman, *See under Love* (New York: Farrar, Straus & Giroux, 1989).

24. See, for instance, Robert Alter, foreword to *Unease in Zionism*, ed. Ehud Ben Ezer (New York: Quadrangle Books, 1974), esp. 12–13. The article was first published in 1970. The other articles in this collection also provide a window onto both the popular atmosphere and critical attitudes of the time.

25. See her "Revisioning the Past: The Changing Legacy of the Holocaust in Hebrew Literature," *Salmagundi* (Winter 1985/Spring 1986): 246.

26. For two examples see Amos Elon, "The Politics of Memory," *New York Review of Books*, 7 October 1993, and Adi Ophir, "On Sanctifying the Holocaust: An Anti-Theological Treatise," *Tikkun* 2, no. 1 (1987): 61–66.

27. Steiner, *The Portage of San Cristobal of A. H.* (London: Faber & Faber, 1981).

28. The open espousal of such attitudes is contained in interviews with Palestinian youth visiting the memorial site of Lahamei Haghetto'ot in Israel as shown in the recent film "Don't Touch My Holocaust." Information on this 1994 film scripted by Asher Tlalim can be found in the catalogue to *The 11th Jerusalem Film Festival* (Jerusalem: n.p., 1994), 45.

29. CNN Saturday Morning Report, 9 December 1995.

30. de Koven-Ezrachi, "Revisioning the Past," 246.

31. James Young, *The Texture of Memory: Holocaust Memorials and Meaning* (New Haven, Conn.: Yale University Press, 1993), 26.

32. I have tried to account for this rather strange affirmation of one's own national identity as essentially murderous in "Archetypes and the German-Jewish

Dialogue: Reflections Occasioned by the Goldhagen Affair," *German History* 15, no. 2 (1997). The essay is reprinted in chapter 9 of this volume.

33. Victor Klemperer, *Ich will Zeugnis ablegen bis zum letzten. 1. Tagebuecher, 1933–1941. 2. 1942–1945* (Berlin: Aufbau-Verlag, 1995). *Schindler's List*, dir. Steven Spielberg, 195 min., 1993, motion picture. This "saviour" theme was suggested by Frank Stern in a lecture entitled "Siegfried's Cinematic Quest: From the Germanic Forest to Olympic Virtues" given at an International Workshop in Jerusalem on "Paganism, 'Volk Religion' and Antisemitism: 19–20th Centuries," 21–23 October 1996.

34. See the provocative but insightful article by Scott L. Montgomery, "What Kind of Memory? Reflections on Images of the Holocaust," *Contention* 5 (Fall 1995): 79–103.

35. Ibid.

36. See Shiraz Dossa, "Human Status and Politics: Hannah Arendt on the Holocaust," *Canadian Journal of Political Science* (June 1980): see esp. 319–20.

37. See his extremely insightful "An Age of Genocide," *New Republic* (29 January 1996), 27–36. The quote appears on 36. Rieff too makes the point that, given the incomparability of the Shoah with other genocides, "in this way the Holocaust may be used to exonerate many crimes and many criminals" (36).

38. Jay, "The Manacles of Gavrilo Princip," 21.

39. These words, Levi tells us, were written as early as 1947 and published for the first time in *The Truce* in Italy in 1963. See his chapter "Shame" in *The Drowned and the Saved*, trans. Raymond Rosenthal (London: Abacus, 1988), 52–67. The quote appears on 54.

CHAPTER 5. EXCURSUS

1. This is a slightly revised version of an essay, "The German-Jewish Legacy beyond America: A South African Example," that appeared originally in "The German-Jewish Legacy in America, 1938–1988: A Symposium," in *American Jewish Archives* (November 1988): 359–64, and then in Abraham J. Peck, ed., *The German-Jewish Legacy in America 1938–1988: From Bildung to the Bill of Rights* (Detroit: Wayne State University Press, 1989).

2. Most importantly see his *German Jews beyond Judaism* (Bloomington: Indiana University Press, 1985). See too, in the present volume, chapter 14, "George Mosse at 80: A Critical Laudatio."

3. See "German Jews beyond *Bildung* and Liberalism: The Radical Jewish Revival in the Weimar Republic" in my *Culture and Catastrophe: German and Jewish Confrontations with National Socialism and Other Crises* (New York: New York University Press, 1996).

CHAPTER 6. ASSIMILATION AND ITS IMPOSSIBLE DISCONTENTS

1. Moritz Goldstein, "Deutsch-jüdischer Parnass," *Der Kunstwart* 25 (1912): 281–94. The quote appears on 283.

2. Moritz Goldstein, "German Jewry's Dilemma: The Story of a Provocative Essay," *Leo Baeck Institute Year Book* 2 (1957): 236–54. The quote appears on 244.

3. Ph. Stauff, "Die Juden in Literatur und Volk," *Der Kunstwart* 25 (1912): 251–59.

4. Julius Bab, "Assimilation," *Der Freistaat* 1 (1913–1914): 172–76.

5. Franz Oppenheimer, "Stammesbewusstein und Volksbewusstein," *Jüdische Rundschau* 15, no. 8 (25 February 1910): 86–88.

6. Goldstein, "Deutsch-jüdischer Parnass," 291.

7. G. Wollstein, "Neue Kompromisse," *Der Jüdische Student* 15 (January 1917): 353–54.

8. Goldstein, "German Jewry's Dilemma," 250.

9. Goldstein, "Deutsch-jüdischer Parnass," 291.

10. Ernst Lissauer, "Deutschtum und Judentum," *Der Kunstwart* 25 (1912): 6–12.

11. Ludwig Strauss (Franz Quentin), "Aussprache zur Judenfrage," *Der Kunstwart* 25 (1912): 236–44.

12. Lissauer, "Deutschtum und Judentum," 6–12.

13. Hannah Arendt, *The Origins of Totalitarianism* (New York: Meridian Books, 1958), 66.

14. Heinrich Heine, "The New Israelite Hospital in Hamburg" (1841) and "Moses" (1854) appear in *The Poetry and Prose of Heinrich Heine*, ed. Frederic Ewen, trans. Margaret Armour (New York: Citadel, 1948), 285, 665–66.

15. "Ost und West," *Ost und West* 1, no. 1 (1901).

16. Ludwig Geiger, "Zionismus und Deutschtum," *Die Stimme der Wahrheit: Jahrbuch für wissenschaftlichen Zionismus* (Würzburg: N. Philippi,1905).

17. This story is recounted by Erich Kahler in "What Are the Jews?" in his *The Jews Among the Nations* (New York: Frederick Ungar, 1967), 6.

18. See Paul Breines, "The Jew as Revolutionary: The Case of Gustav Landauer," *Leo Baeck Institute Year Book* 12 (1967): 76.

19. See Gershon Weiler, "Fritz Mauthner: A Study in Jewish Self-Rejection," *Leo Baeck Institute Year Book* 7 (1963): 144.

20. Strauss, "Aussprache zur Judenfrage."

21. Richard Wagner, "Judaism in Music," *Richard Wagner's Prose Works*, vol.3, *The Theatre*, trans. William Ashton Ellis (London: K. Paul, Trench, Trubner, 1907).

22. Oskar Panizza, "The Operated Jew," trans. Jack Zipes, *New German Critique* 21 (Fall 1980): 63–79.

23. Ibid., 79.

24. Martin Buber, "Judaism and the Jews," in *On Judaism*, ed. Nahum Glatzer (New York: Schocken, 1967), 11–21. The quote appears on 15.

25. See Strauss, "Ein Dokument der Assimilation," *Der Freistaat* 1 (1913–1914) and also his "Aussprache zur Judenfrage."

26. Parts of the Benjamin-Strauss correspondence have been published in Walter Benjamin, *Gesammelte Schriften*, ed. Rolf Tiedemann with Theodor Adorno and Gershom Scholem (Frankfurt: Suhrkamp, 1977), 836–44.

27. Quoted in the illuminating chapter, "The German-Jewish Parnassus," in Paul Mendes-Flohr, *German Jews: A Dual Identity* (New Haven, Conn.: Yale University Press, 1999), 45–65. The quote appears on 53.

28. Ibid., 54.

29. On this theme see my *Brothers and Strangers: The East European Jew in German and Geman-Jewish Consciousness, 1800–1923* (Madison: University of Wisconsin Press, 1982).

30. See Michael Brenner, *The Renaissance of Jewish Culture in Weimar Germany* (New Haven, Conn.: Yale University Press, 1996).

31. See "German Jews beyond Bildung: The Radical Jewish Revival in the Weimar Republic" in my *Culture and Catastrophe: German and Jewish Confrontations with National Socialism and Other Crises* (New York: New York University Press, 1996).

32. "On Being a Jewish Person," in *Franz Rosenzweig,* ed. Nahum N. Glatzer (New York: Schocken, 1962), 216.

33. Quoted in Yosef Haim Yerushalmi, *Freud's Moses: Judaism Terminable and Interminable* (New Haven, Conn.: Yale University Press, 1991), 12.

34. Ibid. See generally chap. 1, "The Fourth Humiliation," esp. 14–15.

CHAPTER 7. HANNAH ARENDT IN JERUSALEM

1. The nature of, and reasons behind, this reception are well analyzed in Seyla Benhabib, *The Reluctant Modernism of Hannah Arendt* (Thousand Oaks, Calif.: Sage, 1996). See especially her "Introduction: Why Hannah Arendt?" See too the introduction to Richard J. Bernstein, *Hannah Arendt and the Jewish Question* (Cambridge, Mass.: MIT Press, 1996). The most powerful postmodern reading to date can be found in Dana R. Villa, *Arendt and Heidegger: The Fate of the Political* (Princeton, N.J.: Princeton University Press, 1996). For the relation to identity politics and feminism, see Bonnie Honig, ed., *Feminist Interpretations of Hannah Arendt* (University Park: Pennsylvania State University Press, 1995). For a post-Marxist reading see Phillip Hansen, *Hannah Arendt: Politics, History, and Citizenship* (Stanford, Calif.: Stanford University Press, 1993).

2. See the revised and enlarged edition, *Eichmann in Jerusalem: A Report on the Banality of Evil* (New York: The Viking Press, 1964).

3. An older view, that Arendt's portrait in *The Origins of Totalitarianism* (Cleveland, Ohio: Meridian Books, 1958) of the powerful centrality of the Jew in the economy and polity of the absolutist state replicates the Nazi version, is held by some leading Israeli historians and political scientists to this day. See Tom Segev, *The Seventh Million: The Israelis and the Holocaust,* trans. Haim Watzman (New York: Hill & Wang, 1993), 360.

4. Indeed, I recognize that the very title "Hannah Arendt in Jerusalem" has a rather provocative ring, conjuring up, as it intentionally does, Arendt's extremely contentious *Eichmann in Jerusalem.* The title was suggested by Prof. Wolfgang Schieder when the idea of this conference was broached. It appears, however, that this theme confirms the existence of a *Zeitgeist.* In the recent special issue of

History & Memory 8, no. 2 (Fall/Winter 1996), entitled *Hannah Arendt and Eichmann in Jerusalem,* and devoted to Arendt, both Richard Wolin and Jose Brenner have similar titles. See "The Ambivalences of German-Jewish Identity: Hannah Arendt in Jerusalem" and "Eichmann, Arendt, and Freud in Jerusalem" respectively. Moreover, Idith Zertal presented a paper (which I have not yet seen) entitled "Arendt in Zion" at a 1997 International colloquium on Arendt in Potsdam. See too Amos Elon's insightful "The Case of Hannah Arendt," *New York Review of Books,* 6 November 1997, 25–29. I only came upon this piece after writing my own article but many of its conclusions are very similar to my own.

5. This is made all the more mysterious by Arendt's comment to Karl Jaspers in 1966: ". . . the Hebrew edition of *Eichmann* is finally coming out in Israel. I think the war between me and the Jews is over." See Letter 394, 26 March 1966 in Hannah Arendt & Karl Jaspers, *Correspondence 1926–1969,* ed. Lotte Kohler & Hans Saner, trans. Robert & Rita Kimber (New York: Harcourt Brace Jovanovich, 1985), 632. See too Tom Segev, *Seventh Million,* 465.

6. For some of the relevant writings, see her *Rahel Varnhagen: The Life of a Jewish Woman,* rev. ed., trans. Richard & Clara Winston (New York: Harcourt Brace Jovanovich, 1974); a collection of her Jewish essays, *The Jew as Pariah: Jewish Identity and Politics in the Modern Age,* ed. Ron H. Feldman, (New York: Grove Press, 1978); and *Essays in Understanding, 1930–1954,* ed. Jerome Kohn (New York: Harcourt & Brace, 1994).

7. This is, to be sure, still a rather fringe, avant-garde affair. But it is rather significant that the Tel Aviv journal *History & Memory* recently devoted a special issue to Arendt. See *History & Memory* 8, no. 2 (Fall/Winter 1996). The hall in which Richard Bernstein gave his 1997 lecture in Jerusalem on "Arendt and the 'Banality of Evil'" was packed beyond capacity. To be sure, these were all English-language events. Nevertheless, a Hebrew panel on Arendt held in Jerusalem in March 1997 under the auspices of the Leo Baeck Institute publication met with similar interest.

8. For her appreciation of the extraordinary nature of that experience ("nothing comparable to it is to be found even in the other areas of Jewish assimilation") and the challenge of historically understanding it, see her preface to *Rahel Varnhagen,* xvii.

9. See Dan Diner, "Hannah Arendt Reconsidered: On the Banal and the Evil in Her Holocaust Narrative," *New German Critique* 71 (Spring-Summer 1997): 177–90.

10. For a superb portrait of this tradition see George L. Mosse, *German Jews beyond Judaism* (Bloomington: Indiana University Press, 1983).

11. "The trouble with the educated philistine was not that he read the classics but that he did so prompted by the ulterior motive of self-perfection, remaining quite unaware . . . that Shakespeare or Plato might have to tell him more important things than how to educate himself . . . he fled into a region of 'pure poetry' in order to keep reality out of his life . . . or to look at it through a veil of 'sweetness and light.'" See "The Crisis in Culture" in Arendt's *Between Past and Future: Six Exercises in Political Thought* (Cleveland, Ohio: Meridian Books, 1961). See too *Rahel Varnhagen,* esp. 9–10.

12. See "Die jüdische Armee—der Beginn einer jüdischen Politik?" in *Auf-*

bau 7 (14 November 1941). Robert Meyerson's 1972 doctoral dissertation, "Hannah Arendt: Romantic in a Totalitarian Age, 1928–1963," University of Minnesota Department of History, contains useful information about these earlier years.

13. The relevant biographical information is to be found in the still-definitive biography by Elisabeth Young-Bruehl, *Hannah Arendt: For Love of the World* (New Haven, Conn.: Yale University Press, 1982).

14. See Scholem to Shalom Spiegel, 17 July 1941, Letter 119, in Gershom Scholem, *Briefe Band I 1914–1947*, ed. Itta Shedletzky (Munich: C. H. Beck, 1994), 285.

15. Arendt to Jaspers, 26 March 1966, Letter 394, in Arendt & Jaspers, *Correspondence*, 632.

16. Arendt to McCarthy, 17 October 1969, in Hannah Arendt & Mary McCarthy, *Between Friends: The Correspondence of Hannah Arendt and Mary McCarthy 1949–1975*, ed. Carol Brightman (New York: Harcourt Brace & Company, 1995), 249. On Arendt's response to the Yom Kippur war, see Arendt to McCarthy, 16 October 1973, *Between Friends*, 349–50 and esp. n. 5 where Brightman describes her reaction as one of "panic."

17. Arendt to Jaspers, 1 October 1967, Letter 421, in Arendt & Jaspers, *Correspondence*, 674–75.

18. This may be the very reason why Arendt was so compelling during the 1950s and early 1960s to previously unengaged non-establishment American Jewish intellectuals. Her capacity to integrate Jewish matters into the storm's eye of world history, to make them explanatory factors in the great catastrophes of twentieth-century history, provided a kind of dignity and importance to a previously marginalized, even derided, existence. See, for instance, Irving Howe, *The Decline of the New* (New York: Harcourt Brace, 1970), 244–45, and Alfred Kazin, *New York Jew* (New York: Knopf, 1978), esp. 299.

19. "[M]any Jews such as myself," she wrote to Jaspers, "are religiously completely independent of Juda*ism* yet are still Jews themselves." Arendt to Jaspers, 4 September 1947, Letter 61, Arendt & Jaspers, *Correspondence*, 98.

20. See especially chap. 2 of Michael Walzer, *Interpretation and Social Criticism* (Cambridge, Mass.: Harvard University Press, 1987).

21. For letters documenting all these qualities see Gershom Scholem to Theodor W. Adorno, 29 February 1968, Letter 131, and Scholem to Hans Paeschke, 24 March 1968, Letter 133, in Gershom Scholem, *Briefe Band II 1948–1970*, ed. Thomas Sparr (Munich: C. H. Beck, 1995), 206–7, 209–10 respectively. See too the interesting comments by Raymond Aron, "The Essence of Totalitarianism according to Hannah Arendt," *Partisan Review* 60, no. 3 (1993): 366–76. This appeared originally in the French journal *Critique* in 1954.

22. Arendt to Scholem, 24 July 1963, reprinted in Arendt, *Jew as Pariah*, 247.

23. See Arendt to Jaspers, 7 September 1952, Letter 135, in Arendt & Jaspers, *Correspondence*, 196–201. The quote appears on 197.

24. Scholem recommended this work to Benjamin. See his *Walter Benjamin: The Story of a Friendship*, trans. Harry Zohn (Philadelphia: Jewish Publication Society, 1981), 213–14.

25. Jaspers added that more justice would have been done to

> see her not just in the context of the Jewish question but, rather, in keeping with Rahel's own intentions and reality as a human being in whose life the Jewish problem played a very large role but by no means the only one. . . . everything you cite from "enlightened" thinking is illustrated with negative examples . . . But it was the greatness of the Enlightenment . . . that carried Rahel. . . . What starts to take shape in your work but is then lost in sociological and psychological considerations (which should not in any way be omitted but should be incorporated into a higher level) is the unconditional aspect of Rahel . . . the quality of her personal influence, the totality of her insight . . . all the things for which being a Jew is only the outward guise and only the point of departure.

See Jaspers' brilliant letter to Arendt, 23 August 1952, Letter 134, in Arendt & Jaspers, *Correspondence*, 192–96.

26. See her 1959 Lessing Prize address "On Humanity in Dark Times: Thoughts about Lessing" in *Men in Dark Times* (New York: Harcourt Brace Jovanovich, 1968), esp. 18.

27. See her letter to Jaspers, 17 December 1946, Letter 50, in Arendt & Jaspers, *Correspondence*, 70.

28. Ibid.

29. Arendt to Scholem, 24 July 1963, in Arendt, *Jew as Pariah*, 246–47.

30. Postmodernist, feminist critics, while admiring of Arendt's resistance to Scholem's definitions—seeing in his "identity politics insidous resources for the homogenizing control of behavior and the silencing of independent criticism"—take her to task for insisting on the private nature of Jewish identity.

> Arendt would have done better to contest the terms of Scholem's construal of Jewishness as identity . . . Both she and Scholem treat Jewish identity as a univocal, constative fact . . . They disagree on whether it is a public or private fact . . . In treating Jewish identity as constative, Arendt relinquishes the opportunity to engage or even subvert Jewish identity performatively, to explore its historicity and heterogeneity, to dislodge and disappoint its aspirations to univocity, to proliferate its differentiated possibilities.

See Bonnie Honig, "Toward an Agonistic Feminism: Hannah Arendt and the Politics of Identity" in Honig, ed., *Feminist Interpretations*, 153–54.

31. Young-Bruehl, *Hannah Arendt*, 127. Unfortunately Young-Bruehl provides no explanation for this extraordinary step.

32. Arendt to Jaspers, 29 January 1946, Letter 34, in Arendt & Jaspers, *Correspondence*, 29.

33. See letter of 8 August 1936 in Hannah Arendt & Heinrich Bluecher, *Briefe 1936–1968* (Munich: Piper Verlag, 1996), 38–40. The quote appears on 39.

34. See Hannah Arendt & Hermann Broch, *Briefwechsel: 1946–1951*, ed. Paul Michael Luetzeler (Frankfurt am Main: Juedischer Verlag, 1996).

35. See the remarkable letter, Arendt to Bluecher, 24 August 1936, in Arendt & Bluecher, *Briefe*, 57–60.

36. See Arendt to Blumenfeld, 28 November 1955, Letter 49, in Hannah Arendt & Kurt Blumenfeld, *". . . in keinem Besitz verwurzelt": Die Korrespon-*

denz, ed. Ingeborg Nordmann & Iris Pilling (Hamburg: Rotbuch Verlag, 1995), 135–36.

37. *Origins of Totalitarianism,* 66. The work appeared first in 1951.

38. On this atmosphere see "German Jews beyond Liberalism: The Radical Jewish Revival in the Weimar Republic" in my *Culture and Catastrophe: German and Jewish Confrontations with National Socialism and Other Crises* (New York: New York University Press, 1996).

39. See, especially, her "Franz Kafka: A Revaluation" in Arendt, *Essays in Understanding,* 69–80 (written originally in 1944). In her famous essay, "The Jew as Pariah: A Hidden Tradition," Kafka is, of course, one of her main examples. See Arendt, *Jew as Pariah,* esp. 81–89.

40. See her essay "Walter Benjamin: 1892–1940," in Arendt, *Men in Dark Times,* esp. 195.

41. Ibid., 190.

42. Arendt to Jaspers (written from the Pension Reich, Beth Hakerem), 13 April 1961, Letter 285, in Arendt & Jaspers, *Correspondence,* 434–36. The quote appears on 435. The last sentence of this paragraph softens things a little: "The major impression, though, is of very great poverty."

43. The debate is by now exceedingly well known. Less familiar is Scholem's reply to Arendt (in a letter only recently published) regarding her belief that if the Jews had "been organized and leaderless" the number of victims would have been considerably less. Had the Jews done that, Scholem argues, "we would have reproached them now. More organization, we would claim, would have helped to save lives!" See Scholem to Arendt, 12 August 1963, Letter 66, in Scholem, *Briefe Band II,* 107–8.

44. The most comprehensive review of responses can be found in Richard I. Cohen, "Breaking the Code: Hannah Arendt's *Eichmann in Jerusalem* and the Public Polemic—Myth, Memory and Historical Imagination," *Michael* 13 (1993): 29–85. The quote appears on 84.

45. This is a quote from McCarthy's review "The Hue and Cry." See Arendt & McCarthy, *Between Friends,* 167, n. 6.

46. Arendt to McCarthy, 23 June 1964, in Arendt & McCarthy, *Between Friends,* 168.

47. See Scholem's published letter, of 23 June 1963, to Arendt in their exchange over the Eichmann book reprinted in Arendt, *Jew as Pariah,* 240–45. We have already examined Arendt's response to Scholem's accusation of lacking *Ahavath Israel.* It is only fair to point out, however, that as Scholem emphasizes in his later reply, he described her as belonging to the Jewish people in order to distance himself from those who regarded her as no longer part of it. See Scholem to Arendt, 12 August 1963, Letter 66, in Scholem, *Briefe Band II,* 105–8. The quote appears on 106.

48. Arendt to Jaspers, 20 July 1963, Letter 331, in Arendt & Jaspers, *Correspondence,* esp. 510–11; Jaspers to Arendt, 20 October 1963, Letter 336, in Arendt & Jaspers, *Correspondence,* 521–25.

49. Jaspers to Arendt, 25 October 1963, Letter 338, in Arendt & Jaspers, *Correspondence,* 527.

50. This is reprinted in Arendt, *Jew as Pariah,* 131–63.

51. See Scholem to Arendt, 28 January 1946, Letter 131, in Scholem, *Briefe Band I*, 309–14.

52. See her reply to Scholem, 24 July 1963, in Arendt, *Jew as Pariah*, 246.

53. Scholem to Hans Paeschke, 24 March 1968, Letter 133, in Scholem, *Briefe Band II*, 210.

54. Scholem to Hannah Arendt, Letter 131, in Scholem, *Briefe Band I*, 310.

55. As it does for the person they both deeply admired, Walter Benjamin.

56. David Suchoff, "Gershom Scholem, Hannah Arendt, and the Scandal of Jewish Particularity," *Germanic Review* 72, no. 1 (Winter 1997): 57–76. The quotes appear on 57–58. I thank Paul Mendes-Flohr for drawing my attention to this piece.

57. For Scholem's attitude, see Letter 133 in Scholem, *Briefe Band II*, 209–10.

58. Arendt to Kurt Blumenfeld, 9 January 1957, Letter 65, in Arendt & Blumenfeld, "*. . . in keinem Besitz verwurzelt*," 174–77. The quote appears on 176.

59. Dana Villa has most recently and radically underlined these aspects of Arendt's thought in his *Arendt and Heidegger*.

60. Elzbieta Ettinger, in *Hannah Arendt, Martin Heidegger* (New Haven, Conn.: Yale University Press, 1995), never goes beyond the merely gossipy. The links and differences are best analyzed in Villa, *Arendt and Heidegger*. See too Bernstein, *Hannah Arendt and the Jewish Question*, 191–92, esp. n. 6.

61. See the suggestive piece by Bonnie Honig, "Toward an Agonistic Feminism" in Honig, ed., *Feminist Interpretations*, 135–66. The quote appears on 149.

62. "Arendt's warnings," writes Amos Elon, "displayed considerable foresight. Today's readers may be more willing to accept both her essays and her book [*Eichmann*] on their merits." See his essay "The Case of Hannah Arendt," 25.

63. See, for instance, Arendt's letter to Bluecher, 18 October 1955, in Bluecher, *Briefe*, 413:

> dies Ländchen, wo man immerzu die Grenzen sieht. Es ist trauriger und weniger erbittend, als ich dachte. Vielleicht, weil meine Umgebung hier verhaeltnismaessig vernuenftig geblieben ist, vor allem auch die sehr reizenden Kinder, von denen die Juengere etwas Besonderes ist. Die Angst ist sehr gross und ueberschattet alles, aussert sich darin, dass man nichts sehen und hoeren will. Schliesslich werden natuerlich die 'aktivischen Element' die Oberhand bekommen . . . Allles, was ueberhaupt den Mund aufmacht, erbittert nationalistisch; die Araber, die noch im Lande sind, haette man auch rausjagen sollen, na usw.

64. Arendt to Bluecher, 22 October 1955, in Bluecher, *Briefe*, 414–16.

65. See the remarkable Letter 61 to Jaspers, 4 September 1947, defining her attitude to Judaism and its future, Zionism, and the "extraordinary" achievements in Palestine in Arendt & Jaspers, *Correspondence*, 96–99, esp. 96. For a balanced treatment of this whole question see "Zionism: Jewish Homeland or Jewish State?" in Bernstein, *Hannah Arendt and the Jewish Question*, chap. 5.

66. Arendt to Bluecher, 20 April 1961, in Bluecher, *Briefe*, 522.

67. See her "To Save the Jewish Homeland: There Is Still Time" in Arendt, *Jew as Pariah*, 191.

68. Many of these have been republished in Arendt, *Essays in Understanding*. See especially "Approaches to the 'German Problem,'" "Organized Guilt and Universal Responsibility," "The Image of Hell," "Social Science Techniques and the Study of Concentration Camps," and others.

69. Arendt, "What Remains? The Language Remains: A Conversation with Guenter Gaus," in Arendt, *Essays in Understanding*, 14.

70. See her letter of 19 July 1947 in Arendt & Blumenfeld, *". . . in keinem Besitz verwurzelt*," 43.

71. Much history writing is a matter of tone, context, and underlying motivation. In the *Historikerstreit* of the1980s, Ernst Nolte was widely perceived as employing the thesis of Nazi-Soviet equivalence as a form of softening or relativizing the indictment against National Socialist atrocities. No one would have dreamed of accusing Arendt of this.

72. Saul Friedlander has incisively analyzed the differences between the original "totalitarian" school and the *Historikerstreit* approach. If both employed the comparative method, the former never sought to relativize but "ultimately maintained the Nazi case as the nec plus ultra, in relation to which the other crimes were measured." See his "A Conflict of Memories? The New German Debates about the 'Final Solution,'" *The Leo Baeck Memorial Lecture* 31 (New York: Leo Baeck Institute, 1987), esp. 7–10.

73. Raul Hilberg's pathbreaking *The Destruction of the European Jews* (Chicago: Quadrangle Books) only appeared in 1961. For the rather absurd, yet symptomatic tensions between Hilberg and Arendt, see Hilberg's *The Politics of Memory: The Journey of a Holocaust Historian* (Chicago: Ivan R. Dee, 1996), esp. 147–57. See too Arendt to Jaspers, 20 April 1964, Letter 351, in Arendt & Jaspers, *Correspondence*, 549–51.

74. See his "From Anti-Semitism to Extermination: A Historiographical Study of Nazi Policies Toward the Jews and an Essay in Interpretation," *Yad Vashem Studies* 16 (1984): 16.

75. Alfred Kazin, *New York Jew*, 298.

76. I have dealt with all this at length in "Nazism, Culture, and *The Origins of Totalitarianism*: Hannah Arendt and the Discourse of Evil," first published in *New German Critique* 70 (Winter 1997): 117–39. The essay also appears in chapter 11 of this volume.

77. Arendt, "Nightmare and Flight," in Arendt, *Essays in Understanding*, 134. She contrasted this with "death [which] became the fundamental problem after the last war."

78. See Arendt, *Origins of Totalitarianism*, 459, and her letter to Jaspers, 4 March 1951, in Arendt & Jaspers, *Correspondence*, 166.

79. For an interesting review of the background and genesis of these theories, see Leon Bramson, *The Political Context of Sociology* (Princeton, N.J.: Princeton University Press, 1961).

80. She wrote this already in 1945. See her "Approaches to the 'German Problem,'" in Arendt, *Essays in Understanding*, 108.

81. See Ernst Gellner, "From Koenigsberg to Manhattan (or Hannah, Rahel, Martin and Elfriede or Thy Neighbour's *Gemeinschaft*)" in *Culture, Identity, and Politics*, ed. Ernst Gellner (Cambridge: Cambridge University Press, 1987) and Richard Wolin, "Hannah and the Magician: An Affair to Remember," *New Republic*, 9 October 1995, 27–37.

82. Arendt, "Approaches to the 'German Problem,'" in *Essays in Understanding*, 109.

83. While this is so, Arendt also consistently criticized Zionism for its desire to believe in the eternality of anti-Semitism and its political instrumentalization of this condition. This prompted Scholem, in his critique of "Zionism Reconsidered," to comment that he did indeed believe in its "eternality" as witnessed by the fact that, despite all rational analyses, it seemed to renew itself in ever-new constellations. Scholem to Arendt, 28 January 1946, Letter 131, in Scholem, *Briefe Band I*, 310.

84. For a sustained comparative analysis, see my "Post-Holocaust Jewish Mirrorings of Germany: Hannah Arendt and Daniel Goldhagen," *Tel Aviver Jahrbuch für Deutsche Geschichte* 26 (1997): 345–53. The essay is reprinted in chapter 12 of this volume.

85. See my "Archetypes and the German-Jewish Dialogue: Reflections Occasioned by the Goldhagen Affair," originally published in *German History* 15, no. 2 (1997): 240–50. Reprinted in chapter 9 of this volume.

86. See Arendt to Blumenfeld, 19 July 1947, in Arendt & Blumenfeld, ". . . *in keinem Besitz verwurzelt*," 43.

87. Arendt, "Social Science Techniques and the Study of Concentration Camps," in *Essays in Understanding*, 235.

88. Interestingly, in his reply to Arendt's "Zionism Reconsidered," Scholem replied that he did indeed subscribe to the notion of an "eternal" anti-Semitism for, despite all rational analyses, it succeeded in reproducing itself in ever-new constellations. See Letter 131, in Scholem, *Briefe Band I*, 310.

89. See Moshe Zimmermann, "Chameleon and Phoenix: Israel's German Image," *Tel Aviver Jahrbuch für deutsche Geschichte* 26 (1997): 265–80.

90. Arendt, "Nightmare and Flight," in *Essays in Understanding*, 134.

91. For one perspective on this, see Richard Bernstein's essay "From Radical Evil to the Banality of Evil: From Superfluousness to Thoughtlessness," in *Hannah Arendt and the Jewish Question*, chap. 7.

92. On her earlier struggles with a kind of "demonizing" tendency see "Hannah Arendt and Karl Jaspers: Friendship, Catastrophe, and the Possibilities of German-Jewish Dialogue," chapter 6 in my *Culture and Catastrophe*. For the various critics who took Arendt to task for such "demonizing," see my "Nazism, Culture, and *The Origins of Totalitarianism*," chapter 11 of this volume.

93. Arendt to Jaspers, 17 August 1946, Letter 43, in Arendt & Jaspers, *Correspondence*, 51–56. The quote appears on 54.

94. Arendt to Jaspers, 5 February 1961, Letter 277, in Arendt & Jaspers, *Correspondence*, 423.

95. Arendt, *Origins of Totalitarianism*, 290.

96. This has already begun. Thus Adi Ophir, quoting Arendt to the effect

that "Totalitarian solutions may well survive the fall of totalitarian regimes," adds: "Indeed, they have survived, even in the State of the survivors." See his piece "Between Eichmann and Kant: Thinking on Evil after Arendt" in *History & Memory* 8, no. 2 (Fall/Winter 1996): 89–136. The brilliant article, in the same issue, by Leora Y. Bilsky, "When Actor and Spectator Meet in the Courtroom: Reflections on Hannah Arendt's Concept of Judgment," 137–73, demonstrates a sophisticated and critical knowledge of Arendt and a willingness and ability to employ her categories in ways that were not available ten years ago.

97. See Hilberg, *Politics of Memory*, 147. In a communication on 4 November 1997, Antonia Gruenenberg informed me that the "Hannah Arendt" is an Inter City Express that goes from Stuttgart to Hamburg-Altona and (on the way back) from Kiel to Stuttgart. The postage stamp, she reports, has been sold out!

98. Jaspers to Arendt, 25 October 1963, Letter 338, in Arendt & Jaspers, *Correspondence*, 527.

CHAPTER 8. GERMAN HISTORY AND GERMAN JEWRY

1. The following essay was presented, with minor changes, at the workshop on "Varieties of Multiculturalism in Modern European History: The Case of the Jews" in Jerusalem (5–9 January 1997) as part of an ongoing project on "The Integration of Jewish History into Modern European History Curricula." Originally published as "German History and German Jewry: Boundaries, Junctions and Interdependence" in *Leo Baeck Institute Yearbook* XLIII (London: Leo Baeck Institute, 1998): 315–22. Reprinted by permission of Leo Baeck Institute.

2. Also in the same volume, see the articles by Evyatar Friesel, "The German-Jewish Encounter as a Historical Problem. A Reconsideration"; Christhard Hoffmann, "The German-Jewish Encounter and German Historical Culture"; Samuel Moyn, "German Jewry and the Question of Identity. Historiography and Theory"; Shulamit Volkov, "Reflections on German-Jewish Historiography. A Dead End or a New Beginning?"

3. Volkov, "Reflections on German-Jewish Historiography," *Leo Baeck Institute Yearbook* XLI (1996): 320.

4. See David Sorkin, *The Transformation of German Jewry 1780–1840* (New York: Oxford University Press, 1987), esp. 6ff.

5. John R. Gillis, "The Future of European History," *Perspectives: American Historical Association Newsletter* 34, no. 4 (April 1996): 5.

6. Till van Rahden, "Mingling, Marrying, and Distancing: Jewish Integration in Wilhelmian Breslau and its Erosion in Early Weimar Germany," in Peter Pulzer, ed., *Jews in Weimar Germany*, Schriftenreihe wissenschaftlicher Abhandlungen des Leo Baecks Instituts, no. 57 (Tübingen: Mohr Siebeck, 1997).

7. Perhaps for that reason this analysis has been forwarded by a young non-Jewish German scholar, questioning the wisdom of his historiographical elders. For another analysis of why an increasing number of young German non-Jewish scholars are entering the field, see Hoffmann, "The German-Jewish Encounter and German Historical Culture."

8. For an analysis of this in another context see my "'The Jew Within': The Myth of 'Judaization' in Germany," in Jehuda Reinharz & Walter Schatzberg, eds., *The Jewish Response to German Culture: From the Enlightenment to the Second World War* (Hanover, N.H.: University Press of New England, 1985), 212–41.

9. See my "Assimilation, German Culture, and the 'Jewish Spirit': The Moritz Goldstein Affair (1912)" in Sander Gilman & Jack Zipes, eds., *A History of Jewish Writing in Germany* (New Haven, Conn.: Yale University Press, 1997). The essay is reprinted in chapter 6 of this volume.

10. See Jacob Katz, *From Prejudice to Destruction: Anti-Semitism, 1700–1933* (Cambridge, Mass.: Harvard University Press, 1980) and "Misreadings of Anti-Semitism," *Commentary* 73 (July 1983): 39–44.

11. Peter Gay, *Weimar Culture: The Outsider as Insider* (New York: Harper & Row, 1968).

12. This applies too—perhaps especially—to the post-liberal, radical, apocalyptic sensibility of those intellectual creations (of people like Gershom Scholem, Franz Rosenzweig, Walter Benjamin, and Ernst Bloch) that today seem most vital to the vaunted Jewish renaissance and which most quintessentially replicate a mood characteristic of what today we understand by Weimar culture (including such right-wing thinkers as Ernst Jünger, Oswald Spengler, and Martin Heidegger). See my "German Jews beyond *Bildung* and Liberalism: The Radical Jewish Revival in the Weimar Republic" in my *Culture and Catastrophe: German and Jewish Confrontations with National Socialism and Other Crises* (New York: New York University Press, 1996). See too Michael Brenner, *The Renaissance of Jewish Culture in Weimar Germany* (New Haven, Conn.: Yale University Press, 1996).

13. I owe this formulation to Eugene Sheppard.

14. Walter Laqueur, *Weimar Culture: A Cultural History* (New York: Capricorn Books, 1976), 73.

15. See the introduction to his *Freud, Germans, and Jews: Masters and Victims in Modernist Culture* (New York: Oxford University Press, 1978), 21.

16. Ibid.

17. Ibid., 77.

18. Benjamin to Florens Christian Rang, 18 November 1923, Letter 122, in Walter Benjamin, *The Correspondence of Walter Benjamin 1910–1940*, ed. Gershom Scholem & Theodor W. Adorno, trans. Manfred R. & Evelyn M. Jacobson (Chicago: University of Chicago Press, 1994), 214–17. The quote appears on 215. I thank Zvi Jagendorf for drawing my attention to this reference.

19. When in 1924 Edmund Husserl, a convert to Protestantism of many years standing, suggested that the longstanding confessional restriction on the chair of Christian philosophy at the University of Freiburg be removed ("the Catholic internationale had been accommodated to a very large extent during the war"), the Catholic scholar Heinrich Finke responded: "This is the kind of thing we have to listen to from an Austrian Jew. I've never in my life been an anti-Semite; but today I find it hard not to think along anti-Semitic lines." See Hugo

Ott, *Martin Heidegger: A Political Life,* trans. Allan Blunden (London: Fontana Press, 1993), 114–15.

20. Once such an essentializing logic is unleashed, the ironies entailed in this commonplace of German cultural criticism become virtually endless. Martin Heidegger's mammoth and engaged efforts to formulate the outlines of an authentic "German spirit" are well known—although his *explicit* linking of this with the Jewish Question is far less so. This becomes apparent in a letter (written to Viktor Schwoerer on 2 October 1929) where he states: ". . . what is at stake here is nothing less than the need to recognize without delay that we face a choice between sustaining our *German* intellectual life through a renewed infusion of genuine, native teachers and educators, or abandoning it once and for all to the growing Jewish influence—in both the wider and the narrower sense." But, obviously the respective German and Jewish "spirits" possessed remarkable flexibility and protean qualities, at times within the same person. Thus, while in 1929 Heidegger championed Eduard Baumgarten as the "great white hope of German intellectual life, a bulwark against the rising tide of Jewish influence," by 1933 he described him as "a Jewish protégé." Clearly here was a casuistic tool of political labeling that could easily boomerang against its user. Erich Jaensch, a Nazi philosopher opposed to Heidegger, wrote in a report to the National Socialist authorities that Heidegger obsessively indulged in the same "hairsplitting distinctions as Talmudic thought," a fact that inevitably attracted Jews to him. If Heidegger would acquire influence "our universities and intellectual life will favour those of Jewish stock . . . These people, even if the non-Aryan blood entered their family a long time ago, will invariably take up this hairsplitting nonsense with alacrity . . . their academic careers will prosper accordingly, while our fine young Germans cannot compete because their minds are too healthy and they have too much common sense." See Ott, *Martin Heidegger,* 378, 379, and 257 respectively.

21. The quote appears in Yosef Hayim Yerushalmi, *Freud's Moses: Judaism Terminable and Interminable* (New Haven, Conn.: Yale University Press, 1991), 97.

22. For an English translation of Jung's comments, see Frederic V. Grunfeld, *Prophets Without Honour* (New York: McGraw-Hill, 1979), 58–59.

23. The need for addressing this distinction was stressed by Shulamit Volkov at the conference where this paper was originally presented.

24. Moyn, "German Jewry and the Question of Identity," 295.

25. See Friedrich Kluge, *Etymologisches Wörterbuch,* 17th ed. (Berlin: Walter de Gruyter, 1957), 129.

26. Jacob Grimm and Wilhelm Grimm, *Deutsches Wörterbuch* 2 (Leipzig, 1860), 1053.

27. Jakob Wasserman, *My Life as German and Jew,* trans. S. N. Brainin (New York: Conrad-McCann, 1933), 220–21.

28. Walter Benjamin to Gerhard Scholem, 22 October 1917, Letter 55, in Benjamin, *Correspondence,* 97–102. The quote appears on 98.

29. Quoted in Max Horkheimer, "The German Jews" (1961) in his *Critique of Instrumental Reason* (New York: Seabury Press, 1974), 111.

30. On Freud see especially chapter 5 of Yerushalmi, *Freud's Moses;* on Buber see his "Judaism and the Jews" in his *On Judaism,* ed. Nahum N.Glatzer (New York: Schocken Books, 1972); on Rosenzweig, see my *Brothers and Strangers: The East European Jew in German and German-Jewish Consciousness, 1800–1923* (Madison: University of Wisconsin Press, 1982), 106.

31. Quoted in Karl Löwith, *My Life in Germany before and after 1933,* trans. Elizabeth King (Urbana: University of Illinois Press, 1986), 138–39.

CHAPTER 9. ARCHETYPES AND THE
GERMAN JEWISH DIALOGUE

1. This essay was originally presented at an International Conference of the Richard Koebner Centre for German History on "Rethinking German Anti-Semitism" in Jerusalem (26–28 November 1996). It was very slightly enlarged and updated before being published in *German History* 15, no. 2 (1997): 240–50. Reprinted here by permission of *German History.* Once again, I want to thank John Landau for helping me to formulate and think through the problem. I could not have written this essay without him.

2. Such meetings and the quest for a common understanding carry with them the danger of an overly placatory stance. Upon being confronted with a desperately apologetic German friend, a colleague of mine reported that she was tempted to respond that what had happened "wasn't *all that* bad!"

3. Daniel Jonah Goldhagen, *Hitler's Willing Executioners: Ordinary Germans and the Holocaust* (New York: Alfred A. Knopf, 1996). The present discussion revolves around the publication of this book and its translation into German, *Hitler's willige Vollstrecker: Ganz gewöhnliche Deutsche und der Holocaust,* trans. Klaus Kochmann (Berlin: Siedler Verlag, 1996). The sales in both languages have been quite extraordinary. The book has been translated into numerous languages and more are planned.

4. Goldhagen, *Hitler's Willing Executioners,* 45. See also 28.

5. For a sample of diverse reactions to the book (prior to its publication in Germany) see Julius H. Schoeps, ed., *Ein Volk von Mördern: Die Dokumentation zur Goldhagen-Kontroverse um die Rolle der Deutschen im Holocaust* (Hamburg: Hoffmann und Campe Verlag, 1996).

6. "Reconceiving the Holocaust?" *Tikkun* 11, no. 4 (July-August 1996): 62–65. The present article is an attempt to view the issue from a quite different perspective. "Reconceiving the Holocaust?" is reprinted in chapter 13 of this volume.

7. For Goldhagen's reply to his German critics, unprecedented in length for a newspaper article, see his "Das Versagen der Kritiker," *Die Zeit,* 2 August 1996, 9–14. For his reply to his English-language critics, see Daniel Jonah Goldhagen, "Motives, Causes, and Alibis," *New Republic,* 23 December 1996, 37–45.

8. See her conversation with Günter Gaus, "What Remains? The Language Remains," in Hannah Arendt, *Essays in Understanding 1930–1954* (New York; Harcourt, Brace & Company, 1994), 14.

9. Louis Kaplan has written a wonderful (as yet unpublished) evocation of

the multi-leveled nature of the meeting entitled "'Geistreiche Wiederjudmachung': Jewish Joke Reparations and Mourning in Post-Holocaust Germany.'"

10. See, for instance, Saul Friedlander, "Trauma and Transference," in his *Memory, History, and the Extermination of the Jews of Europe* (Bloomington: Indiana University Press, 1993), 117–37, and Dominick LaCapra, *Representing the Holocaust: History, Theory, Trauma* (Ithaca: Cornell University Press, 1994).

11. See these formulations in Hans Kellner's insightful, "Never Again Is Now," in *History & Theory* 33, no. 2 (1994): 127.

12. Quoted in John Bayley, "Poet of Holy Dread," *New York Review of Books*, 14 November 1996, 38–40. The quote appears on 38.

13. Henryk Broder, "Ich bin sehr stolz," *Der Spiegel* 21 (1996).

14. Goldhagen, "Motives, Causes, and Alibis," 45.

15. See, for instance, Schoeps's "Vorwort" in *Ein Volk von Mördern*, 11.

16. See the critical analysis of this tendency by Andrei Markovits, "Störfall im Endlager der Geschichte," in Schoeps, *Ein Volk von Mördern*, 228–40. These dubious tones were not limited to Germany. See, for instance, "Taki," "Book Burning Lights up the Big Bagel," *Sunday Times*, 17 April 1996.

17. See Volker Ulrich, "Goldhagen und die Deutschen," *Die Zeit*, 13 September 1996. The sub-title reads: "Die Tournee wurde zum Triumphzug."

18. "Kinkel weist These von Kollektivschuld zurück," *Süddeutsche Zeitung, Feuilleton*, 9 May 1996, 13.

19. For an attempt to analyze this, see Josef Joffe, "Goldhagen in Germany," *New York Review of Books*, 28 November 1996, 18–21. The cover of the review calls the article "Goldhagen Conquers Germany."

20. See Gunter Hoffmann, "Die Welt ist, wie sie ist," *Die Zeit* 40, 27 September 1996, and the interview with Hans Mommsen, "Im Räderwerk," *Frankfurter Allgemeine Zeitung* 209, 7 September 1996, 37.

21. Bayley, "Poet of Holy Dread," 39.

22. Maxim Biller, "Und Sonst?" *Die Zeit* 46, 8 November 1996.

23. Again, this is a general tendency, not an ironclad rule. Gordon Craig originally gave the book a rather positive evaluation (which he later quite severely qualified) as did Volker Berghahn and Dietrich Orlow. This is also true for the Israeli Holocaust historian, Israel Gutman. It should be pointed out, however, that most Israeli historians—among others, Gulie Ne'eman Arad, Yehuda Bauer, Robert Wistrich, Moshe Zimmermann, and myself—have received the book very critically.

24. In a letter sent to Professor Henry Friedlander on 5 April 1996, he writes: "Please feel free to share this letter with anyone."

25. Quoted in Gordon A. Craig, "The New Germany," *New York Review of Books*, 31 October 1996, 61.

26. See Martin Broszat and Saul Friedlander, "A Controversy about the Historicization of National Socialism," *Yad Vashem Studies* 19 (1988): 1–47. The quote appears on 7.

27. Ibid., 13.

28. For an early example of these different empathic frames see "The German-Jewish Dialogue at Its Limits: The Case of Hermann Broch and Volkmar

von Zuehlsdorff," in my *Culture and Catastrophe: German and Jewish Confrontations with National Socialism and Other Crises* (New York: New York University Press, 1996). For an analysis of current popular and scholarly, German empathic and non-empathic biases, see Omer Bartov, "'. . . seit die Juden weg sind': Germany, History, and Representation of Absence," *German Studies as Cultural Studies: A User's Manual,* ed. S. Denham, et al. (Ann Arbor: University of Michigan Press, 1997).

29. For good analyses of this controversy, see Charles S. Maier, *The Unmasterable Past: History, Holocaust, and German National Identity* (Cambridge, Mass.: Harvard University Press, 1988) and Richard J. Evans, *In Hitler's Shadow: West German Historians and the Attempt to Escape from the Nazi Past* (New York: Pantheon Books, 1989).

30. See Shoshana Felman & Dori Laub, *Testimony: Crises of Witnessing in Literature, Psychoanalysis, and History* (New York & London: Routledge, 1992). For a critical examination of some of these issues, see S. Friedlander, ed., *Probing the Limits of Representation: Nazism and the 'Final Solution'* (Cambridge, Mass.: Harvard University Press, 1992).

31. Quoted in Joffe, "Goldhagen in Germany," 21.

32. Such statements reinforce the view that many problematic, traditional German attitudes may remain in place, albeit under the surface. Ironically, these critics are asserting the opposite of what Goldhagen claims for the post-1945 period: that Germany has been transformed into a firmly liberal and democratic society, possessed of a political culture that has rendered anti-Semitism virtually nonexistent.

33. See M. M. Bakhtin, *The Dialogic Imagination: Four Essays,* ed. Michael Holquist, trans. Caryl Emerson & Michael Holquist (Austin: University of Texas Press, 1982).

34. For this view see Friedlander, *Memory, History, and the Extermination,* esp. the introduction. See too the introduction to Amos Funkenstein, *Perceptions of Jewish History* (Berkeley & Los Angeles: University of California Press, 1993) and Omer Bartov, *Murder in Our Midst: The Holocaust, Industrial Killing, and Representation* (New York: Oxford University Press, 1996).

35. The notion of archetypes as I use it here fits both definitions given in *Webster's New Collegiate Dictionary:* "The original pattern or model of which all things or types are representations or copies" and Jung's notion of an "inherited idea or mode of thought . . . that is derived from the experience of the race and is present in the unconscious of the individual."

36. See Nina Sutton, *Bettelheim: A Life and Legacy* (New York: Basic Books, 1996).

37. See my "Nazism, Culture, and *The Origins of Totalitarianism:* Hannah Arendt and the Discourse of Evil," chapter 11 of this volume.

38. This is, of course, a speculative matter. For a suggestive analysis that touches upon the question see Dan Diner, "Hannah Arendt Reconsidered: On the Moral and Evil in Her Holocaust Narrative," *New German Critique* 71 (1997): 177–90.

39. "Simple explanations," Goldhagen writes in his recent rebuttal, "are not

to be rejected merely because they are simple . . . The call for complexity is sometimes the refuge of those who find certain conclusions unpalatable." (Goldhagen, "Motives, Causes, and Alibis," 39). This may be so, but even "simple explanations" are not unmediated reflections of a directly accessible historical reality but products of the ascriptive, interpreting historian.

40. See the interesting article by Wulf Kansteiner, "From Exception to Exemplum: The New Approach to Nazism and the 'Final Solution,'" *History & Theory* 33, no. 2 (1994): 158.

41. Victor Klemperer, *Ich will Zeugnis ablegen bis zum letzten. 1. Tagebuecher, 1933–1941. 2. 1942–1945* (Berlin: Aufbau-Verlag, 1995). *Schindler's List,* dir. Steven Spielberg, 195 min., 1993, motion picture. As yet unpublished lecture entitled "Siegfried's Cinematic Quest: From the Germanic Forest to Olympic Virtues," given at an International Workshop in Jerusalem on "Paganism, 'Volk Religion' and Antisemitism: 19–20th Centuries," 21–23 October 1996.

42. See his insightful "Kitsch and Sadism in Ka-Tzetnik's Other Planet: Israeli Youth Imagine the Holocaust," *Jewish Social Studies* 3, no. 2 (Winter 1997): 42–76. The quote is on 76.

43. Quoted in Diner, "Hannah Arendt Reconsidered," 384. The correspondence was originally published in *Merkur,* April 1965, 380–85.

CHAPTER 10. NAZISM, NORMALCY, AND
THE GERMAN *SONDERWEG*

1. This essay has been slightly revised and updated from the original version, which appeared in *Studies in Contemporary Jewry, vol. 4, The Jews and the European Crisis,* ed. Jonathan Frankel. Copyright © 1988 by Oxford University Press, Inc. Used by Permission of Oxford University Press, Inc.

2. Hannah Arendt, *The Origins of Totalitarianism* (Cleveland, Ohio: Meridian Books, 1958).

3. For a history of Marxist approaches, see Pierre Aycoberry, *The Nazi Question: An Essay on the Interpretations of National Socialism, 1922–1975* (New York: Pantheon Books, 1981), chaps. 4, 9.

4. For a useful analysis of such tendencies, see Georg G. Iggers, *The German Conception of History: The National Tradition of Historical Thought from Herder to the Present* (Middletown, Conn.: Wesleyan University Press, 1983).

5. See Gerhard Ritter, *The German Problem: Basic Questions of German Political Life, Past and Present* (Columbus: Ohio State University Press,1965). The work was published originally in 1962. This, in turn, was a revised and expanded version of Ritter's 1948 treatise *Europa und die deutsche Frage* (Munich: F. Bruckmann Verlag, 1948). See too Friedrich Meinecke, *The German Catastrophe* (Boston: Beacon Press, 1950). This was published originally in German in 1946.

6. See, for instance, H. U. Wehler, *Bismarck und der Imperialismus* (Cologne: Kiepenheuer u. Witsch, 1969); H. U. Wehler, *Das deutsche Kaiserreich, 1871–1918* (Göttingen: Vandenhoeck & Ruprecht, 1973); and Ralf Dahrendorf, *Society and Democracy in Germany* (Garden City, N.Y.: Doubleday, 1969). This,

of course, is a minimal listing. I leave aside for the moment examples of *Sonderweg* intellectual history as this will be discussed in detail shortly.

7. David Blackbourn & Geoff Eley, *The Peculiarities of German History: Bourgeois Society and Politics in Nineteenth-Century Germany* (Oxford: Oxford University Press,1984). In the text I refer to Eley's essay "The British Model and the German Road: Rethinking the Course of German History Before 1914" and Blackbourn's "The Discreet Charm of the Bourgeoisie: Reappraising German History in the Nineteenth Century." See too Blackbourn's *Class, Religion, and Local Politics in Wilhelmine Germany* (New Haven, Conn.: Yale University Press, 1980) and Eley's *Reshaping the German Right: Radical Nationalism and Political Change after Bismarck* (New Haven, Conn.: Yale University Press, 1980).

8. There were clear political implications in this debate. *Sonderweg* theorists by and large happened to be liberal-left historians who felt impelled to counter previous conservative German historical attitudes. Eley is quite aware of this and respectful of their achievement, although the political ramifications go further than this. The *Sonderweg* historians, Eley writes, have argued

> against the accumulated complacency of a society which actively suppressed the questions of deeper-rooted historical responsibility for fascism, and against the obdurate resistance of conservatives in the profession who commanded enormous reserves of institutional power. . . . Their struggle . . . has been conducted as a two-front war—not only with the hulking dinosaurs of the *Zunft* [the "guild" of German historians], but also with the Marxist-Leninist beast. Since the early 1970s, "critical historians" have carefully negotiated a middle path, exposing the limitations of traditional history of whatever stripe, but strictly demarcating themselves from the German Democratic Republic. (5–6)

This is important as Eley claims that their "proscription of Marxism has extended not just to the works of orthodox communist [sic] historiography, but to all forms of a Marxist approach, whatever their distance from the latter" (6). The last remark is clearly self-referential. See the introduction to Eley's series of essays, *From Unification to Nazism: Reinterpreting the German Past* (Boston: Allen & Unwin, 1986).

9. Blackbourn & Eley, *Peculiarities of German History*, 10.

10. Blackbourn, "Discreet Charm of the Bourgeoisie," in Blackbourn & Eley, *Peculiarities of German History*, 169.

11. Eley, "The British Model and the German Road," in Blackbourn & Eley, *Peculiarities of German History*, 80–81.

12. Blackbourn & Eley, *Peculiarities of German History*, 16.

13. Eley, "The British Model and the German Road," in Blackbourn & Eley, *Peculiarities of German History*, 85.

14. Ibid., 84.

15. For some German reactions to the work see, for instance, H. J. Puehle, "Deutscher Sonderweg: Kontroverse um eine vermeintliche Legende," *Journal für Geschichte* 4 (1981); H. U. Wehler, "'Deutscher Sonderweg' oder allgemeine Probleme des westlichen Kapitalismus? Zur Kritik einigen 'Mythen deutscher Geschichtsschreibung,'" *Merkur* 35, no. 5 (1981). For a more complete listing and a

sense of their perspective on the debate, see Blackbourn & Ely, introduction to *Peculiarities of German History*.

16. Gordon Craig, "The German Mystery Case," *New York Review of Books*, 30 January 1986, 20–23.

17. James Joll, "Exactions of Empire," *Times Literary Supplement*, 2 August 1985, 861.

18. Blackbourn & Eley, *Peculiarities of German History*, 6.

19. Eley, "The German Right, 1860–1945: How It Changed," in Eley, *From Unification to Nazism*, 234.

20. R. D. O. Butler, *The Roots of National Socialism* (London: Faber and Faber, 1941), 277f.

21. Peter Viereck, *Metapolitics: From the Romantics to Hitler* (New York: A. A. Knopf, 1941), esp. chaps. 5, 6.

22. Crane Brinton, *Nietzsche* (Cambridge, Mass.: Harvard University Press, 1941).

23. Georg Lukács, *The Destruction of Reason*, trans. Peter Palmer (Atlantic Highlands, N.J.: Humanities Press, 1981). This was first published in German under the title *Die Zerstörung der Vernunft* in 1953.

24. Geoff Eley, review of Roderick Stackelberg, *Idealism Debased*, in *Studies in Contemporary Jewry* 1 (1984): esp. 544. Subsequent to the writing of this essay, I published *The Nietzsche Legacy in Germany 1890–1990* (Berkeley & Los Angeles: University of California Press, 1992). I hope that this can be regarded as an example of the kind of cultural and intellectual history for which I was pleading here.

25. It is of significance that George L. Mosse's *Toward the Final Solution* (New York: H. Fertig, 1978) is subtitled "A History of European Racism." Moreover Mosse stresses the scavenger nature of racism and its compatibility with a wide number of political positions. He specifically departs from a simplistic *Sonderweg* determinism and argues that prior to 1914 it was France, not Germany, that exhibited the most pernicious racist, anti-Semitic and proto-fascist tendencies (168).

26. To document this, see the series of essays in David C. Large & William Weber, eds., *Wagnerism in European Culture and Politics* (Ithaca, N.Y.: Cornell University Press, 1984).

27. There is a contemporary danger of going to the opposite extreme. R. Hinton Thomas, in *Nietzsche in German Politics and Society, 1890–1918* (Manchester: Manchester University Press, 1983), for instance, regards Nietzsche's influence through the Great War as exerted almost totally on progressive circles. The "deconstructionist" Nietzsche—as I note in chapter 2 of the present volume, "Thinking the Nietzsche Legacy Today"—has also largely excised the problematic aspects of Nietzsche's work. Hopefully my *Nietzsche Legacy in Germany* has helped to correct these imbalances.

28. Alfred Kelly, *The Descent of Darwin: The Popularization of Darwinism in Germany, 1860–1914* (Chapel Hill: University of North Carolina Press, 1981).

29. For this whole development, see the instructive and controversial essay by Zeev Sternhell, "Fascist Ideology," in *Fascism: A Reader's Guide*, ed. Walter Laqueur (Harmondsworth: Penguin Books, 1979).

30. George Mosse, *Nationalism and Sexuality: Respectability and Abnormal Sexuality in Modern Europe* (New York: H. Fertig, 1985).

31. George Mosse interview with Michael A. Ledeen in *Nazism: A Historical and Comparative Analysis of National Socialism* (New Brunswick, N.J.: Transaction Books, 1978), 43.

32. See H. Rauschning, *The Revolution of Nihilism* (New York: 1939), and E. Nolte, *The Three Faces of Fascism* (New York: Holt, Rinehart and Winston, 1965).

33. J. Edward Chamberlin & Sander L. Gilman, eds., *Degeneration: The Dark Side of Progress* (New York: Columbia University Press, 1985), viii.

34. Ibid., 290.

35. Geoff Eley, "Holocaust History," *London Review of Books*, 3–11 March 1982, 6–9.

36. For reviews of this school, see Tim Mason, "Intention and Explanation: A Current Controversy About the Interpretation of National Socialism," in G. Hirschfeld & L. Kettenacker, eds. *Der "Führerstaat," Mythos und Reaität* (Stuttgart: Klett-Cotta, 1981); Saul Friedlander, "From Anti-Semitism to Extermination: A Historiographical Study of Nazi Policies Toward the Jews and an Essay in Interpretation," *Yad Vashem Studies* 16 (1984); Otto D. Kulka, "Major Trends and Tendencies in German Historiography on National Socialism and the 'Jewish Question' (1924–1984)," *Leo Baeck Institute Yearbook* 30 (1985).

37. Jeffrey Herf, *Reactionary Modernism: Technology, Culture and Politics in Weimar and the Third Reich* (London: Cambridge University Press, 1984).

38. It is unfortunate that Herf never makes the differences with Blackbourn and Eley explicit as such a confrontation is directly germane to his major thesis. Given the 1980 date of the German publication of their work, there was ample time to include it. Such a confrontation, indeed, may well have toughened Herf's text. After Blackbourn and Eley, one cannot speak, as Herf does in his book, of "the failure of the bourgeois revolution" in Germany (217) as if it were a self-evident historical fact rather than a deeply contested thesis in need of detailed substantiation.

39. Herf, of course, is not alone in this. See, too, Anson Rabinbach, "The Aesthetics of Production in the Third Reich," in George Mosse, ed., *International Fascism* (Beverly Hills, Calif.: Sage Publications, 1979); Karl Heinz Ludwig, *Technik und Ingenieure im Dritten Reich* (Königstein: Athenäum; Düsseldorf: Droste Verlag, 1979).

40. Herf, *Reactionary Modernism*, 11.

41. Ibid., 48.

42. Ibid., 13.

43. Eley, "The German Right, 1860–1945: How It Changed," in Eley, *From Unification to Nazism*, 244.

44. Blackbourn & Eley, *Peculiarities of German History*, 26.

45. See Blackbourn's "Discreet Charm of the Bourgeoisie," in Blackbourn & Eley, *Peculiarities of German History*, esp. 206–21.

46. Norbert Elias, *The Civilizing Process: The History of Manners*, trans. Edmund Jephcott (Oxford: Blackwell, 1978), chap. 1. The work was published originally in 1939.

47. For an interesting treatment of a countervailing (though not triumphant) humanist tradition within German nationalism, see Christoph Prignitz, *Vaterlandsliebe und Freiheit: Deutscher Patriotismus von 1750 bis 1850* (Wiesbaden: Steiner, 1981).

48. George Mosse, *The Crisis of German Ideology: Intellectual Origins of the Third Reich* (New York: Grosset & Dunlap, 1964).

49. Chamberlin & Gilman, *Degeneration*, viii.

50. Blackbourn & Eley, *Peculiarities of German History*, 26. See, too, Blackbourn's "The Politics of Demagogy in Imperial Germany," *Past and Present* 113 (November 1986): 152–84.

51. Eley argues that he offers "a careful Marxist approach explicitly distanced from orthodox Marxist-Leninist ones." At least in terms of the value of their critique of the *Sonderweg* position, I do not believe that Blackbourn and Eley present "just another rendition of the old vulgar Marxist line." It is their alternative theories that are open to question. See Eley's introduction to *From Unification to Nazism*, 18, n. 16.

52. Geoff Eley, "What Produces Fascism: Pre-Industrial Traditions or a Crisis of the Capitalist State?" *From Unification to Nazism*, 270.

53. There is no need here to list the massive relevant literature concerning anti-Semitism and racism. On the question of *Lebensraum* and related matters, see Woodruff D. Smith, *The Ideological Origins of Nazi Imperialism* (New York: Oxford University Press, 1986). On varying conceptions of "national socialism," see Sternhell, "Fascist Ideology."

54. Franz Neumann, *Behemoth: The Structure and Practice of National Socialism* (New York: Oxford University Press, 1944), 125.

55. Herf, *Reactionary Modernism*, see esp. chaps. 8 and 9.

56. Ibid., 229.

57. Blackbourn and Eley are not alone in challenging liberal interpretations. One such challenge that explicitly sought to displace the centrality of racism and genocide as the historical key was Geoffiey Barraclough's series of articles in the *New York Review of Books,* 9 October 1972; 2, 16 November 1972. Barraclough did make some trenchant criticisms. But Nazism's historical significance can surely not be satisfactorily summed up in terms of its (largely unintended) modernizing side-effects. Was its capitalist activity more important than its racial revolution? If Blackbourn and Eley are correct, Germany had experienced its capitalist transformation long before the Nazis appeared. The argument with them remains whether an understanding of Nazism is best comprehended in terms of the dynamics of this crisis.

58. On this point, see George L. Mosse, "Der erste Weltkrieg und die Brutalisierung der Politik: Betrachtungen über die politische Rechte, den Rassismus, und den deutschen Sonderweg" in Manfred Funke et al., eds. *Demokratie und Diktatur. Geist und Gestalt politische Herrschafi in Deutschland und Europa,* Festschrift für Karl Dietrich Bracher (Dusseldorf: Droste, 1987). But Juergen Kocka is correct to point out that in many crucial ways Nazism possessed a dynamic that far transcended "the old German Sonderweg." The Sonderweg thesis, he argues, is helpful in explaining why there were so few barriers to fascism in

Germany but less so when accounting for Nazism's unique radical impulse. See his "German History before Hitler: The Debate about the German 'Sonderweg,'" *Journal of Contemporary History* 23 (1988): 3–16.

CHAPTER II. NAZISM, CULTURE, AND *THE ORIGINS OF TOTALITARIANISM*

1. Hannah Arendt, *The Origins of Totalitarianism*, 2d enl. ed. (Cleveland, Ohio: Meridian Books, 1958). "Nazism, Culture, and *The Origins of Totalitarianism*: Hannah Arendt and the Discourse of Evil" was first published in *New German Critique* 70 (Winter 1997): 117–41. Reprinted by permission of *New German Critique*.

2. Indeed, there is a compulsion to reminisce about it in almost confessional terms! For instance, in a recent paper Michael Marrus reports how taken aback he was when a reviewer of his first book, *The Politics of Assimilation: A Study of the French Jewish Community at the Time of the Dreyfus Affair* (London: Oxford University Press, 1971), rebuked him for taking Hannah Arendt seriously ("a bad sign"): "I first read *The Origins of Totalitarianism* . . . in 1963 and I recall packing a heavily underlined copy among the few possessions I took with me to graduate school in the summer of that year. And so the put-down . . . did not sting at the time. But I remember being puzzled at the very nature of the accusation. Could there be people who did *not* take Hannah Arendt seriously, I wondered?" See Marrus, "Hannah Arendt and the Dreyfus Affair," *New German Critique* 66 (Fall 1995): 147. Even readers more critical than Marrus write similarly of the power exerted by the book. Abbot Gleason, who has just written a kind of retrospective balance-sheet of the notion of totalitarianism reports that upon first reading the *Origins* in 1958, "I was disturbed and enthralled by its vision and rhetoric," although he adds that even then "its post-war atmosphere of Armageddon seemed anachronistic." See Gleason's *Totalitarianism: The Inner History of the Cold War* (New York: Oxford University Press), 5.

3. Raul Hilberg's pathbreaking *The Destruction of the European Jews* only appeared in 1961.

4. I owe this formulation to Melvin Richter in conversation, 6 November 1995.

5. Alfred Kazin, *New York Jew* (New York: Knopf, 1978), 299.

6. A good introduction to this and Arendt's context can be found in Elisabeth Young-Bruehl, *Hannah Arendt: For Love of the World* (New Haven, Conn.: Yale University Press 1982).

7. See the review in the *New Leader*, 15 August 1951.

8. McCarthy to Arendt, 26 April 1951, in Arendt & McCarthy, *Between Friends: The Correspondence of Hannah Arendt and Mary McCarthy 1949–1975*, ed. Carol Brightman (New York: Harcourt Brace,1995), 1–2.

9. See Phillip Rieff, "The Theology of Politics: Reflections on Totalitarianism as the Burden of Our Time," *Journal of Religion* 32, no. 2 (April 1952): 119.

10. Judith N. Shklar, "Hannah Arendt as Pariah," *Partisan Review* 50 (1983): 69.

11. See Leon Botstein, "The Jew as Pariah: Hannah Arendt's Political Philosophy," *Dialectical Anthropology* 8 (1983): 57. Arendt's "views on writing history, despite an enduring insistence on understanding how fact differs from opinion, showed traces of Heidegger, Nietzsche and Walter Benjamin's challenge to the claims of historical objectivity and the static character of historical fact. She stuck to her didactic story telling."

12. Marrus, "Hannah Arendt and the Dreyfus Affair," 14.

13. See Martin Jay, "Name-Dropping or Dropping Names? Modes of Legitimation in the Humanities," in his *Force Fields: Between Intellectual History and Cultural Critique* (New York: Routledge, 1993), 168.

14. For a "left" view see Phillip Hansen, *Hannah Arendt: Politics, History, and Citizenship* (Stanford, Calif.: Stanford University Press, 1993). See too Bonnie Honig, ed. *Feminist Interpretations of Hannah Arendt* (University Park: Pennsylvania State University Press, 1995).

15. For a good exposition of the place of anti-Semitism in her overall scheme, see the article by Ben Halpern, "The Context of Hannah Arendt's Concept of Totalitarianism" in *Totalitarian Democracy and After* (Jerusalem: Magnes Press, 1984), 386–98. Arendt's totalitarianism was a product of the nation-states and essentially international. As Halpern puts it: "For it was the Protocols of the Elders of Zion that became the model the fascists followed; taking the extraterritorial survival of the Jewish people as their example, the fascists developed an essentially anti-national, global conspiracy of their own, with anti-Semitism as its essential base" (394). Both Jaspers and Arendt were very critical of Halpern. See their *Correspondence 1926–1969*, ed. Lotte Kohler & Hans Saner, trans. Robert & Rita Kimber (New York: Harcourt Brace Jovanovich, 1992), 121–23, 162. Halpern was aware of this hostility and prefaced his article by stressing that he would "perform the task with all the empathy she deserves" (387).

16. Irving Howe, *The Decline of the New* (New York: Harcourt Brace Jovanovich, 1970), 244–45.

17. Arendt's portrait in *Origins* not only reflected her overall existentialist posture that all historical actors exercised certain historical choices for which they were responsible (at least in the pre-totalitarian phase) but also a defiantly anti-apologetic form of Jewish history inspired partly by her "post-assimilationist" mentor Kurt Blumenfeld.

18. See the 1972 Hebrew University M. A. dissertation by Yerahmiel Cohen (supervised and approved by the leading modern Jewish historian at that time, Shmuel Ettinger), "On the Question of the Responsibility of the Jews for Their Extermination by the Nazis as Expressed in the Writings of Bruno Bettelheim, Raul Hilberg, and Hannah Arendt, and the Debate Surrounding Them," 45 ff. Cohen has since then clearly moderated his views (see the next note) but, based upon various conversations I have had in the very recent past, it would not be wrong to say that some of Israel's leading historians and political scientists hold this view to this day.

19. Indeed, Yerahmiel Cohen, the author of the views quoted in the above note has now (in much cooler fashion) comprehensively surveyed attitudes in this respect in his "Breaking the Code: Hannah Arendt's *Eichmann in Jerusalem* and

the Public Polemic—Myth, Memory, and Historical Imagination," in *Michael* 13 (1993): 29–85.

20. Leon Wieseltier, "Understanding Anti-Semitism: Hannah Arendt on the Origins of Prejudice," *New Republic*, 7 October 1981, 29–32. The quote appears on 32.

21. This was published for the first time much later in 1957 and in English. For the latest revised edition, see *Rahel Varnhagen: The Life of a Jewish Woman*, trans. Richard & Clara Winston (New York: Harcourt Brace Jovanovich, 1974). Many years later Blumenfeld, her Zionist mentor from Weimar days onward, reformulated his position to Arendt thus: "Genuine relationships between Jews and non Jews will first occur when the Jew too will not be embarrassed to express his opinions about other Jews . . . ." See Letter 104, 25 July 1969, in Hannah Arendt & Kurt Blumenfeld, ". . . *in keinem Besitz verwurzelt" Die Korrespondenz*, Heraugegeben von Ingeborg Nordmann und Iris Pilling (Hamburg: Rotbuch Verlag, 1995), 237–38.

22. As one commentator has recently put it, *Origins* "is best read as an ontologically informed account of a distinctive and frightening political reality which threatens in a powerful and unprecedented way our human status as political beings." See Hansen, *Hannah Arendt*. The quote appears on 133.

23. Relatively early (1978), Martin Jay critically suggested that Arendt's overall views were indelibly stamped by a Heideggerian kind of existentialism and Weimarian "decisionism" that produced a politics devoid of any guiding and substantial norms. See "The Political Existentialism of Hannah Arendt" in Jay's collection *Permanent Exiles: Essays on the Intellectual Migration from Germany to America* (New York: Columbia Press, 1985), 237–56. For a more recent, highly detailed depiction of Arendt as a postmodern political theorist who inherited and creatively reworked the Heideggerian (and Nietzschean) predicament and the collapse of metaphysics but who avoided their pernicious political conclusions see Dana R. Villa, *Arendt and Heidegger: The Fate of the Political* (Princeton, N.J.: Princeton University Press, 1996).

24. It should be very obvious that this was by no means a consensual view. Apart from the fury and pain Arendt evoked with her Eichmann book, many other fine minds were far from persuaded as to the quality of hers. Isaiah Berlin is an extreme example of this: "I do not greatly respect the lady's ideas . . . I think she produces no arguments, no evidence of serious philosophical or historical thought. It is all a stream of metaphysical free association." See Ramin Jahanbegloo, *Conversations with Isaiah Berlin* (London: Peter Halban, 1992), 82.

25. Rieff, "Theology of Politics," 119.

26. "The behaviour patterns of assimilated Jews, determined by this continuous concentrated effort to distinguish themselves, created a Jewish type that is recognizable everywhere. Instead of being defined by nationality or religion, Jews were being transformed into a social group whose members shared certain psychological attributes and reactions, the sum total of which was supposed to constitute 'Jewishness.' In other words, Judaism became a psychological quality and the Jewish question became an involved personal problem for every individual Jew." See Arendt, *Origins*, 66. See generally chap. 3, "The Jews and Society."

27. Arendt, *Origins*, 277. In this chapter (9), entitled "The Decline of the

Nation-State and the End of the Rights of Man," Arendt is especially illuminating on the latter and hopelessly confusing (and perhaps confused) on the former.

28. Ibid., 479.

29. Ibid., 437–59. The quote appears on 437.

30. "From Koenigsberg to Manhattan (Or Hannah, Rahel, Martin and El-friede or Thy Neighbour's Gemeinschaft)" in Ernest Gellner, *Culture, Identity, and Politics* (Cambridge: Cambridge University Press, 1987), 89–90.

31. On the concept of totalitarianism in general and Arendt's in particular, see Abbott Gleason, *Totalitarianism: The Inner History of the Cold War* (New York: Oxford University Press, 1995). For general treatments of *Origins* (fair but also critical) see Stephen Whitfield, *Into the Dark: Hannah Arendt and Totalitarianism* (Philadelphia: Temple University Press, 1980) and Margaret Canovan, *The Political Thought of Hannah Arendt* (New York: Harcourt Brace Jovanovich, 1974). For a defense of the work in the light of such criticisms see Bernard Crick, "On Rereading *The Origins of Totalitarianism*," *Social Research* 44, no. 1 (Spring 1977): 106–26. For one important and perhaps surprising rejection (given the fact that his name was intimately associated with Arendt over the *Eichmann in Jerusalem* controversy), see Raul Hilberg, *Unerbetene Erinnerung: Der Weg eines Holocaust-Forschers* (Frankfurt am Main: S. Fisher, 1994), 128.

32. Raymond Aron, "The Essence of Totalitarianism according to Hannah Arendt," *Partisan Review* 60, no. 3 (1993): 366–76. Originally in the French journal *Critique*, 1954.

33. For a still interesting review of these theories and their problems as well as their ideological biases, see Leon Bramson, *The Political Context of Sociology* (Princeton, N.J.: Princeton University Press, 1961). A recent attempt to argue that Arendt's use of the mass society hypothesis was not conservative can be found in Hansen, *Hannah Arendt*.

34. See his essay on Arendt, "The Survivor" in Jean-François Lyotard, *Toward the Postmodern* (Atlantic Highlands, N.J.: Humanities Press, 1993), 156–58. The burden of the essay, in rather Marcuseian fashion, is to argue that given the ongoing psychological anxieties that both produce and sustain totalitarianism, the totalitarian threat remains not only intact but a reality within advanced contemporary industrial society. There is something absurdly inappropriate in the—badly translated?—text: "The historical names for this Mr. Nice Guy totalitarianism are no longer Stalingrad or Normandy (much less Auschwitz) but Wall Street's Dow Average and the Tokyo Nikkei Index." (159).

35. Jaspers to Arendt, 12 January 1952, Letter 14, in Arendt & Jaspers, *Correspondence*, 174.

36. Hannah Arendt, "A Reply," *Review of Politics*, January 1953, 78.

37. Thus wrote Mary McCarthy in a letter, 26 April 1951, in Arendt & McCarthy, *Between Friends*, 2.

38. Margaret Canovan, *The Political Thought of Hannah Arendt*, 42.

39. As Walter Laqueur has recently noted, Arendt does not deal with Communism "except in passing"; much is said of Dreyfus and Rhodes and hardly anything of Lenin. See his "Postfascism, Postcommunism," *Partisan Review* 3 (1995): 383–96. The reference appears on 389.

40. The work was begun already in 1946, impelled, as Gleason says, "by

her increasing realization of the scale of the death camps and the radicality of Nazi intentions" (*Totalitarianism*, 108). Even before that, in 1945, Arendt published relevant reflections upon Nazi mass murder. See her "Organized Guilt and Universal Responsibility" reproduced in Hannah Arendt, *Essays in Understanding, 1930–1954*, ed. Jerome Kohn (New York: Harcourt, Brace & Co., 1994), 121–32.

41. See Arendt's letter of 19 July 1947 in Arendt & Blumenfeld, " . . . *in keinem Besitz verwurzelt*," 43.

42. Arendt, "What Remains? The Language Remains: A Conversation with Günter Gaus" in Arendt, *Essays in Understanding*, 14.

43. Kazin, *New York Jew*, 298.

44. Arendt, "Approaches to the 'German Problem,'" *Partisan Review* 12, no. 1 (Winter 1945): 93–106; reproduced in Arendt, *Essays in Understanding*, 106–20.

45. I treat these different conceptions in chapter 1 of my *Culture and Catastrophe: German and Jewish Confrontations with National Socialism and Other Crises* (New York: New York University Press, 1995).

46. Arendt, "Approaches to the 'German Problem.'" The quotes appear on 108–9.

47. Arendt to Jaspers, 4 March 1951, in Arendt & Jaspers, *Correspondence*, 166.

48. For an interpretation placing Arendt squarely on the left (perhaps even more radically than Marx) and defending her reading of mass society as proceeding from a radical rather than conservative viewpoint see Hansen, *Hannah Arendt*.

49. Elisabeth Young-Bruehl, *Hannah Arendt, For Love of the World*, 200. Hansen argues that Arendt does not indict modernity as such but rather its specifically bourgeois component as the culprit in the rise of totalitarianism. See Hansen, *Hannah Arendt*, 133.

50. George L. Mosse, *The Crisis of German Ideology: Intellectual Origins of the Third Reich* (New York: Grosset & Dunlap, 1964); Fritz Stern, *The Politics of Cultural Despair: A Study in the Rise of Germanic Ideology* (Berkeley & Los Angeles: University of California Press, 1961).

51. Gellner, "From Koenigsberg," 89.

52. Ibid., 85.

53. One should note that shortly before his death Gellner sought to resuscitate the usefulness of the concept of totalitarianism. See his "Coming to Terms," *New Republic*, 4 December 1995, 42–45.

54. This debate has been fueled by the appearance of Elzbieta Ettinger, *Hannah Arendt/Martin Heidegger* (New Haven, Conn.: Yale University Press, 1995). The most reductionist argument representing Arendt's view of Nazism as "*kulturlos*" as a function of her attempt to rehabilitate Heidegger is to be found in Richard Wolin's piece, "Hannah and the Magician: An Affair to Remember," *New Republic*, 9 October 1995, 27–37.

55. Gellner, "From Koenigsberg," 86.

56. Arendt to Blumenfeld, 19 July 1947, in Arendt & Blumenfeld, " . . . *in keinem Besitz verwurzelt*," 43.

57. Arendt, "Nightmare and Flight," in Arendt, *Essays in Understanding*, 134.

58. In an unpublished letter for instance, Arendt wrote that Raul Hilberg's ork on the destruction of European Jewry was almost "perfect" except for the "foolish" first chapter (that sought to locate Nazi anti-Semitism within the continuity of German—and Western—history). See Hilberg, *Unerbetene Erinnerung*, 135.

59. Kazin, *New York Jew*, 307.

60. Thus, Arendt remarked of Hermann Broch (whom she deeply admired) that his categories and values, and especially his emphasis on death, were characteristic of the generation of World War I. He "remained limited to this . . . horizon of experience; and it is decisive that this horizon was broken through by the generation for whom not war but totalitarian forms of rule were the basic, the crucial experience. For we know today that killing is far from the worst that man can inflict on man and that on the other hand death is by no means what man most fears." See her "Hermann Broch: 1886–1951" in *Men in Dark Times* (New York: Harcourt, Brace, & World, 1968), 126–27.

61. See the insightful comments by George Kateb, "The Questionable Influence of Arendt (and Strauss)" in *Hannah Arendt and Leo Strauss: German Emigres and American Political Thought after World War II*, ed. P. G. Kielmansegg (Washington, D.C.: German Historical Institute, 1995).

62. Raymond Aron, "The Essence of Totalitarianism." The review is a masterly "common-sense" critique.

63. See the English version of this famous work, *The Question of German Guilt*, trans. E. B. Ashton (New York: Dial Press, 1947).

64. Arendt to Jaspers, 17 August 1946, in Arendt & Jaspers, *Correspondence*, 51–56. The quote appears on 54.

65. Jaspers to Arendt, 19 October 1946, in Arendt & Jaspers, *Correspondence*, 60–63. The quote appears on 62.

66. In a review of Denis de Rougemont's *The Devil's Share* in *Partisan Review* 12, no. 2 (1945): 259–60; reproduced in Arendt, *Essays in Understanding*, 133–35.

67. The "metaphysical" temptation is great indeed, perhaps a given, in this kind of extreme situation. Sidney Hook, for instance, was acutely aware of the problem from early on and sought a different, far more concrete mode of analysis in his "Hitlerism: A Non-Metaphysical View," *Contemporary Jewish Record* 7, no. 2 (April 1944): 146–56.

68. Arendt to Jaspers, 17 December 1946, in Arendt & Jaspers, *Correspondence*, 68–70. The quote appears on 69.

69. "My mother," writes Andrew Delbanco, "told me with tears in her eyes that Joseph Goebbels had been the devil incarnate—Mephistopheles she called him." In his recent book *The Death of Satan*, he writes that America is a culture that has lost a necessary sense of evil, incapable of constructing an acceptable symbolic language for describing what nevertheless remains an ongoing experience. See *The Death of Satan: How Americans Have Lost Their Sense of Evil* (New York: Farrar, Straus and Giroux, 1995), esp. 5 and 224.

70. Arendt, "Nightmare and Flight," in Arendt, *Essays in Understanding*, 134.

71. Arendt to Jaspers, 4 March 1951, in Arendt & Jaspers, *Correspondence*, 165–68. The quotes appear on 166. If the camps resemble "nothing so much as medieval pictures of Hell," she wrote in *Origins*, it did not reproduce "what made the traditional conceptions of Hell tolerable to man: the Last judgement, the idea of an absolute standard of justice combined with the infinite possibility of grace" (447).

72. Arendt, *Origins*, 459. In addition, she writes:

> It is the appearance of some radical evil, previously unknown to us, that puts an end to the notion of developments and transformations of qualities. Here, there are neither political nor historical nor simply moral standards but at the most, the realization that something seems to be involved in modern politics that actually should never have been involved in politics as we used to understand it, namely all-or-nothing—all, and that is an undetermined infinity of forms of human living-together, or nothing . . . inexorable doom for human beings. (443)

73. See chapter 1 of Aschheim, *Culture and Catastrophe*.

74. As Greil Marcus puts it: Arendt "does not explain it, because that is not what one does with an abyss; instead . . . she locates it. Without in any way removing Nazism from history," she demonstrates its radically transgressive, novel nature, the ways in which it "altered the limits of action." See his "Götterdämmerung after Twenty-One Years" (1976) but republished as still valid and relevant in his recent *The Dustbin of History* (Cambridge, Mass.: Harvard University Press, 1995). The quotes appear on 61–62.

75. Arendt to Jaspers, 17 August 1946, in Arendt & Jaspers, *Correspondence*, 54.

76. George Steiner, for instance, is quite candid about this. "The atrocities," he writes, "did not spring up in the Gobi desert or the rain forests of the Amazon." See the preface to Steiner's *Language and Silence: Essays on Language, Literature and the Inhuman* (New York, 1977), viii–ix. "My own consciousness is possessed by the eruption of barbarism in Europe," he writes. Yet this simultaneously indicates his Eurocentrism as well as its saving critical capacity: "I do not claim for this hideousness any singular privilege; but this is the crisis of rational, humane expectation which has shaped my own life and with which I am most directly concerned" (viii).

77. See my *Culture and Catastrophe*, 9. I have also just come across Scott L. Montgomery's provocative but insightful article, "What Kind of Memory? Reflections on Images of the Holocaust," *Contention* 5, no. 1 (Fall 1995): 79–103.

78. See, for instance, Shiraz Dossa, "Human Status and Politics: Hannah Arendt on the Holocaust," *Canadian Journal of Political Science* 8, no. 2 (June 1980): 309–23, and Anne Norton, "Heart of Darkness: Africa and African Americans in the Writings of Hannah Arendt," in Honig, ed., *Feminist Interpretations of Hannah Arendt*, 247–61.

79. Arendt, *Origins*, 192.

80. Ibid., 443.

81. Norton, "Heart of Darkness," esp. 252–54.

82. Dossa, "Human Status and Politics," 319–20.

83. Marcus, "Götterdämmerung," in *Dustbin of History*, 53.

84. Montgomery, "What Kind of Memory?" 79–80; 88; 98–99.

85. Ibid., 100–101.

86. His heated denials notwithstanding, this, I would argue, is the effect created by Steven Katz in his massive *The Holocaust in Historical Context: The Holocaust and Mass Death before the Modern Age* (New York: Oxford University Press, 1994).

87. See the very insightful review of Katz's book by David Biale in *Tikkun* 10, no. 1 (January-February 1995): 79–80, 88.

88. Alain Finkielkraut, *Remembering in Vain: The Klaus Barbie Trial and Crimes against Humanity*, trans. Roxanne Lapidus with Sima Godfrey, introduction by Alice Y. Kaplan (New York: Columbia University Press, 1992).

89. Ibid. "Nothing inherent makes a discussion of colonialism cancel out a discussion of the shoah; nothing inherent makes a discussion of the shoah cancel out a discussion of the Third World. The political rift between two world perspectives is both tragic and emblematic of our times." See Kaplan's introduction (xxi).

90. For a rounded discussion of this problem see Saul Friedlander, ed., *Probing the Limits of Representation: Nazism and the "Final Solution"* (Cambridge, Mass.: Harvard University Press, 1992).

CHAPTER 12. POST-HOLOCAUST JEWISH MIRRORINGS
OF GERMANY

1. This essay was originally presented at an International conference on "Mirroring Germany: Imagination, Representation, Memory" sponsored by the Institute for German History, Tel Aviv University, 25–26 May 1997, and originally published in *Tel Aviver Jahrbuch für deutsche Geschichte* 26 (1997): 345–53. Reprinted by permission of Institute for German History, Tel Aviv University.

2. See, for instance, Dominick Le Capra, *Representing the Holocaust: History, Theory, Trauma* (Ithaca, N.Y.: Cornell University Press, 1994) and Saul Friedlander, "Trauma and Transference" in his *Memory, History, and the Extermination of the Jews of Europe* (Bloomington: Indiana University Press, 1993).

3. Her present revival is nothing short of remarkable. Virtually every political and cultural strain is currently claiming and appropriating her. For a neo-Marxist reading, see Phillip Hansen, *Hannah Arendt: Politics, History, and Cizitenship* (Stanford, Calif.: Stanford University Press, 1993). Bonnie Honig has edited a collection entitled *Feminist Interpretations of Hannah Arendt* (University Park: Pennsylvania State University Press, 1995). The postmodernist angle is most thoroughly examined in Dana R. Villa, *Arendt and Heidegger: The Fate of the Political* (Princeton, N.J.: Princeton University Press, 1996). These, one must note, are all general appropriations. Her more familiar role as a "Jewish" thinker also continues to fascinate. See, most recently, Richard J. Bernstein, *Hannah Arendt and the Jewish Question* (Cambridge, Mass.: MIT Press, 1996). Because of her critical attitude to Zionism and, most infamously, her book on Eichmann, until very recently Arendt has been virtually taboo in Israel. This now appears to be changing. See the admirable special issue "Hannah Arendt and *Eichmann in*

Jerusalem," published in the Tel Aviv University journal *History & Memory* 8, no. 2 (Fall/Winter 1996). In addition, a Hebrew University international conference on "Arendt in Jerusalem" was held in December 1997, and the ensuing volume will be published by the University of California Press.

4. My admiration for Arendt, however critically tempered, is evident in the pieces I have written on her work. See "Hannah Arendt and Karl Jaspers: Friendship, Catastrophe and the Possibilities of the German-Jewish Dialogue" in my *Culture and Catastrophe: German and Jewish Confrontations with National Socialism and Other Crises* (New York: New York University Press, 1996) and chapter 11 of this volume, "Nazism, Culture, and *The Origins of Totalitarianism*: Hannah Arendt and the Discourse of Evil." Goldhagen's stature as an historian and thinker is, of course, a quite different matter. See my very critical review of his book, "Reconceiving the Holocaust?" in *Tikkun* 11 (July/August 1996): 62–65 and reproduced as chapter 13 of this volume. The present comparative juxtaposition does not point to any symmetry of importance and depth but only to their visible roles in the geneses, formulations, and receptions of these central paradigms.

5. On this theme see my "Archetypes and the German Jewish Dialogue: Reflections Occasioned by the Goldhagen Affair," in chapter 9 of this volume.

6. "Approaches to the 'German Problem,'" in Hannah Arendt, *Essays in Understanding 1930–1954,* ed. Jerome Kohn (New York: Harcourt Brace, 1994), 108–9. The article was first published in *Partisan Review* 12 (Winter 1945): 93–106.

7. As she wrote to her mentor on January 6, 1933: "What troubled me first of course is the term 'German character.' You say yourself how misused it is. For me it is almost identical with misuse. Even if I were to just to hear the term, as if you were to speak of it for the first time, I would still balk at it. Perhaps I have not understood what you meant by an emerging historical totality. I took it to mean that this character manifests itself from time to time in history. It would remain, then, despite its basic indeterminateness, something absolute, something untouched by history and Germany's destiny. I cannot identify with that, because I do not have in myself, so to speak, an attestation of 'German character.'" See Arendt to Jaspers, Letter 24, in Hannah Arendt & Karl Jaspers, *Correspondence 1926–1969* (New York: Harcourt Brace Jovanovich, 1992), 18–19.

8. Arendt, "Approaches to the 'German Problem,'" *Essays in Understanding,* 97.

9. See Ernest Gellner's provocative "From Königsberg to Manhattan (Or Hannah, Rahel, Martin and Elfriede or Thy Neighbour's Gemeinschaft)," in his *Culture, Identity, and Politics* (Cambridge: Cambridge University Press, 1987).

10. This point is interestingly developed in Ben Halpern, "The Context of Hannah Arendt's Concept of Totalitarianism," *Totalitarian Democracy and After* (Jerusalem: Magnes Press, 1984), 386–98.

11. Ibid., 97.

12. See the postscript to *Eichmann in Jerusalem* (New York: The Viking Press, 1965), 287.

13. This is rather a speculative matter. For some interesting suggestions see

Dan Diner, "Hannah Arendt Reconsidered: On the Moral and Evil in Her Holocaust Narrative," *New German Critique* 71 (1997): 177–90.

14. See her "Nightmare and Flight" in Arendt, *Essays in Understanding*,
154.

15. The work that caused all the furor is *Hitler's Willing Executioners: Ordinary Germans and the Holocaust* (New York: Alfred A. Knopf, 1996).

16. Daniel Jonah Goldhagen, "Motives, Causes, and Alibis: A Reply to My
Critics," *New Republic*, 23 December 1996, 37–45. The quote appears on 39.

17. Even *prior* to its German translation a whole critical volume appeared
in Germany! See Julius H. Schoeps, ed., *Ein Volk von Mördern? Die Dokumentation zur Goldhagen-Kontroverse um die Rolle der Deutschen im Holocaust*
(Hamburg: Hoffmann und Campe, 1996).

18. Goldhagen, *Hitler's Willing Executioners*, 45. See also 28.

19. Clearly this is a complex, long-term process that goes well beyond its
early connection with Arendt. The simple passage of time, the notion that somehow survivors carry with them a form of "mythical" memory and the postmodernist problematization of representation and memory are all components of this
process. Most recently Istvan Deak, has written: "An accurate record of the Holocaust has been endangered in my opinion, by the uncritical endorsement, often
by well-known Jewish writers or public figures, of virtually any survivor's account
or related writings." See his "Memories of Hell," *New York Review of Books*, 26
June 1997, 38.

20. In a recent essay Anson Rabinbach puts it thus:

> Goldhagen's Holocaust is violent, demonizing, particularistic, judeocentric and con-
> crete . . . It reestablishes the hierarchy of hatred among the victims, so overwhelm-
> ingly rejects the pluralist inclusivity that is so manifest in the new public memory
> of Holocaust. . . . Goldhagen's version of the story has a transgressive dimension
> that restores many of the motifs that prevailed when Jewish memory did not have
> to contend with its public presence or its universalist instrumentalization. The im-
> pact of Goldhagen's book therefore should be first and foremost considered an
> event in the public sphere, and as such serves as a counterdiscourse to the "Ameri-
> canization of the Holocaust."

See his "Explosion to Erosion: Holocaust Memorialization in America from Bitburg to Goldhagen," *History & Memory* 9, nos. 1/2 (Fall 1997): 250–51.

21. See Diner, "Hannah Arendt Reconsidered."

22. See Bartov's insightful comments in "Kitsch and Sadism in Ka-Tzetnik's
Other Planet: Israeli Youth Imagine the Holocaust," *Jewish Social Studies* 3, no.
2 (1997): 42–76. The quote appears on 76.

23. This correspondence is to be found in *Merkur*, April 1965, 380–85.

CHAPTER 13. RECONCEIVING THE HOLOCAUST?

This essay was first published in *Tikkun* 11, no. 4 (July/August 1996).

1. Daniel Jonah Goldhagen, *Hitler's Willing Executioners: Ordinary Germans and the Holocaust* (New York: Alfred A. Knopf, 1996).

2. Eric A. Johnson, *Nazi Terror: The Gestapo, Jews, and Ordinary Germans* (New York: Basic Books, 1999).

3. Saul Friedlander, "The 'Final Solution': On the Unease in Historical Interpretation," in his *Memory, History, and the Extermination of the Jews of Europe* (Bloomington: Indiana University Press, 1993), 110.

4. Weil to Georges Bernanos, quoted in Alfred Kazin, "A Genius of the Spiritual Life," *New York Review of Books,* 18 April 1996, 21.

5. Daniel Jonah Goldhagen, "False Witness," *New Republic,* 17 April 1989, 39–44.

6. Elie Wiesel, "Little Hitlers," *Observer Review,* 31 March 1996, 14.

7. Goldhagen, *Hitler's Willing Executioners,* 45.

CHAPTER 14. GEORGE MOSSE AT 80

This essay was first published in *Journal of Contemporary History* 34, no. 2 (April 1999).

1. This chapter, written prior to George Mosse's death, consists of a compilation, but also a considerable elaboration and reworking, of my piece "Between Rationality and Irrationalism: George L. Mosse, the Holocaust, and European Cultural History" that appeared in the *Simon Wiesenthal Center Annual 5* (1988): 187–202 and a talk given on the occasion of a celebration of George Mosse's 80th birthday in Madison, Wisconsin, in September 1998. It has gained immeasurably—and I have indeed had the pleasure of having some of its insights confirmed and deepened—by George Mosse generously providing me access to, and granting me permission to quote from, his autobiography, *Confronting History: A Memoir* (Madison: University of Wisconsin Press, 2000). See Mosse's introduction to his *The Culture of Western Europe: The Nineteenth and Twentieth Centuries* (Chicago: Rand McNally, 1961), 1–10.

2. Mosse was born in 1918 into the upper-middle class of acculturated Berlin Jewry. His maternal grandfather was the founder of the prestigious liberal newspaper the *Berliner Tageblatt.* Mosse fled Germany soon after the Nazi assumption of power, and received his education in England and the United States. See the interview with Michael Ledeen, in *Nazism: A Historical and Comparative Analysis of National Socialism* (New Brunswick, N.J.: Transaction Books, 1978), chap. 1, 21–31. See also Sterling Fishman, "GLM: An Appreciation," in *Political Symbolism in Modern Europe: Essays in Honor of George L. Mosse,* ed. Seymour Drescher, David Sabean, & Allen Sharlin (New Brunswick, N.J.: Transaction Books, 1982), 275ff.

3. The homosexual aspect of Mosse's life, its importance as a sensitizing influence on the themes, emphases, and insights of his work, has only recently been made explicit and I shall return to this subject later in the essay. See Mosse's biography, especially the chapter "Confronting History."

4. Accessible analyses of Mosse's work may be found in the introduction to Seymour Drescher et al., eds., *Political Symbolism in Modern Europe* and in the protracted interview with Mosse conducted by Michael Ledeen in *Nazism.*

5. See *Culture of Western Europe,* 2. The work was originally published in 1961.

6. George L. Mosse, *Masses and Man: Nationalist and Fascist Perceptions of Reality* (New York: H. Fertig, 1980), 14–15.

7. This is true too in more general terms. Moshe Zimmermann has documented the ways in which Mosse prefigured trends that later dominated German historiography but where the willingness to embrace and acknowledge his work was exceedingly slow. See his "Mosse and German Historiography" in *George Mosse: On the Occasion of His Retirement* (Jerusalem: n. p., 1986). That situation has, of course, been remedied and over the last few years Mosse's work has been extensively recognized in Germany and he has been the recipient of various academic honors.

8. George L. Mosse, *Nazi Culture: Intellectual, Cultural, and Social Life in the Third Reich* (New York: Grosset & Dunlap, 1966).

9. In a sense one could argue that Mosse's career has been a kind of application of Malcolm Muggeridge's retort to Goebbels: "Every time I hear the word 'revolver' I reach for my culture!" Mosse is, in many ways (as I shall try to show later) the incarnation of the German Jewish *Bildung* Jews he so masterfully analyses. But this too must be qualified as he has often criticized these same intellectuals for their overestimation of "culture" and for an ensuing, idealized politics, quite cut off from more brutalized political realities. See, for instance, the lengthy essay "Left-Wing Intellectuals in the Weimar Republic" in *Germans and Jews: The Right, The Left, and the Search for a "Third Force" in Pre-Nazi Germany* (New York: H. Fertig, 1970).

10. Many of these have been through numerous editions. See, respectively, *The Struggle for Sovereignty in England, from the Reign of Queen Elizabeth to the Petition of Right* (East Lansing: Michigan State University Press, 1950); *The Reformation* (New York: Holt, Rinehart & Winston, 1963); *The Holy Pretence, a Study of Christianity and Reason of State from William Perkins to John Winthrop* (Oxford: Blackwell, 1957). Mosse has not entirely ignored the earlier period even in his second phase. See his remarkably successful *Europe in the Sixteenth Century*, co-authored with H. Koenigsberger (London: Longmans, 1968).

11. *The Crisis of German Ideology: Intellectual Origins of the Third Reich* (New York: Grosset & Dunlap, 1964).

12. Klemens von Klemperer, in *American Historical Review* 71 (1966): 608–10.

13. Mosse, *Crisis of German Ideology*, 315.

14. George L. Mosse, *Toward the Final Solution: A History of European Racism* (London: J. M. Dent, 1978), 168. For an example of his more recent comparative work, see Mosse's "Toward a General Theory of Fascism," in *Masses and Man*, 159–96. See too his *Confronting the Nation: Jewish and Western Nationalism* (Hanover, N.H.: University Press of New England, 1993).

15. "Der erste Weltkrieg und die Brutalisierung der Politik: Betrachtungen über die Politische Rechte, den Rassismus, und den deutschen Sonderweg," in *Demokratie und Diktatur: Geist und Gestalt politischer Herrschaft in Deutschland und Europa*, ed. Manfred Funke et al. (Düsseldorf: Droste, 1987), 135–36.

16. *Confronting History*, 182. The rest of the quote is also revealing: "and if I have shown how what was latent or inherent in nationalism or in the discrimi-

nation of the outsider became overt through these movements, then I have filled in a neglected piece of history which is also relevant to the present."

17. George L. Mosse, *Fallen Soldiers: Reshaping the Memory of the World Wars* (New York: Oxford University Press, 1990).

18. George L. Mosse, *The Nationalization of the Masses: Political Symbolism and Mass Movements in Germany from the Napoleonic Wars through the Third Reich* (New York: H. Fertig, 1975). For this quote, see *Confronting History*, 177.

19. J. L. Talmon, *The Origins of Totalitarian Democracy* (London: Secker & Warburg, 1952). See *Nationalization of the Masses*. For his criticism of Talmon, see Mosse, "Political Style and Political Theory—Totalitarian Democracy Revisited," in *Totalitarian Democracy and After: international colloquium in memory of Jacob L. Talmon, Jerusalem, 21–24 June 1982* (Jerusalem: Israel Academy of Sciences and Humanities, 1984), 167–76.

20. Mosse, *Nationalization of the Masses*, 168.

21. Mosse, *Toward the Final Solution*.

22. Ibid., xiii–xiv.

23. See Mosse's response in *George Mosse: On the Occasion of His Retirement* (Jerusalem: The Hebrew University, The Koebner Chair of German History, n.d.), xxviii. This book also contains a full bibliography of Mosse's work until mid-1985.

24. See "The Secularization of Jewish Theology," in *Masses and Man*, 249–62.

25. See "The Jews and the German War Experience," in *Masses and Man*, 263–83.

26. See "The Influence of the Völkisch Idea on German Jewry," one of Mosse's most original, influential, and provocative essays, in *Germans and Jews*, 77–115.

27. George L. Mosse, *Nationalism and Sexuality: Respectability and Abnormal Sexuality in Modern Europe* (New York: H. Fertig, 1985).

28. George L. Mosse, *The Image of Man: The Creation of Modern Masculinity* (New York: Oxford University Press, 1996).

29. See the interview with David Strassler in the *Jerusalem Post*, 17 September 1991, 8.

30. Arthur Mitzman, "Fascism and Anti-Sex," *Stichtung Theoretische Geschiedenis* 12 (1986): 339–43, esp. 340.

31. This critique of the bourgeoisie and this analysis of its place within the Nazi scheme must be firmly distinguished from Marxist and neo-Marxist interpretations. Although both approaches indict the bourgeoisie, Mosse's analysis stresses perceptual and ideological factors, not material ones. He does not argue that Nazism was a tool of or served the interests of finance capitalism, as do the Marxists. His analysis is pitched at a different level. For some of the relationships and dissonances between these analyses, see my "Nazism, Normalcy, and the German *Sonderweg*," chapter 10 in the present volume.

32. Mosse, interview with David Strasser, *Jerusalem Post*, 17 September 1991, 8.

33. Mosse, *Confronting History*, 178–80.

34. Mosse, *Nazism*, 43.

35. See Mosse's review, "E. Nolte on Three Faces on Fascism," *Journal of the History of Ideas* 27 (1966): 621–26.

36. For a critical but sympathetic review of *Nationalism and Sexuality*, see Peter N. Stearns, in *Journal of Modern History* 58 (1986): 256–58.

37. This problem is discussed in more detail in this book in "On Saul Friedlander," chapter 15 of this volume.

38. Mosse, *Confronting History*, 5.

39. Ibid., 180

40. See "Conclusion: Everyone's Morality," in Mosse, *Nationalism and Sexuality*, chapter 9, esp. 191.

41. Mosse, *Confronting History*, 180–81.

42. Mosse discusses Croce in *Culture of Western Europe*, esp. 302–7. See also *Nazism*, 28–29.

43. "Ever since I left Harvard I had lived largely among historians committed to their subject. While this furthered my own research and writing, it also made me intolerant of those historians for whom writing history seemed to be only a profession like any other. . . . I sometimes said publicly—and certainly unjustly—that some of my present-day colleagues could just as well have been accountants." Mosse, *Confronting History*, 171.

44. Michael Steinberg, "Aby Warburg's Kreuzlingen Lecture: A Reading" in Aby M. Warburg, *Images from the Region of Pueblo Indians of North America* (Ithaca, N.Y.: Cornell University Press, 1995), esp. 73 n. 27 and 111. The only place, I would argue, that a celebratory view of such a "fortress rationality" may still be discerned in Mosse's work is in his portrait of the rational project of German-Jewish intellectuals, a subject to be dealt with presently.

45. Paul Breines has published two splendidly evocative articles chronicling Mosse's influence as a man and as a teacher: "Germans, Journals, and Jews—Madison, Men, Marxism, and Mosse: A Tale of Jewish-Leftist Identity Confusion in America," *New German Critique* 20 (1980): 81–103; and "With George Mosse in the 1960s" in *Political Symbolism in Modern Europe*, ed. Drescher et. al., 285–99. For similar influence in Jerusalem, see Ze'ev Mankowitz, "George Mosse and Jewish History," in *George Mosse: On the Occasion of his Retirement*, xxi ff.

46. George L. Mosse, "Jewish Emancipation between *Bildung* and Respectability," in *The Jewish Response to German Culture*, ed. Jehuda Reinharz & Walter Schatzberg (Hanover, N.H.: Published for Clark University by University Press of New England, 1985), 1–16. It has also been reproduced in *Confronting the Nation*.

47. See Mosse, *Toward the Final Solution*, chap. 1, 1–16, and Mosse, *Nazism*, esp. 94–95.

48. Mosse, "Political Style and Political Theory," 176, also 170–71.

49. George L. Mosse, *German Jews beyond Judaism* (Bloomington: Indiana University Press, 1985).

50. This is a highly astute portrait of the inner essence and the best explanation of the astonishing creativity of German-speaking Jewry that I know. I have questioned aspects of this analysis but this only strengthens the greater validity of

the whole. See "German Jews beyond *Bildung* and Liberalism: The Radical Jewish Revival in the Weimar Republic" in my *Culture and Catastrophe: German and Jewish Confrontations with National Socialism and Other Crises* (New York: New York University Press, 1996).

51. Mosse, *German Jews beyond Judaism*, 14.

52. Ibid., 3.

53. Mosse, *Confronting History*, 184.

54. See "Left-Wing Intellectuals in the Weimar Republic," in Mosse, *Germans and Jews*, 214–15.

55. Even in the famous essay, "The Influence of the Völkisch Idea on German Jewry," where Zionism's problematic sources are highlighted, Mosse underscores the fact that these Zionists always emphasized the more universal, humanist side of nationalism, rejecting its racist and other exclusivist implications.

56. "Gershom Scholem as a German Jew," in Mosse, *Confronting the Nation*.

57. See, most recently, "Can Nationalism Be Saved? About Zionism, Rightful and Unjust Nationalism," *Israel Studies* 2, no.1 (Spring 1979): 156–73; "Central European Intellectuals in Palestine," *Judaism* 45, no. 2 (Spring 1996): 134–42; and the contribution to a symposium in *New Republic*, 8 & 15 September 1977, 19–20. In the latter piece he also proclaims that "Zionism, in the last resort, is about solidarity and how this can be strengthened in future generations."

58. See his introduction to Nordau's *Degeneration* (Lincoln: University of Nebraska Press, 1993) and his "Max Nordau: Liberalism and the New Jew," in Mosse, *Confronting the Nation*.

59. Mosse, *Confronting History*, 185.

60. Ibid., 190. And, Mosse adds, "I myself was far from immune to the irrational forces which as a historian I deplored and that especially when it came to that group which I regard as my own."

61. Ibid., 6.

62. See George L. Mosse, "Friendship and Nationhood: About the Promise and Failure of German Nationalism," *Journal of Contemporary History* 17 (1982): 351–67, and Mosse, *German Jews beyond Judaism*, esp. 32.

CHAPTER 15. ON SAUL FRIEDLANDER

Essay originally published in *History & Memory* 9, nos. 1/2 (Fall 1997): 11–46. Reprinted by permission of Indiana University Press.

1. "It would be ridiculous," writes Dominick LaCapra, "if I tried to assume the voice of Elie Wiesel or of Saul Friedlander. There is a sense in which I have no right to these voices. . . . while any historian must be 'invested' in a distinctive way in the events of the Holocaust, not all investments (or cathexes) are the same, and not all statements, rhetorics, or orientations are equally available to different historians." See "Reflections on the Historian's Debate" in LaCapra, *Representing the Holocaust: History, Theory, Trauma* (Ithaca, N. Y.: Cornell University Press, 1994), 46.

2. Saul Friedlander, *When Memory Comes*, trans. Helen R. Lane (New York: Farrar, Straus & Giroux, 1979). The French original was published in 1978.

3. As Leon Wieseltier put it in his review, the most remarkable feature of the work is

> its composure, an elegance that is unnerving . . . his language seems armored (even more formidably so in the French) against the dissolution he describes. Yet dissolution triumphs. The pieces of memory do not cohere. . . . Friedlander's life remains disrupted, despoiled of its dreams; not least because of the honesty with which he has attempted to discover what the death of the Jews might mean . . . Even the structure of his memoir thus seems disconsolate; he refuses to impose narrative order upon his account of the catastrophes.

See "Between Paris and Jerusalem," *New York Review of Books,* 25 October 1979, 3–4.

4. These quotes appear in Friedlander's *When Memory Comes,* on 45, 120–22, and 137–38 respectively.

5. Of course, unlike these other writers, Friedlander was never placed in a Nazi camp.

6. Friedlander, *When Memory Comes,* 144.

7. Ibid., 29 and 37 respectively.

8. This essay is an attempt to elaborate on some of the suggestions I make in my *Culture and Catastrophe: German and Jewish Confrontations with National Socialism and Other Crises* (New York: New York University Press, 1996), 115–16 and 192, n. 6.

9. For an overview of Friedlander's career, writings, and reviews thereof through 1994, see *Contemporary Literary Criticism* 90 (1996): 98–123.

10. Friedlander, *Hitler et les Etats-Unis, 1939–1941* (Geneva: Droz, 1963). English translation: *Prelude to Downfall: Hitler and the United States, 1939–1941* (New York: A. Knopf, 1966).

11. Edwin Tetlow, "Of Diplomatic Thrust and Counterthrust," *Christian Science Monitor,* 15 December 1967, 13.

12. Friedlander, *Pius XII and the Third Reich: A Documentation* (New York: A. Knopf, 1966), xv and 236 respectively. French original published in 1964.

13. This, indeed, was the burden of a hostile review arguing that, given the lack of availability of all the documents, selections were necessary. "But the act of selection is, conversely, the act of exclusion . . . Inevitably, it must appear that he is not engaged in an objective scholarly inquiry so much as in grinding an ax." Given Friedlander's emphasis on the partial nature of the documents, the reviewer asks: "Why did he not wait until he *had* more material and could venture *definite* answers, rather than rush into print now with nothing more than conjectures and insinuations?" See E. H. Wall, "Tragic Dilemma," *National Review,* 23 August 1966, 843–44.

14. Friedlander, *Pius XII,* 236 ff.

15. Ibid., 238.

16. Arthur A. Cohen, *New York Times Book Review,* 13 April 1969, 10.

17. Friedlander, *Kurt Gerstein: The Ambiguity of Good,* trans. Charles Fullman (New York: A. Knopf, 1969). The French original appeared in 1967.

18. Ibid. The quotes are culled from pp. 226–28. Italics in the original. See generally the "Final Remarks." If most critics were struck by the restrained nature

of this book, this was not true for all. Thus Norbert Muhlen complained that Friedlander "attempts to set himself up as a supreme moral judge of the large majority of people as well of Gerstein himself. Given his hostile personal bias and his superficial treatment of moral as well as factual questions, which he often answers by cut-rate psychoanalysis and by comic-strip styled over-simplifications, . . . he appears poorly equipped for such a final judgement. His ambiguous verdict on the 'ambiguity of good' remains as meaningless as its fashionable model and companion piece, Hannah Arendt's banal charge against the 'banality of evil.'" See Norbert Muhlen, *America* 120, no. 15 (12 April 1969): 454–55. The suggestion about some kind of relation to Arendt is interesting though asserted not argued. Would it be unfair to suggest that the tone of the critique, written by a German-born American journalist, who points out that Friedlander is "an Israeli historian" may serve as an early example of Friedlander's analyses of the tensions between "German" and "Jewish" memory?

19. Quoting from Arendt's concluding lines of *Eichmann in Jerusalem,* Friedlander's comment that "Hannah Arendt may have unintentionally given us a clue as to what distinguished Nazi crimes from others" is mysterious. There was nothing unintentional about it—in fact it formed a cornerstone of Arendt's thinking on this point. See Friedlander's "Reflections on the Historicization of National Socialism" in his *Memory, History, and the Extermination of the Jews of Europe* (Bloomington: Indiana University Press, 1993), 82–83.

20. Apart from Friedlander, perhaps the best known attempt in this (very well ploughed) field is the concluding chapter ("A Case-study in Collective Psychopathology") of Norman Cohn's *Warrant for Genocide: The Myth of the Jewish World Conspiracy and the Protocols of the Elders of Zion* (London: Eyre & Spottiswoode, 1967). Interestingly, Cohn later omitted this chapter in a revised edition claiming that he now regarded his own interpretation as "somewhat primitive" and in its stead recommended Friedlander's more "adequate" work.

21. *L'antisémitisme nazi. Histoire d'une psychose collective* (Paris: Seuil, 1971).

22. The most bizarre example of this rather large literature is Rudolf Binion's, "Hitler's Concept of *Lebensraum:* The Psychological Basis," *History of Childhood Quarterly* 1, no. 2 (Fall 1973), where the Holocaust is related to Hitler's perception that the Jewish doctor, Dr. Bloch, was responsible for his mother's death. All speculative psychological considerations aside, the plausibility of this theory, one would think, is somewhat dented by the fact that Hitler went out of his way to protect Dr. Bloch!

23. See Jacob Katz's illuminating comments on psycho-history in general and Friedlander's work in particular, "Misreadings of Anti-Semitism," *Commentary,* July 1983, 39–44. The pertinent passages can be found on 40–41.

24. See his later, critically nuanced, general study, *History and Psychoanalysis: An Enquiry into the Possibilities and Limits of Psychohistory* (New York: Holmes & Meier, 1978). The French original appeared in 1975.

25. See *Reflections of Nazism: An Essay on Kitsch and Death,* trans. Thomas Weyr (New York: Avon, 1986), 121. The work was first published in French in 1982 and in English in 1984.

26. See his important and revealing essay, "The 'Final Solution': On the Unease in Historical Interpretation," in Peter Hayes, ed., *Lessons and Legacies: The Meaning of the Holocaust in a Changing World* (Evanston, Ill.: Northwestern University Press, 1991), 23–35. The quotes appear on 25.

27. Ibid., 30.

28. Whether "simple" or "complex" in their nature, such theories are never "immediate" reflections of an unmediated historical reality but are inevitably shaped by a degree of ascriptive and speculative interpretation. See my "Archetypes and the German Jewish Dialogue: Reflections Occasioned by the Goldhagen Affair" in chapter 9 of this volume.

29. See the essay "Trauma and Transference" in Friedlander's collection of essays *Memory, History*, 117–37. The quote appears on 123.

30. See Martin Broszat & Saul Friedlander, "A Controversy about the Historicization of National Socialism," *Yad Vashem Studies* 19 (1988): 1–47. The quote appears on 12.

31. Ibid., 7.

32. Ibid., 12–13.

33. Ibid., 41.

34. Thus, in discussing various modes of avoiding confrontation with this murderous past, Friedlander argues for a fundamental distinction between non-German and German strategies: "The fifteen or twenty years of 'latency' that followed the war in regard to talking or writing about the Shoah, particularly in the United States, should not be equated with massive repression exclusively, in contradistinction to the German scene." See Friedlander, "Trauma and Transference," in *Memory, History*, 126.

35. Friedlander, *Reflections of Nazism*, 9–10.

36. Though the book was greeted in general with great admiration, it must be said that some objected to the book precisely on the grounds that it was too psycho-symbolic and insufficiently historical. As one critic put it:

> If Friedlander gets nowhere, it is because from start to finish he goes nowhere. Though he is a master of the neat phrase . . . the substance of these observations tend to be trite and unhistoric. For instance, Hitler in victory sits on the mountain, in defeat he cowers in his bunker. That, according to Friedlander, is the "parabola" of his career. Actually, Hitler took to his air raid shelter as early as the fall of 1940, during Molotov's visit to Berlin; and the subsequent locus operandi of the fuehrer was determined not by the evolution of symbols but by the growth of allied air superiority. . . . the book has a lot to say about death worship, much of it quite out of context: Hitler's cult of the martyrs of his movement reflected no particular fixation, merely a commonplace practice to sugarcoat death as an act of heroism. For this there were so many models that one wonders whether this involved even conscious imitation.

See Hans A. Schmitt, "Hitler: Obsession without End," *Sewanee Review* 1 (January-March 1988): 158–68. The quote appears on 165.

37. Friedlander, *Reflections of Nazism*, xi.

38. Ibid., 15–16: "The important thing is the constant identification of Na-

zism and death; not real death in its everyday horror and tragic banality, but a ritualized, stylized, and aestheticized death." On the juxtaposition of kitsch and death, see 3 ff. On the synthesis—kitsch death as "a means to digest the past"— see esp. 13.

39. Ibid., xv.

40. Ibid., xvii.

41. See "The Shoah in Present Historical Consciousness," in *Memory, History,* 42.

42. Friedlander, *Reflections of Nazism,* 62.

43. See his "Some Aspects of the Historical Significance of the Holocaust," *Jerusalem Quarterly* 1 (Fall 1976): 36–59. The quote appears on 37.

44. Ibid., 39.

45. See his "From Anti-Semitism to Extermination: A Historiographical Study of Nazi Policies Toward the Jews and an Essay in Interpretation," *Yad Vashem Studies* 16 (1984): 1–50. The quote appears on 16. The italics are in the original.

46. Ibid.

47. Friedlander, "The 'Final Solution,'" in Hayes, ed., *Lessons and Legacies,* 33. That may be so but it is also true that, however sublimated, Arendt's *The Origins of Totalitarianism* was one of the first serious efforts to think through the grounds of the Jewish genocide. See my "Nazism, Culture, and *The Origins of Totalitarianism*: Hannah Arendt and the Discourse of Evil," chapter 11 of this volume.

48. Friedlander, "From Anti-Semitism to Extermination," 6.

49. See the splendid *Nazi Germany and the Jews: Volume One: The Years of Persecution, 1933–1939* (New York: HarperCollins, 1997), 4. See the review by Gulie Ne'eman Arad, "Nazi Germany and the Jews," *History & Memory* 9, nos. 1/2 (Fall 1997): 409–33. Friedlander's always carefully differentiated analyses differ in fundamental ways, of course, from Daniel Jonah Goldhagen's work, which Friedlander curtly dismisses thus: "An interpretation of the events assuming the widespread presence in German society at large, throughout the modern era, of an 'eliminationist anti-Semitism,' craving the physical annihilation of the Jews, is not convincing on the basis of the material presented in this study" (387, n. 53).

50. See Friedlander, "From Anti-Semitism to Extermination," 3 ff.

51. Friedlander, "The Shoah in Present Historical Consciousness," in *History, Memory,* 57.

52. Friedlander, "From Anti-Semitism to Extermination," 27–28, 49. Friedlander's sense of functionalism's affinity with Arendt's "banality of evil" thesis was later validated when its leading analyst Hans Mommsen wrote an introduction for a later German edition of the book. For the English version see Mommsen's "Hannah Arendt and the Eichmann Trial" in his *From Weimar to Auschwitz: Essays in German History,* trans. Phillip O'Connor (Princeton, N.J.: Princeton University Press, 1991), 254–78.

53. The literature on this is enormous. For an accessible analysis of the debate within the largest political and intellectual context, see Charles S. Maier, *The Unmasterable Past: History, Holocaust, and German National Identity* (Cambridge, Mass.: Harvard University Press, 1988).

54. See "A Conflict of Memories? The New German Debates About the 'Final Solution,'" *The Leo Baeck Memorial Lecture* 31 (New York: Leo Baeck Institute, 1987), 7.

55. Ibid. The last two quotes appear on 8.

56. Ibid., 9–10.

57. Ibid., 12.

58. Ibid., 14–15.

59. See Friedlander's "West Germany and the Burden of the Past: The Ongoing Debate," *Jerusalem Quarterly* 42 (Spring 1987): 3–18. The quote appears on 9–10.

60. See Martin Broszat, "A Plea for the Historicization of National Socialism," in Peter Baldwin, ed., *Reworking the Past: Hitler, the Holocaust, and the Historians' Debate* (Boston: Beacon Press, 1990), 77–87. The article appeared originally in German in 1985. Baldwin's volume also includes Friedlander's "Some Reflections on the Historicization of National Socialism" (88–101). Their famous correspondence is also republished there (102–34). This is not the place to go into the rights and wrongs of their debate. It must be mentioned here, however, that already in his first letter, Broszat insisted that such singularity would not go away for National Socialism itself provided a sufficient guarantee by the very magnitude of its crimes. See Broszat & Friedlander, "A Controversy," 4–5.

61. I have analyzed both these correspondences in chapters 5 and 6 respectively in *Culture and Catastrophe*.

62. Broszat & Friedlander, "A Controversy," 39.

63. Ibid., 29–30.

64. Ibid., 20–21 for these respective quotes.

65. Ibid., 25–26.

66. Ibid., 27–28.

67. Ibid., 38.

68. See his respectful piece written after Broszat's death, "Martin Broszat and the Historicization of National Socialism" in *Memory, History*, 95. It should be noted that Friedlander has lately considerably modified his opposition to what he took to be a crucial methodological tool of historicization—*Alltagsgeschichte* (the history of everyday life)—and his suspicion that it essentially served "normalizing" tendencies. Indeed, in his new book, *Nazi Germany and the Jews*, the use of such a method precisely for illuminating a Friedlanderian perspective is explicitly acknowledged:

> Nazi persecutions and exterminations were perpetrated by ordinary people who lived and acted within a modern society not unlike our own, a society that had produced them as well as the methods and instruments for the implementation of their actions; the goals of these actions, however, were formulated by a regime, an ideology, and a political culture that were anything but commonplace. It is the relationship between the uncommon and the ordinary, the fusion of the widely shared murderous potentialities of the world that is also ours and the peculiar frenzy of the Nazi apocalyptic drive against the mortal enemy, the Jew, that give both universal significance and historical distinctiveness to the "Final Solution of the Jewish Question" (6–7).

In this book, Friedlander puts into practice his strictures concerning the role of the historian, the nature of narration, as well as some of the ways in which the debates between intentionalists and functionalists, and concerning historicization have been resolved in his mind and work.

69. Although it is not exhaustive, the most accessible and representative collection (his autobiography apart) of Friedlander's analyses of memory and history in general, and of German, Jewish, and Israeli inscriptions in particular, is to be found in *Memory, History.*

70. For a general outline of these issues see chapter 1 of my *Culture and Catastrophe.*

71. See "The Shoah in Present Historical Consciousness," in *Memory, History,* 48–49.

72. Ibid., 43, 47.

73. Friedlander, *Memory, History,* esp. introduction, chap. 1, "German Struggles with Memory," and chap. 3, "The Shoah in Present Historical Consciousness," where he states: "Major catastrophes such as the Shoah become centrally significant for the collective self-perception of the groups directly involved in one way or another, while the reworking of these catastrophes through time mobilizes central symbolic systems at the disposal of these groups" (47).

74. Friedlander, *Memory, History,* xii.

75. Ibid., "German Struggles with Memory," 2.

76. It should be noted that I have concentrated in this essay on Friedlander's main areas of interest. He has, however, also pursued many other subjects—on international relations, French politics and so on. He has also written prominently on general issues related to Israeli society and the Palestinian-Arab-Israeli problem. See, for instance, the books *Reflexions sur l'Avenir d'Israel* (Paris: Seuil, 1969); with Mahmud Hussein, *Arabs and Israelis: A Dialogue* (New York: Holmes & Meier, 1978), and the many relevant articles and book reviews in the bibliography accompanying *Arabs and Israelis.*

77. See, for instance, his piece with Adam Seligman, "The Israeli Memory of the Shoah: On Symbols, Rituals and Ideological Polarization," in *Nowhere: Space, Time and Modernity,* ed. Roger Friedland and Deidre Boden (Berkeley & Los Angeles: University of California Press, 1994), 356–71. See too "The Shoah in Present Historical Consciousness," 43–47.

78. See the introduction to Friedlander, *Memory, History,* xi–xii.

79. Ibid., xii–xiii.

80. Friedlander, "West Germany and the Burden of the Past: The Ongoing Debate," *Jerusalem Quarterly* 42 (Spring 1987): 17.

81. For a more general discussion of the ways in which the intellectual atmosphere attendant upon a postmodernist sensibility affects the discussion on Nazism and the Shoah, see Aschheim, *Culture and Catastrophe,* esp. 12 ff.

82. See *Probing the Limits of Representation: Nazism and the "Final Solution"* (Cambridge, Mass.: Harvard University Press, 1992), which was edited by Friedlander and for which he wrote the introduction. The volume has had a considerable impact.

83. Friedlander, *Probing the Limits,* 4–5.

84. On this point see Friedlander, "The Shoah in Present Historical Consciousness," 55.

85. Friedlander, "German Struggles with Memory," in *Memory, History*, 10. Italics in the original.

86. Ibid., 5.

87. See the important essay with that phrase, "'The Final Solution': On the Unease in Historical Interpretation," 23–35.

88. Friedlander, "The Shoah in Present Historical Consciousness," 48.

89. Friedlander, *Probing the Limits*, 2.

90. Friedlander, "Some Aspects of the Historical Significance," 42.

91. Friedlander, "Trauma and Transference," in *Memory, History*, 32. In many ways Friedlander has applied this technique in his new book—with striking success. We eagerly await the second volume.

92. Friedlander, *Memory, History*, x.

93. Friedlander, "Trauma and Transference," in *Memory, History*, 134.

94. Friedlander, *Probing the Limits*, 2–3.

95. Friedlander, "The Shoah in Present Historical Consciousness," 49.

96. This is a pastiche of quotes drawn from *Reflections of Nazism*, 89 ff.

97. Friedlander, "'The Final Solution,'" in *Lessons and Legacies*, ed. Hayes, 31. Italics in the original.

98. Friedlander, *Reflections of Nazism*, 106.

99. Friedlander, "'The Final Solution,'" 32. Italics in the original.

100. Friedlander, *Reflections of Nazism*, 106.

101. Friedlander, "'The Final Solution,'" 34.

102. Friedlander, "Trauma and Transference," in *Memory, History*, 133.

103. Friedlander, "'The Final Solution,'" 35.

104. Friedlander, "Trauma and Transference," in *Memory, History*, 129.

105. Ibid., 131.

106. Ibid., 134.

107. Broszat & Friedlander, "A Controversy about the Historicization of National Socialism," 30–31.

108. Friedlander, "Trauma and Transference," in *Memory, History*, 131.

109. Michael R. Marrus, *The Holocaust in History* (London: Penguin Books, 1989), 7.

110. See the instructive piece by Hans Kellner, "'Never Again' Is Now," *History & Theory* 33, no. 2 (1994): 127–44. See too chapters 1 and 7 of my *Culture and Catastrophe*. Martin Broszat put it thus in a letter to Friedlander, concerning the latter's insistence that scientifically positive work had to keep the ideological and criminal dimensions of Nazism at the center: ". . . the wish to prescribe what should or should not be done scientifically . . . leads us astray, forcing us into a constrictive narrowing of the possibility to ask scientific questions." See Broszat & Friedlander, "A Controversy about the Historicization," 34.

111. Friedlander, "German Struggles with Memory," in *Memory, History*, 5–6.

112. James Young, *The Texture of Memory: Holocaust Memorials and Meaning* (New Haven, Conn.: Yale University Press, 1993), 21.

113. Arno Mayer, *Why Did the Heavens Not Darken? The "Final Solution" in History* (New York: Pantheon Books, 1988), xiii.

114. Ibid. For critical comments on this book see chapter 4 of Christopher R. Browning's *The Path to Genocide: Essays on Launching the Final Solution* (Cambridge: Cambridge University Press, 1992) and Aschheim, *Culture and Catastrophe*, 121–24.

115. See chapter 7 of Aschheim, *Culture and Catastrophe*, esp. 124–25.

116. This important new perspective on Auschwitz can be found in Deborah Dwork and Robert Jan van Pelt, *Auschwitz: 1270 to the Present* (New York: W. W. Norton, 1996).

117. Friedlander, *Nazi Germany and the Jews*, 3. Friedlander specifically distinguishes this "redemptive" anti-Semitism from Goldhagen's "exterminationist" notion and argues that the former "represented an ideological trend shared at the outset by a small minority only, and, in the Third Reich, by a segment of the party and its leaders, not by the majority of the population" (337, n. 6).

118. Friedlander, "Some Aspects of the Historical Significance," 41.

119. See Friedlander's new book, *Nazi Germany and the Jews*, 42. See esp. the introduction and chap. 1.

120. Ibid., 157. Italics in the original.

121. See, most prominently, Michael Burleigh & Wolfgang Wippermann, *The Racial State: Germany 1933–1945* (Cambridge: Cambridge University Press, 1991). See also Henry Friedlander, *The Origins of Nazi Genocide: From Euthanasia to the Final Solution* (Chapel Hill: University of North Carolina Press, 1995).

122. See the very instructive critique by Wulf Kansteiner, "From Exception to Exemplum: The New Approach to Nazism and the 'Final Solution,'" *History & Theory* 33, no. 2 (1994): 145–71. Friedlander's "inverted specificity of the event," he argues, "tends to undermine its own foundation whenever the notion of opaqueness and uneasiness solidifies" (151). Therefore he links the inexplicability of the Holocaust alternatively to the event as "inherent in the phenomenon itself" or presents it as a value judgement, arrived at *a posteriori* (161).

Index